The Blackwell Encyclopedic Dictionary of Accounting

UNIVERSITY OF
GLOUCESTERSHIRE
at Cheltenham and Gloucester

THE BLACKWELL ENCYCLOPEDIA OF MANAGEMENT

EDITED BY CARY L. COOPER AND CHRIS ARGYRIS

Blackwell Encyclopedic Dictionary of Accounting
Edited by A. Rashad Abdel-khalik

Blackwell Encyclopedic Dictionary of Strategic Management
Edited by Derek F. Channon

Blackwell Encyclopedic Dictionary of Management Information Systems
Edited by Gordon B. Davis

Blackwell Encyclopedic Dictionary of Marketing
Edited by Barbara R. Lewis and Dale Littler

Blackwell Encyclopedic Dictionary of Managerial Economics
Edited by Robert McAuliffe

Blackwell Encyclopedic Dictionary of Organizational Behavior
Edited by Nigel Nicholson

Blackwell Encyclopedic Dictionary of International Management
Edited by John J. O'Connell

Blackwell Encyclopedic Dictionary of Finance
Edited by Dean Paxson and Douglas Wood

Blackwell Encyclopedic Dictionary of Human Resource Management
Edited by Lawrence H. Peters, Charles R. Greer, and Stuart A. Youngblood

Blackwell Encyclopedic Dictionary of Operations Management
Edited by Nigel Slack

Blackwell Encyclopedic Dictionary of Business Ethics
Edited by Patricia H. Werhane, and R. Edward Freeman

The Blackwell Encyclopedic Dictionary of Accounting

Edited by A. Rashad Abdel-khalik

University of Florida

BLACKWELL
Business

Copyright © Blackwell Publishers Ltd 1997, 1998
Editorial organization © A. Rashad Abdel-khalik, 1997, 1998

First published 1997
First published in paperback 1998

2 4 6 8 10 9 7 5 3 1

Blackwell Publishers Inc.
350 Main Street
Malden , Massachusetts 02148
USA

Blackwell Publishers Ltd
108 Cowley Road
Oxford OX4 1JF
UK

Library of Congress Cataloging-in-Publication Data

The Blackwell encyclopedic dictionary of accounting / edited by Rashad
Abdel-khalik.
    p.   cm.
    Includes bibliographical references and index.
    ISBN 1–55786–941–3 (alk. paper)
    ISBN 0–631–21187–X (pbk)
    1.   Accounting–Dictionaries. I. Abdel-khalik, A. Rashad.
HG5621.B54   1997   96–33131
657'.03—dc20   CIP

British Library Cataloguing in Publication Data

A CIP catalogue record for this book is available from the British Library.

Typeset in 9½ on 11pt Ehrhardt by Page Brothers, Norwich
Printed in Great Britain by TJ International Limited, Padstow, Cornwall

This book is printed on acid-free paper

Contents

—— Preface ——

In any group or organizational setting, having access to information facilitates the process of management and control. Although it is not the only source of information, accounting has been the basic conventional business activity that drives the formal information structure within organizations. Measurement and evaluation of performance transcend all business activities from the level of individual responsibility, to divisions, to the entire firm. Many of these methods appeal to some theoretical reasoning, while others are governed by pragmatic criteria. Whereas the criteria for revenue recognition have withstood the test of time, novel and new transactions create new challenges for which no theoretical support exists. In those situations, professional accounting rule-making bodies promulgate stop-gap rules that would help serve short-term needs. Accounting for new financial instruments, swaps, and derivatives has come to the forefront and is the most formidable task facing accountants in the late 1990s.

In past years, accounting for transactions such as debt defeasance was considered too complex for the traditional accounting model to handle. But in more recent times, the ingenuity of capital market participants in creating new financial instruments for which no known accounting treatment exists continue to pose challenges to accountants. Even some familiar types of executory contracts such as leases continue to frustrate rule makers as they vacillate between well specified criteria that can be evaded in writing lease contracts and professional judgments that allow more freedom for accountants. Accounting for leases join other executory contracts such as pensions and post retirement benefits in their being measured by accounting standards that could end up providing more garbled than precise information. Many users of financial information do not have a reasonable appreciation for the degree of latitude allowed accountants in the measurement and reporting of financial information. Indeed managers are often assumed to use the accounting flexibility allowed them to manage earnings. The complexity of the business has created diversity within and among different nations. Accounting for goodwill and foreign currency translations are good examples of this diversity. Because of the high degree of judgment involved in the measurement and reporting of information, international harmonization of accounting is not likely to materialize in our lifetime.

In addition, many of those pragmatically driven rules become accepted as a common body of knowledge merely because accountants and users of financial statements have grown accustomed to them. Accounting for inventory valuation is one example. Although lacking theoretical support, it enjoys unusual longevity in the field. In many countries, it is the lower-of-cost or market rule that perpetuates the conservative mind set of accounting policy makers. The conservative policy-making posture has led to other accounting problems for activities such as research and development that essentially ignore the investment nature of the activity. Conservatism and adherence to historical cost has reduced the interest in alternative valuation models such as current cost or other market valuation basis. In some countries, the accounting profession allows asset revaluation to reflect market prices, while in most countries the revaluation is allowed only for conditions of asset impairment. Because investors and other external users make use of the publicly reported accounting information, understanding these concerns is important in making ratio analysis and other uses of financial reports.

Because acounting is a process of mesurement and reporting that is subject to a great deal of judgment, independent accountants (i.e., auditors) must assess the extent to which the reported information *faithfully represent the economic conditions of the firm*. The process of auditing financial statements has thus become an important function. First, because of the complexity of business and the cost, auditors must sample transactions for verification and audit sampling has become more specialized. Second, the audit sampling as well as other evidence-generating processes is subject to certain levels of risk. Auditors are required to follow a particular audit risk model. Third, undertaking the audit process requires analysis of trends and analysis of deviations of information from their expectations, an area known as analytical review. Fourth, in searching for evidence, auditors exercise judgment on what processes to use and what information cues are relevant. Fifth, in making those judgments, auditors apply various technical as well as rules-of-thumb methods and use different approaches to testing audit evidence. The final outcome of an audit is a report that must state whether or not the disclosed financial statements are prepared in accordance with accepted methods and whether or not they reflect the underlying economic conditions within the accepted bounds of audit risk. The format of the report, but not the substance, differ slightly among different countries.

Accounting information is used not only by capital market participants who continue to monitor the information content of different signals, but also by insiders who manage the firm. Planning and budgeting for normal operating activities as well as for capital projects are major functions that require use of and generate accounting information. Analysis of deviations from cost standards and budgets constitute important input for managerial decisions. Evaluating divisional performance requires identification of the managerial unit, perhaps setting a set of transfer prices, as well as devising allocation schemes for the cost of shared resources. Much of these activities are dependent on the level of technology employed by the firm. Integrated manufacturing technology and strategic cost analysis are elements of a new perspective on accounting for internal purposes.

The level of technology employed by the firm has a pervasive effect on all of these elements of the accounting domain. Management information systems, database management, technological auditing are all manifestations of the effect of technology.

A. Rashad Abdel-khalik
University of Florida
Gainesville, Florida, USA

Contributors

A. Rashad Abdel-khalik
University of Florida

Mohammad J. Abdolmohammadi
Bentley College

Noel Addy
Mississippi State University

Anwer Ahmed
University of Florida

Bipin B. Ajinkya
University of Florida

Mimi L. Alciatore
Southern Methodist University

Steven A. Allen
Xavier University

K. B. Ambanpola
Nanyang Technological University, Singapore

Stephen K. Asare
University of Florida

Frances L. Ayres
University of Oklahoma

William R. Baber
The George Washington University

Kashi R. Balachandran
New York University

Sasson Bar Yosef
The Hebrew University

Lynn Barkess
University of New South Wales

Jan Barton
University of Alabama

Martin Benis
Baruch College, CUNY

Jane Bozewicz
Baruch College, CUNY

Lawrence D. Brown
State University of New York – Buffalo

Peter Brownell
The University of Melbourne

Barry Byran
Auburn University

H. Francis Bush
Virginia Military Institute

Jeffrey L. Callen
New York University

Robert Capettini
San Diego State University

Mary Ellen Carter
Massachusetts Institute of Technology

Kung H. Chen
University of Nebraska – Lincoln

C. S. Agnes Cheng
University of Houston

Payyu Cheng
Feng Chia University, Taiwan

Jang Youn Cho
University of Nebraska – Lincoln

Frederick D. S. Choi
New York University

Tom Clausen
University of Illinois at Urbana-Champaign

Thomas R. Craig
Illinois State University

B. Michael Doran
Iowa State University

Jean M. DuPree
Tennessee Technological University

Aasmund Eilifsen
Fisher School of Accounting, Florida

Leslie G. Eldenburg
University of Arizona

Samir M. El-Gazzar
Pace University

Amal El-Sabbagh
Concordia University

Patricia Fairfield
Georgetown University

Haim Falk
Rutgers University – Camdem

M. Ali Fekrat
Georgetown University

Ehsan H. Feroz
University of Minnesota, Duluth

Thomas J. Frecka
University of Notre Dame, Indiana

Alan H. Friedberg
Florida Atlantic University

Dipankar Ghosh
University of Oklahoma

James Godfrey
James Madison University

Jayne M. Godfrey
University of Tasmania

Jenny Goodwin
Nanyang Technological University, Singapore

Severin V. Grabski
Michigan State University

Teoh Hai Yap
Nanyang Technological University, Singapore

Susan Haka
Michigan State University

Clyde Herring
Mississippi State University

Gillian Yeo Hian Heng
Nanyang Technological University, Singapore

Joanna L. Ho
University of California – Irvine

William S. Hopwood
Florida Atlantic University

Keith A. Houghton
The University of Melbourne

Alicja A. Jaruga
University of Lodz, Poland

Cynthia Jeffrey
Iowa State University

Christine A. Jubb
The University of Melbourne

Steven J. Kachelmeier
University of Texas at Austin

Sok-Hyon Kang
Carnegie Mellon University

Joseph Kerstein
Baruch College, CUNY

Devaun Kite
Northeast Louisiana University

M. Chris Knapp
University of Oklahoma

Larry A. Kreiser
Cleveland State University

Ellen L. Landgraf
Loyola University Chicago

Meng Hye Lee
Nanyang Technological University, Singapore

Peter Lee
Nanyang Technological University, Singapore

Stewart A. Leech
University of Tasmania

Margarita Maria Lenk
Colorado State University

Barbara Brockie Leonard
Loyola University Chicago

Steven B. Lilien
Baruch College, CUNY

Joan Luft
Michigan State University

Marc F. Massoud
Claremont McKenna College and Claremont Graduate School

Charles L. McDonald
University of Florida

James C. McKeown
Pennsylvania State University

Yaw M. Mensah
Rutgers University, New Brunswick

William F. Messier, Jr
University of Florida

Shane Moriarity
University of Oklahoma

Roger P. Murphy
Iowa State University

S. M. Khalid Nainar
McMaster University

John D. Neill
Florida State University

Eng Juan Ng
Nanyang Technological University, Singapore

Hugo Nurnberg
Baruch College, CUNY

Felix Pomeranz
Florida International University

Brenda A. Porter
Massey University (NY) and Cranfield University (UK)

David N. Ricchiute
University of Notre Dame, Indiana

Diane H. Roberts
University of San Francisco

Joshua Ronen
New York University

Bernadette M. Ruf
Florida International University

William Ruland
Baruch College, CUNY

Oded Sarig
Tel Aviv University

R. W. Schattke
University of Colorado

Herbert P. Schoch
Nanyang Technological University, Singapore

Wayne H. Shaw
University of Colorado at Boulder

David Shields
University of Houston

John K. Simmons
University of Florida

Roger Simnett
University of New South Wales

Ferhad Simyar
Concordia University

Ira Solomon
University of Illinois at Urbana-Champaign

Aldona Kamela-Sowinska
Poznan School of Economics, Poland

Nasser A. Spear
University of Melbourne

Anthony Steele
University of Warwick

James D. Stice
Brigham Young University

Mary Stone
University of Alabama

Norman C. Strong
University of Manchester

Richard H. Tabor
Auburn University

Pearl Tan
Nanyang Technological University, Singapore

Gregory M. Trompeter
Boston College

Ken T. Trotman
University of New South Wales

Trevor A. Wilkins
National University of Singapore

John Joseph Williams
Nanyang Technological University, Singapore

Patricia A. Williams
Fordham University, New York

Teri L. Yohn
Georgetown University

A

accounting for defeasance Defeasance is a procedure that allows a firm to remove debt from its financial statement without having to formally retire the debt issue. There are two types of debt defeasance transactions: legal and in-substance. In a legal defeasance the firm ceases to be the party primarily liable for the payment of the interest and principal of the debt.

Under the provisions of Statement of Financial Accounting Standards No. 76 (SFAS 76, 1983) a firm can also remove debt from its financial statements by executing an in-substance defeasance transaction: the firm transfers risk-free securities, or cash, sufficient to meet the interest and principal payments of a specified debt issue to an irrevocable trust. This effectively eliminates the firm's obligation to make future payments to the debt holders.

At the date of transfer, the firm removes both the debt issue and the companion investment securities from its books, with the difference between them generating an extraordinary gain or loss from early debt retirement.

However, the firm is not legally released from the terms of the covenants nor from its legal standing as the primary obligor of the debt. In addition, an in-substance defeasance transaction does not affect the status of publicly traded debt.

SFAS 76 imposes two criteria that must be met for an in-substance defeasance transaction to qualify as an early extinguishment of debt. First, the sole purpose of the trust must be to administer the cash flow obligation of the debt issue. Second, the trust must own only securities that are "essentially risk free" with regard to the amounts and timing of their future cash payments. This is typically satisfied by US government securities that are matched in the timing and amount of cash as the debt being extinguished.

When the debt is denominated in a currency other than US dollars, the same requirements hold except that the risk-free securities must be denominated in the same currency.

In-substance defeasance can also be used to eliminate callable bonds and long-term lease obligations from the firm's balance sheet. However, in-substance defeasance accounting is permitted only if the firm irrevocably commits itself to exercising the call option at a specific date. Once this is done, the firm can retire the debt using in-substance defeasance accounting.

Under current tax laws, the gain or loss that results from an in-substance defeasance of debt is not taxable. Following the provisions of Statement of Financial Accounting Standards No. 96, issued December 1987, the firm must, however, report the gain or loss on early extinguishment of debt net of the related tax effect.

Effects of Defeasance

Permitting firms to eliminate debt from their balance sheet through an in-substance defeasance is controversial. Accordingly, before undertaking an in-substance defeasance a firm's management must evaluate the effect of an in-substance defeasance on the firm's financial position and assess the reaction of the firm's existing and potential creditors and shareholders to the transaction.

Much of the controversy surrounding in-substance defeasance is traceable to the fact that defeasance also affects the amount of net income reported by the firm. If market interest rates have risen since the issuance of the debt, then the *book value* of the liability will exceed the cost of acquiring the risk-free securities. Therefore, under current accounting rules, a firm can generate an accounting gain in its net income statement by retiring the debt. The financial community became concerned that the firms would engage in defeasance transactions for the sole purpose of generating increases in reported net income.

Incentives For Defeasance

The accounting and finance literature contains several possible explanations for why a firm's management would decide to execute an in-substance defeasance transaction. One explanation that is frequently advanced in accounting texts is that the firm's management has concluded that the best use of the firm's resources is to retire outstanding debt, but that a direct repurchase of debt is prohibitively costly. The management then chooses to achieve this goal through an in-substance defeasance. This explanation implies that the market value of the defeased debt issue should increase and the value of the firm's equity should decrease. Research shows that, on average, following defeasance transactions the increase in bond values is less than would be predicted solely on the basis of defeased debt being made less risky by the defeasance.

In practice, it appears that the underlying reason for a firm's management electing to retire debt is simply that the firm lacks alternate profitable investment opportunities. In other cases, it appears that the firm's management is concerned that the firm is operating too close to the accounting based covenants in its lending agreements. To reduce the likelihood of violating these constraints, the firm's management seeks to improve its debt to equity position by retiring some portion of the firm's debt. Either of these motivations raises questions about the firm's long-term performance. Consequently, analysts and investors may interpret the defeasance as a negative indicator of firm value.

A defeasance transaction may also be a part of financing strategy in which new debt is to be issued. Thus, analysts and investors may interpret the defeasance as a favorable indicator of firm value.

STEVEN A. ALLEN

accounting for fixed assets Long-lived assets are those income-producing resources that expect to benefit more than one accounting period. They are often called "fixed" assets. Tangible fixed assets, such as machinery and buildings, often make up a large part of an enterprise's total assets, especially for nonfinancial enterprises. Accounting for fixed assets includes recognizing the assets in the accounts at date of acquisition, charging their cost to expense over the periods expected to benefit from their use through the process known as depreciation, accounting for related costs subsequent to acquisition, and removing the amounts and related contra asset account amounts for accumulated depreciation upon disposal.

U.S. accounting principles currently require fixed assets to be recorded at historical cost, which is the amount expended for the asset on the acquisition date including freight, installation, setup costs, and other charges to get the asset ready for its intended use. Arguments for the use of historical cost usually center on its objective and reliable nature and its representation of fair market value of the asset on the date it is acquired. It is a conservative measure; the amount reflected in the balance sheet subsequent to acquisition does not reflect replacement costs, and income for the period does not include gains or losses from holding the asset.

Accounting Measures

Land acquired for productive use is recorded at cost, which includes the contract price and amounts expended for title search, title insurance, past due taxes, legal fees, recording and notary fees, surveys and any amounts necessary to prepare the land for its intended use. Demolition costs to raze an existing structure, net of salvage value, are included in the cost of the land if needed to ready the land for its intended use. Generally land is not depreciated, and accounting practices do not record its appreciation, except in special circumstances. The land is carried in the account at cost until the time of disposal.

The cost of a building acquired includes the amount paid for the building plus any expenditures to ready the building for use. If the building is substantially renovated prior to use or if a new building is constructed, related costs of designing, net demolition costs, costs of securing bids and permits, and actual costs of construction are included in the cost of the building. Unlike land, buildings gradually deteriorate and they ultimately will require expenditures to renew or replace them. Their cost is charged to current and future operations as depreciation expense.

Other fixed assets such as equipment, machinery, and furniture and fixtures are recorded on the date of acquisition at cost, including all amounts paid to install and prepare the assets for their intended productive use. Additional expenditures include freight and insurance charges for the asset in-transit, setup charges, and leveling and testing costs incurred.

Self-constructed assets require consideration of interest costs and fixed overhead costs incurred. Financial Accounting Standards Board (FASB), Statement of Financial Accounting Standards (SFAS) No. 34 (1979) requires interest costs to be capitalized based on actual amounts borrowed when an entity constructs a qualifying asset for its own use. This practice enables more accurate measurement of an asset's cost, and it more accurately matches expenses with revenues for the periods benefited by expenditures. Imputed interest is not allowed; the amount of interest that should be charged to the asset account is the amount that theoretically could have been avoided. It is calculated by applying the interest rate to the average cumulative invested costs for the asset during the capitalization period. Total interest incurred during the period must be disclosed, and the amount that has been capitalized should be disclosed separately as well.

Fixed overhead costs incurred when an entity constructs an asset, such as building occupancy costs and depreciation, are most commonly allocated proportionately to that asset. Arguments are made that no overhead should be included in the cost of the asset if overhead is not affected by the construction, and that only the incremental fixed overhead incurred should be included in the asset's cost when excess capacity exists. Allocating a portion of the fixed overhead is most justifiable when the entity is operating at full capacity and usable production is therefore foregone, but it is used in most circumstances.

Transactions other than "cash for asset" arise as well. When dissimilar fixed assets are acquired as a group for one sum, the amount must be prorated to the individual assets acquired. The basis for the allocation is the relative fair market values of the individual assets. When fixed assets are acquired by issuing securities, the general rule is that the assets should be recorded at the more reliable of the fair market value of the assets acquired or the stock issued. When a series of deferred payments is established to pay for the acquisition of an asset, the cost of the asset is the more reliable of its fair value or the fair value of the liability on the date of the transaction. According to US Accounting Principles Board (APB) Opinion No. 21 (1971), the present value of the deferred payments computed at the stated rate may be used if neither fair value is readily determinable and if the stated rate is not materially different from the market rate of interest. If an asset is donated to the entity, the "cost" to be reflected in the accounting records is the fair value on date of acquisition. SFAS No. 116 (1994) requires that this amount be reflected in income for the period.

Exchanging Nonmonetary Assets

Accounting for exchanges of nonmonetary assets, including fixed assets, is somewhat complex. US Accounting Principles Board (APB) Opinion No. 29 (1973) indicates that the general rule is to record an asset acquired in this manner at the fair value of the asset surrendered, recognizing a gain or loss on the exchange if the fair value of the asset given up is different from its carrying value. If money is paid or received as part of the transaction, the cost of the asset acquired includes any amount paid or is net of any amount received. If the fair value of the asset surrendered is less reliable than the fair value of the asset acquired, then the latter amount should be used. This rule applies in the exchange of dissimilar productive assets that are not employed in the same line of business.

When similar productive assets are exchanged between two dealers or two non-dealers, the rules are modified to the extent that the earning process is not considered to be complete as the transaction closes. Revenue is not recognized, based on the conservatism principle. In the case where gain is not recognized, the acquired asset is recorded at the carrying value of the asset surrendered. When an amount of money is received as part of the exchange, a gain is recognized in proportion to the amount of money received to the total consideration received. If the amount of money involved in the transaction exceeds 25 percent of the total consideration, the exchange is considered to be monetary in nature and fair value is used by both parties to the transaction. In any case, a loss incurred on the exchange should be recorded.

Costs incurred after the productive asset has been placed in service should be added to the amount in the account if the expenditures increase the future economic benefits of the asset over those initially expected. The cost of an addition should be capitalized. Improvements and replacements typically extend the useful life or increase an asset's productivity, so their costs should be capitalized. The particular circumstances determine whether the costs should be added to the asset account, used to reduce the related accumulated depreciation account, or substituted for the carrying value of the original asset.

Depreciation

The matching concept requires that cost be allocated to expense in the periods when related revenues are recognized. According to US Accounting Terminology Bulletin No. 1 (1953), the primary consideration is that the allocation be systematic and rational. For fixed assets, depreciation is the means by which the cost of the assets is charged to expense. In some cases, the amount is shown in the income statement as "depreciation expense." Depreciation on factory facilities, however, is included as an inventoriable item and, therefore, is shown in the income statement as part of "cost of goods sold" when the related inventory items are sold. Regardless of format, several depreciation methods are acceptable and widely used. Two types of methods predominate. Time-based methods include the straight line and decreasing charge methods; activity methods typically base depreciation charges on units produced or hours operated.

Since an asset's cost is spread over its service life, an estimate must be made of the service life.

It is usually based on experience with similar assets, and engineering or economic studies can assist in making the determination. Physical deterioration is an important factor, as is technological obsolescence. Frequency and quality of maintenance can affect the former, while market studies can help predict the latter.

The easiest method used is the straight line method. The amount of depreciation each period is the cost less salvage value divided by the estimated useful life. Since an equal amount is charged to expense each year, an implicit assumption is that the process of asset consumption or deterioration occurs uniformly over time. While this might be true for some fixed structures, other assets such as machinery deteriorate more as a function of use than time. Another criticism of this method is that the loss of productivity and increased maintenance costs in the later years of an asset's life are implicitly ignored. It is a popular method, however, due to its simplicity.

Accelerated depreciation methods charge decreasing amounts to expense as time passes. One argument in their favor is that lower depreciation charges in later years would offset the higher maintenance costs likely during those periods. In addition, the higher depreciation charges in the earlier years would reflect the uncertainty about obsolescence in future periods. Many companies have used some variant of accelerated depreciation for financial reporting since it was first sanctioned by the US Internal Revenue Service for tax purposes in 1954.

The sum-of-the-years' digits method computes depreciation expense each period by multiplying the cost less salvage value by a reducing fraction each period. The denominator of the fraction is constant at the sum of the digits from one to the number of years of life of the asset. (It can be computed as $n(n+1)/2$, with n being the expected life of the asset.) The numerator changes each year; it is the number of years remaining of the useful life as of the beginning of the period.

Decreasing charge methods apply a constant percentage to the declining carrying value of the asset each period to determine the amount of depreciation expense for the period. A formula can be used to compute a rate that will reduce the asset balance to the salvage value at the end of the estimated useful life. That rate is calculated as follows:

$$[1 - (salvage\ value/cost)^{1/n}]$$

Although this formula is not used often, a variant known as the declining balance method is in common use. Double-declining-balance is a common application of this procedure wherein 200 percent of the straight line rate is used as the percentage applied to the carrying value each period. No higher rate is used, but lower rates are often applied. Salvage value is ignored in the computation; however, the asset should not be depreciated below this amount. Many entities will switch to straight line from the declining balance rate at either the midpoint in the asset's life or when the amount of depreciation computed using the straight line rate exceeds that amount computed with the declining balance rate. If used systematically, such a procedure is acceptable.

Intensity of use or activity is the basis for computing depreciation for some entities. The amount of depreciation per unit of activity is computed as cost less salvage value divided by the estimated total number of units of activity (hours or units produced for example) over the asset's expected useful life. This fraction is then multiplied by the actual number of units of activity during a period to determine the depreciation expense for that period. This method yields a constant per-unit charge, but depreciation expense varies from period to period depending on the rate of activity each period.

The method selected by an entity should be systematic and rational, and ideally it would consider the rate of usage of the asset as well as the expected repair and maintenance expenditures over the asset's service life. The objective in this case is to achieve a matching of the total cost of the asset (including any costs required to keep it operating as planned) with the revenues generated by the asset. In the USA, most companies use the straight line method of depreciation. This is also true of companies in the UK. In some countries, such as Germany, Switzerland, France, and Italy, depreciation methods used for financial reporting are driven largely by tax requirements.

Regardless of the method of depreciation used, the actual recording of depreciation expense each period is straightforward. It requires a debit entry (an increase) to "depreciation expense" and a credit entry (an increase) to "accumulated depreciation," which is a contra asset account, for the amount of depreciation expense for that period. Assets are often acquired during a period. In this event, one of several conventions is usually used to compute depreciation expense for the partial period. Most common methods are to record depreciation to the nearest month or nearest year, or to record one-half year's depreciation on all assets acquired during the year (with dispositions being treated in a similar manner).

Disclosures related to depreciation required by US Accounting Principles Board (APB) Opinion No. 12 (1967) include the following:

- A general description of the method(s) used in computing depreciation with respect to the major classes of depreciable assets.

- Depreciation expense for the period.

- The balance in the accounts of the major classes of depreciable assets at the balance sheet date.

- The balance in the accumulated depreciation accounts as of the balance sheet date, either by major classes of depreciable assets or in total.

Disposal of Long-lived Assets

When an asset is retired, the capitalized cost amount must be removed from the asset account, and the related accumulated depreciation amount should be removed from the contra asset account. If retired during a period, depreciation should be recorded on the asset using one of the conventions discussed above. A gain or loss computed as the amount of net proceeds minus the net carrying value of the asset is usually included in ordinary income. If the transaction meets the criteria in US Accounting Principles Board (APB) Opinion No. 30 (1973) for recording as an extraordinary item or as the disposal of a segment, then the gain or loss would be shown below income from continuing operations on the income statement.

Accounting for fixed assets varies across countries. Some countries, such as Germany and Japan, have adhered even more strictly to the historical cost principle than has the USA. Other countries, including the UK, the Netherlands, and Switzerland, have allowed more flexibility with respect to revaluations of fixed assets to market values. The US accounting standards still indicate historical cost should be used, with the possible exception of impairment in the value of a long-lived asset. In Australia and New Zealand, accounting practice allows revaluing assets up or down as market values deviate from recorded values.

NANCY D. WEATHERHOLT

accounting for leases standards   This entry provides a comparison of the various standards on the accounting for leases that have been issued by the standard setting bodies in the USA, UK, Australia, and New Zealand, and by the International Accounting Standards Committee (IASC). These are the US Statement of Financial Accounting Standard No. 13, "Accounting for Leases" (SFAS 13); the Australian Statement of Accounting Standard No. 17, "Accounting for Leases" (now titled Approved Accounting Standard ASRB 1008 "Accounting for Leases") (AAS 17); the UK Statement of Standard Accounting Practice No. 21, "Accounting for Leases and Hire Purchase Contracts" (SSAP 21); the New Zealand Statement of Standard Accounting Practice No. 18, "Accounting for Leases and Hire Purchase Contracts," (SSAP 18); and the International Accounting Standard No. 17, Accounting for Leases (IAS 17).

Accounting policy-makers in these countries have usually been concerned with accounting for leases following a rapid growth in lease financing. In Australia, the value of all lease agreements increased rapidly in the decade up to 1976 and then subsequently almost doubled in real terms in the next three years to A$5.8 billion (US$4.1 billion) (Bazley et al. 1985, p. 45). Similarly, the UK Accounting Standards Committee issued its standard, SSAP 21, in 1984 following a decade where annual expenditure on leased assets by the leasing industry increased tenfold (from 288 million (US$450 million) in 1973 to 2,894 million (US$4,560 million) in 1983) (Deloitte et al., 1985, p.1). A similar sequence of events was noted in India.

Analysis of Standards

Conceptually, the various regulations governing the accounting for and reporting of lease transactions in published financial statements of lessees and lessors are based on the same general principles as those of SFAS 13 in the USA. All of the standards require lessees to capitalize leases that are considered finance, financial or capital leases, but only to recognize and disclose separately the total amount of annual lease rental expenses charged to income for other leases. Since a finance lease is considered, in substance, equivalent to a purchase with debt financing, the various pronouncements require that a finance lease be recorded by lessees as a lease asset and as a lease obligation in the lessee's balance sheet. The various pronouncements also set standards for the determination of the initial values of capitalized lease assets and liabilities, the amortization of the lease asset, the reduction of the lease liability, and the required disclosures for both finance and operating leases. (Capitalizing a finance lease requires the present value of the minimum lease payments to be recorded as an asset and a liability. The capitalized asset should then be depreciated in accordance with normal depreciation requirements and policies over the shorter of the asset's useful life or the lease term, while the lease rental payments should be apportioned between the finance or interest charge to income and the capital portion that reduces the outstanding lease liability.)

Lessors are also required to classify leases as finance or operating on the basis of whether the lessor "transfers substantially all the risks and rewards incident to the ownership of the leased property" to the lessee. Thus, lessors would treat rentals receivable under a finance lease as repayments of principal and finance income to reimburse and reward the lessor for the investment and services. However, under an operating lease, "the risks and rewards incident to ownership" remain with the lessor. Thus, lessors would treat assets held for operating leases as depreciable assets, and would include rentals receivable in periodic income over the lease term. (The particular accounting and disclosure requirements for lessors depend upon whether the leases are classified as being either direct financing, sales type, or leveraged leases. There are also additional requirements for sale and leaseback transactions and leases involving land and buildings.)

There is little agreement as to what constitutes a finance lease and an operating lease. Because of this difficulty and the significant impact of such a classification on financial statements and key financial indicators, in particular lessee leverage ratios, the issue of economic consequences of lease capitalization has added to policy-makers' difficulties. Consequently, the chosen criteria are considered "too arbitrary," or "too ambiguous in interpretation," or "too easily circumvented by judicious structuring of lease contracts to avoid capitalization rules or tests" and mark most differences among countries.

In the USA (SFAS 13, para. 7), a finance lease is one that satisfies any one or more of the following four criteria:

(1) The present value of the minimum lease payments at the beginning for the lease term is equal to or greater than 90 percent of the fair market value of the leased asset ("90 percent test").
(2) The lease term is equal to 75 percent or more of the estimated remaining economic life of the leased asset ("75 percent test").
(3) The lease transfers ownership of the leased asset to the lessee at the end of the lease term.
(4) The lease contains a bargain purchase option.

A lease that does not meet any of the above criteria is classified as an operating lease.

However, the criteria in the UK and Australian regulations and in the IASC pronouncement are less prescriptive and leave more room for judgment. The Australian AAS 17 (paras 8 to 9) provides only guidelines and relies upon management interpretation of "economic substance" as the basis for classification, rather than prescribing specific criteria. In circumstances where "substantially all the risks and benefits incident to ownership effectively pass to the lessee," the lease should be classified as a finance lease. Prima facie evidence of such a transfer are:

(1) the lease is non-cancellable; and
(2) either of the first two SFAS 13 tests is met (para. 10).

The UK SSAP 21 (para. 15) defines a financial lease similarly and offers one criterion: at the inception of the lease the present value of all minimum lease payments must amount to substantially all (normally 90 percent or more) of the fair value of the leased asset. Otherwise, a lease is classified as operating.

In contrast to the SFAS 13 criteria, the SSAP 21 "90 percent test" and the three Australian conditions (non-cancellability, "90 percent test," and "75 percent test") only give rise to a rebuttable presumption that a lease is a finance lease. Consequently, it is possible to classify similar leases in different ways under the different standards.

By providing criteria as guidelines for classification, rather than strict rules, the Australian profession was attempting to discourage the practices of structuring lease contracts in order to avoid the strict capitalization rules (McGregor, 1985). Australian regulators amended the standard in November 1987. This new Australian regulation begins with a definition of an operating lease and then defines a financial lease as any lease other than an operating lease. However, as noted by Shanahan (1981) and discussed in Whittred & Zimmer (1988, p. 237), the new drafting was not effective. Thus, by constructing a lease which intentionally avoids "transferring substantially all the risks and benefits incident to ownership," a lease could still be classified as an operating lease.

Similar experiences in applying SSAP 21 in practice in the UK also indicate that leases were often constructed to avoid or "fail" the "90 percent test." In response, the Institute of Chartered Accountants in England and Wales even made a submission to the UK Accounting Standards Board in 1992 which recommended that the "90 percent test" be relegated in importance or even abandoned, and be replaced by the use of a number of suggested qualitative tests (Paterson, 1993, p. 42).

International Accounting Standard No. 17, issued in 1982, defines a finance lease as "a lease that transfers substantially all the risks and rewards incident to ownership of an asset" (para. 2), which is identical to that given in SSAP 21. IAS 17 also relies upon management interpretation of "economic substance over form" as the basis for classification of leases (para. 5). However, unlike other standards, IAS 17 does not prescribe any definitive rules or tests or attach any rebuttable presumptions to the definition. Instead, it gives four examples of *situations* where a lease "would normally be classified as a finance lease," and these situations are virtually identical to the four criteria prescribed in SFAS 13 in the USA.

The disclosure requirements under IAS 17 are also less onerous than those required under the USA, UK, and Australian equivalents. (IAS 17 does not prescribe disclosure of the depreciation and finance charges for finance leases, nor the total amount of rental expenses for operating leases. However, it does state that these may be "appropriate" or are sometimes disclosed, and that other disclosures, such as the nature of any renewal options, purchase options, or escalation clauses, may also be "appropriate.") There are also some minor differences in the accounting requirements, such as the discount factor to be used in calculating the present value of the minimum lease payments (defined as"the interest rate implicit in the lease, if it is practicable to determine; if not, the lessee's incremental borrowing rate" (para. 9)). However, in general, compliance with the much less-detailed and less onerous requirements of IAS 17 enables compliance with the USA, UK, Australian, and New Zealand equivalents.

The New Zealand SSAP 18, issued only in 1986 and amended in 1990, is the most recent of the standards. Much of the terminology and some of the definitions of terms used in this standard are similar or identical to those used in other countries (especially SSAP 21 and IAS 17). However, this New Zealand standard differs in applying the classification criteria. For example, paragraph 4.4 provides that a lease would normally be classified as a finance lease in circumstances where the lease is non cancellable and the four criteria of SFAS 13 (or "situations" given as examples in IAS 17), are satisfied. However, this standard· also imposes the additional requirements of "collectibility of the minimum lease payments is reasonably predictable" (para. 4.4b), and "in the case of the lessor the amount of unreimbursable costs yet to be incurred by the lessor under the lease can be ascertained with reasonable certainty" (para. 4.4d). Disclosure requirements for both finance and operating leases are also more stringent than those prescribed by IAS 17.

Expected Developments

Empirical research in at least the USA and Australia indicates there are incentives for firms, especially those that are "high lease" or highly levered, to avoid lease capitalization requirements (e.g., El-Gazzar et al., 1986; Imhoff & Thomas, 1988; Imhoff et al., 1991; Wilkins & Mok, 1991). Some of the many methods that innovative lessees and their contracting parties can use to mitigate or avoid perceived adverse effects of capitalization are discussed in some undergraduate texts (e.g., Whittred & Zimmer, 1988 ch. 9) and in professional journals. Indeed, the use of some of these methods by US firms was noted soon after Statement of Financial Accounting Standard (SFAS) 13 was first implemented (Abdel-Khalik, 1981). The Financial Accounting Standards Board Action Alert No. 79–10 (March 8, 1979) also reports that a majority of the Board members then expressed the tentative view that if SFAS 13 were to be reconsidered, they would support a property-right approach in which all leases would be included as rights to the use of property and as lease obligations in the lessee's balance sheet.

Since that time there have been a number of similar statements and suggestions by policy-makers and professions in other countries. These various policy-makers are concerned that the past attempts to develop lease accounting standards within the conventional accounting framework have "failed in their objective" and have been "largely ineffective in putting assets and liabilities relating to leasing transactions onto the balance sheet" (McGregor, 1993) Paterson (1993, Ch. 5) also reports that the property-right approach is hinted at in the UK Accounting Standards Board's draft *Statement of Principles* (Ch. 4); although the existing SSAP 21 rules presently take precedence in that country.

Bibliography

Abdel-khalik, A. R. (1981). *The economic effect on leases of FASB Statement No. 13, Accounting for Leases.* Research report, Stamford, CT: FASB.

Bazley, M., Brown, P. & Izan, H. Y. (1985). An analysis of lease disclosures by Australian companies. *Abacus*, 21, May, 44–62.

Deloitte, Haskins & Sells (1985). *Accounting by lessees following SSAP 21*, London: Deloitte, Haskins & Sells.

El-Gazzar, S., Lilien, S. & Pastena, V. (1986). Accounting for leases by lessees. *Journal of Accounting and Economics*, 8, Oct., 217–37.

Imhoff, E. A. & Thomas, J. K. (1988). Economic consequences of accounting standards: The lease disclosure rule change. *Journal of Accounting and Economics*, 10, Dec., 277–310.

Imhoff, E. A., Lipe, R. C. & Wright, D. W. (1991). Operating leases: Impact of constructive capitalization. *Accounting Horizons*, 5, Mar., 51–63.

McGregor, W. (1985). Accounting for leases: The impact of AAS17. *The Australian Accountant*, June, 90–2.

McGregor, W. (1993). Accounting for leases – A new framework. *The Australian Accountant*, May, 17–20.

Narayanaswamy, R. (1992). Accounting for leases by lessees in India: Some evidence of economic impact. *International Journal of Accounting*, 3, 255–61.

Paterson, R. (1993). *Off balance sheet finance*. London: Macmillan.

Shanahan, J. B. (1981). *Leasing in Australia*. Sydney: CCH Australia.

Whittred, G. & Zimmer, I. (1988). *Financial accounting: Incentive effects and economic consequences*. Sydney: Harcourt Brace Jovanovich.

Wilkins, T. A. & Mok, W. M. (1991). An analysis of lease accounting and disclosures by Australian firms subsequent to AAS 17. In S. G. Rhee & R. P. Chang (eds), *Pacific Basin capital markets research*, 2, Amsterdam: Elsevier Science Publishers B. V. (North-Holland).

TREVOR A. WILKINS

accounting income concepts Economic gain is and has been a significant motivating factor underlying activities of both individuals and business entities, although the nature of the specific activities varies across different cultures and over the centuries. While the concept of economic gain remains a constant motivating factor underlying human behavior, its measurement varies considerably. In some cultures economic gain might be measured by the number of cows, horses, or camels one owns or the number of households one can maintain. In other cultures it might be measured by the quantity of some monetary unit that can be exchanged for desired possessions. Even where the measurement unit is universal, the measurement process is subject to the exercise of extensive judgment and even debate.

"Income" is a term commonly used in modern society to describe economic gain. But there is no universal agreement on a single definition of income, partly due to the need to measure income over short and somewhat arbitrary time periods. Lifetime income is a reasonably simple concept. One can compare an accepted basic measure of wealth commanded by an individual or other economic entity at the end of its life to the same measurement at the beginning of its life with the difference being income. One measurement of lifetime income is the quantity of cash commanded by an individual or other entity at the end minus the quantity of cash commanded at the beginning of its life. This assumes that all net assets are converted to cash. In other words, lifetime income is the net cash flow over the life of an entity. Net cash flow could be used to measure income over shorter interim time periods but most would argue that the ability to command future positive net cash flows is a better measure of economic gain than past cash flows for a short period of time. This opens the path for considerable judgment and debate on the measurement of economic gain or income.

A complication to the clarification of the concept of income is created by the existence of other closely related terms. Terms such as "profit" and "earnings" have often been used interchangeably with "income." There is also sometimes confusion about whether one is referring to a gross or a net measurement. In Statement of Financial Accounting Concepts No. 5 (1984) (SFAC 5), "Recognition and Measurement in Financial Statements of Business Enterprises," the US Financial Accounting Standards Board (FASB) chooses to use the term "earnings" rather than "income" and also introduces a concept described as "comprehensive income" (paras 33 to 42). Here we will consider the concept of income as a net measurement, more precisely described as the net change in economic position for an individual or other economic entity from specified sources. Economic position can be defined and measured in various ways and is sometimes referred to as "net wealth."

In discussing various concepts of income one might begin with current accounting practice. However, significant difficulties arise from this approach due to differences in the concept of income as well as the specific measurements across countries. Furthermore, income is commonly defined and measured according to specified rules rather than by the application of a clearly defined concept. In the USA the measurement of income is primarily governed by the application of rules relating to the measurement of revenue and expense. Thus, income is not clearly defined as a concept in accounting practice. Rather it is the result of the application of revenue recognition and expense matching concepts. In addition to articulation of the concepts of revenue recognition and expense matching, many rules have been promulgated by the FASB and other standard setting bodies to guide the measurement of revenues and expenses in specific situations, including specialized industries. Gains and losses are distinguished from revenues and expenses and are also included in the computation of income according to specific rules.

Although current accounting practice does not offer a clear concept of income, several concepts exist in the accounting and economic literature. The writings of the economist J. R. Hicks offer a good starting point. In his book *Value and Capital* he states that "it would seem that we ought to be able to define a man's income as the maximum value which he can consume during a week, and still be as well off at the end of the week as he was at the beginning" (p. 172). In order to apply this definition some measurement rules must also be specified. In a world of certainty, the measurement of all relevant future net cash flows discounted to the present by an appropriate discount rate would receive strong support among accounting theorists as the best measure of "well off." The change in this measure during a period becomes the basis for determining income. (For a more complete discussion of the determination of income under certainty see R. K. Jaedicke & R. T. Sprouse, 1965).

There is much disagreement on the measurement of income in the real world – the world of uncertainty. The discounting of estimated future cash flows offers one possibility. But the subjectivity inherent in this measurement

process and the notion that such estimations may fall beyond the scope and responsibility of accounting drives one quickly to consider other measurement processes. As one evaluates other measurement processes and, therefore, alternative income concepts, it becomes paramount to consider the purpose of income measurement.

The conceptual framework articulated by the FASB offers one source of arguments concerning the purpose of income measurement. Statement of Financial Accounting Concepts No. 1 (1978) (SFAC 1), "Objectives of Financial Reporting by Business Enterprises," indicates that the basic purpose of financial reporting is to provide information that will assist in the prediction of future net cash flows (para. 37). The measurement and reporting of income is considered important in fulfilling this objective. It is often described as a measure of enterprise "performance." The FASB indicates that the primary focus of financial reporting is information about an enterprise's performance provided by measures of earnings and its components (SFAC 1, para. 43).

In Statement of Financial Accounting Concepts No. 2 (1980) (SFAC 2), "Qualitative Characteristics of Accounting Information," relevant information is described as information that is capable of making a difference in decisions. This occurs by improving decision-makers' capacities to predict or by confirming or changing earlier expectations. "Relevance" includes the characteristics of predictive value, feedback value, and timeliness (SFAC 2, paras 51 to 57). One might focus on the notion of feedback value and conclude that an income concept that focuses solely on completed or past events is sufficiently relevant. However, when considered in the context of the objectives of financial reporting, with the emphasis on providing information to assist in the assessment of future cash flows especially for investment decisions, predictive value seems to assume a higher degree of relevance. The theoretically preferred concept of income that discounts future cash flows under conditions of certainty adds further weight to the importance of predictability. In other words, income should measure economic gain in such a way that the prediction of future economic gains is enhanced.

Income and Capital Maintenance

Income concepts are best described through various definitions of capital maintenance. Although not identical in concept, capital maintenance can be related to notions of economic position, net wealth, and "as well off as" that are commonly used. The US Financial Accounting Standards Board (FASB) recognized the importance of explaining income concepts through reference to capital maintenance and attempted to describe the earnings (income) concept used in current accounting practice with reference to the maintenance of financial capital. But this is a nebulous concept that did little to clarify the nature of income.

Although not often described as a capital maintenance concept, one could argue that the strongest definition of capital maintenance is the maintenance of the ability to generate future net cash inflows. The direct measurement of this concept through the discounting of estimated future net cash flows is generally believed to be impractical under conditions of uncertainty and perhaps beyond the scope of current accounting responsibility.

A capital maintenance concept that has been discussed widely in the literature is the maintenance of physical capital. This is also sometimes referred to as the maintenance of productive or operating capacity. The underlying theory behind this concept is that an entity must provide for the replacement of all income-generating factors that have been consumed during a period before income occurs. The measurement process in the application of this theory focuses on the determination of replacement costs for consumed income-generating factors (expired assets). A potential problem inherent in this measurement process is that there are several replacement cost figures that may be available for a particular item. For example, the current and estimated future replacement costs of an item may differ. Also, an item may no longer be available or available only with improved technology. Conventional wisdom tends to favor using a replacement cost that best reflects the current cost of replacing a similar asset even if the asset is not available. This is commonly referred to as the "current cost." In periods of rising prices the use of replacement costs to measure expenses, as compared to the alternative of actual past prices paid, tends to reduce the computed income.

There are several potential variations in the suggested use of replacement costs in the measurement of income that do not strictly conform to the concept of physical capital maintenance. One variation is to subtract estimated replacement costs for expired assets from revenues to obtain an operating income and then adjust for the difference between estimated replacement and actual past costs of the expired assets to obtain net income. This results in a final income figure that is equal to the income obtained under current FASB guidelines and rules. This procedure yields income figures for both the physical and financial capital maintenance concepts. The operating income is the income figure according to the physical capital maintenance concept, while the final income figure is the income according to the FASB notion of financial capital maintenance.

A second variation is to consider any price changes during the period on assets still held at the end of the period as holding gains and losses. Those who support this approach argue that a gain or loss occurs due to the acquisition of an item at a price that differs from the current acquisition price. Thus, an item held during a period of changing prices creates a holding gain or loss. A price increase or holding gain would be added in arriving at income while a price decrease or holding loss would be deducted. Some have suggested disclosing this figure separately after income rather than adding or subtracting it directly in arriving at income. The FASB experimented during the early 1980s with supplemental disclosures that computed income under the physical capital maintenance concept with separate disclosure of holding gains and losses (Statement of Financial Accounting Standard No. 33 (1979), "Financial Reporting and Changing Prices.")

Recognizing a distinction between general price level and specific price changes is another important issue for income measurement. Specific price changes are derived from the replacement costs for specific items. General price level changes are measured by an average of all price changes for a broad cross-section of items in the total economy through an index relating to some base year. This is often described as reflecting the changes in purchasing power of the basic monetary unit in a country, such as the dollar in the USA. In capital maintenance terms, computing income using general price indices is described conceptually as the maintenance of invested purchasing power. There are several problems and complexities associated with the recognition of general price level changes in computing income. Business entities, even very large entities, operate only in segments of the total economy. General price movements as determined by a large cross-section of items in the economy may not reflect the price changes experienced by a particular business entity. Another issue raised by consideration of general price level changes is the potential divergent impact of the changes on monetary versus nonmonetary items. Since general price level changes reflect a change in the purchasing power of the basic monetary unit, it is argued that a purchasing power gain or loss occurs on monetary items as they are held through periods of changing prices. For example, in a period of rising prices (decline in purchasing power) a loss occurs on monetary assets while a gain occurs on monetary liabilities. This potential gain or loss is further complicated by interest rates that often are attached to financial instruments considered as monetary items. If an interest rate attached to a monetary item such as a bond includes a charge for "inflation expectations," the theoretical purchasing power gain or loss is reduced.

Under the invested purchasing power concept of capital maintenance, nonmonetary items are restated by adjusting for the changes in the monetary unit that have been experienced since the acquisition of the item. The historical acquisition price of the item is typically restated by multiplying by the current general price level index over the index at the time of acquisition. Although the restatement does not result in a gain or loss on the item, the restatement does affect the measurement of income as adjusted expenses are related to adjusted revenues.

A business entity may experience general and specific prices moving in opposite directions. For example, the computer industry has recently experienced falling specific prices while general prices have increased mildly. The potential divergence between the general price level movement and the change in specific prices experienced by a particular entity during a period may affect the predictive quality of income computed for that entity when adjusting for general price level changes while items are replaced at specific prices. But the use of the specific price or replacement cost framework in computing income has potential predictive weaknesses as well. Actual replacement cost when an item is replaced may differ from the replacement cost estimated at the time the item was utilized and expensed. Also, a particular item may not be replaced by the same or even by a similar item. Changing technology, modification of product lines, and other changes can cause replacement costs to vary and muddle the predictive characteristics of income computed under a replacement costing framework. The use of the "current cost" system may improve the matching of revenues and expenses but may not necessarily be highly predictive of actual future replacement costs and/or future operating margins.

Adjustments for general price level changes may affect the measurement of lifetime income since general price level changes reflect the underlying fluctuations in the purchasing power of the monetary measuring unit. Cash remaining upon liquidation may not have the equivalent purchasing power as the beginning cash. A change in the purchasing power would cause the measured income to be different from the total difference in cash. Adjustment for specific price changes only, in the current or replacement cost framework, will not change lifetime income since fluctuations in the purchasing power of the monetary unit are not considered. Changes in specific replacement prices affect the measurement of income only while items are being held and replacement is anticipated. Therefore, the lifetime cash difference remaining after liquidation will be equal to the lifetime measured income.

There is some support for the use of exit market prices in measuring income. Accounting practice in the USA requires this for some items such as certain marketable securities held for sale. Agricultural products and precious metals are some other examples where this may occur. In these cases income is recognized before the item is sold. There are advocates who favor an increase in the use of exit market prices for items held and readily salable in the measurement of income. This would tend to advance the measurement of income to earlier periods in most cases but would not change total lifetime income.

To summarize, the measurement of income is a difficult task in the complex real world of economic uncertainties. Measurement is especially difficult in periods of changing prices. Both the concept of income and its measurement are subject to variations. Yet, income measurement is arguably the most important dimension of financial reporting and essential in meeting the basic objectives and purposes of accounting. Current accounting practice has generally relied on measurement rules for revenues, expenses, gains and losses in determining income. Prior debate and research have not resulted in agreement on a concept of income for accounting practice. Furthermore, clarification and agreement on a single concept of income is difficult in a world of changing prices and technology with potentially differing capital maintenance objectives.

Bibliography

Bedford, N. M. (1965). *Income Determination Theory: An Accounting Framework*. Reading: Addison Wesley.

Hicks, J. R. (1946). *Value and Capital*. Oxford: Clarendon Press. Second Edition.

Jaedicke, R. K. & Sprouse, R. T. (1965). *Accounting Flows: Income, Funds and Cash*. New Jersey: Prentice-Hall.

Johnson, L. T. & Storey, R. K. (1982). Recognition in Financial Statements: Underlying Concepts, and Practical Conventions. Stamford, CN.

Report of the Committee on Corporate Financial Reporting (1972). *Supplement to the Accounting Review*, **47**.

Revsine, L. (1973). *Replacement Cost Accounting*. New Jersey: Prentice-Hall.

Solomons, David (1961). Economic and Accounting Concept of Income. *The Accounting Review*, July.

JOHN K. SIMMONS

accounting misstatements   If reported accounting information is in violation of generally accepted accounting principles (GAAP), it would be erroneous and should be corrected upon its detection. GAAP specifies the requirements for correcting misstatements of a prior period financial statements. A misstatement is distinguished from a change in estimate inherent in the accounting process within GAAP. A major distinguishing feature of a correction of an accounting misstatement is that the financial statements of the affected prior periods, when originally issued, should have reflected the adjustment. For example, a change from an unacceptable accounting principle to one that is generally accepted is a correction of a misstatement (APB 20, para. 13).

Accounting misstatements could be mistakes (unintentional errors) or they could be intentional (irregularities). Intentional misstatements are made by the management to mislead users and accompanied by actions to mislead the auditor, i.e., fraudulent financial reporting. The intent is often difficult to determine, particularly in matters involving the use of judgement (Statement of Auditing Standard No. 53). In the absence of evidence to the contrary, a misstatement arising from selecting and applying accounting principles or in making accounting estimates is considered as unintentional.

GAAP requires that net income for an accounting period reflect all items of profit and loss recognized during the period, with the exception of prior period adjustments (APB Opinion No. 9, para. 3). The accounting treatment and the necessity for disclosure depend on materiality of the correction, which should be considered in relation to both the effects of each correction separately and the combined effect of the correction (APB 20, para. 38). If the correction has a material effect on income or on the trend of earnings, GAAP requires the following accounting and disclosures for the corrections:

(1) An item of profit or loss related to the correction of an error in the financial statements of a prior period should be accounted for and reported as a prior period adjustment and excluded from the determination of net income for the current period (FASB Statement No. 96, para. 205). The correction should be accounted for as an adjustment of the opening balance of retained earnings (FASB 16, para. 16).

(2) The correction should be reflected by restating the financial statements for all prior periods affected by the misstatement

(FASB 16, para. 41). The corresponding adjustments should be made of the amount of net income (and the components thereof) and retained earnings balance (as well as of other affected balances) for all the periods reported therein to reflect the retroactive effect of the adjustment (APB 9, para. 18).

(3) The nature of an error and the effect of its correction on income before extraordinary items, net income, and the related per share amounts should be disclosed in the period in which the error was discovered and corrected (APB 20 para. 37). Disclosures should include the amounts of income tax applicable to the prior period adjustments. Disclosure of restatements in annual reports issued subsequent to the first such post-revision disclosure would ordinarily not be required (APB 9, para. 26).

(4) When historical summaries of financial data are presented, the reported amounts of net income (and the components thereof) as well as other affected items for any of the periods included therein should be appropriately restated, with disclosure in the first summary published after the adjustment (APB 9, para 27).

Empirical research shows that accounting misstatements resulting in reporting an improved financial condition, e.g., higher income or larger assets, are more frequent than misstatements resulting in reporting less favorable conditions had GAAP been properly applied (Neter & Loebbecke, 1975; Ramage et al., 1979; Johnson et al., 1981; Hylas & Ashton, 1982; Kinney & McDaniel, 1989; El-Sabbagh, 1993). Based on traditional materiality guidelines in auditing standards of 5 to 10 percent (Ricchiute, 1982, p. 43), accounting misstatements, on average, are material (Johnson et al., 1981; Kinney & McDaniel, 1989; El-Sabbagh, 1993). The major cause of all known accounting misstatements tends to be related to misapplication of accounting principles, e.g., improper revenue recognition and deferrals of costs and expenses (El-Sabbagh, 1993).

Business and Legal Implications of Accounting Misstatements

As accounting information is a primary source of information available to the public, the effect of accounting misstatements extends beyond their apparent effect on accounting records and reports. Accounting research shows that the use and detection of accounting misstatements subsequent to the issuance of financial statements result in different financial and social adverse effects. Effects include: (1) dilution of public confidence in the fairness of financial reporting, which damages the effective functioning of financial markets (Barret et al., 1975); (2) lower public confidence in the firm, leading to unfavorable terms of contracts, e.g., higher cost of capital (Trueman & Titman, 1988; Foster, 1987; El-Sabbagh, 1993); (3) litigation and substantial costs and compensations (Kellog, 1984; Feroz et al., 1991); (4) damage of employee reputations and morale (Barret et al., 1975); and (5) adverse impact on securities prices (Kellog, 1984; Anderson & Pincus, 1984; Elliott & Swieringa, 1985; Foster, 1979 & 1987; Kinney & McDaniel, 1989; El-Sabbagh, 1993).

In addition, in the USA, provisions of federal securities laws preserve accountability of financial information. The Securities and Exchange Act of 1934 prohibits fraudulent financial reporting and promotes fair and sufficient disclosure that makes information not misleading. Also, the requirements of the Foreign Corrupt Practices Act of 1977 (FCPA) ensure that companies meet their financial disclosure obligations, by keeping accurate books and records and maintaining a system of internal accounting control that preserves preparation of financial statements in conformity with GAAP.

Under the Exchange Act, the enforcement program of the Securities and Exchange Commission (SEC) provides a motivation to deter improper financial reporting and to improve the reliability of information, to maintain the integrity of financial reporting. Enforcement efforts are extended to cover acts needed against auditors to strengthen the audit function. If violations take place, penalties are enforced. Enforcement activities include court injunctions; administrative proceedings; litigation; and referrals of cases to the Justice Department, state regulatory agencies, prosecutor's offices, or state Boards of Accounting (Pincus et al., 1988, p. 45). Civil injunctive actions order the defendant to comply with the appropriate securities laws in the future. Administrative proceedings provide other types of remedies in financial reporting cases, e.g., denials, suspensions, or prohibitions against trading securities, and censures. Generally, enforcement actions are directed toward a company's officers, directors, auditors, or employees or other parties involved in committing the misstatements. Violations of financial disclosures, civil and criminal, may also lead to the enforcement of the accounting provisions of the FCPA.

The choice of action depends upon the degree of the violation. In 1982, the SEC began issuing Accounting and Auditing Enforcement Releases (AAERs) to publicize the facts and outcomes of enforcement actions. Prior to 1982, enforcement actions were publicized through Accounting Series Releases (ASRs). Violations discovered included misapplications of accounting principles within financial statements, inadequate disclosures of material facts, and false disclosures.

The requirement that publicly-held corporations produce annual audits by independent accountants provides the front-line protection against improper financial reporting. Nonetheless, the number of accounting improprieties and their dollar magnitudes have increased in recent years, and, hence, the demand for accountability and greater protection to the public has been growing. In response, the profession has acknowledged a greater auditor's responsibility in detecting accounting errors and irregularities to increase the value of the audit process: Statement of Auditing Standard (SAS) No. 1, SAS No. 16, and SAS No. 53. The profession's emphasis on the enhancement of auditors' role and responsibilities of detection is anticipated to continue, by strengthening standards of professional performance of accountants and emphasizing professional ethics. Also, positive regulatory steps that deter accounting fraud and encourage compliance with the securities laws are expected to be undertaken to enhance the credibility of financial reporting to protect interests of users and society.

Bibliography

Accounting Principles Board (1966). Reporting the results of operations. *Opinion No. 9.*

Accounting Principles Board (1971). Accounting Changes. *Opinion No. 20.*

American Institute of Certified Public Accountants (1988). The auditor's responsibility to detect and report errors and irregularities. *Statement of Auditing Standards No. 53.*

Anderson, J. & Pincus, M. (1984). Market efficiency and legal liability: Some extensions and an illustration. *Accounting and Business Research,* Spring, 169–81.

Barret, M., Baker, D. & Radde, L. (1975). Top management fraud: Definitional problems, external auditor responsibilities and top management controls.American Accounting Association Collected Papers of the 1975 AAA's Annual Meeting.

Elliott, J. & Swieringa, R. (1985). Aetna, the SEC and tax benefits of loss carry forwards. *The Accounting Review,* July, 531–46.

El-Sabbagh, A. (1993). Market evaluation of discovery of distorted earnings signals: Empirical tests of changes in cash flow expectations, riskiness, and earnings quality hypotheses.Ph.D. dissertation.

Financial Accounting Standard Board (1977). Prior Period Adjustments. *Statement of Financial Accounting Standards No. 16.*

Financial Accounting Standard Board (1987). Accounting for Income Taxes. *Statement of Financial Accounting Standards No. 96.*

Feroz, E., Park, K. & Pastena, V. (1991). The financial and market effects of the SEC's accounting and auditing enforcement releases. *Journal of Accounting Research,* (supplement),, 107–42.

Foster, G. (1979). Briloff and the capital market. *Journal of Accounting Research,* Spring, 262–74.

Foster, G. (1987). Briloff and the capital market. *Journal of Accounting, Auditing, and Finance,* Fall, 409–30.

Hylas, R. & Ashton, R. (1982). Audit detection of financial statement errors. *The Accounting Review,* Oct., 751–64.

Johnson, J., Leitch, R & Neter, J. (1981). Characteristics of errors in accounts receivable and inventory audits. *The Accounting Review,* Apr., 270–93.

Kellog, R. (1984). Accounting activities, security prices, and class action lawsuits. *Journal of Accounting and Economics,* **6,** 185–204.

Kinney, W. & McDaniel, L. (1989). Characteristics of firms correcting previously reported quarterly earnings. *Journal of Accounting and Economics,* **11,** 71–93.

Neter, J. & Leobbecke, J. (1975). *Behavior of major statistical estimates in sampling accounting populations.* New York: American Institute of Certified Public Accountants, Inc.

Pincus, K., Holder, W. & Mock, T. (1988). *Reducing the incidence of fraudulent financial reporting: The role of the Securities and Exchange Commission.* SEC and Financial Reporting Institute Center for Accounting Research. Report No. 3.

Ramage, J., Krieger, A. & Spero, L. (1979). An empirical study of error characteristics in audit populations. *Journal of Accounting Research*, (supplement), 72–102.

Ricchiute, D. (1992). *Auditing*. Cincinnati, OH: South-Western Publishing Co.

Trueman, B. & Titman, S. (1988). An explanation for accounting income smoothing. *Journal of Accounting Research*, (supplement), 127–39.

AMAL EL-SABBAGH

accounts receivables: recognition, valuation, and reporting

Recognition of accounts receivables

Accounting receivables (A/R) arise from the sale of goods or services on account. They are normally collectible within 30 to 60 days and represent "open accounts" resulting from short-term extension of credit. There are four basic issues in accounting for A/R: recognition, valuation, disposition, and presentation of A/R.

Although the exchange price may be blurred in practice, the amount to be recognized is the exchange price established in the transaction. Many companies offer cash discounts as an inducement for prompt payment. Examples are: 2/10, n/30 (2% if paid within 10 days, gross amount due in 30 days), or 2/10, E.O.M. (2% if paid within 10 days of the end of the month). The common way to record sales and related sales discount is to record the receivable and sales at the gross amount. Under this gross method, sales discounts are recognized when payment is received within the discount period. Sales discount would then be shown in the income statement as a deduction from sales to arrive at net sales. The other practice used contends that sales discount not taken reflect penalties added to an established price. Under this net method, sales and receivables are recorded net, and any discount not taken is recorded subsequently as "sales discount forfeited." In practice the gross method is widely used, because it is easy to apply. However, theoretically net method is preferable because under the net method the A/R is stated closer to its realizable value.

For the purposes of generally accepted accounting principles (GAAP), A/R must be reported at net realizable value. Net realizable value is equal to the gross amount of receivables less an estimated allowance for uncollectible receivables. Two common procedures are available for recording uncollectibles:

(1) *Direct write-off method*
This method recognizes a bad debt expense only when a specific account is determined to be uncollectible. This method is theoretically deficient because it usually does not match costs with revenues of the period. Besides, A/R is likely to be overstated, because no provision is made for the unknown bad debts. Therefore, use of the direct write-off method is considered a departure from GAAP. However, the direct write-off method is required for income tax purposes as a result of the Tax Reform Act of 1986.

(2) *Allowance method*
An estimate is made of the expected uncollectibles from each period's (credit) sales or from the balance of outstanding A/R. The amount is charged to bad debt expense and the credit is made to a valuation account such as allowance for doubtful debt. Because the collectibility is considered a loss contingency, the allowance method is appropriate in situations when the following two conditions are met (Statement of Financial Accounting Standards No. 5, "Accounting for Contingencies"): (a) it is probable that an asset has been impaired as of the date of the financial statement, and (b) the amount of the loss can be reasonably estimated.

The allowances are estimated on either the basis of percentage of (credit) sales or the basis of outstanding receivables.

Under the percentage of (credit) sales approach, the estimate is based on a historically determined percentage of each period's total (or credit) sales. This percentage may be modified by expectations based on current experience. Unless there is considerable periodic fluctuation in the proportion of cash and credit sales, the percentage of sales method (rather than credit sales) will give satisfactory results.

Under the basis of outstanding receivables approach, companies may base their estimates on a percentage (or percentages) of account receivables outstanding. Two methods are in practice. The percentage of receivable may be applied either using one composite rate or using different rates based on past experience to the various age categories of receivables outstanding. The aging approach categorizes the individual receivables according to age and applies a historical collection loss percentage to each age category to determine the required ending allowance balance. Companies may transfer accounts receivable to others to obtain immediate access to cash. The receivables are generally transferred to a third party in one of three ways:

(1) assignment of receivables, which is a borrowing arrangement with receivables pledged as security on the loan;
(2) factoring receivables, which is a sale of receivables without recourse;
(3) transfer of receivables with recourse, which is a hybrid of the other two forms of receivables financing.

(1) Assignment of A/R

The owner of receivables assigns receivables as collateral for a loan. The assignor usually continues to receive payments from customers (non-notification basis), and bears the risks of bad debt. A formal note allows the assignee (lender) to seek payment directly from the receivables if the loan is not paid when due.

(2) Factoring of Accounts

A sale of A/R without recourse is commonly referred to as A/R factoring, and the buyer is referred to as a "factor." Customers are usually notified that their bills are payable to the factor, and this party assumes the burden of billing and collecting accounts.

(3) Transfer of A/R with recourse

If receivables are sold with recourse, a transfer of receivable can be accounted either as a sale or as a borrowing transaction. The US Financial Accounting Standards Board requires that if the transaction is treated as a sale:

(1) The transferor surrenders control of future benefits of receivables.
(2) The transferor's obligation can be reasonably estimated.
(3) The transferee cannot require the transferor to repurchase the receivables.

If the transaction is treated as a sale, then journal entry is the same as factoring (transfer without recourse). If the transfer of receivables is recorded as a borrowing, then the discount on transferred A/R is amortized to interest expense over the borrowing period.

Receivables that are expected to be collected within one year or one operating cycle, whichever is longer, are reported as current assets in the balance sheet. Receivables from employees and officers should be disclosed separately. Allowances for doubtful accounts should be reported as contra asset accounts and subtracted from the A/R balance and any receivables pledged as security for loans also should be disclosed. Further, US Statement of Financial Accounting Standards No. 105, "Disclosure of Information about Financial Instruments with Off-Balance Sheet and Financial Instruments with Disclosure of Credit Risk," requires disclosure of credit risk from receivables and financial instruments. A concentration of credit risk occurs when a firm has receivables from different entities whose ability to pay is subject to common business risks (e.g., oil price change).

JANE YOUN CHO

advanced manufacturing technologies

Management Accounting

The advent of inexpensive computers, programable controllers, microprocessors, numerically controlled machine tools, and robotics has dramatically changed the face of manufacturing around the world from labor-intensive process and job shop production to automated, flexible, and computer-integrated manufacturing systems. An automated manufacturing system (AMS) consists of an integrated assembly of machines and ancillary equipment necessary for carrying out production with the minimum of manual attention together with the means for transferring components automatically through the system, all operating under fully programable control. An AMS is either an automated transfer lines system (ATLS) or a flexible manufacturing system (FMS) or some combination of both. In an ATLS, the machines are dedicated to manufacturing only one type of product in each transfer line. Such lines are characterized by high steady volume and efficiency born of economies of scale. An FMS, on the other hand, is capable of producing any of a range or family of products with minimum manual intervention. An FMS trades off economies of scale for economies of scope where the latter refers to the economic advantages associated with producing a variety of similar products. On the production side, these economic advantages derive from the firm's ability to produce different products within the same product family at minimum or no setup costs. On the demand side, these economic advantages derive from the firm's ability to satisfy demand for a variety products with little or no delay.

A computer-integrated manufacturing system (CIMS) is an AMS for which all numerically controlled production machinery as well as the materials handling system are controlled and run by a central computer. In a true CIMS, all phases of manufacturing from the design stage, using computer-aided design, through the production planning, production scheduling, quality control inspection, and delivery scheduling stages are controlled by a central computer. Not only does a CIMS provide fully assembled, inspected, and ready-to-use products, it is also capable of providing much of the information required to optimize the system given demand conditions. The numerical controllers and microprocessors provide the central computer with a wealth of data about machine usage and specific products processed. These data can be used for cost management purposes, especially product costing, to provide accurate and up-to-date analyses. These data can also be used to calculate physical and financial measures of plant productivity.

Product Costing

In a typical job shop operation, manufacturing costs are broken down into three categories: direct materials, direct labor, and factory overhead. In advanced manufacturing technologies (AMTS), this classification scheme is somewhat less useful.

Direct materials. This category of costs is also important in AMTS. Direct materials used in a job can be tracked by the central computer from the time the materials are released from the stockroom until final assembly. This is made possible by bar-codes, optical characters, or magnetic strips attached to the materials. In effect, bar coding (or its alternatives) has allowed firms to integrate their materials

resources planning (MRP) system with their accounting systems. Given the production schedule, the MRP system schedules the delivery of parts and components inventory needed for production from the stockrooms and warehouses to the production floor or to the automated materials handling system (AMHS). The primary effect of integrating the MRP system with the accounting system is to reduce and often times eliminate the paperwork associated with tracking direct materials in a conventional job shop environment. Errors in tracking direct material costs are also minimized.

Direct labor. Direct labor in AMTS is minimal by comparison to conventional technologies. In a conventional job shop operation, for example, an operator is typically needed at each machine for loading, unloading, set-ups, machine-control, and so on. In AMTS, these functions are handled by programable controllers and the central computer in conjunction with the AMHS. Operators are nevertheless required to load and unload the AMHS. Troubleshooting operators make sure that production machinery are running smoothly and service the machines when necessary. Technicians and computer operators also perform maintenance duties. Tool setters get the tools ready for the job and setup operators are used to setup special dies, fixtures, and jigs. In most cases, it is next to impossible to trace a specific operator to a particular job or product. A load operator may load 10 units of product A, then 5 of B, and 7 of C, all within a limited range of time. For all intents and purposes, most labor in AMTS is fixed factory overhead rather than variable direct labor. The amount of direct labor may be sufficiently minimal so that very little costing bias is introduced by treating all labor as fixed factory overhead.

Factory overhead and service support costs. Except for direct materials, almost all costs in AMTS are factory overhead or service support costs. The important question from a management accounting prospective is how to allocate these overhead costs to the product so that the resultant product costs truly reflect long-run resource usage.

Unlike a typical job shop, processors and computers keep accurate data on machine usage in AMTS. Specifically, the central computer collects processing times for each job on all numerically controlled machines. This means that it is possible to use each machine or assembly of homogeneous machines or manufacturing cell as a cost center (machine center) to both accumulate costs in cost pools and allocate these costs to products.

Consider the factory overhead item "equipment depreciation expense." One potential method of allocating this cost to products is to cumulate the acquisition cost of machinery in each machine center. The cost of common equipment like the central computer and the AMHS could be allocated to each machine center based upon the proportion of each machine center's equipment costs to the total equipment costs of all machine centers. The rationale here is that more costly machine centers are also more likely to place greater demands on the common equipment resources. The cost of each machine center, inclusive of allocated common equipment costs, could then be divided by the expected productive capacity of the machine center (in hours) over its economic lifetime. This calculation yields a depreciation rate for each machine center based upon hourly usage of that center. Products could then be costed based on this hourly rate and the actual usage of the machine center by the product.

Operating expenses could be allocated to each product either on the basis of machine center equipment cost, or machine center physical area, or by machine power usage depending upon the specific expense. Maintenance expenses, for example, tend to vary with the complexity, automation, and speed of the machine center so that maintenance is probably best allocated on the basis of machine center equipment costs. Building depreciation, custodial services, water, etc. should probably be allocated on the basis of machine center area. Power and electricity charges are best allocated to machine centers on the basis of the rated capacity of the machine or, if available, actual power usage of the machine center.

Activity-Based Costing

Activity-based costing (ABC) maintains as its primary tenet that product costs are generated by non-volumetric cost drivers such as product complexity, setups, quality control inspections, and materials handling, to name only a few, as well as the volume of production. This insight is particularly pertinent to AMTS where most costs, except for direct materials, are of an overhead or service support nature and are usually not driven by the volume of production. Take setup costs, for example. It is generally immaterial whether the setup is for a run of 10,000 units or 10 units. The setup costs are likely to be the same. Allocating setup costs by volume rather than the number of setups (the cost driver) would lead to overcosting high volume products and undercosting low volume products. If, in turn, prices are cost determined, as in markup pricing, this would result in high volume products being overpriced and low volume products being underpriced.

The nature of cost in AMTS is such that the relevant cost drivers must be carefully defined. Consider setup costs again. In AMTS there are two types of setups; initial setups and subsequent setups. New products have to be programed, and their production scheduling simulated and tested by trial runs in order that they mesh effortlessly within an automated system. These initial setups are quite costly, involving the time and effort of computer analysts and process engineers. Essentially, these costs are driven by demand for the product over its life cycle. Therefore, initial setup costs should be capitalized in an ABC analysis and allocated to the product based on the total number of units to be manufactured over the product's life cycle. In other words, initial setup costs are driven by the volume of production. Subsequent setup costs, on the other hand, are driven by the number of setups rather than the volume of production.

Just-In-Time Inventory and Management Accounting

Advanced manufacturing technologies, especially flexible manufacturing system (FMS) plants, typically adopt just-in-time (JIT) inventory systems. In a JIT system, delivery of inventory components and parts takes place immediately prior to production. Ideally, there is almost no standing inventory of direct materials or work in process. Therefore, a sine qua non for JIT is that the demand for the product family – although not necessarily for the specific product – be relatively stable. Firms adopting JIT typically reduce the number of their suppliers dramatically. Long-term contracts stipulating price and acceptable quality levels are negotiated with the remaining suppliers. In most cases, suppliers are required to do in-house quality inspections prior to delivery. Inventory is normally delivered in shop-ready containers to facilitate materials handling.

JIT typically simplifies the management accounting system in a number of ways. JIT increases the direct traceability of costs by reducing joint overhead costs such as warehousing and materials handling. The reduction or elimination of these costs also reduces the number of cost pools used to accumulate costs. As a consequence, JIT changes the basis for allocating indirect costs to production departments. Instead of using warehouse space as an allocation basis for purchases and material handling costs, the dollar value of materials or the number of deliveries are used. JIT also simplifies the internal accounting system by reducing the frequency and detail of purchase deliveries. Since JIT induces constant flow manufacturing and minimizes spoilage and reworked units, firms adopting it change from more complex job costing systems to simpler process costing or even to backflush costing systems.

Performance Measurement

Computer integration in advanced manufacturing technologies has given manufacturing firms the capability of developing physical and financial performance measures at a fairly disaggregated level. Such performance measures include (1) partial productivity measures (e.g., output per employee) and indices of total factor productivity; (2) partial quality measures (e.g., product quality) and indices of total quality; (3) partial flexibility measures (e.g., process flexibility) and indices of total flexibility in FMS; and (4) disaggregated inventory turnover ratios for all types of inventories and for each product line in JIT plants. Other performance measures now in use in advanced manufacturing technologies plants include manufacturing cycle time, idle time, scrap and rework costs, material cost variances, percent of on-time delivery, percent of orders filled, and so on. There have also been attempts to integrate a number of these

performance measures (e.g., quality, flexibility, and productivity) into one integrated performance measure.

In a JIT plant, purchase price variances are de-emphasized and other productivity factors such as availability, delivery timeliness, and quality are emphasized instead. Labor variances are also de-emphasized because of the team effort required to successfully implement and maintain a JIT philosophy.

Investment

Accounting information is a potentially important input into the decision to invest in advanced manufacturing technologies (AMTS). The problem is that many of the benefits and costs of AMTS such as the benefits and costs of productivity, quality, and flexibility are difficult to quantify. A related problem is that manufacturing systems tend to be too dynamic and too complex to describe adequately in mathematical terms. Therefore, although a discounted (after-tax) cash flow (DCF) model is appropriate for AMTS as well as conventional technologies, it is far more difficult to estimate the cash flows of the former. Research in this area has concentrated on integrating simulation models of the manufacturing firm with DCF models to evaluate investment in AMTS versus conventional technologies. Unfortunately, these models are highly sensitive to the discount rate and it is not all clear what discount rate is appropriate, especially since the risk structure of AMTS is very different from conventional technologies. The decision to invest in flexible manufacturing is a case in point. If the FMS and the conventional plant have similar cost structures, the FMS would clearly dominate the conventional technology. FMS plants, however, require extremely large initial capital outlays by comparison to conventional technologies. On the other hand, FMS plants are more susceptible to swings in the business cycle (which may affect the demand for the entire product family) yet less susceptible to unpredictable changes in demand for any given product within a product family. The upshot is that in many cases investments in AMTS are never fully rationalized and the decisions to invest in AMTS are primarily made on the basis of "feel" rather than the underlying economics. In point of fact, accounting has had far less of an impact on the decision to adopt AMTS than is prudent.

Bibliography

Barlev, B. & Callen, J. L. (1986). Total factor productivity and cost variances: Survey and analysis. *Journal of Accounting Literature*, 5, 35–56.

Callen, J. L. & Sarath, B. (1995). Risk aversion, generalized correlation and investment in manufacturing capacities. *Journal of Operations Management*, (forthcoming).

Cooper, R. & Kaplan, R. S. (1992). Activity-based systems: Measuring the cost of resource usage. *Accounting Horizons*, 6, September, 1–13.

Dhavale, D. G. (1989). Product costing in flexible manufacturing systems. *Journal of Management Accounting Research*, 1, Fall, 66–88.

Foster, G. & Horngren, C. T. (1988). Cost accounting and cost management in a JIT environment. *Journal of Cost Management*, 2, 4–14.

Gosse, D. I. (1993). Cost accounting's role in computer-integrated manufacturing: An empirical field study. *Journal of Management Accounting Research*, 5, Fall, 159–179.

Mensah, Y. M. & Miranti, Jr, P. J. (1989). Capital expenditure analysis and automated manufacturing systems: A review and synthesis. *Journal of Accounting Literature*, 8, 181–207.

Hilton, R. W. (1994). *Managerial accounting*. 2nd edn, McGraw Hill.

Merchant, E. (1985). The importance of flexible manufacturing systems to the realisation of full computer-integrated manufacturing. *Flexible manufacturing systems*, in H. J. Warnecke and R. Steinhilper 27–43.

Son, Y. K. (1991). A Framework for modern manufacturing economics. *International Journal of Production Research*, 29, Dec., 2483–99.

Young, S. M. & Selto, F. H. (1991). New manufacturing practices and cost management: A review of the literature and directions for research. *Journal of Accounting Literature*, 10, 265–297.

KASHI R. BALACHANDRAN and
JEFFREY L. CALLEN

advisory services While auditing has traditionally been considered the accounting profession's most significant service to the public, research indicates that the share of audit firm revenue from providing audit services has fallen while the percentage of fee revenue from providing other advisory services, its revenue has increased. Over the past decade, audit firms have become multi-service providers and how this trend affects the public perception of the accounting profession is an issue that continues to stimulate controversy. This debate has centered on independence and pricing issues associated with the provision of advisory services by the incumbent auditor. However, research mostly by authors in the USA has resulted in knowledge of "no instance in which it can be demonstrated that the provision of MAS (management advisory services) to an audit client interfered with independence in performing the audit function" (AICPA Public Oversight Board, 1986).

Regulation of Advisory Services

Standards issued by international accounting bodies in order to regulate MAS reflect differing points of view. A comparison of standards is provided in Table 1.

The Australian Corporations Law (Schedule 5 (Cl. 27 1 & 2) requires the disclosure, in the company's financial reports, of the remuneration earned by the company auditor for both audit and advisory services. Further, while the Australian Statement of Auditing Practice, AUP 32, "Audit Independence" (1992), does not prohibit auditors from providing advisory services to their clients, it prohibits the auditors from performing and auditing the same work or recovering the audit costs from fees charged for advisory services. AUP 32 also suggests considering the effect on audit independence when total fees for an audit client or group of audit clients exceed 15 percent of the gross fees of the practice.

In the USA the Securities and Exchange Commission (SEC) issued Accounting Series Release (ASR) No. 250 in response to the Cohen Commission Report (1978). This regulation required the disclosure of the ratio of non audit fees to audit fees paid by US companies to the incumbent auditor. Under pressure, the regulation was canceled in February, 1982. However, the SEC Practice Section of the American Institute of Certified Practicing Accountants (AICPA) requires member firms to refrain from performing for their clients those services that are inconsistent with the firm's responsibilities to the public or that consist of certain types of services. The requirement to maintain independence becomes more explicit

Table 1   Provision of advisory services to audit clients[a].

Country	Possible[b]	Forbidden	Disclosure in financial statements
Australia	X		Disclosure of both audit fees and advisory services fees paid to company auditor(s)[c]
New Zealand	X		No disclosure
USA	X		No disclosure
EEC Countries			
Denmark	X		New law to be implemented requiring such disclosure
France		X	Not applicable
Germany	X		No disclosure
Greece		X	Not applicable
Ireland	X		Disclosure of audit fees only
Luxembourg		X	Not applicable
Netherlands	X		No disclosure
UK	X		Disclosure of audit and advisory services fees mandatory

[a]   Table 1 was adapted from table NAS201093 provided by Fédération des Experts Comptables Europeans.
[b]   Possible if it does not impair the independence and objectivity of the statutory auditor, otherwise forbidden. It is consequently a matter of interpretation.
[c]   In the Australian public sector, the Australian National Audit Office prohibits the independent auditor of Commonwealth public secytor organizations from providing advisory services to their audit clients without the prior consent of the Auditor-General.
[d]   Legislation is currently in the process of being amended. If the draft new law is adopted in its current format, the answer will become "possible."

when a practitioner also provides audit services to that client.

One of the most strongly debated issues concerning the Eighth Directive of the European Community (EC) dealing with the qualifications of statutory auditors was whether auditors should provide advisory services to their audit clients. Some countries recommended the total separation of audit and advisory services in order to ensure independence, while other countries felt that the provision of taxation and other advisory services would not impair auditor independence. The Eighth Directive, in the form adopted by the Council of Ministers of the EC in 1984, requires statutory auditors to comply with the existing national regulations in each country when determining the conditions relating to audit independence (Radebaugh & Gray, 1993).

In 1986, the UK Department of Trade and Industry also suggested that auditors should be prohibited from supplying non-audit services to

their clients. However, as a result of pressure from various professional bodies, this proposal was not adopted. Changes to the regulations to the Companies Act, 1989, now require UK companies to disclose in their annual reports all fees paid to their auditors, as from October 1, 1991. This includes both audit and non audit fees.

Research on Advisory Services

The US SEC monitored information provided by ASR 250 over the two-year period 1979–1980 during which the requirement was in effect and identified widespread provisions of advisory services by incumbent auditors. These services included tax work, accounting services, and other management advisory services (SEC, 1983). Information provided as a result of ASR 250 was also examined by Scheiner & Kiger (1982). They found that most of the services provided by audit firms were in traditional accounting areas and suggested that prohibiting the provision of non-accounting services by audit firms would have little impact on accounting practice.

Audit Pricing with Advisory Services

Taking advantage of disclosure requirements in Australia, Barkess & Simnett (1994) examined the annual reports of publicly listed Australian companies between 1986 and 1990. The study identified an overall increase of 6 percent in the numbers of clients purchasing advisory services from their auditors over the period, with 91 percent of the clients of the "Big Eight" auditors disclosing the purchase of advisory services from their auditor in 1990. These results are consistent with Read & Tomczyk (1992) who also found a steady growth in the Big Eight firm's proportion of revenue earned from nonaudit services during the 1980s.

One commonly mentioned advantage of auditors providing both audit and advisory services to their clients is the potential cost advantages arising from "knowledge spillovers" (Barkess & Simnett, 1994). Several researchers, including Simunic (1984), Palmrose (1986), Abdel-khalik (1990) Davis et al. (1993), and Barkess & Simnett (1994), have investigated the relationship between audit fees and fees for advisory services to determine whether knowledge spillovers exist, and, if so, whether the cost benefits are passed on to the client. Much of the evidence offered mixed results.

Davis et al. (1993) examined the relationship between audit fees and advisory services fees. They incorporated audit-hour and billing-rate information to control for audit effort. By controlling for audit effort, this study identified an association between increased audit fees and increased audit effort. Thus this study provided no empirical support for the argument that providing nonaudit services for audit clients results in auditors compromising their objectivity in relation to the pricing of audit services.

Effects of Audit Tenure

A study by DeBerg et al. (1991) investigated the allegation that audit firms would be more likely to retain clients who purchased high levels of advisory services. While they found no evidence of any association between the decision to change auditors and the provision of advisory services by the incumbent auditor, a significant decrease in the level of advisory services purchased from the incumbent auditor immediately after changing auditor was identified. Conflicting results from a study of Australian companies (Barkess & Simnett, 1994) identified a significant increase in the amount of advisory services purchased from the new auditor. However, this study found no relationship between the provision of advisory services and audit tenure

Although the debate surrounding the provision of advisory services by auditors remains topical, none of the published empirical research, to date, has been able to establish a relationship between a lack of independence or objectivity and the provision of advisory services by auditors to their clients.

Bibliography

Abdel-khalik, A. R. (1990). The jointness of audit fees and demand for MAS: A self-selection analysis. *Contemporary Accounting Research*, 6, Spring, 295–322.

AICPA Public Oversight Board of the SEC Practice Section (1986). *Public perceptions of management advisory services performed by CPA firms for audit clients.* Oct.

Barkess, L. & Simnett, R. (1994). The provision of other services by auditors: Independence and pricing issues. *Accounting and Business Research*, 24, Spring, 99–108.

Davis, L. R., Ricchiute, D. N. & Trompeter, G. (1993). Audit effort, audit fees, and the provision of nonaudit services to audit clients. *The Accounting Review*, 68, Jan., 135–150.

DeBerg, C. L., Kaplan, S. E. & Pany, K. (1991). An examination of some relationships between non audit services and auditor change. *Accounting Horizon*, 5, Mar., 17–28.

Delaney, P. R. (1994). *CPA Examination Review Volume 1 Outlines and Study Guides.* 21st edn, New York: John Wiley & Sons.

Palmrose, Z. (1986). The effect of nonaudit services on the pricing of audit services: Further evidence. *Journal of Accounting Research*, 24, Autumn, 405–411.

Radebaugh, L. H. & Gray, S. J. (1993). *International accounting and multinational enterprises.* New York: John Wiley & Sons, Inc.

Read, W. J. & Tomczyk, S. (1992). An examination of changes in scope of services performed by CPA firms. *Accounting Horizons*, 6, Sept., 42–51.

Scheiner, J. & Kiger, J. E. (1982). An empirical investigation of auditor involvement in non-audit services. *Journal of Accounting Research*, **20**, Autumn, 482–496.

SEC (1983). *SEC Accounting Rules – Accounting Series Releases*. 3001–3311. Commerce Clearing House, Inc.

Simunic, D. (1984). Auditing, consulting, and auditor independence. *Journal of Accounting Research*, **22**, Autumn, 679–702.

LYNN BARKESS

analytical procedures in auditing Analytical procedures consist of evaluations of financial information made by an auditor of plausible and expected relationships among both financial and nonfinancial data. They range from simple comparisons (e.g., the current year with the preceding year) to the use of complex models involving many relationships and elements of data (e.g., regression analysis).

According to US Statement on Auditing Standards (SAS) No. 56, issued in 1988, "*Analytical Procedures*" (American Institute of Certified Public Accountants (AICPA), *Professional Standards*, vol. 1, AU section 329) –

A basic premise underlying the application of analytical procedures is that plausible relationships among data may reasonably be expected to exist and continue in the absence of known conditions to the contrary. Particular conditions that can cause variations in these relationships include, for example, specific unusual transactions or events, accounting changes, business changes, random fluctuations, or misstatements. [para. 2]

History and Authoritative Pronouncements

The term analytical review procedures (changed to analytical procedures by US Statement on Auditing Standards (SAS) No. 56) was introduced in the authoritative auditing literature in 1970 when Statement on Auditing Procedures (SAP) No. 54 (AU section 320.70) was issued. The Statement specified that sufficient competent evidential matter "is obtained through two general classes of auditing procedures: (a) tests of details of transactions and balances and (b) analytical review of significant ratios and trends and resulting investigation of unusual fluctuations and questionable items."

Analytical procedures were being used, however, in audits prior to 1970. In fact, in 1950 the American Institute of Accountants (subsequently changed to the American Institute of Certified Public Accountants (AICPA)) states:

One way this (the analysis and review of data) is accomplished is by comparison of balances in the trial balance at the balance-sheet date with those in the trial balance at the end of the previous comparable period, noting for investigation any items which appear to be out of line with previous experience. Another comparison is that of the gross profit percentage during the current period with the corresponding percentages in previous periods. (*Audits by Certified Public Accountants*, 1950)

Subsequent to the issuance of SAP No. 54, the AICPA required, recommended, or discussed the use of analytical procedures in the following authoritative pronouncements:

SAS No. 21, 1977, "Segment Information."
SAS No. 23, 1978, "Analytical Review Procedures."
SAS No. 36, 1981, "Review of Interim Financial Information."
SAS No. 39, 1981, "Audit Sampling."
SAS No. 56, 1988, "Analytical Procedures" (SAS No. 56).
SAS No. 59, 1988, "The Auditor's Consideration of an Entity's Ability to Continue as a Going Concern."

In 1987, the Report of the National Commission on Fraudulent Reporting (the Treadway Commission) recommended that standards should be established "to require independent public accountants to perform analytical review procedures in all audit engagements and should provide improved guidance on the appropriate use of these procedures." The Auditing Standards Board of the AICPA responded to this recommendation by issuing SAS No. 56.

SAS No. 56 Analytical Procedures

In April 1988, in the USA, Statement on Auditing Standards SAS No. 56 was issued. It *requires* auditors to use analytical procedures to assist in planning the nature, timing, and extent of other auditing procedures and as an overall review of the financial statements in the final review of the audit. The Statement also indicates that analytical procedures may be used "as a substantive test to obtain evidential matter about particular assertions related to account balances on classes of transactions."

The next section discusses the broad categories of analytical procedures, and the section after that contains a general discussion on the use and effectiveness of those procedures. The three sections after the general discussion section describe uses of analytical procedures in the planning, evidence accumulation, and final review phases of an audit, as well as research concerning the procedures applied in those three phases.

Categories of Analytical Procedures

Analytical procedures may be classified as follows:

(1) Comparisons of absolute numbers.
(2) Comparisons of the results of mathematical computations.
    (a) Ratio analysis.
    (b) Common-size financial statements.
    (c) Trend analysis.
(3) Regression analysis.

Comparisons of absolute numbers This procedure involves the comparison of current year's unaudited financial data with the prior year's audited financial data.

Comparison of the results of mathematical computations Ratio analysis involves the computation of the relationship between two numbers. For income statement data, the relationship is usually based on ,sales; therefore, the gross profit percentage is the relationship of gross profit to sales. Interstatement ratios may also be computed. For example, the inventory turnover ratio is the relationship of average inventory (a balance sheet item) to cost of sales (an income statement item). After ratios are computed, they are compared with company ratios from prior years or industry ratios. Industry ratios may be obtained in the USA from commercially

available data published by Standard & Poor's Corp., Dun & Bradstreet, Robert Morris Associates, or industry trade associations.

A common-size financial statement is one in which all numbers are converted to percentages. For example, the dollar amounts of cash, receivables, inventory, and other assets in the balance sheet are converted to percentages based on the relationship of each asset to total assets. For income statement items, costs and expenses are converted to percentages based on their relationship to sales. Those percentages may be compared to prior years' percentages or industry percentages. Industry percentages may be obtained in the USA from the organizations noted in the previous paragraph.

Trend analysis indicates the relative changes in data from period to period based on the data of a base year. Trend statements may be computed for any financial statement item. The statements may be computed for any financial statement item. The statements highlight departures from the norm in a company's operations.

Regression analysis Regression analysis is the means by which presumed cause-and-effect relationships are used to make predictions. The relationships are expressed in terms of a dependent variable and one or more independent variables. Regression analysis is used to estimate or predict what an account balance should be for comparison with what that account balance is.

General Analytical Procedures

In today's highly competitive auditing environment, auditors must use effective and more efficient procedures in their audits. When applying analytical procedures, the auditor will, generally, do the following:

(1) develop expectations;
(2) define what will be considered a material difference between expected and recorded amounts;
(3) identify significant differences;
(4) investigate the causes of the significant differences; and
(5) reach a conclusion.

Research has been conducted for over twenty years to determine when analytical procedures are used, the effectiveness of those procedures, and the impact they have on auditors' decisions.

Questions have been raised concerning the effectiveness of analytical procedures as a means of accumulating audit evidence. One study concludes that "many auditors lack confidence in analytical procedures because of the perceived low precision of the procedures and the perceived unreliability of the data that are necessary for the procedures, for example, monthly (or annual unaudited) data."

On the other hand, a study of audit workpapers found that of 281 errors requiring financial statement adjustments on 152 audits 27.1 percent of those errors were detected through the use of analytical procedures (Hylas & Ashton, 1982). What is not known, however, is the number and frequency of errors not detected when analytical procedures are used.

Another study concludes that "analytical procedures are useful for the auditor with respect to detecting overstatements of revenue, fictitious sales and receivables, fictitious and overvalued inventory, understated bad debts and allowances for doubtful accounts, unrecorded purchase liabilities, underaccrual of expenses, and inappropriate expense capitalization. Analytical procedures, used effectively in those situations, would have revealed unusual relationships and significant changes in relationships. By following up the unusual relationships and the changes in relationships with other audit procedures, the auditor could have detected large errors in the financial statements" (Coglitore & Berryman, 1988).

A number of studies conclude that the auditor's knowledge of the client and the client's industry influenced the use and effectiveness of analytical procedures (Kinney & Felix, 1980; Lev, 1980). One study concludes that the auditor's knowledge of analytical procedures and perception of the effectiveness of those procedures affected the auditor's tendency to use those procedures and rely on the results of their application (Tandy, 1992).

Auditor's experience is a factor in the effectiveness of analytical procedures. When a procedure indicates that the actual data deviates from the expected data, the auditor must determine the cause. One of the advantages of experience is the ability to generate a greater number of plausible explanations for the deviation. The more experienced auditor is also more efficient in that he or she first investigates the more likely explanations for the deviation (Libby & Frederick, 1990). At times, deviations from expected values are not caused by accounting errors but by environmental factors. One study concludes that "audit experience was positively associated with the number and ranking of environmental factors selected. Thus, accumulated direct experience does affect plausibility assessment and appears to enable auditors to understand that significant fluctuations in ratios do not necessarily indicate the occurrence of accounting errors."

Other factors influence the use and effectiveness of analytical procedures. When those procedures produce deviations from expected results, auditors seek explanations from management. Auditors consider managers' competence when evaluating the reliability of their explanations of deviations. That is, the greater the managers' competence the more willing the auditor is to accept their explanations of deviation (Anderson et al., 1994).

The use and effectiveness of the more common analytical procedures depends on other factors. For example, if the auditor determines that a client's internal control structure is strong, the auditor will have greater flexibility in planning the mix between analytical procedures and tests of details. That is, the quality of the client's internal control structure influences the extent to which the auditor applies analytical procedures (Kinney, 1979).

Use of Analytical Procedures in Planning the Audit

In the audit planning phase, analytical procedures serve as an attention-directing device. They are used by auditors to help determine the nature, timing, and extent of their substantive procedures. The objective of using analytical procedures in this phase is to increase the auditor's understanding of the client and identify specific audit risks by considering unusual or unexpected balances or relationships in aggregate data.

Analytical procedures used in planning the audit might include the following:

1. *Account balance comparison*. Compare unadjusted trial balance amounts with adjusted tried balance amounts of the prior year.
2. *Computation of significant ratios*. Compare current year ratios to current industry ratios and prior year computing ratios.
3. *Computation of ratios using nonfinancial and financial data*. E.g., sales per square foot of sales space.
4. *Regression analysis*. This procedure is discussed in a separate section below.

A question arises concerning the auditor's response to the results of analytical procedures in the planning stage. One study indicates that when the results signal possible errors, the auditor assigned more hours to testing than when the results indicated the possibility of no errors. However, when the results indicated the possibility of no errors, the auditor did not reduce the hours preliminarily assigned to testing (Cohen & Kida, 1989). Those results provide some confirmation of the auditor's tendency toward conservation. That conservative tendency is one explanation why auditors increase their type I error risk (the risk of not accepting a materially correct balance) and decrease their type II error risk (the risk of accepting a materially incorrect balance). Those results should not negate the fact that analytical procedures can increase audit efficiency by allowing the auditor to reduce sample sizes for substantive tests if the results of those procedures are favorable. Also, favorable results of analytical procedures will increase audit effectiveness by reducing the auditor's risk of accepting an incorrect balance (Knechel, 1988).

Most auditors use relatively simple types of analytical procedures in planning the audit. In one study it was found that simple quantitative techniques involving ratio and trend analysis were most commonly used (Holder, 1983). Another study found that the most commonly used analytical procedure in the planning stage was a comparison of the current year's unaudited account balance with last year's corresponding audited account balance (Coakley, 1982).

The effectiveness of analytical procedures in the planning stage is, to some degree, determined by the investigation threshold of the auditor: the extent of deviations from expected values after which an auditor modifies the audit plan. Investigation thresholds usually are arbitrary. One study found that the most widely used decision rule in planning the audit was to investigate if the account balance had changed by more than 10 percent from the previous year (Coakley, 1982). It has been recommended that investigation thresholds be computed more rigorously by using univariate and bivariate statistical distributions (Harper et al., 1990).

Studies also have concluded that analytical procedures in the planning phase can increase audit efficiency because if the results of those procedures are favorable, many auditors will reduce the extent of their substantive tests.

Use of Analytical Procedures As a Substantive Test

Although US Statement on Auditing Standards SAS No. 56 does not require the auditor to use analytical procedures as a substantive test, auditors use them for that purpose. The extent to which the auditor uses analytical procedures as a substantive test depends on the level of assurance the auditor wants in achieving a particular audit objective and the tolerable error for a specific account balance. The higher the level of assurance desired, the more predictable must be the relationship used. The higher the tolerable misstatement, the less predictable must be the relationship used. As a general rule, relationships involving income statement accounts are more predictable than relationships involving only balance sheet accounts.

The results of one study indicate that analytical procedures may enhance audit effectiveness, especially when employed in conjunction with a minimum level of substantive auditing procedures. The auditor should, however, exercise caution in determining the degree of reliance to be placed solely on analytical procedures (Wheeler & Pany, 1990).

Another study – a protocol study of five experienced auditors in the performance of an analytical review of inventory – concludes that conventional analytical procedures have limited effectiveness. The most effective procedure was the gross profit percentage trend, and the most effective auditors were those who used that procedure and relied on it (Blocher & Cooper, 1988).

Conventional analytical procedures – comparisons, ratios, trend analysis – do not have the precision necessary for the auditor to rely on them alone as a substantive test. Auditors believe that those procedures provide limited negative assurance, and therefore their use as a substantive test is limited. Some researchers believe that the expected effectiveness of analytical procedures depends on the assertion being audited and the design of the procedure. Analytical procedures may be somewhat more effective than tests of details for tests of completeness and reasonableness of reserves (e.g., doubtful accounts and depreciation). Tests of details will be more effective in testing the existence or ownership assertion (Blocher & Loebbecke, 1993).

Auditors who use analytical procedures as a substantive test consider deviations between the expected amount and the client's amount as a likely error. At the conclusion of the audit if the total of the known error, likely error, and allowance for undetected error is less than the acceptable error established by the auditor, no further action is required. If, however, the total exceeds the amount of acceptable error, the auditor must investigate those deviations further.

Use of Analytical Procedures in Final Review of the Audit

The application of analytical procedures in the final review of the audit is one of the last audit tests. Those procedures assist the auditor in assessing conclusions reached concerning certain account balances and in evaluating the overall financial statement presentation. Procedures such as the following may be applied:

1. Comparisons with similar financial data of the prior year or of the client's industry.
2. Ratio analysis.
3. Trend analysis.
4. Development of common-size financial statements.

The objective of analytical procedures in the final phase of the audit is similar to that in the planning phase – attention directing. Unfavorable results will require the auditor to investigate the reasons for those results.

As a final step in the audit, the auditor must determine if the company has the ability to continue in business for at least one year from the balance sheet date (US Statement on Auditing Standards SAS No. 59, "The Auditor's Consideration of an Entity's Ability to Continue as a Going Concern" 1988). Ratios such as the current ratio and the debt-to-equity ratio aid the auditor in making this assessment.

In assessing a company's ability to continue as a going concern, auditors apply models using ratios and trends that have been developed to predict bankruptcy. Those models use various ratios. One of the models was developed using a statistical technique (multiple discriminant analysis) and five ratios. Those ratios for a public company are:

1. Working Capital/Total Assets
2. Retained Earnings/Total Assets
3. Earnings before Interest and Taxes/Total Assets
4. Market Value of Equity/Book Value of Total Debt
5. Sales/Total Assets

Coefficients were determined for those ratios. The total of the five produces a "Z" score which, if below a certain level, indicates the strong possibility of impending bankruptcy within a year or two (Altman & McGough, 1947).

Use of Regression Analysis in Analytical Review

Analytical procedures discussed above give little comfort to auditors as a substantive test because of the absence of measurable precision. Auditors are, therefore, looking for more rigorous and more precise analytical procedures. Those procedures require the use of statistical techniques. The most common statistical technique for analytical procedures is regression analysis. Because of its relative complexity, however, regression analysis is not yet a widely used procedure.

Regression analysis uses the relationship between two or more variables so that one variable, the dependent variable, can be predicted from one or more independent or explanatory variables. A simple regression model involves only one independent variable and is expressed as $Y = a + bX$, where Y is the dependent variable and X is the independent variable. Multiple regression analysis involves more than one independent variable to predict the value of the dependent variable and is expressed as $Y = a + b_1X_1, + b_2X_2 \ldots b_nX_n$. The auditor uses the regression model to estimate or predict the value of the dependent variable (Y), conditional on the independent variables used, and compares that value with the client's corresponding value.

After determining the dependent and independent variables and assembling a series of observations of those variables, the auditor computes the statistical attributes of the model, including a precision interval and a confidence interval. Given the statistical attributes, the auditor computes a point estimate of the dependent variable and determines a range around that estimate based on the precision interval. If the client's account balance falls within that range, the auditor will have a certain degree of confidence (the confidence interval) that the client's true account balance falls within that range. If, however, the client's account balance is outside the range, the auditor will have to investigate further.

The development of regression models is relatively more costly than ratio analysis and requires statistical expertise. Regression analysis is, however, superior to other analytical procedures in detecting material hours. With the development of statistical based computer software, this procedure will be more frequently used.

Conclusion

Competition has become intense in the accounting profession in recent years. This condition has put pressure on auditors to become more efficient in their audits. The use of analytical procedures is one method of increasing auditor efficiency.

Simple analytical procedures – comparisons, ratio analysis, trend analysis, and common size financial statements – are effective as attention – directing tools in the planning and final review stages of the audit. Those procedures are also effective when used in conjunction with a minimum level of tests of details as a substantive test.

As computer technology continues to develop, auditors will use regression models as an analytical procedure. It is the most effective and ultimately most efficient of the analytical procedures.

Bibliography

Altman, E. I. & McGough, T. P. (1974). Evaluation of a company as a going concern. *Journal of Accountancy*, **138**, 6, 50–7.

Anderson, U., Koonce, L. & Marchant, G. (1994). The effects of source–competence information and its timing on auditors' performance of analytical procedures. *Auditing: A Journal of Practice and Theory*, **13**, 1, 137–48.

Blocher, E. & Cooper, J. C. (1988). A study of auditors' analytical review performance. *Auditing: A Journal of Practice and Theory*, **7**, 2, 1–28.

Blocher, E., Esposito, R. S. & Willingham, J. J. (1983). Auditors' analytical review judgments for payroll expense. *Auditing: A Journal of Practice and Theory*, **3**, 1, 75–91.

Blocher, E. & Loebbecke, J. K. (1993). Research in analytical procedures: Implications for establishing and implementing auditing standards. *The expectation gap standards*. New York: AICPA. 177–226.

Coakley, J. R. (1987). Analytical review: A comparison of procedures and techniques used in auditing.Unpublished Ph.D. dissertation (University of Utah, 1982), cited by J. K. Loebbecke & P. J. Steinhart, An investigation of the use of preliminary analytical review to provide substantive audit evidence. *Auditing: A Journal of Practice and Theory*, **6**, 2, 74–89.

Coglitore, F. & Berryman, R. G. (1988). Analytical procedures: A defensive necessity. *Auditing: A journal of practice and theory*, **7**, 2, 150–63.

Cohen, J. & Kida, T. (1989). The impact of analytical review results, internal control reliability and experience on auditors' use of analytical review. *Journal of Accounting Research*, **27**, 2, 263–276.

Harper, R. M., Jr, Strawser, J. R. & Tang, K. (1990). Establishing investigation thresholds for preliminary analytical procedures. *Auditing: A Journal of Practice and Theory*, **9**, 3, 115–33.

Holder, W. W. (1983). Analytical review procedures in planning the audit: An application study. *Auditing: A Journal of Practice and Theory*, **2**, 2, 100–7.

Hylas, R. & Ashton, R. (1982). Audit detection of financial statement errors. *Accounting Review*, **57**, 4, 751–65.

Kaplan, S. E., Moechel, C. & Williams, J. D. (1992). Auditors' hypothesis plausibility assessments in an analytical review setting. *Auditing: A Journal of Practice and Theory*, **11**, 2, 50–65.

Kinney, W. (1979). The predictive power of limited information in preliminary analytical review: An empirical study. *Journal of Accounting Research*, **17** (supplement), 148–65.

Kinney, W. & Felix, W. L. (1980). Analytical review Procedures. *Journal of Accountancy*, **150**, 4, 98–103.

Knechel, W. R. (1988). The effectiveness of non-statistical analytical review procedures used as substantive audit tests. *Auditing: A Journal of Practice and Theory*, 8, 1, 87–107.

Lev, B. (1980). On the use of index models in analytical review by auditors. *Journal of Accounting Research*, 18, 2, 524–50.

Libby, R. & Frederick, D. M. (1990). Experience and the ability to explain audit findings. *Journal of Accounting Research*, 28, 2, 348–67.

Tandy, P. R. (1992). The influence of auditor and client characteristics on auditor use of analytical procedures. *Journal of Applied Business Research*, 8, 14, 87–96.

Wheeler, S. & Pany, K. (1990). Assessing the performance of analytical procedures: A best case scenario. *The Accounting Review*, 65, 3, 557–77.

MARTIN BENIS

asset revaluation accounting Australian firms frequently revalue noncurrent assets in balance sheets through an adjustment to a shareholders' funds item called asset revaluation reserve. Although similar procedures are also common in at least the UK and New Zealand, asset revaluations, except for asset impairment, have been effectively banned in the USA since 1930 through an administrative decision of the Securities and Exchange Commission (Walker, 1992). The revaluation procedure results in material differences in total assets reported under Australian accounting rules compared to US generally accepted accounting principles (GAAP). In a recent survey of large Australian firms that provide reconciliations between their financial statements (prepared under Australian accounting standards) and US rules, asset revaluations are shown to cause the net assets in Australian financial statements to be decreased by up to 40 percent when converted to US GAAP (Arthur Anderson, 1994).

Institutional Background

Revaluation accounting procedures in Australia are regulated by accounting standard AASB 1010, which was issued by the Australian Accounting Standards Board in 1987. Essentially, this requires that the increment arising from an upward revaluation of a noncurrent asset be adjusted directly to shareholders' equity by a credit to asset revaluation reserve; in other words, the income statement is not usually affected. A number of implications of this requirement and other features of the standard are worth noting.

(1) Upward and downward revaluations have asymmetric treatment. Upward revaluations generally are posted directly to an asset revaluation reserve in the owner's equity section; downward revaluations generally flow through the income statement. However, both of these rules are reversed if the revaluation effectively offsets a previous revaluation of the same asset. That is, an upward revaluation can go to the income statement if it offsets a previous devaluation, and a downward (re)valuation may be posted directly to an asset revaluation reserve in the owner's equity in the balance sheet if it offsets a previous revaluation.

(2) If the asset is sold, the profit on sale would be the difference between the sale price and the updated book value, which includes any revaluation increments. This can be a disincentive to revalue assets whose sales may be contemplated, as the revaluation increment "never gets to the income statement."

(3) If the economic conditions justify a revaluation the decision whether or not to revalue is at the discretion of management; it is not compulsory. Furthermore, not all assets have to be revalued; however, all assets "within the same class" have to be similarly treated – either all revalued or all not revalued. This has resulted in tangible long-lived assets typically being revalued from time to time whereas revaluations of plant and equipment are rare. With respect to *intangible* assets, while Australian rules do not allow goodwill to be revalued (and require it to be amortized over a period not more than 20 years), the current lack of an Australian accounting standard on identifiable intangible assets implies that items such as magazine mastheads, patents, and so on are frequently revalued and not amortized. Therefore, revaluations of either tangible or intangible noncurrent assets rarely have a material affect on subsequent depreciation charges in the income statement.

(4) The amount of the revaluation is not required to be an unbiased estimate of the current value of the asset; although all noncurrent assets need to be carried at above their "recoverable amount." To illustrate, if the cost of the asset (or previous revaluation) is $100, and the recoverable amount is $200 managers have the discretion to revalue the asset up to any amount between $100 to $200 inclusive.

(5) Recoverable amount is defined to be "the net amount that is expected to be recovered through the cash inflows and outflows arising from its continued use and subsequent disposal." A particularly controversial feature of AASB 1010 is that it does not require the cash flows attributable to the asset to be discounted back to present value when determining the recoverable amount (although it does require disclosure of the extent to which discounting is used). This can lead to some counter-intuitive calculations of recoverable amount. Furthermore, the recoverable amount can be materially higher than the amount the asset would realize if sold in the short term.

For example, consider a situation where a firm owns a central business district property that has a market value of $5 m if sold within the next accounting period and a book value of $8 m. Assume further that operating cash inflows are equal to operating cash outflows for the asset. The management intends to retain the asset for another five years, at which time it expects that the asset will be sold for $10 m. If a discount rate of 20 percent is applicable to an asset of this risk class, then the present value of the future cash flows is ($10 m x 0.4019 =) $4,019.000. However, as the accounting standard does not *require* that discounting be used, the management can maintain that the recoverable amount is $10 m; hence the asset does not have to be written down! On the other hand, if management prefers to take the option of writing down the asset, they are permitted to use discounting, and write the asset down to $4,019,000.

(6) While of course the revaluations are audited, they can be based on either a "directors' valuation" or an independent valuation by a qualified valuer or appraiser.

Certain disclosures are required by the Corporations Law, including the date of the revaluation, whether the valuation was made by an officer of the company, a related entity, or an independent valuer, and, in the latter case, the name and qualifications of the valuer. In at least this respect, regulations differ between Australia and New Zealand. In New Zealand SSAP 28 requires that revaluations must always be by a qualified valuer, although the valuer can be internal provided that the valuation is reviewed by an independent valuer.

Two other aspects of the institutional background tend to mitigate the intent of the accounting standard. First, the standard does not preclude alternative treatments of asset revaluations to be used in supplementary financial statements or even in extra "comparative" columns. Hence, some Australian firms (notably some property developers) provide "extra column comparative financial statements" that effectively take the credit for upward revaluations to the income statement rather than asset revaluation reserve as required by the standard. Second, by law, the asset revaluation reserve can be "distributed" as a cash dividend. More correctly, a cash dividend can be paid with the debit going to asset revaluation reserve rather then retained earnings. Thus, a company with nonprofitable operations may be able to distribute dividends through asset revaluation, which is a discretionary decision.

Treatment in Debt Agreements

Surveys of Australian debt agreements (e.g. Whittred & Zimmer, 1986) indicate that most Australian debt agreements contain a "borrowing limitations clause" that requires management to maintain a specified debt-to-assets ratio throughout the term of the loan (for industrial companies this is typically 0.6). Of course, if managers are unconstrained in terms of their asset revaluation decisions, such a leverage covenant would not be an effective constraint. Managers' discretion is limited by the accounting standard requiring the assets not to be reported at above recoverable amount together with the requirement for an audit; however, lenders often go a step further. Whittred & Zimmer (1986) show that for the purpose of debt-to-assets ratios in at least public debt agreements the contracts do not recognize asset revaluations unless the revaluations are carried out by an independent valuer approved by the lenders' representative (trustee). Furthermore, if the revaluation relates to an intangible asset it is ignored regardless of who does the revaluation, because the contracts typically require intangible assets to be written off for the purpose of the covenant.

Determinants of Revaluation Decisions

Given that managers have such discretion over when to revalue noncurrent assets, a number of research studies have investigated the incentives of managers to exercise this option.

Brown et al. (1992) propose that managers revalue assets upwards to minimize contracting and political costs. More specifically, they hypothesize that revaluers are large companies with higher leverage (and hence closer to covenants in debt agreements) and are more likely to be in strike-prone industries (in other words, subject to higher political costs) than firms that do not undertake asset revaluations. Furthermore, they hypothesize that revaluers are more likely to have less "financial slack" (reserve borrowing capacity), and might be under threat of takeover than firms that do not revalue. Their study involves empirical tests that compare samples of firms that do and do not revalue across these hypothesis variables. The results generally support their propositions.

Whittred & Chan (1992) argue that growth firms have relatively more severe problems with lenders because a higher proportion of the assets of such firms tend to be intangibles. This causes lenders to be reluctant to lend to such firms. To mitigate lenders' concerns (and hence be able to borrow at lower interest rates), managers are likely to try to convince lenders that their firm has a "reasonable" proportion of tangible assets. Whittred & Chan propose that managers frequently try to achieve this by revaluing their tangible assets. In particular, they hypothesize that revaluers, when compared to non-revaluers, have more growth opportunities and higher leverage, as well as less ability to finance growth internally. Their results generally confirm these propositions.

The Whittred & Chan (1992) study is extended by Cotter & Zimmer (1995) who propose that firms have more incentive to undertake an upward revaluation of noncurrent assets when experiencing declining current cash flows. They also address the question of why some revaluations are made by directors (in other words, based on an assessment by management), whereas others are based on assessments by independent professional valuers. Given that the placement of secured debt often requires an independent valuation to determine the adequacy of loan security, Cotter & Zimmer propose that independent valuations are more likely to occur when the firm increases the amount of secured borrowings. Their empirical results support these propositions.

Share Prices

A number of researchers have investigated the relation between asset revaluations and share prices. Overall, the conclusions are that while asset revaluations increase the alignment between values reported in financial statements and values reflected in share prices, such revaluations are not "timely" information. That is, the changes in asset values are reflected in stock prices prior to disclosure of asset revaluations in financial statements. However, these conclusions are only tentative, because there are other "confounding events" (such as announcements of bonus share issues, earnings and dividend policy changes) that occur at precisely the same time as the announcement of asset revaluations. Statistically, researchers have found it difficult to disentangle the share price effect of these other events from the effect of the revaluation announcement.

Brown & Finn (1980) pointed out that the majority of the announcements of revaluations occurred in months where there were either annual reports or interim reports released or a bonus issue was announced. Therefore, an earlier finding of an asset revaluation effect by Sharpe & Walker (1975) is not supported. Consistent with Brown and Finn, a study of UK asset revaluations by Standish & Ung (1982) found that revaluations were only significant when interpreted as a signal of subsequent favorable information about the firm. More recently, Easton, Eddey and Harris (1993) found that asset revaluations are statistically associated with changes in share prices over long periods (e.g., three years). A more solid and consistent evidence on the issue remains to be developed.

Bibliography

Arthur Andersen *FINAC*, (1994). April. Melbourne. p. 5.

Brown, P., Izan H. Y. & Lowe, A. L. (1992). Fixed asset revaluations and managerial incentives. *Abacus*, Mar., 36–57.

Brown, P. & Finn, F. (1980). Asset revaluations and share prices: Alternative interpretations of a study by Sharpe and Walker.In R. Ball, P. Brown, F. Finn, R. Officer (eds), *Share markets and portfolio theory*. University of Queensland Press.

Cotter, J. & Zimmer, I. R. (1995). Asset revaluations and the assessment of borrowing capacity.Submitted to *Abacus* for possible publication at time of writing.

Sharpe, I. & Walker, R. G. (1975). Asset revaluations and stock market prices. *Journal of Accounting Research*, Autumn, 293–310.

Standish, P. & Ung, S. (1982). Corporate signalling, asset revaluations and the stock prices of British companies. *The Accounting Review*, Oct., 701–15.

Walker, R. G. (1992). The SEC's ban on upward revaluations and the disclosure of current values. *Abacus*, Mar., 3–36.

Whittred, G. P. & Chan, Y. K. (1992). Asset revaluations and the mitigation of under-investment. *Abacus*, Mar., 58–74.

Whittred, G. P. & Zimmer, I. R. (1986). Accounting information in the market for debt. *Accounting and Finance*, Nov., 19–23.

IAN ZIMMER

audit evidence   Audit evidence refers to the information obtained by an auditor in arriving at the conclusions on which an audit opinion is based. Decisions on the quantity and quality of the audit evidence to be obtained in any audit and the procedures for obtaining this evidence are central to the overall audit process. Guidance on these decisions is provided in the following auditing standards: International – 500; Australian – 502; Canada – 5300; UK – 400; USA – 326.

The International Standard on Auditing 500 (ISA 500) states that audit evidence is obtained from an appropriate mix of tests of controls and substantive procedures or entirely from substantive procedures. Substantive procedures include (1) tests of details of transactions and balances, and (2) analysis of significant ratios and trends including the resulting investigation of unusual items (referred to as "analytical procedures.")

Obtaining Audit Evidence

ISA 500 suggests the following procedures for obtaining audit evidence: inspection, observation, inquiry and confirmation, computation and analytical procedures.

Inspection consists of examining records, documents, or tangible assets. Documentary audit evidence may consist of evidence created and held by third parties (e.g., securities or stock certificates held at a bank), evidence created by third parties and held by the client (e.g., listing of securities held by the bank and sent to the client, and evidence created and held by the client) (e.g., internal records detailing purchases and sales of investments). Inspection of tangible assets such as inventory and property plant and equipment is a direct way of verifying that an asset exists.

Observation involves the auditor looking at a process or procedure being performed by others, usually client staff. For example, an auditor could observe client staff clocking on or observe from a tour of the factory that some plant appears obsolete.

Inquiry involves seeking information from client staff or other knowledgeable individuals independent of the client. For example, client staff could be asked about reasons for a drop in sales revenue. Inquiries may be made of individuals outside the organization about a variety of items including movements in real estate values in a particular area, expected sales of various products, new technological developments that may affect the client, etc. Corroborative evidence should be obtained from the client.

Confirmation refers to the receipt of a written response from an independent third party to corroborate information contained in the accounts.

Computation involves checking the arithmetical accuracy of source documents and accounting records. For example, the auditor may check such items as depreciation calculations, a listing of accounts receivable, invoice totals, and the sales journal.

Analytical review procedures consist of the analysis of significant ratios and trends including the investigation of fluctuations and relationships that are inconsistent with expectations
Analytical review procedures include:

(1) comparison of the financial information with information for the comparable prior period(s);
(2) comparison of the financial information with anticipated results (e.g., budgets and forecasts);
(3) comparison of the financial information with similar information based on industry averages, results of competitors or other operations in the same industry;
(4) study of the relationships among elements of financial information that would be expected to conform to a predictable pattern based on the entity's experience (e.g., gross margin percentages);
(5) study of the relationships between the financial information and relevant nonfinancial information (e.g., payroll costs to number of employees).

Analytical review procedures vary from simple comparisons to reasonably complex regression analysis and time series modeling. In recent years there has been an increased emphasis on analytical review as part of substantive testing. Research has shown that analytical review can be a very effective means of detecting errors (e.g., Hylas & Ashton, 1982; Wright & Aston, 1989).

Role of Judgment

The professional and academic auditing literature has recognized for a number of decades the importance and pervasiveness of judgment in auditing (see JUDGMENT IN FINANCIAL STATEMENT AUDITS). More recently, professional standards have discussed the need for auditors' judgments in an extensive number of areas. Some examples of auditor judgments include establishing materiality, identifying important audit objectives and assertions, assessing the inherent risk environment, evaluating internal controls, developing an audit strategy, selection and evaluation of analytical review procedures, evaluating the results of audit testing and determining whether the going concern basis

is appropriate (Bamber et al., 1995). With respect to audit evidence Bamber et al. suggest the following questions need to be considered: What audit procedures should be performed? In what areas should audit effort be focused, and on what issues? What should be the nature, timing and extent of audit procedures? How should the evidence obtained from a variety of sources be aggregated? What audit conclusions may be drawn?

Sufficient Appropriate Evidence

Auditors are required to obtain sufficient appropriate audit evidence in order to draw reasonable conclusions on which to base their audit opinions. The judgments that will be examined here are those judgments needed to be made by the auditor in order to obtain sufficient appropriate audit evidence.

In deciding what is appropriate audit evidence, the auditor's judgment will be influenced by such factors as:

– the auditor's assessment of the nature and level of inherent risk at both the financial report level and the account balance or class of transactions level;
– the nature of the internal control structure and the assessment of control risk;
– the materiality of the item being examined;
– the experience gained during previous audits;
– the results of audit procedures, including fraud, other illegal acts and errors which may have been found; and
– the source and reliability of information available.

The research evidence on each of these will be discussed in turn.

First, a number of studies have examined what factors are important to auditors in assessing the level of inherent risk. In general, it has been found that auditors perceive variables pertaining to characteristics of management and history of errors to be major determinants of the assessment of inherent risk (e.g., Monroe et al., 1993). While auditing standards suggest that the auditors' assessment of inherent risk should affect the level of testing, early studies have found that changes in inherent risk do not have an effect on the amount of actual or planned audit testing (Mock & Wright, 1993).

Second, auditors' judgments with respect to internal control systems are one of the most frequently studied issues in auditing. Most of these studies have extended Ashton (1974) who examined auditors' internal control judgments over payroll. Ashton found that auditors placed greatest significance on the segregation of duties cues and that the extent of consensus between auditor judgments on the strength of the internal control systems was relatively high compared to the consensus found in studies of other types of expert judges, e.g., stockbrokers and radiologists. The Ashton (1974) study has been extensively replicated and extended by subsequent research. Trotman & Wood (1991) identify 17 studies that examine consensus in internal control judgments. They conclude that while there is considerable variation in consensus between studies, overall the results show higher mean consensus than is typically reported in non audit studies. This level of consensus was increased by use of the review process (Trotman & Yetton, 1985). Many of these studies also examined cue usage, judgment stability over time, and self-insight into cue usage. In all of the studies that examined cue usage, a policy-capturing model explained almost all of the variance in subjects' judgments. Normally about four to six cues were found to be significant and there were considerable individual differences in cue usage across auditors (Solomon & Shields, 1994). Bonner (1990) found that differences in consensus in cue weighting between experienced and inexperienced auditors was greater for analytical risk assessments (expert task) than control risk assessments (novice task). While earlier auditing studies found almost no evidence of configural cue usage, more recent studies by Brown & Solomon (1990; 1991) provided evidence of configural cue processing in situations where the nature of the configural processing was specified ex ante based on the context of professional evaluations. Studies that have also examined judgment stability over time have found that stability has been higher than consensus across subjects which is consistent with studies in other areas of judgment/decision-making. Auditors have also demonstrated a reasonably high level of self-insight in connection with their use of information.

In forming an opinion about an account balance, class of transactions, or a control, the auditor generally does not examine all of the information available. Instead, the auditor uses judgmental or statistical sampling procedures. While there has been reasonably high levels of consensus on internal control evaluations, this has not been the case for sample sizes. A study by Mock & Turner (1981), for example, found large differences in recommended sample sizes by experienced auditors working on detailed workpapers.

Third, there have been a number of studies that have examined materiality. When planning an audit, auditors need to consider what factors could generate material misstatements in the financial accounts. Most studies have found that the percentage effect of an item on profit is the most important factor in deciding if an item is material (Messier, 1983; Chewing et al., 1989). Other factors found to be significant included earnings trend and total assets. Studies have also found differences between users of accounts and auditors as well as large differences in materiality thresholds between auditors (e.g. Chewing et al., 1989).

Fourth, prior knowledge of clients gained during previous audits can also affect the extent of testing needed. For example, Houghton & Fogarty (1991) carried out a survey to determine the characteristics of auditor-detected errors and whether areas in which errors occur could be determined during the planning process. They found that 73 percent of errors examined were or could have been identified during the planning stage based on prior knowledge of the client.

The fifth factor is the results of audit procedures, including fraud, illegal acts, and errors which have been found. The usage of a checklist of potential fraud indicators has become an important part of the risk assessment process in practice (see Cushing et al., 1995). With respect to other errors, Bedard & Biggs (1991) show that auditors can improve hypothesis generation of possible errors by examining patterns of discrepancies.

The final factor relates to the source and reliability of information available. In contrast to non auditing studies, research that has examined auditors' sensitivity to the reliability of the source of the evidence has generally found that auditors are relatively sensitive to the reliability of evidence (e.g. Hirst, 1994).

Heuristics and Biases

Early studies of probabilistic judgments by auditors suggest that auditors are also subject to many of the heuristics and biases found in the psychology literature, such as representativeness and anchoring and adjustment. This research has recently been extended in a number of areas directly related to auditors' collection and evaluation of evidence. For example, auditing researches have used the Hogarth & Einhorn's (1992) belief-adjustment model, which assumes that belief-adjustment follows an anchoring and adjustment process, to study audit evidence which is obtained in a sequential manner. Several studies (e.g. Ashton & Ashton, 1988; Tubbs, 1990) have found that auditors place more weight on evidence received most recently. This is known as a recency effect. Such an effect has major implications for audit practice, since this suggests that the order in which auditors receive and evaluate evidence may have a substantial impact on decision-making. That is, two auditors may receive exactly the same evidence but in varying order and subsequently arrive at different conclusions, thus potentially reducing audit effectiveness or efficiency.

Biases may not only occur in processing evidence but also in the search for evidence. A number of studies (e.g. Kida, 1984) have investigated evidence-search strategies used by auditors. Auditors often explicitly or implicitly formulate hypotheses to explain certain factors (e.g., a change in key ratios during preliminary analytical review) and then search for evidence to test the hypothesis. Kida (1984) examined whether the hypothesis-testing strategies employed by auditors affect their search for evidence. Kida noted that audit tasks require auditors to sift through a number of pieces of information, some of which can provide confirming evidence and some disconfirming. The overwhelming conclusion from the psychology literature is that individuals preferentially collect evidence that tends to confirm rather then disconfirm their hypothesis. Although Kida found limited support for the existence of

confirmatory strategies, the effect was less powerful than found in many psychological studies. Subsequent research has provided very little confirmation of the presence of confirmatory strategies in the information search and recall process of auditors.

There has also been audit research to suggest that the search for confirming and disconfirming evidence related to a hypotheses can be influenced by an already-generated hypothesis. This is known as interference effects and has been found in studies examining analytical procedures (e.g., Libby, 1985; Libby & Frederick, 1990; Heiman, 1990).

In conclusion, research on how auditors select, interpret, combine, and evaluate evidence and what decision aids improve these judgments is likely to continue to be an important research issue in auditing in the future.

See also **analytical procedures in auditing; substantive auditing tests**

Bibliography

Ashton, R. H. (1974). An experimental study of internal control judgments. *Journal of Accounting Research*, **12**, 143–57.

Ashton, A. H. & Ashton, R. H. (1988). Sequential belief revision in auditing. *The Accounting Review*, **63**, 623–41.

Bamber, E. M., Gillett, P. R., Mock, T. J. & Trotman, K. T. (1995). Audit judgment.In *Auditing practice, research & education: A productive collaboration*, T. B. Bell & A. Wright (eds), American Accounting Association: Auditing Section.

Bedard, J. C. & Biggs, S. E. (1991). Pattern recognition, hypothesis generation, and auditor performance in an analytical task. *The Accounting Review*, **66**, July, 622–43.

Bonner, S. E. (1990). Experience effects in auditing: The role of task-specific knowledge. *The Accounting Review*, **65**, Jan., 72–92.

Brown, C. E. & Solomon, I. (1990). Auditor configural information processing in control risk assessment. *Auditing: A Journal of practice & Theory*, **9**, 17–38.

Brown, C. E. & Solomon, I. (1991). Configural information processing in auditing: The role of domain-specific knowledge. *The Accounting Review*, **66**, 100–19.

Chewing, G., Pany, K. & Wheeler, S. (1989). Auditor reporting decisions involving accounting principle changes: Some evidence on materiality thresholds. *Journal of Accounting Research*, **27**, Spring, 78–96.

Cushing, B. E., Graham, L. E., Palmrose, Z. V., Roussey, R. S. & Solomon, I. (1995). Risk orientation. *Auditing practice, research & education productive collaboration*. In T. B. Bell & A. Wright (eds), American Accounting Association: Auditing Section.

Heiman, V. B. (1990). Auditors' assessments of the likelihood of error explanations in analytical review. *The Accounting Review*, **65**, Oct., 875–90.

Hirst, D. E. (1994). Auditors' sensitivity to source reliability. *Journal of Accounting Research*, **32**, 113–26.

Hogarth, R. M. & Einhorn, H. J. (1992). Order effects in belief updating: The belief-adjustment model. *Cognitive Psychology*, 1–55.

Houghton, C. W. & Fogarty, J. A. (1991). Inherent risk. *Auditing: A Journal of Practice and Theory*, **10**, Spring, 1–21.

Hylas, R. E. & Ashton, R. H. (1982). Audit detection of financial statement errors. *The Accounting Review*, **47**, Oct., 751–65.

Kida, T. (1984). The impact of hypothesis testing strategies on auditors' use of judgment data. *Journal of Accounting Research*, **22**, Spring, 332–40.

Libby, R. (1985). Availability and the generation of hypotheses in analytical review. *Journal of Accounting Research*, **23**, Autumn, 648–67.

Libby, R. & Frederick, D. (1990). Experience and the ability to explain audit findings. *Journal of Accounting Research*, **28**, Autumn, 348–67.

Messier, W. F. (1983). The effect of experience and firm type on materiality/disclosure judgments. *Journal of Accounting Research*, **21**, 611–18.

Mock, T. J. & Turner, J. L. (1981). Internal accounting control evaluation and auditor judgment. *Auditing Research Monograph No. 3*. New York: American Institute of Certified Public Accountants.

Mock, T. J. & Wright, A. (1993). An explanatory study of auditor evidential planning judgments. *Auditing: A Journal of Practice and Theory*, **12**, 39–61.

Monroe, G. S., Ng, J. K. L. & Woodliff, D. R. (1993). The importance of inherent risk factors: Auditors' perceptions. *Australian Accounting Review*, **3**, Nov., 34–46.

Solomon, I. & Shields, M. D. (1994). Judgment and decision-making in auditing. *Judgment and decision research in accounting and auditing*. In A. H. Ashton & R. H. Ashton (eds), Cambridge University Press.

Trotman, K. T. & Yetton, P. W. (1985). The effect of the review process on auditor judgments. *Journal of Accounting Research*, **23**, 256–67.

Tubbs, R. M., Messier, Jnr, W. F. & Knechel, W. R. (1990). Recency effects in the auditor's belief-revision process. *The Accounting Review*, **65**, 452–60.

Wright, A. & Ashton, R. H. (1989). Identifying audit adjustments with attention-directing procedures. *The Accounting Review*, **64**, Oct., 710–28.

KEN TROTMAN

audit liability   Price Waterhouse (PW) audited the United Bank of Arizona in 1985 and 1986, from which they received fees of c. $150,000 a year. In January 1987 Standard Chartered Bank, an international bank based in London, bought United, paying $335 million to the thousands of individuals who were its shareholders. By 1988 Standard Chartered realized that United's loan portfolio was poor quality. They had made a commercial error. They sold the bank at a loss. Standard Chartered's lawyers were set to work to recoup the commercial blunder. The former directors and officers of United had insufficient wealth to be worthwhile to pursue. The original shareholders were too disperse a group to recover any money from. The only convenient party left to sue were the auditors. At the first trial, the court awarded damages of $338 million against PW. The legal doctrine of joint and several liability means that any single defendant is liable for the entire loss. In turn, if the judgment is upheld, the partnership organizational form of trading makes every single partner personally liable for the $338 million, more than $350,000 per PW partner.

This is one case against one accounting firm. On 17 November 1990, Lavethol & Horwath, the seventh largest firm in the USA succumbed to more than 100 lawsuits with a potential $2 billion in claims. It became the largest professional service company to file for bankruptcy. Audit liability is serious issue, which is changing the organization, structure, and performance of the audit industry.

Auditors are employed to express an opinion on whether accounts prepared by management are fairly stated. The liability of auditors for their opinion serves two functions: as an economic incentive for auditors, and a means of socializing risk.

To illustrate the first function, consider the situation in Prague, where commentators complain of "coffee break" auditors. This is where the examination is so cursory it is merely long enough for the auditor to drink a cup of coffee. Though the Czech Republic may not be wholly representative of Central Europe, it can be considered the most advanced in terms of implementing legislation and privatizing former state enterprises. The Law on Auditing approved by the Czech National Chamber in October 1992 which imposed a duty on all joint stock companies to have financial statements audited also placed the regulation of auditors in the hands of the auditor's union, the Chamber of Auditors. The absence of liability for an audit opinion tends in the Czech Republic toward the subversion of the audit requirement into a low value, perfunctory, and pointless ritual. The major international firms of accountants, the "Big 6," recognize that audit liability is intimately implicated in establishing auditing as a high value economic service, and are lobbying the Czech Ministry of Finance for change. There is an optimal degree of audit liability, and it is evidently not zero, if only because it removes economic incentives from auditors.

The second function of audit liability, as a means of socializing risk, is succinctly expressed in the US case *Rusch Factors versus Levin* (1968) where the court asked:

> Why should an innocent reliant party be forced to carry the weighty burden of an accountant's professional malpractice? Isn't the risk of loss more easily distributed and spread by imposing it on the accounting profession which can pass the cost of insuring the risk onto its customers, who can in turn pass the cost onto the consuming public?

This articulates the so-called "deep pocket theory," where professional indemnity insurance is at the core of a chain of redistribution. Provided auditors can obtain insurance, and are able to price the insurance through to their clients, audit liability merely serves as a link in the chain. The technical problems of the underwriting industry in pricing audit liability were recognized in the German legislature as Fleiss (1986) recounts, and were among the reasons for imposing a legal cap. Under the German Commercial Code, an auditor's obliga-

tion to compensate for damages is limited to DM 500,000.

In both the USA and the UK auditors face unlimited liability for their opinions. In the UK section 310 of the 1985 Companies Act explicitly voids any private contract whose object is to limit auditor's liability. In practice, the liability position of auditors to third parties is limited by the concept of "privity of contract." That is, if there is a private contract between A and B, then C, or D, or E as third parties have no rights under that contract. Under this view the contract for audit services is between an audit firm and a company, and not between an audit firm and the company's bank or individual shareholders, or potential investors, or customers and so on. Arguments of the "hidden principal" (B is really an agent for C on whose behalf the contract with A was undertaken) have been accepted by the courts as extending the classes of claimants to whom a duty of care is owed. This has led to an erosion of the protection to auditors that a narrow interpretation of the doctrine of privity has afforded. In the 1970s litigation costs including settlements, self-insurance reserves, internal and external legal costs on average for the audit industry were no more than 2 to 3 percent of fees. In the 1990s this was the fastest-growing expense line and had reached 14 percent of fee income. Uncertainty regarding the scope and nature of the auditor's legal liability has resulted in a substantial literature analyzing auditor's professional responsibilities. Pound & Courtis (1980), Davidson (1982), and Gwilliam (1987) discuss the evolution of audit liability over time through the analysis of UK and Commonwealth case law. Davies (1979), Minow (1984), and Brecht (1988) discuss the evolution of US legal thinking. The empirical research regarding factors associated with lawsuits in the USA is presented in St Pierre & Anderson (1984), Palmrose (1988; 1991), and Stice (1991). A political factor that commentators identify is the "expectations gap," where public opinion formers expect the audit opinion to provide a warranty, a guarantee against fraud, a certification of solvency. Such expectations contribute to a climate in which there is an acceleration of litigation against auditors. In response, the audit firms are changing the organizational form in which they trade. In the USA, all major audit firms have become limited liability partnerships (LLPs). This protects the personal assets of partners from the potential claims of litigants. In the UK an LLP is only available for those partners that have a passive or sleeping status, any active partners retaining unlimited liability. Incorporating the professional organization as a limited liability company is costly. Disclosure and reporting requirements are more extensive, and payroll taxes for the partners are higher if they are employees of a company. Despite this, already one of the Big 6 firms has incorporated in the UK. Audit liability is changing, and it is changing auditing.

Bibliography

Brecht, H.D (1988). Auditors' duty of care to third parties: A comment on judicial reasoning underlying US cases. *Accounting and Business Research*, Spring, 175–8.

Davidson, A. G. (1982). Auditor's liability to third parties for negligence. *Accounting and Business Research*, Autumn, 257–64.

Davies, J. J. (1979). Accountants' third party liability: A history of applied sociological jurisprudence. *Abacus*, Dec., 93–112.

Fleiss J. W. (1986). German National Paper in *Audit risks and the increasing burden of unlimited liability*. Institute of Certified Public Accountants in Israel.

Gwilliam, D (1987). The auditor, third parties and contributory negligence. *Accounting and Business Research*, Winter, 25–35.

Minow, N. N. (1984). Accountants, liability and the litigation explosion. *Journal of Accountancy*, Sept., 70–86.

Palmrose, Z. (1988). An analysis of auditor litigation and audit service quality. *The Accounting Review*, Jan., 55–73.

Palmrose, Z. (1991). Trials of legal disputes involving independent auditors: Some empirical evidence. *Journal of Accounting Research*, **29** (Supplement), 149–85.

Pound, G. D. & Courtis J. K. (1980). The auditor's liability: A myth? *Accounting and Business Research*, Summer, 29–36.

Stice, J. D. (1991). Using financial and market information to identify pre-engagement factors associated with lawsuits against auditors. *The Accounting Review*, **66**, 516–33.

St Pierre, K. & Anderson J. A. (1984). An analysis of the factors associated with lawsuits against public accountants. *The Accounting Review*, LIX, 2, 242–63.

ANTHONY STEELE

audit planning   During audit planning an auditor develops expectations about likely financial statement error and designs a responsive audit strategy. The professional standards, research, and practice procedures bearing on audit planning follow.

Professional Standards

American Institute of Certified Public Accountants (AICPA) Statement on Auditing Standard No. 22, "Planning and Supervision ," of 1978, defines audit planning as the process of "developing an overall strategy for the expected conduct and scope" of the audit (paragraph 3). Rather than being identical for all audit engagements, the nature, timing, and extent of an audit plan will vary depending on the size and complexity of an entity and on the auditor's experience both with the entity and within the entity's industry. The procedures an auditor performs when planning include (1) reviewing correspondence files and prior year's audit working papers, financial statements, and audit reports; (2) discussing the audit with management, the board of directors, and the board's audit committee; (3) inquiring of management among others about current developments affecting the entity; (4) reading current year financial statements, and establishing the timing of audit work; and (5) coordinating staffing requirements. The auditor's objective in planning is to obtain an understanding of the entity sufficient to perform the audit in accordance with generally accepted auditing standards.

The auditor's planning tasks are typically performed in two stages: first level, performed soon after the first quarter of an audit client's fiscal year, and second level, performed after the second quarter. First level planning is intended to identify important accounting, auditing, or reporting issues. Typical first level planning begins with reviews of prior year audit work (assuming a continuing engagement) and of first quarter financial information for the current year.

The *review of prior year audit work* assesses potentially risky audit areas, identifies audit areas to be emphasized during the engagement, and considers improvements that could be made in the current year. For example, an unusually large number of adjusting journal entries and unexpectedly high actual hours in the audit of receivables last year may prompt the auditor this year to reallocate budgeted audit hours from a low-risk account to receivables. The *review of first quarter financial results* is similarly motivated in that the auditor attempts to isolate unexpected fluctuations or inconsistencies from prior year statements that may signal potentially risky audit areas this year. For example, an intensive January advertising campaign followed by poor first quarter sales may have implications for the valuation assertion in inventory. Thus, the objectives of reviewing prior year audit work and first quarter financial results are to identify problem areas, minimize audit risk, and optimize audit effort.

As part of first level planning, an auditor prepares a *preliminary audit time budget*, an estimate of total planned audit time by staff level and audit activity. For example, a preliminary time budget might allocate 40 audit hours to cash, 20 to marketable securities, and 30 to receivables. First level planning focuses on preliminary evaluations, first-pass first thoughts based on the auditor's general understanding of a client's business, or industry, and other relevant factors.

Second level planning begins with updating the results of first level planning by *reviewing second quarter financial results* and *finalizing the audit time budget*. During second level planning, the auditor also *performs analytical procedures* that are used to assist in planning the nature, timing, and extent of anticipated auditing procedures and in drafting the preliminary audit planning memorandum. Under Statement on Auditing Standard No. 56, "Analytical Procedures" issued by AICPA in 1988, analytical procedures used in planning should focus on enhancing the auditor's understanding of the entity's transactions and on identifying risky audit areas. The sophistication of the analytical procedures applied during planning will vary depending on the engagement, and may range from simple comparisons of account balances between the current and prior year to extensive statistical analyses designed to estimate ranges of expected account balances.

Based on the procedures above, the auditor prepares a *preliminary audit planning memorandum*, which represents an overview of planned audit activity by staff level and includes the final audit time budget. Typically, the planning memorandum describes in general terms the audit approach intended for each audit area. Following completion and approval of the planning memorandum, an auditor schedules available staff members for the audit, and a meeting is held to *coordinate with professional staff assigned to the engagement*. The purpose of the meeting is to introduce each staff member to the engagement and to discuss the planned audit strategy. Since the meeting is ideally held in advance of audit work, the assigned staff should have sufficient time to prepare for the engagement, e.g., by reviewing the planning memorandum, the correspondence and permanent files, and prior year working papers. The auditor should also *coordinate with management* about the scheduled audit dates and anticipated client assistance in preparing working paper schedules, retrieving documents, and providing administrative help.

The final second level planning activity involves drafting *audit programs* – i.e., a detailed list of audit procedures to be performed for each audit area. Individually, an audit program assists an auditor in estimating the time required for a particular audit area, in determining staff requirements, and in scheduling audit work; collectively, all of the programs prepared for an engagement assist in maintaining control as the audit progresses. In general, audit programs cannot be designed until the auditor has reviewed and documented the entity's internal controls. However, in continuing engagements, audit programs can be drafted in advance of field work, since the auditor has prior knowledge of the entity's internal controls and prior information about the results of previous assessments of control risk. If necessary, the programs may be revised when actually used, although the reasons for revision should be justified (e.g., unreliable information during second level planning or accounting system changes). For initial engagements, audit programs are not usually prepared until the entity's internal controls have been reviewed and documented, since the auditor has no prior information about the controls.

Audit planning does not end with second level planning. Rather, planning should continue throughout the engagement. A plan is an overall strategy, subject to revision as more current information becomes available.

Research

Compared to research on, say, evidence gathering or opinion formulations, research on audit planning has not matured significantly in the last three decades, largely because there are no well-established theories of planning for researchers to exploit. Rather, the volume of research is relatively small and the insights limited.

Early research on audit planning addressed the consistency (rather than the appropriateness) of auditors' judgments about planned audit effort, such as audit hours. In short, do auditors agree on the amount of effort required to perform an audit? In an early study of judgment consistency in audit planning, Joyce (1976) found extensive individual differences among 35 practicing auditors who made hypothetical planned audit hours judgments for five categories of audit tasks over varying levels of internal control design variables and two accounting ratios. Like Joyce, Mock & Turner (1981) also reported inconsistent judgments among auditors employed by the same firm. Motivated in part by Joyce's (1976, p. 745) conjecture that the high consensus among auditors on internal control evaluations documented in prior research would not mean that auditors necessarily agree on planned audit effort, Gaumnitz et al. (1982) found consensus among 35 practicing auditors both for internal control evaluation and for planned audit hours.

Research in the 1980s offered considerable evidence that decisions about the nature of planned audit procedures are sensitive to the levels and changes in inherent risk and control risk (e.g. Cohen & Kida, 1989; Kaplan, 1985; Libby et al., 1985). However, little research had addressed the effect of perceived audit risk on the *extent* of planned audit procedures. In response, Mock & Wright (1993) reported the results of a study which – unlike the prior experimental research that placed practicing auditors in hypothetical fact situations – was based on the actual audit planning judgments made for 159 randomly selected manufacturing and merchandising company audits. Interestingly, the results indicate that moderate variation in perceived audit risk across engagements drove little change in the *nature* – but some change in the *extent* – of the audit evidence gathered.

Auditors focus substantive tests in part toward the problems, such as likely financial statement error, identified during audit planning. But, how do practicing auditors represent audit planning problems in memory? Consistent with early research that documents inconsistent audit planning decisions, Christ (1993) found that managers and partners represent audit problems differently in memory than do less experienced seniors and juniors. The study suggests that managers and partners are likely to prepare effective and efficient audit plans, since, compared with seniors/juniors, their free recalls included a higher number and a higher percentage of case-based abstractions.

Bibliography

Christ, M. (1993). Evidence on the nature of audit planning problem representations: An examination of auditor free recalls. *The Accounting Review*, **68**, 2, 304–22.

Cohen, J. R. & Kida, T. (1989). The impact of analytical review results, internal control reliability, and experience on auditor's use of analytical review. *Journal of Accounting Research*, **27**, 2, 263–76.

Gaumnitz, B. R., Nunamaker, T. R., Surdick, J. J. & Thomas, M. T. (1982). Auditor consensus in internal control evaluation and audit program planning. *Journal of Accounting Research*, **20**, 2, 645–755.

Joyce, E. J. (1976). Expert judgment in audit program planning. *Journal of Accounting Research*, **14**, (supplement), 29–67.

Kaplan, S. (1985). An examination of the effects of environment and explicit internal control evaluation on planned audit hours. *Auditing: A Journal of Practice & Theory*, **5**, 1, 12–25.

Libby, R., Artman, J. & Willingham, J. (1985). Process susceptibility, control risk, and audit planning. *The Accounting Review*, **50**, 2, 212–30.

Mock, T. J. & Turner, J. L. (1981). *Internal control evaluation and auditor judgment*. Audit Research Monograph No. 3. New York: AICPA.

Mock, T. J. & Wright, A. (1993). An exploratory study of auditors' evidential planning judgments. *Auditing: A Journal of Practice & Theory*, **12**, 2, 39–61.

DAVID N. RICCHIUTE

audit risk In forming an opinion on the financial statements, the auditor faces various audit-related risks and risk components. Two types of audit-related risk can be distinguished: *audit risk* and *business risk*. Audit risk can generally be defined as the *probability* of incorrectly reporting on the financial statements, and is a function of a number of auditor-and auditee-related risk components. Business risk relates to the adverse consequences to the audit firm arising from any litigation or criticism concerning the auditor's work or the client's audited financial statements. Some major elements of business risk (*see*, for example, Brumfield et al., 1983) are litigation, sanctions imposed by public or private regulatory bodies, and impaired professional reputation.

Two distinct approaches have evolved in the literature (*see*, for example, Cushing & Loebbecke, 1983): the *risk analysis approach* and the *audit modeling approach*. The former approach focuses only on risk related to audit tasks, thereby ignoring business risk. *Audit risk analysis* has been the result of a movement toward the idea of basing audit scope and timing decisions on a more explicit analysis of audit risk. The major purpose of audit risk models is to help the auditor to obtain a *given* degree of confidence that the financial statements do not contain a material error. Economic considerations are not explicitly taken into account, and the focus is rather on effective audit risk control. In the second approach, *audit decision models* are more comprehensive in nature as compared to audit risk models: a broader set of factors are taken into account (such as, audit risk, audit costs, etc.). This type of model may serve as an aid for auditors to identify an efficient and cost-effective way by which a *suitable level* (i.e., cost minimizing) of confidence can be achieved.

The most general definition of audit risk is the risk or probability of incorrectly reporting on the financial statements. This embodies both the risk of incorrect rejection or α-*risk* (also type I error risk) and the risk of incorrect acceptance or β-*risk* (also type II error risk). The distinction between α and β risk types is used both in the context of a single reported book value and at the aggregated level of the financial statements as a whole. The difference between α and β risk is clarified in the article by Elliott & Rogers (1972). It stems from the application of the statistical hypothesis testing approach to the audit setting, which permits the auditor to measure and control both types of risk.

Along another dimension that is directly related to the use of statistical sampling methods in audit testing, audit risk can also be viewed to entail two other types of risk: *sampling* and *nonsampling risk*. Roberts (1978) defined sampling risk as "the portion of audit risk of not detecting a material error that exists because the auditor examined a sample of the account balances or transactions instead of every one." Nonsampling risk then is "the portion of audit risk of not detecting a material error that exists because of inherent limitations of the procedures used, the timing of the procedures, the system being examined, and the skill and care of the auditor." Although both types of risk are defined here in the light of β-risk, a distinction between sampling and nonsampling risk equally applies to α-risk. Roberts further defines another concept, the δ-risk, as the sampling risk of unwarranted reliance in statistical compliance tests.

Finally, there exist three distinct forms of (total) audit risk (*see*, for example, Arens & Loebbecke, 1994; Senetti, 1990). First, there is the *planned level of acceptable audit risk* (or, desired audit risk), specified before the substantive audit procedures are performed; second, there is the *true ex post level of audit risk* (a synonym for ex post audit risk is *achieved audit risk*), which is unknown to the auditor; and third there is the *estimate of ex post audit risk* as made by the auditor.

"Multiplicative" Audit Risk Model

The use of an audit risk model for financial statement auditing has been established in various auditing standards. General statements about risk consideration have evolved into detailed guidance on quantitative risk assessment. An understanding of the importance of risk evaluation was already shown in professional standards in the USA as early as 1963 (*see* AU Section 150.05 of The American Institute of Certified Public Accountants (AICPA) professional standards):

> The degree of risk involved also has an important bearing on the nature of the examination. . . . The effect of internal

control on the scope of the examination is an outstanding example of the influence on auditing procedures of a greater or lesser degree of risk of error; i.e., the stronger the internal control, the less the degree of risk.

The first explicit incorporation of a formula in the standards occurred only in 1972, when the AICPA published Statement of Auditing Procedure No. 54 (which was later incorporated as Section 320 of the Codification of Statements of Auditing Standards (SAS 1)). At that stage of development, the problem was modeled as one of setting the "reliability" level of substantive test of details (S) so that its combination with the subjective reliance on internal accounting control and other relevant factors (C) would provide a combined reliability level (R) sufficient to meet the auditor's overall objectives for the audit. Or:

$$S = 1 - \frac{(1 - R)}{(1 - C)}$$

The relationship with risk was described as follows:

> The combined reliability is the complement of the combined risk that none of the procedures would accomplish the particular audit purpose, and the combined risk is the product of such risks for the respective individual procedures . . . (SAS 1 section 320B.31)

The audit risk model was given further authoritative support by the publication of Statement of Auditing Standard (SAS) 39 (1981) and SAS 47 (1983). SAS 39 proposes the following multiplicative model for audit *planning* purposes:

$$AR = IR \times CR \times AP \times TD$$

Where:

AR = allowable audit risk level that financial statements are materially misstated;

IR = inherent risk of material misstatement; i.e. susceptibility of an assertion to a material misstatement assuming that there are no related internal control structures or procedures;

CR = control risk, or the risk of a material misstatement given that it has occurred and has

not been detected by the system of internal control;

AP = risk that analytical review procedures will fail to detect a material misstatement;

TD = risk that substantive tests of detail fail to detect a material misstatement, given that it has occurred and has not been detected by the system of internal control.

The SAS 39 model is specified in terms of risk factors instead of reliance factors, and includes a factor for analytical review procedures and other relevant substantive tests. SAS 39 also raises the issue of inherent risk, but asserts that this risk is potentially costly to quantify and that for this reason it is implicitly and conservatively set at unity. It further suggests that the proposed model might be used in *planning* a statistical sample by selecting an acceptable ultimate risk, subjectively assessing inherent (IR), control (CR) and analytical review risk (AR) and then solving for tests of detail risk (TD) as follows: TD = AR / (IR * CR* AR). SAS 39 does *not* contemplate the use of the formula to conditionally revise an audit plan or to *evaluate* audit results.

SAS 47 updated the concepts and terminology of SAS 39 to provide further guidance in considering audit risk both at the financial statement level and at the level of individual account balances or classes of transactions. The basic approach remains the same although certain terms have been redefined. SAS 47 explicitly incorporates a factor for inherent risk and combines analytical review risk (AR) and test of details risk (TD) in one risk factor, namely, detection risk (DR). Unlike SAS 39, SAS 47 emphasizes the need of audit risk and materiality "to be considered together in determining the nature, timing, and extent of auditing procedures and in *evaluating* the results of these procedures" (para. 1) (*italics added*). The suggestion to use the ARM for risk evaluation has been heavily criticized in subsequent audit risk literature, as the model is clearly not fit to correctly measure achieved (ex post) audit risk.

An interesting discussion of the assumptions and limitations of ARM has been provided by Cushing & Loebbecke (1983). The major points of their criticism are the following: First, it is assumed that the individual risk components of the ARM are *independent* of each other, whilst there exist interdependencies between these factors. Inherent risk, analytical review risk, and substantive test of detail risk all depend on control risk. Failure to consider these inter-dependencies when internal control is weak tends to understate the risk factor being assessed. As a result the use of the model might expose the auditor to a higher level of ultimate risk than he or she would consider acceptable. Second, the model does not provide any guidance for *aggregating* the risk assess-ments made at the disaggregated level of accounts or transactions to the risk for the financial statements as a whole. Third, the model only considers sampling risk (and β-risk) and assumes that the nonsampling risk compo-nent is negligible. Fourth, the ARM is ill-equiped to explicitly consider other economic factors such as the audit cost or the effect of potential misstatement. Fifth, the ARM should only be used as a *planning* tool, namely, to determine the appropriate level of sampling risk for substantive tests of details, and not as a risk evaluation model.

Although the audit risk model as defined by SAS 39/47 has been accepted by several auditing firms as a planning aid for their audits, there appear to be wide differences in the way in which audit firms in different countries imple-ment the audit risk model. This is not surprising in itself, since little guidance is provided in audit standards about the under-lying determinants of the risk components in the model (in particular w.r.t. inherent risk and control risk), which might result in differences in their conceptual interpretations. A number of empirical studies (*see*, for example, Jiambalvo & Waller, 1984; Daniel, 1988; Strawser, 1990, 1991; Waller, 1993) have investigated some behavioral aspects related to the use of the ARM in practice. From the evidence there seems to be reason to believe that the audit risk model might not be descriptive of risk judgment in practice.

Bayesian Approaches to Modeling Audit Risk

Given the limitations of the "multiplicative" audit risk model for evaluation of (ex post) audit risk, several authors have discussed an alter-native approach for the combination of risk components into an overall ex post audit risk measure, which is derived from the application

of Bayesian theory of *conditional dependence* to the audit judgment process. The approach is fundamentally different from the US Statement on Auditing Standard (SAS) 39/47 model that is a *joint* (multiplicative) ad hoc risk model. From a theoretical perspective the Bayesian approach to risk modeling is superior as it is based on the laws of subjective probability theory.

Several versions of Bayesian audit risk models have been proposed in the literature, based on alternative assumptions about the conditional nature of the various steps in the audit process. Two major categories of models can be distinguished. A first category views inherent risk as the prior probability of material error in the financial statements, but does not recognize the sequential and conditional nature of various audit procedures. The audit risk model intro-duced in 1980 by the Canadian Institute of Chartered Accountants (CICA, 1980) is an example of such a model. In a second category of models (*see*, for example, Kinney, 1989; Sennetti, 1990) the conditional and sequential nature of various audit procedures is explicitly recognized.

Bibliography

Arens, A. A. & Loebbecke, J. K. (1994). *Auditing: An integrated approach*. Englewood Cliffs, NJ: Pre-ntice-Hall.
Brumfield, C. A., Elliott, R. K. & Jacobson, P. D. (1983). Business risk and the audit process. *Journal of Accountancy*, Apr., 60–8.
CICA (1980). *Extent of audit testing: A research study*. Canadian Institute of Chartered Accountants.
Cushing, B. E. & Loebbecke, J. K. (1983). Analytical approaches to audit risk: A survey and analysis. *Auditing: A Journal of Practice and Theory*, 2, Fall, 23–41.
Daniel, S. J. (1988). Some empirical evidence about the assessment of audit risk in practice. *Auditing: A Journal of Practice and Theory*, 7, Spring, 174–81.
Elliott, R. K. & Rogers, J. R. (1972.). Relating statistical sampling to audit objectives. *Journal of Accountancy*, July, 46–55.
Jiambalvo, J. & Waller, W. (1984). Decomposition of audit risk. *Auditing: A Journal of Practice and Theory*, 3, Spring, 80–8.
Kinney, Jr, W. R. (1989). Achieved audit risk and the outcome space. *Auditing: A Journal of Practice and Theory*, 8, Supplement, 867–84.

Roberts, D. M. (1978). *Statistical sampling*. American Institute of Certified Public Accountants.

Sennetti, J. T. (1990). Toward a more consistent model for audit risk. *Auditing: A Journal of Practice and Theory*, **9**, Spring, 103–12.

Strawser, J. R. (1990). Human information processing and the consistency of audit risk judgments. *Accounting and Business Research*, **21**, Winter, 67–75.

Strawser, J. R. (1991). Examination of the effect of risk model components on perceived audit risk. *Auditing: A Journal of Practice and Theory*, **10**, Spring, 126–35.

Waller, W. S. (1993). Auditors' assessment of inherent and control risk in field setting. *The Accounting Review*, **68**, Oct., 783–803.

MARLEEN WILLEKENS

auditor's report Upon completion of the audit process, the auditor issues a report rendering an opinion regarding the financial statements taken as a whole. This report is governed by the profession's ten Generally Accepted Auditing Standards (GAAS), four of which deal with reporting. The reporting standards require that the auditor's report (1) states whether the financial statements are presented in accordance with Generally Accepted Accounting Principles (GAAP); (2) identifies those circumstances in which such principles have not been consistently observed in the current period in relation to the preceding period; (3) indicates that informative disclosures in the financial statements are to be regarded as reasonably adequate unless otherwise stated in the report; and (4) contains either an expression of opinion regarding the financial statements taken as a whole or an assertion to the effect that an opinion cannot be expressed.

The standards of reporting provide general rules regarding the auditor's report. Authoritative guidance regarding the application of these standards in practice is provided in Statements on Auditing Standards (SASs). According to current SAS requirements, if the financial statements present fairly, in all material respects, an entity's financial position (i.e., the balance sheet), results of operations (i.e., the income statement), and cash flows (i.e., the statement of cash flows) in conformity with GAAP and if the audit is performed in accordance with GAAS, then a standard unqualified report can be issued. The auditor is directed to address his or her report to the company, its board of directors and/or its stockholders, but not the management. The standard unqualified report is shown in Box 1.

Box 1: An independent auditor's report

We have audited the accompanying balance sheets of X Company as of December 31, 19X2 and 19X1, and the related statements of income, retained earnings, and cash flows for the years then ended. These financial statements are the responsibility of the company's management. Our responsibility is to express an opinion on these financial statements based on our audits.

We conducted our audits in accordance with generally accepted auditing standards. Those standards require that we plan and perform the audit to obtain reasonable assurance about whether the financial statements are free of material misstatement. An audit includes examining, on a test basis, evidence supporting the amounts and disclosures in the financial statements. An audit also includes assessing the accounting principles used and significant estimates made by management, as well as evaluating the overall financial statement presentation. We believe that our audits provide a reasonable basis for our opinion.

In our opinion, the financial statements referred to above present fairly, in all material respects, the financial position of X Company as of [at] December 31, 19X2 and 19X1, and the results of its operations and its cash flows for the years then ended in conformity with generally accepted accounting principles.

The three paragraphs in Box 1 are referred to as introductory, scope, and opinion paragraphs, respectively. The report is signed by the auditor and is dated as of the last day of field work. However, the auditor may discover major events subsequent to the financial statement date, but before the issuance of the auditor's report. These events are reviewed by the auditor to assess whether they would have affected financial statements had they been known at the financial statement date. If so, the financial statements should be adjusted for the effects of the new information. If subsequent events do not have any effect at the financial statement date, but nevertheless are significant events, they may require disclosure in footnotes to financial statements. In this case, the auditor has two options for dating the report. The first is to date the report as of the day that the discovery occurred, thus extending the auditor's responsibility to the date of the note explaining the subsequent event. The second alternative is to use dual dating where the report date is as of the last day of field work except for the date of the note explaining the subsequent event. In this case the responsibility of the auditor is limited to the first date (i.e., the date of field work) with the exception of the specific subsequent event for which responsibility extends to the second date.

Types of Auditor's Report

Standard unqualified opinion. The standard unqualified report is issued in a majority of audits (*see* AUDITOR'S REPORT, STANDARDS GOVERNING). This fact does not mean that there is no disagreement between the auditor and the auditee in all of these audits. However, in cases where disagreements arise, the auditees resolve the problems to the satisfaction of the auditors so that the standard unqualified report can be issued. Nevertheless, certain conditions may be present that require the auditor to deviate from the standard report. In such circumstances, the auditor adds additional wording or one or more complete explanatory paragraphs to describe the situation or refer the reader to information in financial statements (e.g., footnotes). The resulting opinion is still unqualified, but modified as compared to the standard unqualified report. For example, if the auditor's opinion is based in part on the report of another auditor, the introductory and scope paragraphs are amended to communicate this information. The auditor could also amend the opinion paragraph to reflect the situation.

Other conditions may cause the auditor to add a fourth paragraph to the unqualified report. For example, significant transactions with related parties may be described in a fourth paragraph without a change of wording to the introductory, scope, or opinion paragraphs.

This option is open to the auditor even when probable future contingencies exist for which it is not possible to measure financial effects. This includes conditions when the auditor raises "substantial doubt" regarding the ability of the company to continue as a going concern in the following year. The same treatment is required to explain changes in the application of GAAP or a simple emphasis of a matter. If the departure from GAAP is justified as fair presentation, an unqualified report with a fourth paragraph explaining the departure may be issued by the auditor. In these additional explanatory paragraphs, the auditor either completely explains the departure or refers the reader to notes in the financial statements.

Adverse opinion. If, in the auditor's judgment, pervasive material deviation(s) from (GAAP) exists and the auditee cannot be persuaded to adjust the financial statements to the satisfaction of the auditor, then the auditor must express an adverse opinion. In this condition, the auditor expresses an opinion that the financial statements taken as a whole do not present fairly the financial position of the company in accordance with GAAP.

Qualified opinions. In conditions where the departure from GAAP is viewed by the auditor as material, but not pervasive, the auditor must add an explanatory paragraph before the opinion paragraph describing the departure and then qualify the opinion paragraph by stating that "except for the effects of the [departure] explained in the preceding paragraph, the financial statements present fairly . . ." Such an opinion is called a qualified opinion. Material departure from GAAP is not the only condition resulting in a qualified opinion. The scope of the audit may materially, but not pervasively, be limited by circumstances or by the auditee. In such conditions, the auditor is required to explain the limitation in a paragraph before the opinion paragraph and use an "except for" qualification in the opinion paragraph.

Disclaimer of an opinion. If scope limitation is so pervasive that the auditor cannot be satisfied as to the adequacy of the scope of the audit for a qualified report, he or she will issue a disclaimer. In this situation, the scope paragraph is replaced by an explanatory paragraph regarding the pervasive nature of the scope limitation. The opinion paragraph will then state that due to the pervasive nature of the scope limitation, an opinion cannot be expressed. A disclaimer is also issued when the auditor lacks independence from the auditee. Disclaiming of an opinion is also permitted, but not required, in conditions of pervasive uncertainties about the future of the company.

Piecemeal opinions and negative assurance. Can an opinion be issued on only a part of financial statements? This method was historically allowed, but is no longer permitted. However, in certain specialized engagements, the auditor may issue a negative assurance indicating that nothing came to his or her attention that specified that matters did not meet particular requirements. An example is comfort letters sent to underwriters. Negative assurance should be distinguished from limited assurance. In a limited assurance situation, the auditor is engaged to perform a specific audit procedure for a specific user of the report (i.e., a positive assurance about a specified matter). Limited assurance is allowed by professional standards as a part of a growing body of engagements other than complete audits. These engagements are governed by the Statements on Standards for Attestation Engagements

Effects of the Auditor's Report on Users' Behavior

Investors and creditors and other users of financial statements may take economic actions based on their reliance on the auditor's report. The standard unqualified auditor's report is what the users of financial statements expect to see in annual reports of companies and thus it is looked at by users as evidence confirming expectations. Deviations from the standard unqualified report raise red flags about a company's financial statements that theoretically should alter users' behavior. For example, concern has been raised regarding a self-fulfilling prophecy effect in the auditor's going concern qualification or explanatory paragraph. This effect will occur if in fact the going concern qualification or explanatory paragraph forces the auditee into failure. However, recent empirical results do not provide support for this concern.

A related issue is how well auditor's going concern modification or qualification predicts an auditee's bankruptcy. Empirical evidence indicates that auditor's opinions are not very good predictors of bankruptcy. This conclusion is based on research showing that unless the likelihood of failure is very high, the probability that the auditor will issue a going concern qualification is very low. Given the weak association between going concern qualification or modification and auditee's future bankruptcy, many studies have investigated stock price fluctuations of the auditee before and after going concern qualification. The results of these empirical studies are mixed, indicating perhaps that many going concern qualifications are already known to the market, based on publicly available information. Recent studies that are more precisely controlled for the timing of the information release and the type of qualification have reported significant negative effects on stock prices from unexpected going concern audit opinions and positive effects on stock prices as a result of withdrawn going concern opinions.

Another issue of concern is the effect of the auditor's opinion on the auditee's behavior. For example, faced with the possibility of receiving a qualified opinion, the auditee may switch auditors, in the hope of receiving an improved auditor opinion. Termed opinion shopping, this type of behavior has been of concern to the Securities and Exchange Commission and the popular press.

However, while research indicates a positive association between auditor switching and receipt of qualified audit opinions, recent studies show that companies that switch auditors do not receive improved audit opinions in the year following the switch.

MOHAMMAD J. ABDOLMOHAMMADI

auditor's report: an international comparison   The auditor's report is the culmination of the audit process; it is the most visual part of the auditor's work and frequently constitutes the auditor's sole communication with external parties interested in the reporting entity. Since 1988, a new standard audit report has been widely adopted – e.g., in:

- the USA, by Statement of Auditing Standards No. 58, "Reports on Audited Financial Statements" (US SAS 58);

- Canada, by the Canadian Institute of Chartered Accountants' *Handbook* sections 5400, "The Auditor's Standard Report" (CICA sec. 5400) and 5510, "Reservations in the Auditor's Report" (CICA sec. 5510);

- the UK, by Statement of Auditing Standards 600, "Auditors' Reports on Financial Statements" (UK SAS 600);

- Australia, by Statement of Auditing Practice 3, "The Audit Report on a General Purpose Financial Report" (Aus. AUP 3);

- New Zealand, by Auditing Standard 10, "The Audit Report on General Purpose Financial Reports" (NZ AS 10).

The new "long form" report is also prescribed by the International Federation of Accountants (IFAC) in International Standard on Auditing "The Auditor's Report on Financial Statements" (IFAC/ISA).

The new audit report includes:

- a title, such as "The Auditor's Report" and, except in the USA, the addressee;

- a section identifying the financial information on which the audit opinion is expressed and explaining the respective responsibilities of the entity's directors and auditor for the financial statements;

- a statement that the audit is designed to give reasonable assurance that the financial statements are free of material misstatement, the audit has been conducted in accordance with generally accepted auditing standards, and that the audit includes:
  – examining, on a test basis, evidence supporting the amounts and disclosures in the financial statements;
  – assessing significant estimates made by the directors in preparing the financial statements;
  – assessing whether the accounting policies are appropriate to the entity's circumstances, consistently applied and adequately disclosed;

- the auditor's opinion on the truth and fairness (fair presentation) of the financial statements;

- the auditor's signature, and date of the audit report.

The former "short form" report did not explain the respective responsibilities of the directors and auditor for the financial statements, the level of assurance provided by the auditor's opinion, or the audit process. Thus, the new audit report is longer and more informative than its predecessor.

Audit reports may be either unqualified ("clean") or qualified ("tagged"). As discussed below, the requirements for an unqualified report differ between the various countries. Qualified reports may contain:

- an "except for" opinion – expressed when the auditor disagrees with the treatment or disclosure of a financial statement item but the matter does not undermine the truth and fairness of the financial statements as a whole;

- an adverse opinion – expressed when the auditor disagrees with the treatment or disclosure of a financial statement item and considers the matter undermines the truth and fairness of the financial statements;

- a disclaimer of opinion – expressed when, due to insufficient audit evidence, the auditor is unable to form an opinion on the financial statements.

The accountancy standard setting bodies in the USA, Canada, the UK, Australia, and New Zealand are all members of the IFAC and, as such, have undertaken to follow, to the extent possible given legal and regulatory constraints, the IFAC's auditing standards. This, combined with the domination of auditing in these countries by the "Big Six" international firms of chartered accountants, might be expected to result in audit reports which are very similar. Although the audit reports of the various countries are similar, analysis reveals some marked differences. These are discussed below.

Statements Regarding the Level of Assurance Provided by the Audit Opinion

Audit reports prepared in accordance with US SAS 58, CICA sec. 5400, Aus AUP 3, and IFAC/ISA state the audit has been conducted to obtain reasonable assurance that the financial statements are free of material misstatement. In the UK and New Zealand, the phrase "whether caused by fraud or error" is added – and represents an acknowledgment by auditors in the UK and New Zealand of some responsibility for detecting fraud. The inclusion of the phrase in UK SAS 600 and its exclusion from US SAS 58 reflects differences in the criticism faced by auditors in the USA and the UK. In the UK, particularly in the 1980s, auditors were severely criticized for failing to be more active in combatting corporate fraud. In 1990, the profession responded by issuing an auditing guideline which recognized more exacting duties for auditors in the UK to detect and report fraud than are found elsewhere. In the USA, public and political criticism was more broadly based and resulted, in 1988, in nine new expectation gap auditing standards covering a range of topics. (with respect to the addition of the phrase "wheter caused by fraud or error", New Zealand followed the UK example: NZ AS 10 followed UK SAS 600; meanwhile, CICA sec. 5400 and IFAC/ISA followed US SAS 58.)

Criteria for an Unqualified Audit Opinion

In the USA and Canada, an unqualified opinion is expressed when auditors consider the financial statements present fairly, in all material respects, the entity's financial position, results of operations, and cash flows in accordance with generally accepted accounting principles (GAAP). In Canada (but not in the USA), auditors are explicitly required to consider the appropriateness of the accounting principles adopted for the entity's circumstances. Also, in Canada, a change in an accounting principle which accords with GAAP is not to be referred to in the audit report; in the USA, the change is to be mentioned in an explanatory paragraph.

In the UK, an unqualified opinion requires three criteria to be met: the financial statements must be prepared using appropriate accounting policies which are consistently applied; the statements must accord with relevant legislation or applicable accounting standards; and all information relevant to a proper understanding of the financial statements must be adequately disclosed. In New Zealand, the same criteria must be met and also a further three: the financial report must be prepared in accordance

with generally accepted accounting practice, it must be consistent with the auditor's knowledge of the operations of the entity, and all material matters relevant to the proper presentation of the financial report must be adequately disclosed. The last requirement may seem similar to that requiring adequate disclosure of all information relevant to a proper understanding of the financial report. However, the meaning of "proper presentation" (preparers' perspective) differs from that of "proper understanding" (users' perspective).

The last two requirements noted above can be traced to the previous version of NZ AS 10 (1986) and from there to the IFAC's International Auditing Guideline (IAG) 13 (1983). However, a small but significant change has been introduced in NZ AS 10. AS 10 (1986), like IAG 13, referred to the financial information being consistent with the auditor's knowledge of the *business*, rather than *operations*, of the entity. The former has a broader focus than the latter.

IFAC/ISA has two criteria for an unqualified opinion: the view presented by the financial statements as a whole must be consistent with the auditor's knowledge of the business of the entity (as per IAG 13), and the financial statements must be prepared in accordance with acceptable financial reporting standards and comply with statutory requirements. In Australia, to qualify for an unqualified opinion, the financial report must be presented fairly in accordance with accounting standards and relevant statutory and other requirements, so as to present a view which is consistent with the auditor's understanding of the entity's financial position, results of operations, and cash flows. As in New Zealand, the superseded standard (AUP 3, 1984) followed IAG 13 and included the requirement for financial information to be consistent with the auditor's knowledge of the business of the entity. While NZ AS 10 and UK SAS 600 narrow *business* to *operations*, Aus AUP 3 narrows this further to (in effect) the entity's *financial affairs*. The US and Canadian standards go even further, merely requiring the financial statements to be prepared in accordance with GAAP, with no reference to consistency with the auditor's knowledge/understanding of the entity's business, operations, or financial affairs.

Treatment of Uncertainties

Two categories of uncertainties are generally recognized:

- *inherent uncertainties* – uncertainties whose resolution depends on future events for which audit evidence does not currently exist;

- *limitations on scope* – uncertainties resulting from circumstances or the client denying the auditor access to adequate audit evidence.

Prior to the new audit report, inherent uncertainties generated a "subject to" audit qualification in all of the countries, but a scope limitation resulted in a "subject to" qualification in the USA and Canada and an "except for" qualification in the UK, Australia, and New Zealand. The IFAC's IAG 13 permitted a "subject to" or "except for" qualification for a scope limitation.

"Subject to" qualifications have now been eliminated in all of the countries except Australia. The professional bodies decided that, if an inherent uncertainty is properly accounted for and adequately disclosed, a qualified audit opinion is inappropriate. In Canada, when an unqualified opinion is justified, an uncertainty is not to be referred to in the audit report. By contrast, in the USA, auditors are required to describe, in a paragraph following the opinion paragraph, any uncertainty the resolution of which is reasonably likely to result in a material loss. In its 1989 revision of IAG 13, the IFAC followed the US example.

In the UK and New Zealand, elimination of the "subject to" qualification was more complex because it was used for both inherent uncertainties and scope limitations. Nevertheless, as in North America, the UK and New Zealand professional bodies have eliminated the use of "subject to" qualifications and adopted the "except for" qualification for scope limitations. They have also introduced an explanatory paragraph for "fundamental uncertainties" – uncertainties which, because of their nature and implications, would render the financial statements seriously misleading if not disclosed. Thus, uncertainties qualifying for an explanatory paragraph in the UK and New Zealand are significantly more serious than those warranting such disclosure in the USA. Further, in the

USA, the explanatory paragraph follows the opinion paragraph and is designed to highlight an uncertainty which could materially affect financial statement users' understanding of the entity's financial position and/or performance. In the UK and New Zealand, the explanatory paragraph is included in the "basis of opinion" paragraph and is intended to draw attention to a significant matter the auditor considered when concluding that the financial statements present a true and fair view of the entity's financial affairs.

In Australia, the "subject to" qualification was retained when AUP 3 was revised in February 1994. However, an exposure draft of a new audit report auditing standard, issued in May 1994, proposes that the "subject to" qualification be eliminated, the "except for" qualification be used for scope limitations, and (following the US example), attention be drawn to an inherent uncertainty in an explanatory paragraph following the opinion paragraph.

Audit Report Formats and Location of Audit Qualification Explanations

In the USA, Canada, and Australia, and also under IFAC/ISA, an audit qualification is explained in a paragraph *preceding* the opinion paragraph; in the UK and New Zealand, it is explained *within* the opinion paragraph. This difference results primarily from differing audit report formats.

Audit reports prepared in accordance with US SAS 58, CICA sec. 5400, and IFAC/ISA comprise an introductory paragraph (which refers to the statements audited and the respective responsibilities of the entity's management and auditors for the financial statements); a scope paragraph (which briefly describes the audit process and the level of assurance the audit provides); and an opinion paragraph. Where a qualified opinion is expressed, a paragraph explaining the qualification is inserted between the scope and opinion paragraphs. Additionally, under US SAS 58 and IFAC/ISA, when relevant, a paragraph is added to the audit report explaining an inherent uncertainty. Headings are not used to distinguish the various paragraphs.

Audit reports in the UK have four sections: an (unheaded) introductory paragraph identifying the statements audited; a (headed) paragraph describing the respective responsibilities of the entity's directors and auditors; a (headed) section explaining the basis of the audit opinion (which briefly describes the audit process, the level of assurance the audit provides, and, in appropriate cases, includes a (headed) sub section describing fundamental uncertainties); and a (headed) section setting out the auditor's opinion. When a qualified opinion is expressed, the qualification is first explained, then the opinion is expressed in a second paragraph.

New Zealand audit reports resemble UK reports but, in New Zealand, the respective responsibilities of the directors and auditor(s) are explained in separate (headed) sections and the "basis of opinion" section concludes with a statement regarding any relationship the auditor has with the entity other than as auditor. (This is required by the Financial Reporting Act 1993.) A further difference results from the legal requirement for auditors in New Zealand to state whether they have obtained all the information and explanations they required, and whether the entity has maintained proper accounting records. In the UK, auditors are required to comment on these matters only when something is amiss.

In Australia, an unqualified audit report has two (headed) sections: a "scope" section, which provides all of the information presented in the reports considered above other than the auditor's opinion, and an "opinion" section. Where a qualified opinion is expressed, a paragraph (headed "qualification") is inserted between the scope and opinion sections. Similarly, any reference to the application of Australian Accounting Standards is made in a separate (headed) section following the "scope" section of the report.

Evaluation of the Recently Adopted Audit Report

The new "long form" audit report was adopted primarily to overcome financial statement users' misconceptions regarding auditors' responsibility for financial statements, the level of assurance their opinion provides, and the audit process. Research in the USA and the UK has found that these objectives have been generally

met. However, this has been at the cost of changing the auditor's report into a lengthy, complex document. Questions arise as to the propriety of explaining the respective responsibilities of directors and auditors, and describing the audit process, in *every* audit report. Further, although financial statement users may initially read the new-style report in detail, as they become familiar with it, it is likely that they will treat it, like its predecessor, as a symbol. But, given its length, the new report is less effective as a symbol than the former short form report; any warning messages given by the auditor are likely to be overlooked.

The primary function of the auditor's report is to express an opinion on the accompanying financial statements. Information about the respective responsibilities of directors and auditors, and information about the audit function, differs in nature from a report of audit findings, and such information may divert attention from the auditor's key message. Further, to explain the audit process in a few sentences is to lay oneself open to misunderstanding. In developing the new auditor's report, the professional bodies appear to have focussed on clarifying the responsibilities for which auditors are *not* responsible and the limitations of the service they provide. They seem to have paid inadequate attention to the impact of such additional information on the effectiveness of the auditor's report in fulfilling its primary purpose – conveying the auditor's conclusions with respect to the audit as clearly and succinctly as possible. Additionally, given the similarity of the socioeconomic environments of Anglo-American countries, the growth of multinational corporations and international accountancy firms, and the trend toward increased international harmonization of accounting and auditing standards, the variations in the wording, meaning, and formats of audit reports in the different countries seem to be unnecessary and undesirable.

BRENDA A. PORTER

B

bonds A bond is a financial instrument that arises from a contract known as an *indenture* and denotes a two fold promise. First, it promises to pay a fixed amount of money at a specified maturity date. Second, it promises to pay a periodic interest at a specified rate on the face value of the financial instrument. Bonds are typically evidenced by a certificate and have a usual value of $1,000. The interest payments are usually paid semi-annually.

Bonds come in many variations and some of the more important types are detailed below:

Secured bonds. These bonds have a claim on real estate (mortgage bonds) and other securities (collateral trust, bonds).

Unsecured bonds. These bonds have no specific claim on assets and as such are "unsecured." A prime example of this type is the "junk bonds" one comes across in the popular business press.

Term bonds. These are bonds that mature on a single date.

Serial bonds. These bonds mature in installments.

Convertible bonds. These bonds have a notable feature that enables them to be converted into other securities of the firm.

Registered bonds. These bonds are issued in the name of the owner and require surrender of the certificate and issuance of a new certificate to complete a sale.

Bearer bonds. These are bonds that are not recorded in the name of the owner and may be transferred from one owner to another by mere delivery.

Stripped bonds. Also known as zero-coupon bonds, these are created by deattaching (stripping) interest coupons from a coupon bond and selling the stripped bond as a contract in itself.

Figure 1 outlines the important aspects relating to bond issuance. The issuance of bonds as a financial instrument is a very serious affair and is done with extreme formality. Much planning is done and approval sought at different levels, both within the firm and outside (rating agencies), before a bond issue comes for sale to the public.

Table 1 shows how the inherent relative risk in a bond issue is determined through quality rating made by firms (in the USA) such as Moody's Investors Service and Standard and Poor's Corporation. Typical bond quality designations and rating symbols of these two firms are shown in Table 1. The quality rating typically assigned to a bond issue is an assessment of the firm's ability to pay with regard to a specific borrowing. It should be noted, therefore, that over the life of a bond issue this rating can be notched up or down a rating level.

Figure 1: Bond issuance

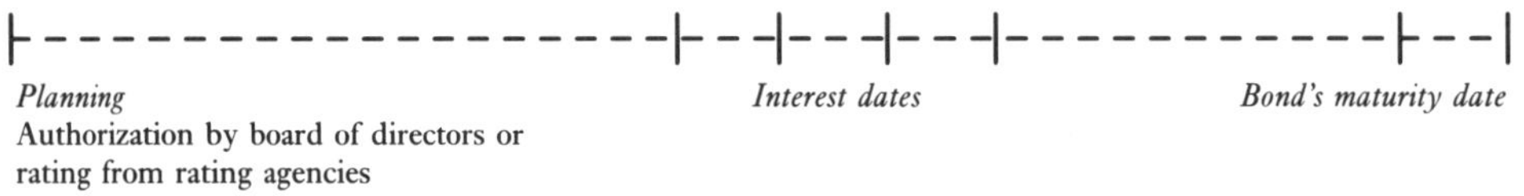

Planning
Authorization by board of directors or
rating from rating agencies

Interest dates

Bond's maturity date

Table 1: Quality rating by two US firms

Quality	Moody's	Standard & Poor's
Prime	Aaa	AAA
Excellent	Aa	AA
Upper medium	A	A
Lower medium	Baa	BBB
Marginally speculative	Ba	BB
Very speculative	B, Caa	B
Default	Ca, C	D

Bond Valuation

Much time-consuming planning is done before a bond issue comes to the fore which means that the market conditions and the financial condition of the issuing firm could alter significantly in the interim. This then impacts the marketability of the bonds by way of their selling prices.

In this context, there are two major issues relating to the bond issue:

(1) bond issued at par, at discount or at premium.
(2) discount (or premium) amortization methods.
   (a) straight line rate method.
   (b) effective interest rate method.

We first look at issue 1. Table 2 shows the way a bond is valued. Thus, the investment community at large values a bond at the present value of its future cash flows which consist of (1) principal and (2) interest payment stream. The interest rate used to compute present value of these cash flows is the market rate that provides an acceptable return on an investment in line with the issuing firm's risk profile and market conditions.

When the market rate is equal to the coupon rate, the present value of future cash flows to the buyer will equal the face value of bonds and the bonds will be issued at par.

When the market rate is greater (less) than the coupon rate, the present value of future cash flows to the buyer will be less (greater) than the face value of bond and the bonds will be issued at a discount (premium). The result of issuing bonds at a discount is that the bond discount represents the interest expense to the issuing firm in addition to the amount of interest paid in cash at each interest period. When bonds are issued at premium, the bond premium represents an amount by which the interest expense to the issuing firm will be less than the amount of the interest paid at each date. For purposes of statement disclosure, bond discount is shown as a non current asset, inasmuch as it is similar to prepayment of asset, and a bond premium is shown as a non current liability, inasmuch as it is similar to advances received.

Next, moving on issue 2, we note that this issue arises only when bonds are issued at a discount or at a premium. It does not arise when these are issued at par.

The straight line rate method of amortizing a premium or discount results in a constant amount being charged to interest expense for each year of the life of the bond. This practice is not conceptually correct, as the relationship of interest expense to carrying value or book value of bonds results in an apparent decrease (for bond discount) or increase (for bond premium) in the interest rate for the various years of the life of the bond. This occurs even though the interest expense is constant; the carrying value increases for each year for discounted bonds and decreases for bonds issued at premium.

The effective interest rate method solves this problem by doing the following:

Thus unlike the straight line method, the effective interest rate method produces a periodic expense equal to a constant percentage of the carrying value of the bond. Although, the

Table 2:

Phrase	Meaning	When
At par rate	Proceeds from bond issue = face value	Market rate = coupon rate
Below par	Proceeds from bond issue < face value	Market rate > coupon rate
Above par	Proceeds from bond issue > face value	Market rate < coupon rate

Bond interest expense

Carrying value   Effective
of bonds at   X   interest   –
             rate
expense
beginning of

Bond interest paid

Face amount   Stated
of bonds   X   interest = Amortization
         rate

total interest expense over the life of the bond is equal under both methods, the annual amounts could be quite different. If the differences are material, then only the effective interest rate method should be used.

Bond Redemption

The life of a bond could come to an end in any of the following ways:

(1) normal redemption
(2) premature termination
   (a) reacquisition
   (b) legal or in-substance defeasance

Normal redemption. Here the issue is simple as the bonds are held to maturity. This implies that all discount or premium will have been fully amortized resulting in the carrying value being equal to the maturity value of the bonds at that time. A common way in which bonds may be retired in this way is by way of a sinking fund. This practice essentially involves setting aside cash or other assets for the retirement of a bond. Such a reserve is also known as a redemption fund.

Premature termination.
Reacquisition. Reacquistion of bonds can happen at any time over the life of a bond issue and at the time of reacquistion, an unamortized premium or discount and any costs of issue applicable to the bonds must be amortized up to the reacquisition date. The amount of money paid on redemption before maturity including any call premium and expense of reacquisition is known as the reacquisition price. The net carrying amount is the amount payable at maturity adjusted for unamortized discount (premium) and the cost of issuance. The difference between the net carrying amount and the reacquisition price is the gain or loss from extinguishment.

Legal/in-substance defeasance

A quite different way to remove the debt is to have a firm provide for the future repayment of bonds by placing cash or other assets in an irrevocable trust. The principal and interest are pledged and are sufficient to pay off the principal and interest of its own bond. Firms may do this because the normal call premium may be high and the cost of purchase of securities may be lower than the carrying value of firm's debt.

In this context, a distinction needs to be made between legal defeasance and in-substance defeasance. Legal defeasance means debtor firms are released from all legal liability as a result of the arrangement. In such cases, the debt is removed from the balance sheet. In-substance defeasance occurs when the firm deposits cash and securities in an irrevocable trust which is used to pay principal and interest on bond but the creditors may not be party to the arrangement and in some cases may not even know it exists. However, it is argued that the economic effects are similar to the above, hence the name in-substance defeasance.

Review of Research Literature

Beginning with Watts & Zimmerman (1978), various studies have explored the relation between accounting method decisions and firm characteristics. The basic theme has been that accounting decisions are determined by political costs which typically cause firms to defer income recognition. The firms understate assets and debt on the one hand and on the other adopt compensation contracts which generally encourage the acceleration of income recognition. With regard to extant literature on bonds, it might enhance our understanding of the issues involved if we divide our focus into three main parts:

(1) Bond characteristics in relation to firm characteristics.

(2) Bond covenants.

(3) Bond redemption/insubstance defeasance.

Bond characteristics

In an early study, Bowman (1980) studied the relationship between firm's risk and the debt – equity ratio. The finance theory suggests that the higher a firm's debt – equity ratio, the higher a firm's risk as proxied by the firm's betas. Bowman's (1980) results hold the above prediction irrespective of whether the debt was measured in market or book values. These results were corroborated later by Mulford (1986) using a later time period and a larger dataset.

Bond covenants. Apart from the above issue of firm characteristics which has occupied researchers' interest, equally important has been the study of bond covenants which form a core part of a bond issue. Briefly, the covenants are a device which enable the creditors to protect themselves from the injudicious acts of the borrowers. Smith & Warner (1979) outline the various types of debt covenants. Duke & Hunt (1990) find that the various debt covenants used in practice are quite effective as measured by their proxies using accounting numbers. However, Press & Weintrop (1990) present evidence that information obtained from public domain sources such as Moody's (in the USA) and annual reports is not comprehensive, particularly with respect to privately-placed debt, and that in these cases one should access original Securities and Exchange Commission (SEC) filings. Leftwich (1983) presents evidence of how some covenants may modify generally accepted accounting principles (GAAP) to protect the interests of the creditors.

In-substance defeasance. Next, with regard to insubstance defeasances that firms undertake when interest rates are high and they want to post gains on retirement of debt, Hand et al. (1990) present evidence from a sample of defeased firms that is consistent with the hypotheses of earnings management, probable bad news leading to bond covenant violations and lack of productive ventures for excess cash. Because of lack of adequate data to better discriminate among the above motivations, they state that one would have to wait till the next

recession when the interest rates are high and more instances of defeasances occur, to conduct more studies into firm behavior in the context of bond retirements.

Bibliography

Bowman, R. G. (1980). The importance of a market-value measurement in assessing leverage. *Journal of Accounting Research*, Spring, 617–30.

Dukes, J. C. & Hunt, H. G. (1990). An empirical examination of debt covenant restrictions and accounting related debt proxies. *Journal of Accounting and Economics*, Jan., 45–63.

Hand, J., Hughes, P. & Sefcik, S. (1990). Insubstance defeasances: Security price reactions and motivations. *Journal of Accounting and Economics*, Jan., 47–89.

Leftwich, R. W. (1983). Accounting information in private markets: Evidence from private lending agreements. *The Accounting Review*, Jan., 23–42.

Mulford, C. W. (1986). The importance of a market value measurement of debt in leverage ratios: Replications and extensions. *Journal of Accounting Research*, Autumn, 897–906.

Press, E. G. & Weintrop, J. B. Accounting-based constraints in public and private debt agreements. *Journal of Accounting and Economics*, Jan., 65–95.

Smith, C. & Warner, J. B. On financial contracting: An analysis of bond covenants. *Journal of Financial Economics*, June, 117–61.

Watts, R. & Zimmerman, J. (1978). Towards a positive theory of the determination of accounting standards. *The Accounting Review*, Jan., 112–34.

S. M. KHALID NAINAR

budgetary participation Budgetary participation (BP) is the process by which managers, whose performance evaluation is at least in part budget-based, are *involved* and are *influential* in the setting of those budgets. While the theoretical foundations for the concept of participation stem from the human relations movement of the 1930s (e.g., Mayo, 1931), it was Argyris (1952) who first introduced the concept of participation to the management accounting literature in the context of budgeting.

BP is theoretically distinct from participation in decision-making more generally, because of the budget's implication in subsequent performance evaluation of the participating manager. As a consequence, much of what was known by the mid-1950s about the cognitive and behavioral effects of participation in decision-making could be generalized to the setting of budgets only with great caution.

Early research work examining the effects of BP was either case-based with small samples (such as Argyris' work) or non-empirical (e.g., Becker & Green, 1962). Organized empirical work in a more scientific tradition began with Stedry (1960). By the mid-1970s, results of this stream of work were inconclusive. Those results ranged from those showing strong positive effects, particularly on cognitive outcomes like job satisfaction (e.g., Cherrington & Cherrington, 1973), to no clear effects (e.g., Milani, 1975) and even negative effects (e.g., Stedry, 1960; Bryan & Locke, 1967). This state of affairs prompted Hopwood (1976) to conclude, somewhat inevitably, that BP's effects were likely to be conditional on contextual factors for which no controls were provided. Instead, the literature until that time appeared preoccupied with the possibility that refinements of research method would produce more consistent evidence. Apparently, the parallel arrival in the management accounting literature of contingency theory triggered the realization that it was deficiencies in theory, rather than method, which accounted for the mixed evidence.

From 1980, therefore, research examining the effects of BP began to adopt contingency theoretic frameworks, and empirical work explicitly accommodated moderating variables thought to govern these effects. In addition, reinterpretations of the earlier seemingly conflicting findings began to produce clear evidence that BP works sometimes, and not at other times (Brownell, 1982a). Contingencies from multiple domains emerged as factors governing the effects of BP. For example, Brownell (1981, 1982b) showed that BP was effective for managers who felt a personal sense of control over their destinies (internal locus of control), but not for those who believed that chance and luck or fate governed the outcome of their actions (external locus of control). Individual level variables therefore have the capacity to moderate BP's effects. National culture also has been shown (Harrison, 1992) to influence the efficacy of BP, some national cultures distinctly preferring BP, others finding it distasteful. Other variables at the interpersonal level, task and environmental variables, and strategy have all been shown to matter.

Also in the beginning of the 1980s there emerged a stream of research rooted in the economics of agency. This work was largely analytical in nature and explored the implications for BP of information asymmetry, moral hazard, and unobservability of subordinate behavior (e.g., Magee, 1980). In a decentralized organization, subordinate managers are likely to enjoy information advantages over superiors and BP is one of several processes that are designed to elicit such information. However, the existence of budget-based rewards, coupled with incomplete observability of subordinate behavior, gives rise to concerns over the truthfulness of the information revealed in the process. The results of empirical work pursuing this line of inquiry are mixed. For example, Dunk (1993) did not produce evidence consistent with the intuitively appealing notion that information asymmetry coupled with budget-based rewards would cause subordinates to use the participative process to negotiate easy-to-achieve ("slack") budgets.

Also more recent is a return to concerns with research method, particularly over the construct validity of operational measures of BP (and other variables). For example Briers & Hirst (1990) raise legitimate questions about the potential slippage between theoretical and operational definitions of constructs and urge the use of multiple methods (triangulation) in the empirical assessment of constructs like BP.

Two themes are suggested to attract research attention in the future. First, work within the agency – theoretic paradigm is likely to pay more attention to issues of theory – and empirical work – which will show more concern with issues of method and measurement. Both of these thrusts will contribute to bringing some further resolution and consensus to what is known about the effects of BP.

Bibliography

Argyris, C. (1952). *The impact of budgets on people*. New York: Controllership Foundation.
Becker, S. W. & Green Jr, D. (1962). Budgeting and employee behavior. *Journal of Business*, Oct., 392–402.
Briers, M. & Hirst, M. (1990). The role of budgetary information in performance evaluation. *Accounting, Organizations and Society*, 15, 373–98.

Brownell, P. (1981). Participation in budgeting, locus of control and organizational effectiveness. *The Accounting Review*, Oct., 844–60.

Brownell, P. (1982a). Participation in the budgeting process: When it works and when it doesn't. *Journal of Accounting Literature*, 1, 124–53.

Brownell, P. (1982b). A field study examination of budgetary participation and locus of control. *The Accounting Review*, Oct., 766–77.

Bryan, J. F. & Locke, E. A. (1967). Goal-setting as a means of increasing motivation. *Journal of Applied Psychology*, June, 274–7.

Cherrington, D. J. & Cherrington, J. O. (1973). Appropriate reinforcement contingencies in the budgeting process. *Journal of Accounting Research*, 11, supplement, 225–53.

Dunk, A. S. (1993.). The effect of budget emphasis and information asymmetry on the relation between budgetary participation and slack. *The Accounting Review*, Apr., 400–10.

Harrison, G. L. (1992). The cross-cultural generalizability of the relation between participation, budget emphasis and job related attitudes. *Accounting Organizations and Society*, 17, Jan., 1–15.

Hopwood, A. G. (1976). *Accounting and Human Behavior*. Englewood Cliffs, NJ: Prentice-Hall.

Magee, R. P. (1980). Equilibria in budget participation. *Journal of Accounting Research*, 18, Autumn, 551–73.

Mayo, E. (1931). *The human problems of an industrial civilization*. New York: Viking.

Milani, K. (1975). The relationship of participation in budget-setting to industrial supervisor performance and attitudes: A field study. *The Accounting Review*, Apr., 274–84.

Stedry, A. C. (1960). *Budget control and cost behavior*. Englewood Cliffs, NJ: Prentice-Hall.

PETER BROWNELL

budgeting Budgeting is the process by which the goals of an organization, and the resources to attain those goals, are quantified and communicated. Specifically, budgets are used to plan and control operations and to make long-term investments. Planning entails coordination, marshalling and allocating resources, and control involves performance evaluation.

In not-for-profit organizations like government agencies and charities, the focus of budgeting has been to balance revenues from taxes or donations with expenditures. Recently governments worldwide have been facing increased pressures to raise efficiency while maintaining balanced budgets. These pressures may change the focus of budgeting to stress efficiency and prioritization of expenditures. The U.S. Government Performance and Results Act of 1993 is an example of this change.

Financial Planning

Planning is achieved through a series of interrelated budgets known as the master budget. The master budget is a coordinated business plan, which summarizes the planned operating, investing, and financing activities of the business for the budget period.

The master budget, portrayed in figure 1, comprises two sets of budgets: (1) operating budgets, and (2) financial budgets. Within these two broad categories of operating and financial budgets, there can be an unlimited number and variety of budgets and sub-budgets, depending on the level of detail desired. Operating budgets summarize the expected operating activities – sales, purchases, labor, overhead, and discretionary expenses – culminating in the income statement. The income statement is sometimes grouped with financial budgets. Here it is included with operating budgets on the premise that it is a summary display of operating results during the budget period. Financial budgets summarize the investing activities, cash flows, and the pro forma balance sheet. These budgets articulate in that they feed into each other and

Figure 1: Amount of $500,000 budget allocated to Manager A (in $1000s). Bargaining zone is noted by x's

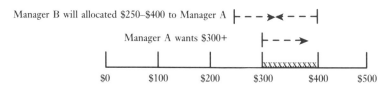

form part of an interdependent whole. But the impetus clearly flows from operations.

At the epicenter of budgeting is the projected sales. Forecasting sales is critical because all other budgeted activities depend on it. Organizations develop demand forecasts in different ways. Some use highly sophisticated models and market surveys, while others rely on simple extrapolations of past year's sales. Many use multiple sources of information including the views of line managers and field sales force. Forecasts from these separate sources are consolidated into the final sales budget.

The sales forecast is used to develop budgets for operating, investing, and financing activities. For operations, the forecast is used to budget for the acquisition of inputs and for discretionary spending. Operating budgets vary by industry and by company. Manufacturing firms develop a production budget showing the product units to be manufactured, ending inventories for work-in-process and finished goods, direct labor, direct materials, and overhead. A budget for selling and administrative expenses is also prepared. Merchandising firms, on the other hand, develop budgets for merchandise purchases together with budgets for labor, inventories, and selling and administrative expenses. Service firms develop a set of budgets that show how the demand for their services will be met.

The sales forecast is also used to prepare the financial budgets. The capital budget summarizes the investing activities – resources that require medium- and long-term advance commitment. The advance commitments ensure that capacity is on hand when expected sales materialize. But they also entail considerable risk, because, once committed, they cannot be altered easily in the short run. These commitments inject rigidity into the cost structure of the firm, magnifying the impact of small variations in sales on profits – a condition known as the operating leverage effect.

The cash budget reflects the cash flows associated with planned operating, investing, and financing activities. The importance of the cash budget stems from its strategic role in cash management – investing surpluses and financing deficits. For global enterprises, these "treasury functions" can become highly com-

plex, not only because of the burgeoning supply of derivatives (futures, options, swaps, caps, floors, collars, etc.), but also because different financing strategies entail different risk profiles. Reliance on debt to leverage the return to shareholders entails additional constraints and higher fixed financing costs. These fixed costs further magnify the impact of demand variability on profits – a condition known as the financial leverage effect.

The pro forma balance sheet incorporates the cumulative results of all the budgeted activities to display the financial position of the firm at the conclusion of the budget period. It shows the projected configuration of assets, liabilities, and shareholders' equity. If desired or mandated configurations are not obtained, then budgets are revised to reconfigure the balance sheet.

When budgets are approved, resources are allocated to implement the planned activities. As implementation proceeds, results are monitored for control and evaluation.

Management Control

Control often centers on operating activities, i.e., profits. To this end, two budgets are used: one for the forecasted level of activity – the master budget – and the other for the level of activity actually attained – the flexible budget. The latter is based on the same input – output ratios for variable inputs as in the master budget. These two budgets together with actual results are used to disaggregate the profit variance between profits under the master budget and actual profits into two components: (1) profits missed or earned because of failing to reach or exceeding the forecasted level, and (2) profits missed or earned because of efficiency and price variances. These aggregate differences are decomposed further into specific volume and price variances. An alternative but less customary formulation is to divide the differences between actual profits and profits under the master budget into (1) a profit-linked productivity measure derived by comparing actual profits with profits based on a flexible budget using budgeted input-output ratios but actual prices, and (2) another component lumping the effects on profits of volume and price differences between the master budget and the flexible budget. But to have confidence in any of these measures, it is imperative not only to have truthful budgets, but also to have knowledge about how different costs behave in response to changes in the level of activities.

Cost Behavior

Accountants have traditionally relied on the economist's short-run cost curves to understand the behavior of costs. They have, therefore, assumed that costs either change with output (variable) or remain constant (fixed). Although this dichotomy has the advantage of providing a quick perspective of the behavior of costs as a function of volume, it is flawed because it suppresses valuable detail about the behavior of costs.

Two momentous events have combined to heighten the need for a better knowledge of costs and to provide the wherewithal to meet that need. One is the growing intensity of global competition; the other is the unrelenting wave of information technology. The former has raised the cost of relying on distorted cost information, while the latter has lowered the cost of getting the needed information. Consequently, the focus on cost behavior has shifted from volume as the cost driver to activities as cost drivers. Under this so-called activity-based costing (ABC), activities drive costs, and products, markets, and customers drive activities. In diversified firms operating in competitive markets, a detailed knowledge of cost drivers can provide a strategic advantage.

Focus on activities undertaken to attain the organization goals raises three types of questions. First, which activities are indispensable for the attainment of organization goals and how can they be done with fewer resources? Second, which activities are dispensable for the attainment of organization goals and how can they be eliminated? Third, which activities can be supplied with and without acquiring a capability in advance? The first two lead to a distinction between value-added and non-value-added activities. For value-added activities, budgets aim at getting *more* output with *fewer* resources. Performance evaluation is driven by the input – output efficiency or productivity. However, the simple model of volume-driven costs is substituted by activity-driven costs. For non-value-added activities, budgets aim at getting *less* output with *fewer* resources, i.e., use less of the non-value-added activities with even lower

costs. Performance evaluation is driven by the progress made toward the eventual elimination of these activities.

The third question has strategic implications. Resources are either acquired on demand or in fixed quantities in advance before actual demand is realized. For resources acquired on demand, costs are flexible. Productivity enhancements immediately translate into profits. For resources acquired in advance, costs are independent of the amount used – at least in the short run. Productivity enhancements do not translate into profits instantaneously. Profits will not improve unless released capacity from one activity is redeployed in another value-added activity or until spending is reduced.

Managerial Behavior

Organizational theorists have posited a positive relationship between subordinate performance and participation in budgeting. Two sets of behavioral issues arise when such budgets are used for performance evaluation: impact of budgeting on behavior and truthful budgeting and reporting. Both fall under the concept of goal congruence – the alignment of individual and organizational goals.

Budgets that emphasize specific rather than firm-wide outcomes may induce myopia and window dressing. Emphasis on cost-cutting may motivate managers to resort to myopic actions like purchasing large quantities of materials to get price discounts and producing large quantities of finished products to avail themselves of economies of scale. But both these actions increase inventories *and* costs. When budgets stress a single measure, managers resort to gaming behavior – window dressing – to manipulate that measure regardless of its side-effects.

A system-wide, integrated control and evaluation system using multiple performance measures alleviates the problem (Kaplan, 1990; Campi, 1992; Atkinson et al., 1995). This approach admits that maximizing the efficiency of sub-units is not equivalent to maximizing the efficiency of the whole firm (Turney, 1991). But multiple performance measures do not necessarily influence the direction and intensity of a manager's effort in the same way. A perfectly congruent and noiseless performance measure will induce optimum results – maximum intensity in the best direction. A performance measure is noisy when events other than the manager's efforts influence the measure. Recent research cautions that if the basic measure is perfectly congruent but noisy, then the primary role for additional performance measures is to reduce noise (Feltham & Xie, 1994). The use of noncongruent performance measures would produce results that differ from the optimum in both direction and intensity. Similarly, if a performance measure is noiseless but noncongruent, then the role for additional measures will be to improve congruence. However, if the additional measures are noisy, then results will again differ from the optimum in both direction and intensity.

Truthful budgeting and reporting are the domain of the agency theory (Jensen & Meckling, 1976). Contemporary literature asserts that misrepresentation of information occurs because of two conditions: (1) the subordinate manager has *private* information that top management needs for budgeting, and (2) the information is used for both budgeting and performance evaluation. These two conditions give rise to what is known as moral hazard, where the subordinate is motivated to misrepresent private information because of the very nature of the evaluation system. The existence of moral hazard creates another phenomenon called information impactedness. This arises when subordinates have valuable private information, but do not communicate it truthfully because of fear of jeopardizing their self-interest.

Internal managerial reporting falls into two categories: managerial reporting as part of contracting process and managerial reporting outside the context of a contracting setting (Baiman & Evans, 1983; Conroy & Hughes, 1987). Under the first category, a common difficulty is devising an appropriate incentive structure to induce truth in budgeting and maximum intensity of effort in execution (Weitzman, 1976). By providing penalties for understating budgets and bonuses for achieving and even larger bonuses for exceeding the budget, managers are induced to avoid slack and shirking. Empirical evidence suggests that risk-averse subordinates create more slack than risk-neutral ones, and that truth-inducing schemes reduce slack for the latter group, not for the former (Young, 1985; Waller, 1988).

The implication is to induce subordinates into risky behavior to reduce slack (Kim, 1992). Nevertheless, the link between participation and slack remains equivocal. In fact, there is old and new evidence that participation reduces slack through better communication, even when budgets are used for evaluation and there is information asymmetry (Dunk, 1993; Cammann, 1976; Merchant, 1985; Onsi, 1973).

The second category involves information impactedness in capital budgeting (Sridhar, 1994). It is shown that truthful reporting depends on the manager's talent. A more talented manager always reports his or her assessment of a project truthfully, while a less talented manager may report truthfully or untruthfully when the magnitude of the difference between the productivities of the more and the less talented managers is small. Otherwise, the less talented manager understates the benefits of a project to discourage investment and guard his or her reputation. Either way, the firm's investment decisions are bound to be distorted.

Bibliography

Atkinson, A. A. et al. (1995). *Management Accounting*. Chapter 14, Englewood Cliffs: Prentice-Hall.

Baiman, S. & Evans III, J. H. (1983). "Predecision Information and Participative Managerial Control Systems". *Journal of Accounting Research*, Autumn, 371–95.

Cammann, C. (1976). "Effects of the use of Control Systems". *Accounting, Organizations and Society*, 301–13.

Campi, J. P. (1992). "It's Not as Easy as ABC,". *Journal of Cost Management*, Summer, 5–12.

Conroy, R. & Hughes, J. (1987). "Delegating Information Gathering Decisions". *The Accounting Review*, Jan., 50–66.

Dunk, A. S. (1993). "The Effect of Budget Emphasis and Information Asymmetry on the Relation Between Budgetary Participation and Slack". *The Accounting Review*, April, 400–10.

Feltham, G. A. & Xie, J. (1994). "Performance Measure Congruity and Diversity in Multi-Task Principal/Agent Relations". *The Accounting Review*, July, 429–53.

Jensen, M. C. & Meckling, W. H. (1976). "The Theory of the Firm, Managerial Behavior, Agency Costs, and Capital Structure". *Journal of Financial Economics*, Oct., 305–60.

Kaplan, R. S. (ed.) (1990). *Measures for Manufacturing Excellence*. Boston: Harvard Business School Press.

Kim, D. C. (1992). "Risk Preferences in Participative Budgeting". *The Accounting Review*, April, 303–18.

Merchant, K. A. (1985). "Budgeting and the Propensity to Create Budgetary Slack". *Accounting, Organizations and Society*, 201–10.

Onsi, M. (1973). "Factor Analysis of Behavioral Variables Affecting Budgetary Slack". *The Accounting Review*, July, 535–48.

Sridhar, S. S. (1994). "Managerial Reputation and Internal Reporting". *The Accounting Review*, April, 343–63.

Turney, P. B. B. (1991). "How Activity-Based Costing Helps Reduce Cost,". *Journal of Cost Management*, Winter, 29–35.

Waller, W. (1988). "Slack in Participative Budgeting: The Joint Effect of a Truth-Inducing Pay Scheme and Risk Preference". *Accounting, Organizations and Society*, Feb., 87–98.

Weitzman, M. L. (1976). "The New Soviet Incentive Model". *Bell Journal of Economics*, Spring, 251–57.

Young, M. (1985). "Participative Budgeting: The Effects of Risk Aversion and Asymmetric Information on Budgetary Slack". *Journal of Accounting Research*, Autumn, 829–42.

M. ALI FEKRAT

business combinations

Pooling

Business combinations will be accounted for using the pooling-of-interests (pooling) method or the purchase method, depending on the circumstances; they are not alternative methods. Twelve conditions must be satisfied in order to use pooling. These conditions are separated into three categories: (1) attributes of the combining enterprises, (2) manner of combining interests, and (3) absence of planned transactions. These conditions are required to insure that combined companies present, as a single interest, two or more common stockholder interests that (1) were previously independent, (2) neither withdraw nor invest assets, (3) combine the rights and risks represented by those interests, and (4) exchange voting common stock in a ratio that determines their interests in the combined entity (Accounting Principles Board Opinion 16, paragraph 45).

Assets and liabilities are recorded at the historical cost-based amounts of the combining entities because there has been no acquisition, simply a combining of interests; and the existing basis of accounting continues. If different accounting bases exist, financial statements of the separate entities may be adjusted to the same basis of accounting if this change would otherwise be appropriate (Accounting Principles Board Opinion 16, paragraph 52). Stockholders equity of the combined enterprise will equal the equity of the separate entities.

Results of operations of the separate entities are combined for the entire year as though the pooling occurred at the beginning of the year. All expenses of the combination are expensed when incurred since no assets (capital) have been acquired (obtained) (Accounting Principles Board Opinion 16, paragraph 56). Prior period financial statements included for comparative purposes shall be restated as though the entities had been combined for those years (Accounting Principles Board Opinion 16, paragraph 57).

Purchase

The purchase method of accounting for business combinations is required if any one or more of the twelve conditions required for a pooling are not met. The purchase method identifies one entity as the acquiring entity and the other entities as the acquired entities. Assets and liabilities (net assets) of the acquired entities are recorded at the purchase price – i.e., the amount of cash disbursed, the fair value of any other assets distributed, the present value of any debt issued, and the fair value of any stock issued (Accounting Principles Board Opinion 16, paragraph 67). If the purchase price is in excess of the fair value of the identifiable net assets, then the excess is goodwill (Accounting Principles Board Opinion 16, paragraph 68). However, if the purchase price is less than the fair value of the identifiable net assets, negative goodwill exists. Negative goodwill reduces noncurrent assets other than investments in marketable securities. If these assets are reduced to zero, the remaining negative goodwill is recorded as a deferred credit and amortized over a period not to exceed 40 years.

Results of operations of the acquired entities shall be included only from the acquisition date. Expenses of the combination fall into three categories: (1) direct costs, (2) indirect and general costs, and (3) costs of issuing securities. Direct costs are included in the purchase price, indirect costs are expensed as incurred, and costs of issuing equity securities are recorded as a reduction of the fair value of the securities (reduces other contributed capital) (Accounting Principles Board Opinion 16, paragraph 76). Costs of issuing debt securities are capitalized as debt issue costs and amortized over the life of the debt.

Business combinations accounted for using the purchase method may provide for additional consideration contingent on specified events or transactions in the future. Contingent consideration based on future earnings is recorded as part of the cost of the acquired entity, whereas contingent consideration based on future security prices shall not change the cost of the acquired entity (Accounting Principles Board Opinion 16, paragraph 79). Prior period financial statements included for comparative purposes are not restated.

Issues For Standard Setters

A significant issue currently being addressed in the USA by the Financial Accounting Standards Board is what constitutes control. Currently, ownership of a majority of voting stock constitutes control. However, factors such as membership on the board of directors, significant intercompany transactions, or wide dispersion of ownership by other stockholders may indicate control even though majority ownership is not present.

A second issue relates to "push down" accounting. Staff Accounting Bulletin 54 requires it for Securities and Exchange Commission companies who have a substantial ownership in the subsidiary. However, it is not required when less than substantial ownership is present or when the subsidiary has outstanding debt or preferred stock held by the public. This allows for flexibility and inconsistency in financial reporting by subsidiaries.

A third issue is accounting for the elimination of intercompany profits with less than wholly owned subsidiaries. Accounting Research Bulletin 51, paragraph 14 allows for intercompany profits to be allocated proportionately between the majority and minority interests, but does not require it. This will affect noncontrolling interest and consolidated net income and,

therefore, allows for inconsistent reporting among affiliated groups.

A fourth issue relates to recording assets and liabilities of less than wholly owned subsidiaries. The common practice is to adjust the book value of assets and liabilities by the ownership percentage times the difference between book value and fair value. However, this practice is not universal and therefore allows for inconsistency in financial reporting.

The last issue discussed relates to reporting noncontrolling interest on the balance sheet as a liability, an equity, or something else. A common but not universal practice is to report noncontrolling interest between liabilities and equity, but neither of the two.

Managers

The choice to combine business is usually only one of several possible actions for management. Companies with substantial profits may choose to use the resources as dividends, repurchase stock or debt, or use the resources for acquisitions of other firms or other forms of expansion. How the resources will be used is partly determined by the forces exerted on management. Strong, expert, boards of directors, and the presence of management compensation plans that emphasize the long run (which may incorporate performance measures based on accounting information), are examples of factors that will influence management to consider which action is in the best interest of shareholders.

There are several factors for bidding management to consider when deciding which firm to target as an acquisition. For example, there are fewer informational asymmetries between companies in the same industry. Accounting policies and procedures, as well as other information sources, are similar for firms within an industry, so interpreting financial statements in the search for a target is less costly. As a result, combinations between companies in the same industry have a cost advantage. Prior experience with acquisitions will make the integration phase less expensive, which is a consideration because combining accounting and information systems, as well as operations, is costly.

There are also tax considerations in selecting a target, and some may favor selecting a target from another industry. Two common tax deductions are losses and interest. Combining two businesses that do not have positively correlated earnings, such as businesses from different industries, provides a greater chance that losses from one entity will provide tax benefits to the other part of the combined entity. Additional interest deductions may be the result of issuing debt as part of the purchase price or may be a byproduct of acquiring a highly leveraged target business.

Because pooling and purchase methods have different effects on the accounting reports, acquisitions can be strategically designed to be accounted for by one method or the other. Pooling tends to increase the income of businesses compared to the purchase method. Management of firms where there is no strong outside ownership, especially when earnings per share are weak, tends to use pooling. An income-increasing accounting method such as pooling would also be expected to be positively related to firm characteristics such as leverage. It would be expected to be negatively associated with the beta of the stock, capital intensity, size of the company, and degree of concentration in the industry. However, pooling is not related to those characteristics, other than the counter-intuitive result of being associated with less leveraged companies.

The target company also possesses alternatives to the business combination. Shareholders might prefer merger to bankruptcy. But, because management of acquired businesses are frequently gone after the combination, target management may not view the alternatives neutrally and select bankruptcy protection.

Financial statements of the combined business provide some audit of the target business's previous financial disclosures. The statements of the combined business are presented by the new management and represent the new management's perspective. This occasionally provides a chance to show the extent of consensus between two sets of management applied to the same set of assets. For example, in some cases supplementary market values presented by the target firm prior to the purchase can be compared to the fair value amounts recorded at the time of the purchase, which confirm or disconfirm prior reports.

Shareholders

The US Securities and Exchange Commission takes as an objective equal access to information by investors. This objective may not be met in the case of business combinations. Both market prices and trading volume of target firms tend to have significant increases many weeks prior to the first public announcement of the merger. Some of these increases may be the result of insider trading, some may be the result of observant outsiders using subtle clues like meetings between management and investment bankers, and some may be the result of technicians reacting to the small, early, price movements caused by insiders. Some of the early price and volume movement may be the result of informal leakage by owners seeking more bids in response to proposals. This implies that information leakage is more likely with owner-controlled firms. Manager-controlled businesses may have an incentive to suppress information about informal offers that might be good for owners but would cause managers to lose their jobs.

A goal of financial accounting is to be useful in investors' buy-and-sell decisions. Accounting information is a poor predictor of which firms will be targets. However, the models to date have been attempts to be parsimonious while considering all possible motives in the acquisition decision. The acquisition decision by the bidder may be sufficiently complex that a single model may not fit all business combinations. Further, since some targets have alternatives to merger, the model must also sort out a merger from, for example, bankruptcy or leveraged buyouts. Nevertheless, the market reacts less for the subset of predicted merger targets that ultimately become actual targets compared to the nonpredicted targets. As a result, there seems to be some impounding of prediction variables in the stock price.

Given that a merger is known, accounting information on liquidity and profitability is useful at diagnosing the direction and extent of market reaction of bidders and targets. For example, controlling for financial characteristics, targets of mergers have higher price increases than leveraged buyouts. Accounting information also helps analysis when liquid firms with limited internal investments opportunities are making acquisitions with high growth potential, with such acquisitions providing the best returns to shareholders of bidding firms.

There is, at least nominally, a greater price increase for pooling compared to purchase methods of implementing a combination. However, because the method of accounting between types of business combinations tends to proxy for financial characteristics (higher leverage is associated with use of the purchase method), the high price reaction of purchases compared to poolings is probably a reaction to the leverage rather than the method of accounting.

Analysis and Auditors

A business combination changes the relation between earnings and stock returns. The relation between earnings and stock returns of the combined entity is a weighted combination of the individual relations of the premerger businesses. The weighting depends on the relative size of the combining firms, and the covariability and variability of the earnings streams of the combining businesses.

The change in earnings behavior affects analysts' ability to forecast earnings. Immediately after a combination the ability to forecast earnings deteriorates, with some recovery in accuracy after time. The extent of deterioration is influenced by the change in leverage and correlation between target and bidding companies' earnings. Because amortization of assets makes up the bulk of the difference between pooling and purchase accounting income, no difference in predictability exists between methods of accounting.

NOEL ADDY and CLYDE HERRING

C

capital budgeting Capital budgeting involves decisions on resource allocation, particularly for the production of future goods and services. Capital budgeting process comprises four phases: **identification, evaluation, selection, and control.**

Identification of Capital Budgeting Projects

Identification of capital budgeting projects can be initiated by top management or come about as a result of an opportunity seen by lower management. Through communication between various management levels, projects should be identified in accordance with company goals and strategies.

Projects can be identified by types based on functional purposes: replacement; expansion; foreign operations; abandonment; general and administrative; research and developing or advertising and promoting; social expenditures and high technology. In addition, capital budgeting projects can be classified as mandatory projects, cost-saving projects, and revenue-generating projects. Mandatory projects are must-do investments (e.g., pollution control) whose identification begins with regulation and industrial trends. Identification of cost-saving projects begins by examining on-going firm activities, and identification of revenue-generating projects starts with either existing activities or newly created activities. Information required for identifying different types of projects can be external or internal, financial or nonfinancial, firm-specific or market-based.

Evaluation and Selection of Capital Projects

Objective means should be developed to quantify capital budgeting projects to form a reasonable base for evaluation. The quantitative parameters of a project typically include the economic life, the future cash flows, the initial cash outlay, and the cost of capital. Table 1 provides examples of different appraisal methods.

Discounted Cash Flow (DCF) Methods

Net present value (NPV): All future cash inflows and outflows are discounted using a selected cost of capital. The NPV is then calculated as the difference between the total present value of net cash inflows and the initial cash outflow. A positive NPV implies that the project is profitable. The cost of capital is based on the financing cost (i.e., the market interest rate of borrowing or lending) and perceived project risk.

Internal rate-of-return (IRR): The IRR is the interest rate that equates the present value of cash outflows and cash inflows. The calculation of IRR is not affected by the cost of capital. A trial-and-error method using different interest rates is applied to find the IRR. If IRR is greater than the selected cost of capital, then the project is considered profitable.

A comparison of NPV and IRR: NPV is expressed explicitly as the effect of an investment on the firm's wealth position and is considered a theoretically preferred method. IRR is only implicitly associated with wealth. In cases where it is necessary to evaluate the additive wealth effect, IRR is not applicable. Moreover, the IRR cannot handle periodical variations of rate of return and is problematic when cash flows have alternative signs. One advantage of IRR, especially as a medium of communication, is that it does not require cost of capital in the initial calculation stage; the cost of capital matters only during the final project selection stage.

Table 1 Comparison of capital budgeting appraisal methods for mutually exclusive projects

Year	Mutually exclusive projects						
	A	B	C	D	E	F	G

Cash flows in nominal dollars

Year	A	B	C	D	E	F	G
0	(100,000)	(50,000)	(100,000)	(200,000)	(200,000)	(30,000)	(250,000)
1	40,000	20,000	30,000	0	0	22,000	0
2	40,000	20,000	30,000	0	0	22,000	0
3	40,000	20,000	30,000	0	300,000	3,000	0
4	40,000	20,000	30,000	0			0
5			30,000	0			0
6			30,000	430,000			0
7							600,000

Discounted cash flows based on 10% interest rate

Year	A	B	C	D	E	F	G
0	(100,000)	(50,000)	(100,000)	(200,000)	(200,000)	(30,000)	(250,000)
1	36,364	18,182	27,273	0	0	20,000	0
2	33,058	16,529	24,793	0	0	18,182	0
3	30,053	15,026	22,539	0	225,394	2,254	0
4	27,321	13,660	20,490	0			0
5			18,628	0			0
6			16,934	242,724			0
7							307,895

Appraisal methods

	A	B	C	D	E	F	G
NPV	26,795	13,397	*30,658*	*42,724*	25,394	10,436	57,895
IRR	*21.86%*	*21.86%*	*19.91%*	13.61%	14.47%	**33.75%**	13.32%
PI	*1.27*	*1.27*	*1.31*	1.21	1.13	**1.35**	1.23
PB	*2.5*	*2.5*	3.33	5.47	*2.50*	1.36	6.42
PB-DCF	*3.02*	*3.02*	4.26	5.82	*2.89*	**1.55**	6.81
ARR	15.00%	15.00%	13.33%	*19.17%*	16.67%	*18.89%*	**23.33%**

NPV: Net present value
IRR: Internal rate of return
PI: profitability index (the NPV divided by initial outlay)
PB: Payback period based on nominal dollars
PB-DCF: Payback period based on discounted cash flows

While NPV and IRR can reach the same conclusion regarding the profitability for a single project, they may lead to inconsistent decisions when evaluating multiple projects as, for example, is shown in Table 1. The IRR method tends to favor projects with shorter lives, smaller sizes, and earlier cash inflows. The differences between IRR and NPV result from the reinvestment rate assumption. When project lives differ in length, the NPV assumes that the reinvestment rate for future projects equals the cost of capital while the IRR assumes that it equals the IRR. The superiority between these two methods depends on the proximity of the cost of capital or the IRR to the real reinvestment rate.

Payback Period

The payback period is the number of periods needed to break even on an investment and it is compared to a threshold payback period to determine the project acceptability. This method provides a measure for project liquidity which affects the project's risk. For a project that has uniform cash flows and an unlimited economic life, the payback period equals the inverse of the IRR. Payback method has two disadvantages: it ignores the time value of money, and it does not measure a project's profitability. The payback method does not consider cash flows beyond the payback period – accordingly, it favors earlier cash flows. A common practice in capital budgeting is to use the payback period as a yardstick to delineate undesirable projects, then the profitability based on the DCF methods can be used to select the best project.

Accounting Rate of Return (ARR)

ARR is calculated as the average annual income divided by the initial or average investment. A target ARR is needed in selecting the project, which may depend on the cost of capital, the project risk, and the division's past performance. Instead of net cash flows, the accounting income (after the deduction of depreciation) is used as the numerator. One important aspect of ARR is that the ex post performance measure is often based on the actual ARR. Many studies show that the stock market employs a firm's overall ARR to evaluate its performance. Moreover, management compensation plans are often based on data which either directly use or relate to ARR. Although ARR has serious theoretical drawbacks in that it does not consider time value of money, it remains to be an important method as an ex post performance measure.

Variation of the Basic Methods

Profitability index (PI): The profitability index measured as the total present value of future net cash inflows divided by the initial investment is a modification of the NPV method. It is consistent with the reinvestment rate assumption employed by the NPV but with a tendency of not favoring large projects. With reference to table 1, the top four projects that PI favors are small projects: A, B, F, and C. While A and B (shorter lives) have higher rankings than C using the IRR, they have lower rankings than C using the PI. For firms with limited fund and high financing costs, the PI may work better than the NPV method.

Payback method based on discounted cash flows (PB-DCF) or break-even time (BET): An alternative way of calculating the payback period is first converting all the cash flows into the present value and then calculating the payback period based on the discounted future cash flows. The payback period represents the break-even time after the basic financing costs are covered. This method is also known as the break-even time (BET). For firms that concern time-to-market as a critical strategy, the BET has the advantage of identifying new projects that will cover at least the financing costs in a relatively short time and still improve the firm's competitive position.

The bailout payback method: This method measures the time that a project will take for the cumulative cash flows from operations plus the disposal value of the equipment in a particular period to equal the initial investment. Projects using general-purpose equipment should be less risky than that using special purpose equipment because the former frequently have disposal values far exceeding that of the latter. The bailout payback considers the differences in the behavior of the disposal values of project investments and is a useful risk indicator.

Depreciation Method and Tax Effect

The choice of depreciation method has no impact on project evaluation for tax-exempt organizations. However, this is not the case when taxes do need to be considered. In evaluating tax effects, aspects that need to be considered include the nature of the institutions (individual, partnership, or corporation), differences in financial and tax accounting treatments, tax rules for allowable depreciation amount, useful lives and allowable depreciation methods, and the resulting marginal tax rate applicable to individual projects. If capital projects involve activities in different countries, the tax benefit in one country often can be a driving force in determining profitability.

Methods for Including Risk Consideration

Simple risk-adjustment methods: Subjective assessment is first conducted based on project characteristics and types. For example, projects with small initial investments, earlier cash flows, and shorter payback times, projects on replacement or expansion of the existing operations, and projects involving domestic instead of foreign operations may be considered less risky projects. For riskier projects, either the selection criterion is raised or the estimated future cash flows are decreased (the *certainty equivalent approach*). Once the cash flows are adjusted for risk, the regular selection criteria can be applied.

Probabilistic risk analysis techniques: Commonly employed techniques include sensitivity analysis, simple probability analysis, decision-tree analysis, and Monte Carlo simulation. Sensitivity analysis examines the consequences of changing key assumptions; it helps to identify the range of change in the assumptions within which the project remains profitable. Simple profitability analysis assigns probability to future cash flows; their expected values are used to assess the level of cash flows and their variance is used to assess the risk. Decision-tree analysis and Monte Carlo simulation apply complicated probability analyses.

Company Practices and Trends

Based on survey studies, the discounted cash flow method is the most popular method and the payback method the second most popular method for countries such as the USA, Australia, Canada, Ireland, South Korea and the UK. The only exception is Japan which uses the payback method as the primary method and the ARR as the secondary method. Studies find that the preference of the simple methods over the complicated methods is affected by firm size, industry, and project type. Among the DCF methods, studies have found that the IRR is preferred to the NPV and the preference is affected by the capital budget size and project type. Studies also show that more companies are using sophisticated capital budgeting techniques. While the IRR is still a method preferred to the NPV, the NPV is gaining popularity in practice.

Control: Post-Completion Audit of Projects

Control of capital budgeting projects is carried out by post-completion audits. This serves three functions: a control mechanism; an implementation mechanism to overcome the psychological and political problems associated with proposing and terminating projects; and a learning mechanism that compares the actual performance with the past estimates to gain insight into improving future investment decisions. To successfully operate the post-completion auditing process, it is important to let the operating managers know that the purpose of the post-completion audit is not to penalize managers for making wrong estimations during the past budgeting stage, but to learn from past experiences.

While the post-completion audit is costly, it should be conducted regularly as long as it is cost-effective. The basis used to select projects should be applied to both the actual and the budgeted data. Empirical studies indicate that many firms select projects based on discounted cash flow (DCF) techniques, but monitor them using reported accounting ratios. This flawed method will lead managers erroneously to the use of simple accounting measures (e.g., the accounting rate of return (ARR)) to select projects. Studies also show that the post-completion audit can play an important role in improving firm performance and an increasing number of managers have implemented this procedure.

C. S. AGNES CHENG

cash flow statement　In the USA, Financial Accounting Standards Board Statements No. 95 and No. 117 require most enterprises to provide a cash flow statement for each period for which results of operations are provided. The cash flow statement explains the change during the period in cash and cash equivalents, and classifies cash receipts and cash payments as relating to operating, investing, or financing activities. Similar requirements are applicable to enterprises in Australia, Canada, France, New Zealand, South Africa, the UK and Ireland, and those countries following International Accounting Standards Committee Statement

No. 7 (IASC No. 7), as well as for proprietary and nonexpendable trust funds and governmental entities that use proprietary fund accounting under the US Government Accounting Standards Board Statement No. 9 and Governmental Entities that use Proprietary Fund Accounting.

The US cash flow statement is designed to provide information about the cash receipts and cash payments of an enterprise. A comparable focus is mandated by the authoritative pronouncements of Australia, France, New Zealand, the UK and Ireland, and by the IASC (*see* Stolowy & Walser-Prochazka, 1992). It is reasoned that information on cash flows is useful to help creditors, investors, and other external parties assess (1) the ability of the enterprise to generate positive future net cash flows, meet its obligations, and pay dividends; (2) the needs for external financing; (3) the reasons for the differences between cash flow from operating activities and net income (or change in net assets); and (4) the effects on financial position of cash and noncash investing and financing activities. Practice varies across countries in distinguishing between operating, investing, and financing cash flows. The following discussion summarizes practice in the USA as specified in Statement of Financial Accounting Standard (SFAS) No. 95.

Operating activities. Operating activities, a residual category, include all transactions and events other than investing and financing activities, and generally relate to producing and delivering goods and providing services. Operating inflows include interest and dividend collections on debt and equity securities of other entities, customer collections from sales of goods and services (including trading securities), and all other receipts not defined as investing or financing inflows, such as supplier refunds, collections on lawsuits, and most insurance proceeds. Operating outflows include interest payments (unless capitalized), payments for inventories (including trading securities), payments to employees, payments to suppliers of other goods and services, payments to governments for taxes, duties, fines, and other fees, and all other payments not defined as investing or financing outflows, such as customer refunds, payments under lawsuits, and charitable contributions.

Investing activities. Investing activities include (1) making and collecting loans, and (2) acquiring and disposing of debt or equity instruments (except cash equivalents and trading securities), and plant assets. Investing outflows include payments to make or acquire loans, payments to acquire debt or equity securities of other entities, and payments to acquire plant assets. Investing inflows include receipts from collecting or disposing of loans, receipts from sales of debt or equity instruments of other entities, and receipts from sales of plant assets.

Financing activities. Financing activities include (1) obtaining resources from owners and providing them with a return on, and a return of, their investment; (2) receiving resources that are donor restricted for long-term purposes; (3) borrowing money and repaying amounts borrowed, or otherwise settling the obligation; and (4) obtaining and paying for other resources obtained from creditors on long-term credit. Financing inflows include proceeds from issuing debt or equity securities, proceeds from contributions and investment income that are donor restricted for long-term purposes, and proceeds from other short- or long-term borrowing. Financing outflows include dividend payments, outlays to reacquire or retire equity securities, and repayments of amounts borrowed.

Classification controversies. There is little world wide consensus as to the classification of interest and dividends in the cash flow statement. US SFAS No. 95 classifies interest and dividend collections as operating inflows, interest payments as operating outflows, and dividend payments as financing outflows. According to Stolowy & Walser-Prochazka (1992, pp. 194 to 195), the French standard conforms to SFAS No. 95, the South African standard classifies all four items as operating flows, the Australian and New Zealand standards classify interest and dividend payments as financing outflows and the New Zealand (but not Australian) standard classifies interest and dividend collections as investing inflows, the Canadian standard and IASC No. 7 permit a choice, and the joint UK/

Irish standard classifies interest and dividends in a separate category. For governmental units in the USA, Government Accounting Standards Board Statement No. 9 classifies interest and dividend collections relating to investing activities as investing inflows and all other interest and dividend collections as operating inflows; it classifies interest payments relating to financing activities as either capital or noncapital financing outflows, and all other interest payments as operating outflows.

There is additional controversy concerning the reporting of income taxes in the cash flow statement. SFAS No. 95 prohibits allocating income taxes among operating, investing, and financing activities in the cash flow statement; all income taxes payments (or refunds) are classified as operating cash flows. As a consequence, net cash flow from operating activities is contaminated by the tax effects of gains and losses relating to investing and financing activities. In contrast, IASC No. 7 classifies income tax payments as operating outflows but permits tax allocation among operating, investing, and financing activities if practicable.

Foreign Currency Translation. Under SFAS No. 95, the cash flow statement of an American multinational enterprise reports the dollar equivalent of foreign currency cash flows using exchange rates in effect on the dates of the cash flows. Similar requirements are applicable to enterprises in Australia, Canada, France, New Zealand, South Africa, the UK and Ireland, and those countries following IASC No. 7 (Stolowy & Walser-Prochazka, 1992).

The effect of exchange rate fluctuations on foreign currency cash balances is reported as a separate component in the reconciliation of beginning and ending cash balances. The resulting cash flow statement is the same, whether the functional currency is the local foreign currency or the US dollar (*see* Huefner et al., p.p. 70 to 71) Conceptually, this involves (1) preparing separate foreign currency cash flow statements for each foreign operation, (2) translating them into dollars, and (3) consolidating them (with appropriate eliminations) with the cash flow statements of domestic operations.

Because translated balance sheet accounts reflect the effect of exchange rate changes as well as transactions, the cash flow statement of a multinational enterprise does not reconcile changes in individual assets and liabilities (other than cash) in comparative balance sheets.

Research Issues

Information content of cash flows. Certain studies provide limited evidence of the information content of cash flows given earnings (*see*, for example, Rayburn, 1986) or given accruals, whereas other studies (*see*, for example, Bernard & Stober, 1989) show that disaggregating earnings into cash flow from operations and accruals does not provide additional information content beyond earnings. However, these studies focus on a single aspect of cash flows, namely, cash flow (or working capital) from operations, and generally ignore information about cash flow components. In contrast, another study (Livnat & Zarowin, 1990) provides limited evidence of the information content of individual component operating and financing cash flows.

A characteristic of these studies is that they assume linear relationships between abnormal security returns and reported accounting information. A more recent study (Ali, 1994) assumes nonlinear relationships between abnormal security returns and accounting information, and provides stronger evidence of the incremental information content of operating cash flow beyond the information content of reported earnings.

A limitation of these studies is that they are not based on reported cash flows because such data are only available since the issuance of US SFAS No. 95 in 1987. Rather, for each enterprise, operating cash flow is estimated by adjusting reported earnings for depreciation, deferred taxes, nonoperating gains and losses, changes in trade receivables/payables and inventories, and similar items, and component cash flows are estimated very imperfectly by adjusting financial statement amounts for some of these items (*see* Drtina & Largay, 1995). Although there is some evidence (Livnat & Sondhi, 1989, p. 8) that such estimates do not differ materially from amounts reported by management under SFAS No. 95, noise may be introduced whenever cash flows are estimated indirectly rather than by aggregating actual cash transactions, especially multinational enterprises which do not disclose the effects of foreign currency exchange rate fluctuations on individual balance sheet accounts. As a result, these studies are in fact examining relationships between abnormal security returns and reported earnings components/balance sheet changes, not actual cash flows.

Analysis of authoritative standard. A number of studies identify ambiguities and inconsistencies in the current pronouncements on the cash flow statement.

Three-way classification. Nurnberg (1993, pp. 61 to 71) shows that the three-way classification under SFAS No. 95 is inconsistent with a comparable trichotomy in the finance literature, and often results in reporting similar cash flows differently and different cash flows similarly. Nurnberg also demonstrates that classifying interest, income taxes, and dividend collections as operating cash flows contaminates cash flow from operating activities with the interest and dividend effects of investing and financing activities as well as with the tax effects of gains and losses relating to investing and financing activities.

Installment purchases and sales of plant assets. Under SFAS No. 95, there are certain inconsistencies in reporting installment purchases and sales of plant assets. For installment *purchases* of plant assets, only early payments of principal, such as advance payments and down payments, are investing cash outflows; subsequent payments of principal are financing outflows. For installment *sales* of plant assets, however, *all* receipts of principal are investing inflows – not just the early receipts.

Additionally, advance payments and down payments are not defined unambiguously. As an example, for assets acquired under capitalized leases by lessees, the early lease payments are comparable to down payments in purchase-borrow transactions, and should be classified as investing outflows. SFAS No. 95 implies, however, that all payments under capital leases are for interest and principal and should be classified as operating and financing outflows, respectively.

Bonded debt. SFAS No. 95 calls for classifying interest payments as operating outflows and principal payments as financing outflows. Over the life of a bond issue, a literal application of this provision results in differences between total financing inflows and total financing outflows whenever bonds are issued at a discount or premium, with offsetting differences between total interest expense and total operating outflows for interest (*see* Stewart et al., 1988, p.p. 7 to 8).

Other ambiguities. Other ambiguities in reporting cash flows relate to life insurance premiums, capitalized interest, and depreciation of manufacturing equipment.

Bibliography

Ali, A. (1994). The incremental information content of earnings, working capital from operations, and cash flows. *Journal of Accounting Research*, **32**, Spring, 61–74.

Bernard, V. L. & Stober, T. L. (1989). The nature and amount of information in cash flows and accruals. *The Accounting Review*, **64**, Oct., 624–52.

Bowen, R. M., Burgstahler, D. & Daley, L. A. (1987). The incremental information content of accrual versus cash flows. *The Accounting Review*, **62**, Oct., 723–47.

Drtina, R. E. & Largay, J. A. (1985). Pitfalls in calculating cash flow from operations. *The Accounting Review*, **60**, Apr., 314–26.

Financial Accounting Standards Board (1987). Statement No. 95. *Statement of Cash Flows*, Stamford, Conn: FASB.

Financial Accounting Standards Board (1993). Statement No. 117. *Financial Statements of Not-for Profit Organizations*, Norwalk Conn: FASB.

Governmental Accounting Standards Board (1989). Statement No. 9. *Reporting Cash Flows of Proprietary and Nonexpendable Trust Funds and Governmental Entries that use Proprietary Fund Accounting*, Norwalk Conn: The GASB.

Huefner, R. J., Ketz, J. E. & Largay, J. A. (1989). Foreign currency translation and the cash flow statement. *Accounting Horizons*, 3, June, 66–75.

International Accounting Standards Committee (1992). Statement No. 7 Revised. *Cash Flow Statements*, London: The IASC.

Livnat, J. & Sondhi, A. (1989). Estimating the components of operating cash flow. Working paper. New York: New York University.

Livnat, J. & Zarowin, P. (1990). The incremental information content of cash-flow components. *Journal of Accounting and Economics*, 13, Apr., 25–46.

Nurnberg, H. (1993). Inconsistencies and ambiguities in cash flow statements under FASB Statement No. 95. *Accounting Horizons*, **7**, June, 60–75.

Rayburn, J. (1986). The association of operating cash flow and accruals with security returns. *Journal of Accounting Research*, **24**, supplement, 112–33.

Stewart, J. E., Ogorzelec, P. R., Baskin, D. L. & Duffy, T. J. (1988). Implementing the new statement of cash flows for banks. *Bank Accounting and Finance*, **1**, Spring, 3–19.

Stolowy, H. & Walser-Prochazka, S. (1992). The American influence in accounting: Myth or reality? The statement of cash flows example. *The International Journal of Accounting*, **27**, 185–221.

Wilson, G. P. (1987). The incremental information content of the accrual and funds components of earnings after controlling for earnings. *The Accounting Review*, **62**, Apr., 293–322.

HUGO NURNBERG

cash versus accrual basis of accounting Present and potential investors and creditors and other users often make their investment, credit, and similar decisions based on (1) expectations about a firm's future performance, and (2) evaluations of a firm's past performance. To that effect, the US Statement of Financial Accounting Concepts (SFAC) No. 1, "Objectives of Financial Reporting," (1978, para. 43), suggests that "the primary focus of financial reporting is information about an enterprise's performance provided by measures of earnings and its components." There are two approaches to measuring the operating performance of a firm: the cash basis of accounting and the accrual basis of accounting provides a better measure of a firm's performance than the cash basis of accounting provides a better measure of a firm's performance than the cash basis of accounting. Standard setting bodies in the USA, the UK, Australia, Canada, and most other developed countries agree that the accrual basis of accounting provides a better measure of a firm's performance than the cash basis of accounting. For example, in the USA, SFAC No. 1 (1978, para. 44) asserts that: "Information about enterprise earnings and its components measured by accrual accounting generally provides a better indication of enterprise performance than information about current cash receipts and payments."

Under the cash basis of accounting a firm recognizes the financial effects of transactions in the periods in which cash is received or paid. Central to the cash basis of accounting is the concept that resources received from providing services and from selling goods are recorded as revenues in periods in which the firm receives cash from customers. Also, resources expended for wages, salaries, raw materials, taxes, interest, rent, and similar items are recorded as expenses in periods in which the firm pays cash to its suppliers, employees, and other creditors.

Professionals, such as lawyers, are the main users of the cash basis of accounting. Most of these users provide services on a cash basis and pay for their expenses in cash. They rarely have operating activities that start in one accounting period and finish in another. Therefore, they will have very few measurement problems.

On the other hand, SFAC No. 1 (1978 para. 44) articulates the essence of the accrual basis of accounting as follows: "Accrual accounting attempts to record the financial effects on an enterprise of transactions and other events and circumstances that have cash consequences for an enterprise in the periods in which those transactions, events, and circumstances occur rather than only in the periods in which cash is received or paid by the enterprise."

The same concept is used in most developed countries. A firm recognizes revenues from providing services and from selling goods when the services have been rendered or when the goods have been sold, regardless of whether those services or goods currently produce cash. At the same time, a firm records expenses in the period when it recognizes the revenues that the expenses helped produce, regardless of whether those expenses currently use cash. This "matching" of efforts and accomplishments results in reporting earnings performance for the period.

Resources received in periods other than those in which related production has occurred will be reflected on the balance sheet. For example, a firm may receive a 10 percent deposit for services to be performed during the next reporting period. In this case, the deposit represents unearned revenues which the firm must record as a liability on its balance sheet. Similarly, resources consumed in periods other than those in which related sales activities have occurred will also be reflected on the balance sheet. For example, in cases where a firm acquires assets that provide benefits over a number of periods, such as the acquisition of machinery, the cost of the machinery will be recorded as an asset on the balance sheet. The firm recognizes a portion of the acquisition cost of the machinery as a period expense in periods when the machinery is used in the production of goods and services.

SFAC No. 1 (1978, para. 37) states that: "Financial reporting should provide *information* to help present and potential investors and creditors and other users in assessing the amounts, timing, and uncertainty of prospective cash receipts from dividends or interest and the proceeds from the sale, redemption, or maturity of securities or loans (*emphasis added*)." "Cash flow information" or any other specific information is neither required or prohibited. However, accrual accounting with its attendant net income is considered to be superior to a system of cash flow information in terms of providing information about the amounts, timing, and uncertainty of prospective cash flows.

Nevertheless, Ijiri (1978) expresses concern over the emphasis on accruals and argues that financial statements should have a cash flow orientation (1) because there is a logical link between past cash flows and future cash flows and (2) because cash flow is less misleading. And in spite of the fact that most accounting standard setting organizations around the world advocate the accrual basis of accounting to measure the performance of a firm, many stock market participants, certain members of the academic community, and some accounting practitioners are voicing a sense of discomfort with the current accrual model. According to Beaver (1989), the challenge to the accrual model is related to a broader issue of aggregation of financial data. He notes that: "Accrual accounting can be viewed as one potentially cost-effective compromise between merely reporting cash flows and a more ambitious system of fuller disclosure." (p. 8).

Bibliography

Beaver, W. H. (1989). *Financial reporting: An accounting revolution.* 2nd edn, Englewood Cliffs, NJ: Prentice-Hall.

Ijiri, Y. (1978). Cash flow accounting and its structure. *Journal of Accounting, Auditing, and Finance*, Summer, 331–48.

NASSER A. SPEAR

classification as a going concern

Going Concern Assumption and The Auditor

External financial statements are prepared on the assumption that the firm is a *going concern*; i.e., that it will continue to operate indefinitely. Based on this assumption, assets are generally recorded at cost and depreciated over their expected useful lives. If the going concern assumption is no longer valid, the company's assets and liabilities should be reported at the amounts estimated to be collected or paid when they are liquidated. What is or should be the role of external auditors in *evaluating* and *reporting* on a company's going concern status?

Historically, the auditor's role in reporting on financial statements has been restricted to an assessment of fair presentation of financial position and results of operations. While management is responsible for reporting on the entity's financial position and results of operation, the auditor's role is to evaluate management's assertions and issue a report on the fairness of the financial statements. Current and future investors make decisions on the company's prospects for survival using the financial statements and other available information.

Over the years, however, the public has perceived the auditor's role in a somewhat larger context – one that also encompasses an assessment of a company's viability. The perception is best reflected by the cries of "where were the auditors?" when a company suffers a financial collapse shortly after receiving an unqualified audit opinion on its financial statements. This expectation gap has been the source of much debate.

The historical role of auditors is predicated on the premise that, in the absence of clear evidence to the contrary, auditors should assume their clients will continue in existence. Continuity is a necessary postulate whose abandonment makes auditing improbable, if not impossible. Moreover, the postulate places an important limit on the extent of an auditor's responsibilities and provides a basis for reducing the extent of his obligation to forecast the future and to have his work judged on the basis of hindsight.

Over the years, this historical role was challenged on three grounds. First, auditors have access to information not generally available to financial statement users. Second, some auditors and financial statement users believe that issuance of a modified opinion may provide auditors protection from lawsuits. Third, the option of a modified opinion provides the auditor with leverage to force disclosures about the continuity of the company that might not otherwise be forthcoming from management.

The going concern question was formally addressed in the USA by the Commission on Auditors' Responsibilities (CAR), an independent study group commissioned in 1978 by the board of directors of the American Institute of Certified Public Accountants (AICPA) to develop recommendations regarding the appropriate responsibilities of independent auditors. CAR concluded that the going concern report was confusing to users, detracted from the functions of the auditor, and often created false expectations among users. In CAR's view, uncertainty about a company's ability to continue in operation is more effectively communicated by a disclosure in, or an adjustment of, the financial statements rather than through any audit reporting requirements.

The Auditing Standard Board (ASB) subsequently reaffirmed CAR's conclusions. However, user opposition that greeted the draft proposal was instrumental in the deferral of formal action. As the incidence of corporate failures escalated in the 1980s, legislators raised additional questions about the auditor's limited role in signaling early warnings about the possibility of business failure.

Faced with various pressures, the ASB issued Statement of Auditing Standard (SAS) No. 59 in 1988. SAS No. 59 requires the auditor to evaluate whether there is substantial doubt about the company's ability to continue as a going concern for a reasonable period of time, not to exceed one year beyond the date of the financial statements being audited. If the auditor has substantial doubt about the entity's ability to continue in existence for that length of time, the auditor should add an explanatory paragraph – highlighting the client's disclosure of the going concern uncertainty – to the standard unqualified report.

Evaluation of the Status

Statement of Auditing Standard (SAS) No. 59 provides guidance to auditors on how to evaluate a client's viability status. The auditor must assess the client's *ability to meet its obligations* as they become due without having to liquidate its assets, restructure debt, be forced by outsiders to revise its operations, or other similar actions. Conditions or events that raise doubts about the client's ability to continue in existence include:

Negative trends – e.g., recurring operating losses, working capital deficiencies, negative cash flow from operating activities, adverse key financial ratios.

Indicators of possible financial difficulties – e.g., default on loan or similar agreements, arrearages in dividends, denial of usual trade credit from suppliers, restructuring of debt, non-compliance with statutory capital requirements, need to seek new sources or methods of financing or to dispose of substantial assets.

Internal matters – e.g., work stoppages or other labor difficulties, substantial dependence on the success of particular projects, uneconomic long-term commitments, or need to significantly revise operations.

External matters – e.g., legal proceedings, legislation, or similar matters that might jeopardize an entity's ability to operate; loss of key franchise, license, or patent; loss of a principal customer or supplier; or uninsured or underinsured catastrophe such as a drought, earthquake or flood.

If the aggregate effect of these conditions and events suggest that the client may have continuity problems, the auditor must consider and evaluate the feasibility of management's plans for dealing with these adverse effects. Management plans include: plans to dispose of assets and the effects of such disposals, plans to borrow money or restructure debt and the effects of such plans on existing covenants, plans to reduce or delay expenditure and the effects of such delayed expenditure on operations, and plans to increase ownership equity.

If substantial doubt about the entity's ability to continue as a going concern remains, the auditor's report must include an explanatory paragraph with the audit opinion that comments on the going concern uncertainty.

Research evidence suggests auditors do follow the guidance in SAS 59. There is also evidence that the going concern decision involves economic tradeoffs of the risks of losing a client, of being exposed to third party lawsuits, and of loss of reputation.

The typical research study examines a client's bankruptcy status subsequent to receiving a going concern report. In effect, the researcher uses the benefit of hindsight to compute auditors' hit rate. As a benchmark, the hit rate of a bankruptcy model, proposed by the researcher, is compared to auditors' hit rate. Research studies generally confirm that ex-post models outperform auditors in predicting bankruptcy. However, since going concern decisions are not equivalent to predicting bankruptcy, these studies do not unambiguously resolve the question of how well auditors evaluate their clients' continuity status.

Evaluation of the Report

Does the auditor's going concern report convey useful information? Four lines of research have addressed this question:

Information content studies: The typical study in this paradigm examines a company's stock price reaction to an auditor's going concern announcement. A company's prior stock market returns (together with the market rate of returns) are used to develop an expectation of future returns. This expected return is compared to the actual return around the time of an issuance of a going concern report. If the actual return varies significantly from the expected return, an inference is drawn that the auditor's announcement conveyed additional information to the market. On the other hand, if the actual return does not differ significantly from the expected return, the auditor's report is considered as not providing useful information to investors.

Research results using this approach have been mixed. Further, to use this paradigm effectively, a researcher must be able to precisely identify the audit report announcement date and ensure that no other concurrent information is released around the announcement date. Both requirements are difficult to overcome.

Publicly available information studies: Studies in this paradigm examine the association between publicly available information and the going concern report. If market participants are able to use readily available public information to predict the issuance of a going concern report, the subsequent release of the report should not convey new information to the market.

Various models using financial statement ratios and stock market variables have been developed that predict the going concern report very accurately. Taken together, these studies suggest that the going concern report provides redundant information.

Survey studies: Survey studies involve direct inquiry of investors to ascertain their views on the usefulness of the going concern report. Such studies consistently indicate that investors consider going concern reports to be useful. Further, investors believe that the issuance of a going concern report should enhance the defensive posture of the auditor in the event of a lawsuit.

Experimental studies: Experimental studies place users in simulated decision-making contexts and examine users' decisions with and without a going concern report. The studies indicate that as long as the going concern uncertainty is disclosed in a footnote to the financial statements, the going concern report is redundant.

STEPHEN K. ASARE and
WILLIAM F. MESSIER JR

communication in accounting To appreciate the difficulty of communication in accounting reports, consider footnote 12 of the 1994 *Annual Report* of Atlantic Richfield Company (ARCO).

ARCO continues to estimate the amount of these [environmental loss contingency] costs in periodically establishing reserves based on progress made in determining the magnitude of remediation costs, experience gained from sites on which remediation has been completed, the timing and extent of remedial actions required by the applicable governmental authorities and an evaluation of the amount of ARCO's liability considered in light of the liability and financial wherewithal of the other responsible parties.

Additionally, consider the following excerpt from paragraph six of Financial Accounting Standards Board (FASB) Statement of Accounting Standard No. 119 (SFAS No. 119), "Disclosure About Derivative Financial Instruments and Fair Value of Financial Instruments" (1994):

> Those [financial] instruments have characteristics similar to options in that they provide the holder with benefits of favorable movements in the price of an underlying asset or index with limited or no exposure to losses from unfavorable price movements, generally in return for a premium paid at inception by the holder to the issuer.

As with the ARCO report, it is difficult to know what information is intended to be communicated to the reader.

While an adjustment to simpler writing takes effort, it should be a worthwhile endeavor for the conscientious accountant. Compare the following example from FASB SFAS No. 119 with the rewritten sample. The same information appears in both versions, but with significant differences in presentation styles.

From SFAS No. 119:

> Entities are encouraged, but not required to disclose quantitative information about interest rate, foreign exchange, commodity price, or other market risks of derivative financial instruments that is consistent with the way the entity manages or adjusts those risks and that is useful for comparing the results of applying the entity's strategies to its objectives for holding or issuing the derivative financial instruments. Quantitative disclosures about the risks of derivative financial instruments are likely to be even more useful, and less likely to

be perceived to be out of context or otherwise misunderstood, if similar information is disclosed about the risks of other financial instruments or nonfinancial assets and liabilities to which the derivative financial instruments are related by a risk management or other strategy.

Plain English

> Disclosing information about the company's exposure to risk in financial markets is desirable for comparing management's results to their goals. Such information on derivatives might include interest rates, foreign currency contracts, and commodity prices. These disclosures are most useful if quantified and related to management's risk strategies.

The argument is often made that complex accounting information cannot be made simple. This is true. However, no justification can be found for making things more unintelligible than necessary. These illustrations reveal that much can be done to improve matters and managers ought to insist on it.

Jargon, as defined by Kenneth Hudson in his book *The Jargon of the · Professions*, possesses four elements:

(1) Jargon reflects a particular profession or occupation.
(2) It is pretentious, with only a small kernel of meaning underneath it.
(3) It is used mainly by intellectually inferior people, who feel a need to convince the general public of their importance.
(4) It is deliberately, or accidently, mystifying.

"It seems charitable to grant the accounting profession the benefit of the doubt on the latter two points. Once one becomes well versed in a technical language, it becomes extremely difficult to scrutinize its comprehensive faculty. It seems reasonable to assume that if the accounting profession were aware of a method for making its disclosures more understandable to all users, there would be no justification for doing otherwise" (Tillery, 1982).

Bibliography

DuPree Tillery, J. (1982). Financial statement users' preferences for descriptive versus technical accounting terminology.Ph.D. dissertation, Georgia State University, p. 91.

JEAN M. DUPREE

comparison of auditing standards Auditing is described in the most simple terms as an "independent examination of, and expression of an opinion on, the financial statements of an enterprise." The cross-cultural factors such as differing legal, social, economic, and political environments give rise to differing perceptions of the audit function. For example, the main objective of an audit in Switzerland is to ensure that the financial statements are an accurate reflection of the company's accounting records, while in Germany the objective is to ensure that financial statements comply with the legislation. Irrespective of the differing perceptions, the overriding contribution an audit opinion makes is the confidence it creates in the users of financial information, thereby adding credibility to the financial statements.

In the UK, Australia, Singapore, and Malaysia, it is a legal requirement for all incorporated companies (with the exception of certain categories of small companies in the UK under Section 249A (1) of the Companies Act, 1985) to have their accounts audited. In the USA, the 1934 Securities Exchange Act requires an audit only in respect of those companies that are listed on recognized stock exchanges and those unlisted large companies with over 500 shareholders.

"Auditing standards" are the basic principles that guide and measure quality of audit performance. They relate to the professional qualities of auditors, the performance of their examination, and the preparation of their report. In the UK, the auditing standards are defined to include "basic principles and essential procedures."

It is important to draw a distinction between auditing standards and auditing practices. Auditing standards are basic principles that provide the framework within which the auditor conducts the audit, while auditing practices relate to the ways in which auditing standards are applied in practice. Thus, auditing standards are on a higher conceptual level than auditing practices and they remain the same from audit to audit while auditing practices change to suit the circumstances of each audit. Knowledge and visibility of auditing standards are a necessary condition for achieving public confidence in the audit opinion. It may thus be said that as much as an audit opinion adds credibility to the financial statements, the auditor's adherence to auditing standards adds credibility to the audit opinion.

Source and Status of Auditing Standards

The UK, the USA, and Australia have a set of formal "auditing standards" that are mandatory to follow when carrying out an independent audit.

In the USA, there are ten "generally accepted auditing standards" (GAAS) that were formulated by the American Institute of Certified Public Accountants (AICPA) as far back as 1947. Since then the AICPA has been issuing extensions and interpretations of GAAS by way of Statements of Auditing Standards that form an integral part of professional auditing standards. The Securities Exchange Commission (SEC), which is a government agency responsible for the registration and exchange of securities, follows a policy of "active oversight" of the standards set although it does not directly interfere with the private standard setters. Its directives issued to publicly traded corporations have a significant impact on the auditing standards issued by the AICPA. The deliberations of the AICPA are also influenced greatly by the findings of some of the Congressional Sub-committees such as the Metcalf Committee and the Moss Committee.

In Australia, auditing standards are set out in the Statements of Auditing Standards (AUS) 1. They are prepared by the Australian Accounting Research Foundation (AARF) and are issued jointly by the Institute of Chartered Accountants in Australia and the Australian Society of Accountants. Failure to observe these standards is regarded by the Institute and the Society as "discreditable," which may expose members to disciplinary action.

In the UK, auditing standards are produced by the Auditing Practices Board (APB), which succeeded the Auditing Practices Committee (APC) in 1991. The APB, like its predecessor, was established by the Consultative Committee of Accountancy Bodies (CCAB) and the members of the CCAB have undertaken to adopt the standards promulgated by the APB. The reports of the Department of Trade inspectors, especially on company failures and suspected fraud, and the requirements of the London Stock Exchange in relation to published accounts, have significant influence on the development of auditing standards. The APB has ventured on reviewing and updating all previous Auditing Standards and Guidelines. Each Statement of Auditing Standard (SAS) will indicate its scope and authority and the "Auditing Standards" included in the statement, with which auditors are required to comply, will be indicated by bold type. Two SASs – the "Auditor's Operational Standard" and the "Statement of Auditing Standard 600 – Auditors' Reports on Financial Statements" – have already been issued by the APB.

At the time of writing, Singapore has no formal set of auditing standards. The Statements of Auditing Guideline (SAG) issued by the Institute of Certified Public Accountants of Singapore (ICPAS) set out what is considered generally accepted auditing practices and the form and contents of audit reports. These SAGs are based on the International Auditing Guidelines (IAG) issued by the International Federation of Accountants (IFAC). The SAGs are not mandatory but carry a high degree of authority in the auditing profession in Singapore. The ICPAS advises members to work toward the implementation of SAGs when and to the extent practicable to improve the degree of uniformity of practices in Singapore in line with the rest of the world. The ICPAS is currently involved in the process of developing auditing standards based on the International Standards on Auditing issued by the IFAC.

In Malaysia, the Malaysian Association of Certified Public Accountants (MACPA) issues approved Auditing Standards comprising of International Auditing Guidelines of the IFAC that are specifically approved by the MACPA, and the Malaysian Auditing Guidelines (MAGs) and Auditing Technical Releases (AT) developed by the MACPA. The Council expects members who assume responsibilities as independent auditors to observe these approved auditing standards in the conduct of an audit.

Failure to comply with these standards is regarded as conduct discreditable to the accountancy profession.

Enforcement of Auditing Standards

Unlike the case in Canada where legal authority is given to the auditing recommendations of the professional accountancy body, many countries' auditing standards have no such legal authority.

In the UK, indirect legal backing is given to auditing standards by virtue of section 25 of the Companies Act 1989. In order to be eligible for appointment as auditors in the UK, persons must be registered with a supervisory body recognized under the Companies Act 1989 and must be eligible for appointment under the rules of that recognized supervisory body (RSB). The Companies Act 1989 requires the RSBs to have rules and practices as to the technical standards to be applied in company audit work and as to the manner in which these standards are to be applied in practice. Each RSB adopts Statements of Auditing Standards (SASs) in order to meet that requirement and has disciplinary and regulatory procedures to ensure compliance with the standards by its members.

In the USA, the American Institute of Certified Public Accountants' (AICPA's) generally accepted auditing standards (GAAS) are enforced through its Code of Professional Ethics. Rule 202 states that an AICPA member must comply with GAAS and under its bylaws any non-compliance exposes members to disciplinary action that could result in penalties such as suspension or expulsion. Likewise, the Australian auditing standards are enforced through the Code of Professional Conduct of the two professional bodies.

In Singapore, although compliance with the provisions of Statements of Auditing Guideline is not mandatory, the Institute of Certified Public Accountants of Singapore (ICPAS) monitors the quality of professional performance of its members in public practice through the Practice Review Programme to reassure the public that the high standards of the profession are being maintained.

In Malaysia, the Council of the Malaysian Association of Certified Public Accountants (MACPA) may inquire into apparent failure by members to observe auditing standards and take disciplinary action against the members concerned.

Basic Principles of Auditing Standards

Apart from minor differences as to the status and enforcement of auditing standards, there are no divergent views internationally as to the basic contents of auditing standards. Some of the major auditing standards are discussed below.

Integrity, Objectivity and Independence

Independence is the keystone of the auditing profession and auditing standards reiterate the need for the auditor to maintain an impartial attitude and both be and appear to be free from any interests that might be regarded as being incompatible with integrity and objectivity. Accordingly, the professional bodies consider the following causes as likely to impair auditor independence: holding significant equity shares in the client company (in Singapore, holding more than 20 percent in a private company and more than 5 percent in a public company); fee dependence; providing non-audit services to clients; or being an officer or employee of the client company.

Adequate Planning and Proper Supervision

Auditing standards require the auditor to plan the audit work to conduct an efficient and effective audit. This demand is to be met by acquiring knowledge about the client's business, accounting system, policies, and internal control procedures. The auditor holds himself or herself responsible for the opinion expressed notwithstanding the fact that auditors generally delegate their work to assistants. This responsibility imposes on the auditor the duty to ensure proper supervision and review of work done by assistants.

Evidence as the Basis for an Opinion

Auditing would have no reason for existence unless the financial information is verifiable and therefore the concept of evidence is basic to the verification process involved in auditing. Every decision or judgment the auditor makes must be justified by reference to sufficient and appropriate audit evidence. The auditor must evaluate the quantity as well as the quality of audit evidence obtained through inspection, observation, mathematical computations, statements by third parties, and satisfactory internal control procedures. The evidence so gathered is required to be documented for review and for future reference.

Nature of Assurance Provided by the Audit Opinion

Due to the test nature and other inherent limitations of an audit and to the fact that the opinion is formed from a combination of fact and judgment, the auditor provides only a reasonable level of assurance and not an absolute one. Auditing standards further warn users not to assume that the auditor's opinion is an assurance as to the future viability of the entity or an opinion as to the efficiency or effectiveness with which management has conducted the affairs of the entity. However, in the USA the auditor is required to, in his or her opinion, refer to the future viability of the entity for the next nine months.

Fraud, Other Irregularities, and Errors

The auditing profession holds the view that it is the entity's management that has the fiduciary role of safeguarding the assets placed under their control and, therefore, it is the management's responsibility to take adequate measures to prevent and detect fraud, other irregularities, and errors. Although a recurring annual audit may act as a deterrent, the auditor is not responsible for preventing fraud, other irregularities, or errors. The auditor, however, will endeavor to plan his/her audit procedures so that he/she has a reasonable expectation to detect material misstatements in the financial statements resulting from irregularities or fraud.

Contents of Audit Report

The audit report is the only communication most users of financial statements receive from an audit and it is imperative that the report should be clear, concise, and as informative as possible. There is, however, no unanimity on the interpretation of the terms "as informative as possible." It is alleged that the traditional short form audit report is too short and creates misconceptions in the minds of the users of financial statements about the role of the auditor and his/her audit function. In an effort to counter this criticism, the American Institute of Certified Public Accountants (AICPA) introduced the "extended form of audit report" in 1988, in which the auditor makes additional statements distinguishing the responsibilities of management vis-à-vis the auditor, stating the nature of an audit and indicating the level of assurance conveyed by the report. The Auditing Practices Board (APB) in the UK followed suit with the issuance of Statement of Auditing Standard (SAS) 600 in May 1993, which requires disclosure of additional information in the audit report.

Australia, Singapore, and Malaysia, however, have not as yet incorporated the additional information in their audit reports.

Responsibility for the Opinion Expressed

In the USA, the principal auditor who reports on the consolidated financial statements may decide to base an opinion in part on the report of another auditor and indicate in his or her report the division of responsibility between the portion of the financial statements examined by him or her and the portion examined by the other auditor(s). In the UK, Australia, Singapore, and Malaysia, the principal auditor has no such option and he or she remains solely responsible for the opinion expressed. If the principal auditor is unable to obtain reasonable assurance as to the reliability of the other auditor's work, he or she is expected to qualify the audit opinion. However, in Singapore and Malaysia, there is the additional requirement that the auditor should disclose in the report the subsidiaries not audited by him or her along with any qualifications made by the subsidiary auditor. There is no such requirement in the UK and Australia.

The "True and Fair" View

Keeping in line with the legal requirement, the auditing standards in the UK, Singapore, and Malaysia require the auditor to express an opinion as to whether the financial statements give a "true and fair" view of the entity's financial affairs and the profit or loss. Neither the law nor the profession has attempted to define what is true and fair and the decision on it will depend on the auditor's professional judgment. Basically, "true" implies consistency with facts while "fair" refers to being just, unbiased, impartial, and equitable. Financial statements will not be considered true and fair

unless the information they contain is sufficient in quantity and quality to satisfy the reasonable expectations of their users.

In the USA and Australia, the phrase "true and fair" has been replaced by "present fairly." The interpretation of "present fairly." is given specific meaning by reference to the generally accepted accounting standards against which the auditor should apply professional judgment concerning fairness of financial statement presentation. In addition, the auditing standards in the USA require the auditor to state whether the accounting standards are "applied on a consistent basis."

Date of the Audit Report

The date of the audit report is important to users of financial statements because it indicates the last day of the auditor's responsibility for the review of significant events that occurred after the balance sheet date and that could have an impact on the financial statements. In the USA and Australia, the date of the audit report is the last day of the field work on which the auditor completed his/her important audit procedures. The auditor has the further option to dual-date the audit report where an important subsequent event occurred after the field work was completed but before the audit report was issued. In such a situation, auditing standards require the auditor to extend audit tests for the newly-discovered subsequent event and indicate in the report the two dates: one relating to all events except the newly-discovered event and the other applicable to the new event only.

In the UK, Singapore, and Malaysia, the date of the audit report is the date on which the auditors sign their reports for distribution with the financial statements rather than the day on which they complete their field work.

Comparative Figures and Audit Opinion

The auditing standards in the USA prescribe that the audit opinion should explicitly refer to the results and financial position of both the current year and the previous year. An auditor may issue a report on the financial statements of one year and in the following year may change that opinion when reporting on comparative statements. In the UK, Singapore, and Malaysia, the auditor's opinion covers only the current year's results and financial position although the comparative figures for the previous year are required to be disclosed by company law in the UK and by the Stock Exchange Authorities in Singapore and Malaysia.

K. B. AMBANPOLA

concurrent auditing techniques Concurrent auditing techniques are tools that auditors use to collect evidence on the reliability of a computer-based application system at the same time as the application system carries out live operational processing of transaction data. They are implemented via program instructions that are embedded within the application software or within the system software, such as the database management system, that supports the application system (Clark et al., Groomer & Murthy, 1989). In sensitive, high-materiality application systems, concurrent auditing techniques may be executed continuously. Alternatively, they may be executed periodically – e.g. during random intervals or during high-risk intervals. The evidence they collect can be reported immediately to the auditor, which is likely to be the case if high-risk errors or irregularities are identified during application system processing. Alternatively, the evidence they collect can be stored and reported periodically, which is likely to be the case when the expected losses associated with the exceptions identified are low.

Development

Concurrent auditing techniques are not new. They were developed in the late 1960s and early 1970s to address certain problems that were emerging in conducting audits of computer systems. These problems were as follows:

Disappearing paper-based audit trail. Historically, auditors have placed substantial reliance on the paper trail used to document the events that occur in accounting systems. They have referenced this paper trail to determine whether errors or irregularities have occurred within a system. With the emergence of computer systems, much of the paper-based audit trail has disappeared. Without purposeful design, adequate recording of events may not occur in a computer system. Concurrent auditing techniques provide a means for auditors to ensure that a system records the events in which they are interested.

Difficulty of performing transaction walkthroughs One way in which auditors have sought to understand an application system is to trace material transaction types through the various processing steps in the system. In most manual systems, this technique is fairly straightforward to use. With increasing use of computer systems, however, the range of functions that could be provided on a cost-effective basis within application systems has expanded. As a result, application systems have become more complex, and transaction walkthroughs have become more difficult to undertake. Auditors have used concurrent auditing techniques to collect evidence on a transaction as it passes through an application system and to assemble and report this evidence in a way that can be easily understood.

The need for timely identification of errors and irregularities. Because of the speed with which computers operate, errors or irregularities have not always been identified on a timely basis. In some cases, organizations have suffered substantial losses as a result. Traditional *ex post* or retrospective auditing has sometimes been inadequate as a means of identifying errors or irregularities on a timely basis. Auditors have used concurrent auditing techniques to identify errors or irregularities immediately they have occurred.

The above reasons for using concurrent auditing techniques remain valid today. Several recent other factors, however, have emerged that motivate more extensive use of concurrent auditing techniques. These factors include the following:

Increased integration of information systems. Information systems are becoming increasingly integrated, both within an organization and externally via links to systems in other organizations. As a result, the complexity of information systems is increasing. Concurrent auditing techniques help auditors to understand how the reliability of different components of an information system impacts on the reliability of other components.

Increased incidence of distributed information systems. The locations where information systems functions are performed are becoming increasingly dispersed. The infrastructure that now supports many information systems comprises physically remote, heterogeneous hardware and software platforms. Auditors may be unable to visit all sites where information processing is conducted. Concurrent auditing techniques can be installed at remote sites to collect evidence on their behalf.

Increased exposures when errors and irregularities occur. As systems become increasingly integrated and perform a greater range of functions (sometimes safety-critical functions), the expected losses from errors and irregularities increase. For example, a computer virus that is introduced into one system can propagate quickly to other systems via communication networks. As a result, timely identification of errors becomes more important. Concurrent auditing techniques permit errors and irregularities to be identified as they occur.

Presence of entropy in systems

All systems suffer entropy – i.e., the tendency toward disorder and eventual collapse. Information systems experience entropy for a variety of reasons. For example, system design errors or programing errors may exist such that they would slowly undermine the effectiveness and efficiency of the system. User information requirements can also change and, as a result, an information system may no longer meet its users' needs. Concurrent auditing techniques provide a means of detecting entropy as it occurs. For example, they can be used to detect increasing error rates during data capture and input.

The need for more effective and efficient audits
During the 1980s and 1990s, auditors have been placed under substantial pressure to improve the effectiveness and efficiency of their audits. Many of their clients have suffered from prolonged periods of economic recession. Moreover, institutional and regulatory changes have occurred that have substantially increased competition in the market-place for audit services. Concurrent auditing techniques sometimes provide a more cost-effective way of performing some types of audit functions, thereby allowing auditors to better cope with client and market place pressures.

Types of Techniques

Over the years, a large number of different types of concurrent auditing techniques have been proposed. Nevertheless, Mohrweis (1988) argues that they all fall into three general categories: (1) those that can be used to test an application system with test data during normal processing; (2) those that can be used to select transactions during normal processing for audit review; and (3) those that can be used to trace, map, or document the state of a system during normal processing.

The subsections below provide a brief description of five concurrent auditing techniques (*see*, further, Weber, 1988). The first, "Integrated Test Facility," is an example of a concurrent auditing technique that is used to collect test data during normal processing. The second and third, "System Control Audit Review Files" and "Continuous and Intermittent Simulation," are examples of concurrent auditing techniques that are used to select transactions during normal processing for subsequent audit review. The fourth and fifth, "Snapshots" and "Extended Records," are examples of concurrent auditing techniques that trace, map, or document the state of a system during normal processing.

Integrated Test Facility

The integrated test facility technique (ITF) involves auditors establishing a minicompany or dummy company on the live files processed by an application system. For example, in a payroll system, auditors might establish a master-file record for a fictitious employee. Auditors then submit test data to the application system as part of the normal transaction data entered into the system. They monitor the effects of their test data on the dummy entity they have established.

Two major design decisions must be made when auditors use ITF. First, auditors must determine what method will be used to enter test data. One approach is to select and tag live transactions. The tagged transactions then update not only their target records but also the dummy entity that has been established. An alternative approach is to design and create test transactions specifically for the application. These test transactions update only the dummy entity. Second, auditors must determine how the effects of test transactions will be masked within the application system being tested. One approach is to submit transactions that have immaterial amounts and which, therefore, are unlikely to be noticed by application system users. A second approach is to submit reversal entries so that the net effect of the test transactions is zero. A third approach is to modify the application system so the test transactions are not counted in the application system's control totals. This third approach is the most expensive, but it is often the most effective.

System Control Audit Review File. With a system control audit review file (SCARF), auditors embed audit routines into an application system and collect data on events that are of interest to them. This data is then written to a file (hence the name of the technique) for subsequent review or subsequent use in other tests that auditors may wish to conduct.

Leinicke et al. (1990) describe an example of how SCARF might be used within an insurance company to detect unauthorized changes to policyholder master records followed by subsequent fund withdrawals. When a name-and-address change is made to a policyholder record, the change can be recorded via SCARF. Any subsequent withdrawal of funds above a material amount can then be monitored by SCARF and reported for audit scrutiny. In this way a fraudulent withdrawal of funds can be detected. For example, without authorization, an insurance company employee may change a policyholder's name and address to their own name and address. The employee then may fraudulently borrow money against the policy or withdraw funds against the policy.

Continuous and Intermittent Simulation. Continuous and intermittent simulation (CIS) has been proposed by Koch (1981) as a means of collecting audit evidence concurrently with application system processing when the application system uses a database management system to support updating and querying of application files.

CIS has two major components. First, like SCARF, the database management system must be able to trap transactions that are of interest to the auditor. Koch initially proposed that the database management system be modified to capture transactions. Some current database management systems, however, provide facilities that allow auditors to write their own software routines that the database management system will execute on their behalf. Second, auditors must write software modules that will replicate the application system processing that is of interest. The database management system then passes the transactions it captures across to these modules. These modules in turn determine the results that should be produced as a result of the transaction. The results produced by the audit modules are then compared with the results produced by the application system. Deviations are written to a file for scrutiny by the auditor.

To illustrate the use of CIS, consider a financial application where auditors are concerned about the accuracy of the calculations relating to the payout value when a customer of the financial institution pays out a loan early. The database management system would identify a payout transaction as being one of the transactions that interest the auditor. It would capture the payout transaction and pass the transaction across to the audit modules. The modules would then calculate the payout value. In the meantime, the application system also would have calculated the payout value. The payout value calculated by the audit modules would then be compared with the payout value calculated by the application system. If a discrepancy existed between the two values, an exception would be written to an audit file.

Snapshot. The snapshot technique is straightforward. As the name implies, it involves taking "snapshots" or "pictures" of a transaction as it winds its way through an application system. In essence, it is an automated version of a manual transaction walkthrough. Snapshots are taken at material processing points in the application system. Auditors must first identify these points and then embed audit modules within the application system at these points. At each of these points, the audit modules typically take a snapshot of the transaction just prior to processing and a snapshot just after processing. The auditor then has the before-image of the transaction and the after-image of the transaction as a basis for evaluating the authenticity, accuracy, and completeness of the application

Table 1:   Survey of usage of concurrent auditing techniques

| | Technique | | |
Study	Integrated text facility	Embedded audit modules/SCARF	Snapshot/extended records
IIA (1977)	5.0%	15.8%	18.4%
Perry & Adams (1978)	15.0%	20.0%	20.0%
Tobinson & Davis (1981)	13.3%	13.3%	4.4%
Langfield-Smith (1987)	22.7%	2.1%	–
Mohrweis (1988)	12.2%	11.9%	9.9%
IIA (1991)	11.0%	11.0%	–

processing carried out. These snapshots are written away to an audit file for subsequent scrutiny by the auditor.

To illustrate use of snapshot, consider an order that is input to a manufacturer's order entry system. The order may pass through a number of processing points that are of audit significance. For example: the customer has to be an authorized customer; the amount of the purchase must be within certain credit limits; a discount might be given depending upon the status of the customer and the type of product that the customer is wanting to purchase; the order might be "exploded" via a bill-of-materials to determine the parts required to make the product ordered; shortages of parts may invoke a purchase order being placed on a supplier. At some or all of these points, snapshots might be taken so the auditor can examine the veracity of processing at each point.

Extended Records. Extended records are a simple extension of the snapshot technique. Using conventional snapshot, individual snapshots are simply written to an audit file. Auditors then must assemble all the snapshots that pertain to a particular transaction and a particular stream of processing that the transaction undergoes. If a large number of snapshots are taken, assembling related snapshots can be onerous.

The extended records technique collects all related snapshots together in a single record. As a transaction passes through the various snapshot points, the snapshots are appended to a record that is eventually written to a file for audit scrutiny. Auditors then do not bear the

overheads of sorting related snapshots together. More timely scrutiny of veracity of the transaction and the application processing stream is possible.

Users of the Techniques

In spite of the apparent benefits of concurrent auditing techniques, they have had a checkered history. Table 1 reports the results of a number of surveys taken periodically since 1978 (*see also* Reeve, 1984). A common definition for the different types of concurrent auditing techniques has not been used in the surveys. Moreover, in some cases, data was not collected on a particular technique, and different types of auditors were surveyed.

Nevertheless, a common theme emerges – namely, concurrent auditing techniques are not in widespread use, and usage has not increased over the years.

The results of the surveys also indicate that several factors seem to affect usage of concurrent auditing techniques. First, internal auditors are more likely to use concurrent auditing techniques than external auditors. Concurrent auditing techniques can require substantial resources to establish and maintain them, and internal auditors are better placed to support and use concurrent auditing techniques. Second, concurrent auditing techniques are more likely to be used if auditors are involved in the development work associated with a new system. It is easier to install concurrent techniques from the outset rather than to retrofit an application system with a concurrent auditing technique. Third, concurrent auditing techniques are more likely to be used if other types of computer-based audit techniques are also in use. Auditors are more likely to have the knowledge to employ concurrent auditing techniques if they use a portfolio of computer-based audit techniques. Fourth, concurrent auditing techniques are more likely to be used as the incidence of automatically-generated transactions increases. The audit trail is less visible for these types of transactions, and there can be high exposures if an error or irregularity occurs.

Limitations

Use of concurrent auditing techniques often is not straightforward. A number of drawbacks exist:

(1) Auditors must have a reasonable level of knowledge about computer systems if they are to design and implement concurrent auditing techniques effectively. In addition, they must have a good knowledge of the application system.

(2) Stakeholders in the application system must support the use of concurrent auditing techniques. For example: management must provide the resources needed to design, implement, and use concurrent auditing techniques; information systems personnel must keep auditors abreast of changes to the application system that might impact any concurrent auditing techniques that have been implemented; application system users must be prepared to bear the costs sometimes associated with the disruption that occurs when concurrent auditing techniques are used.

(3) Concurrent auditing techniques are unlikely to be effective unless they are implemented n application systems that are stable. If application systems are subject to frequent change, the costs of maintaining concurrent auditing techniques are likely to be prohibitive.

Bibliography

Clark, R., Dillon, R. & Farrell T. (1989). Continuous auditing. *Internal Auditor*, **46**, Spring, 3–10.

Groomer, S. M. & Murthy, U. S. (1989). Continuous auditing of database applications: An embedded audit module approach. *Journal of Information Systems*, **3**, Spring, 53–69.

Institute of Internal Auditors (IIA) (1977). *Systems auditability and control study: Data processing audit practices report*. Altamonte Springs, Fl.: The Institute of Internal Auditors Research Foundation.

Institute of Internal Auditors (IIA) (1991). *Systems auditability and control: Module 2: Audit and control environment*. Orlando, Fl.: The Institute of Internal Auditors Research Foundation.

Koch, H. S. (1981). Online computer auditing through continuous and intermittent simulation. *MIS Quarterly*, **5**, 29–41.

Langfield-Smith, K. (1987). The use of computer-assisted audit techniques in Australian Internal Audit Departments. *The EDP Auditor Journal*, **11**, 28–40.

Leinicke, L. M., Rexroad, W. M. & Ward, J. D. (1990). Computer fraud auditing: It works. *Internal Auditor*, **47**, Aug., 26–33.

Mohrweis, L. C. (1988). Usage of concurrent EDP audit tools. *The EDP Auditor Journal*, **111**, 49–54.

Perry, W. E. & Adams, D. R. (1978). Use of computer audit practices. *EDPACS*, **6**, Nov., 3–18.

Reeve, R. C. (1984). Trends in the use of EDP audit techniques. *The Australian Computer Journal*, **16**, May, 42–7.

Tobinson, G. & Davis, G. B. (1981). Actual use and perceived utility of EDP auditing techniques. *The EDP Auditor Journal*, Spring, 1–22.

Weber, R. (1988). *EDP auditing: Conceptual foundations and practice*, 2nd edn, New York: McGraw-Hill Book Company.

RON A. WEBER

consolidated financial statements The US Financial Accounting Standards Board (FASB) defines consolidated financial statements as follows:

> A set of financial statements that presents, primarily for the benefit of the shareholders and creditors of the parent company, the combined assets, liabilities, revenues, expenses, gains, losses, and cash flows of a parent and those of its subsidiaries that satisfy the criteria established for consolidation. (FASB Discussion Memorandum, 1991)

Accounting Research Bulletin (ARB) 51 (1959), issued by the American Institute of Certified Public Accountants and entitled,

"Consolidated Financial Statements," states a presumption that consolidated financial statements are more meaningful than separate statements.

The amount of academic research concerning consolidated financial statements is relatively small and the results of the research performed often give conflicting signals to accounting policy-setters. In general, research in this area has attempted to evaluate the relative amount of information presented by consolidated financial statements as compared to disaggregated information, e.g., segment information or line-of-business (LOB) information.

Studies by Ajinkya (1980), Collins (1975), and Collins & Simonds (1979) examined whether market participants could better assess the risk–return characteristics of firms using consolidated information or disaggregated information (LOB information). The results of these studies, in general, suggest that the use of disaggregated information allowed participants to better assess firm characteristics than the use of consolidated information.

Another area of research examined the effects of US Statement of Financial Accounting Standard (SFAS) 94 on the relative amount of information provided concerning finance subsidiaries. Prior to SFAS 94, many manufacturing and retail parent companies that had wholly-owned finance subsidiaries did not consolidate these type of affiliates. SFAS 94 requires consolidation of the finance subsidiaries. One rationale used by the FASB is that unconsolidated finance subsidiaries are a form of off balance sheet financing. Research by Tosh & Rue (1988), Mian & Smith (1990), Gosman & Meyer (1992), and Rosman (1992) attempted to evaluate the FASB's decision to require consolidation of finance subsidiaries by examining the effects on lenders' decision-making. The study by Tosh & Rue tended to support the FASB's conclusion, while the other studies questioned the conclusion.

The Concept of Control

The concept for requiring consolidated financial statements is control of one entity by another entity. Control of an entity is power over its assets–power to use or direct the use of the individual assets of that entity to achieve the objectives of the controlling entity. In August 1994, the US Financial Accounting Standards Board (FASB) issued its Preliminary Views on consolidation policy. The Preliminary Views is a document that precedes an Exposure Draft and is issued to elicit public comments on the FASB's tentative conclusions regarding an agenda topic. The approach taken by the FASB is to broaden the definition of control beyond legal control (majority ownership) to include effective control. The tentative conclusion on consolidation policy is summarized as follows:

> A controlling entity (parent) shall consolidate all entities that it controls (subsidiaries) unless control is temporary at the time that the entity becomes a subsidiary. For purposes of this requirement, control of an entity is power over its assets–power to use or direct the use of the individual assets of that entity to achieve the objectives of the controlling entity. (FASB Preliminary Views, 1994, "Consolidation Policy")

In the phrase "to achieve the objectives of the controlling entity," the objectives of a business enterprise are defined as being to provide net cash inflows to its owners by enhancing value of the enterprise or by distributing cash or other assets to its owners. The requirement of power over assets means that control by itself is not a sufficient condition for consolidation, but the right to receive the beneficial interest of ownership must also be present.

In the Preliminary Views, the FASB provided a list of factors that would indicate that effective control is so highly probable that control is presumed. These factors are:

> a. Ownership of a large minority voting interest (approximately 40 percent or more) in the absence of another party or organized group of parties with a significant interest (approximately 20 percent or more)
>
> b. An ability demonstrated by a recent election to dominate the process of nominating candidates for an entity's governing board and to cast a majority of the votes cast in an election of board members

c. A unilateral ability to obtain a majority voting interest without significant additional cash outlay, for example, through ownership of securities that may be converted into a majority voting interest at the option of the holder

d. Provisions in a corporation's charter or bylaws that cannot be changed by entities other than the creator (or through legal due process) and that limit the corporation to activities that can be initiated or were scheduled by the creating entity and are designed primarily to provide future net cash inflows or other future economic benefits to its creator. (paragraph 36 of the Preliminary Views, 1994)

The FASB also indicated that effective control may exist in circumstances other than legal or presumed control. It provided some indicators of effective control that include (the following list is not exhaustive):

An ability to cast a majority of the votes cast in an election of directors

A right to a majority of net assets of a corporation in the event of liquidation or to a majority of net assets in a distribution other than liquidation

Beneficial contractual relationships with an entity that continue after previously holding a majority voting interest

Ownership of an option to acquire a majority or large minority voting interest that requires the outlay of a significant amount of additional cash. (paragraph 41)

The Preliminary Views of the FASB are subject to public comment and due process. When a final standard is issued it is likely will have some differences from the Preliminary Views.

In a study of consolidated financial statements in other countries, Price Waterhouse (1990) found that when required, consolidation is applied by all of the surveyed countries when one company controls another company. Most countries surveyed define control as the ability to control more than 50 percent of the voting shares, in the absence of extenuating circum-stances. Several countries, however, are exploring economic concepts of control. For example, France has provisions which require consolidation when 40 percent of the voting shares are controlled and no other independent group controls more shares. The UK provides for consolidation at levels of ownership of less than majority when dominant influence is exercised over the subsidiary or investee. Like the US, Canada is exploring the possibility of broadening the definition of control.

Concept of Majority Ownership in Consolidation

Majority ownership is the primary standard used for consolidation policy, i.e., when consolidated financial statements are required. Accounting Research Bulletin (ARB) 51 (1959), issued by the American Institute of Certified Public Accountant and entitled "Consolidated Financial Statements," states that consolidated statements are necessary when one of the companies in a group directly or indirectly has a controlling financial interest in the other companies. Paragraph 2 of ARB 51 provides the current standard for consolidation policy and it states that the usual condition for a controlling financial interest is ownership of a majority voting interest. Consolidated financial statements generally are indicated when one company, directly or indirectly, owns over 50 percent of the voting shares of another company (paragraph 2). ARB 51 provides for several exceptions to this general standard of majority ownership for consolidation policy. US Statement of Financial Accounting Standards, (SFAS) 94 addresses the ARB 51 exceptions to the general standard for consolidation policy. The Statement leaves intact two exceptions for consolidated financial statements when majority ownership of the voting shares exist: (1) when control of the majority-owned company is temporary, e.g., the majority-owned company is about to be disposed of, and (2) control does not rest with the majority owner because of, for example, corporate reorganization or bankruptcy. The Statement also amends ARB 43, Chapter 12, "Foreign Operations and Foreign Exchange," to eliminate distinctions in consolidation policy between foreign and domestic majority-owned companies (paragraph 9).

ARB 51 allowed three exceptions to the general policy of consolidation of all majority-owned companies. These three exceptions, listed below, were eliminated by SFAS 94:

1. The minority interest (noncontrolling ownership) is so large, in relation to the equity of the shareholders of the owner in the consolidated net assets, that the presentation of separate financial statements for the two companies would be more meaningful and useful.

2. Separate statements may be preferable for the presentation of financial information concerning the activities of companies of heterogeneous character. For example, a finance company owned by a company engaged in manufacturing,

3. Certain other restrictive policies. (paragraph 3)

Rule 3A-02 of Securities and Exchange Commission (SEC) Regulation S-X which is entitled "Form and Content of and Requirements for Financial Statements," indicates that majority ownership should be the primary factor in a registrant's consolidation policy:

Generally, registrants shall consolidate entities that are majority owned and shall not consolidate entities that are not majority owned. The determination of "majority ownership" requires a careful analysis of the facts and circumstances of a particular relationship among entities.

Rule 3A-02 indicates, however, that in some circumstances consolidation may be required even though there is less than majority ownership:

In other situations, consolidation of an entity, notwithstanding the lack of technical majority ownership, is necessary to present fairly the financial position and results of operations of the registrant, because of the existence of a parent-subsidiary relationship by means other than record ownership of voting stock.

Bibliography

Ajinkya, B. B. (1980). An empirical evaluation of line-of-business reporting. *Journal of Accounting Research*, 18, Autumn, 343–61.

Collins, D. W. (1975). SEC product-line reporting and market efficiency. *Journal of Financial Economics*, 2, 125–64.

Collins, D. W. & Simonds, R. R. (1979). SEC line-of-business disclosure and market risk adjustments. *Journal of Accounting Research*, 17, Autumn, 352–83.

FASB (1991). Discussion Memorandum. "Consolidation Policy and Procedures". Financial Accounting Standards Board.

Gosman, M. L. & Meyer P. E. (1992). SFAS 94's effect on liquidity disclosure. *Accounting Horizons*, March, 88–100.

Mian, S. L. & Smith, Jr C. W. (1990). Incentives for unconsolidated financial statements. *Journal of Accounting and Economics*, 12, 141–71.

Price Waterhouse (1990). International Accounting Research Project: Consolidations/Equity Accounting, "A Survey of Analysis of Consolidations/Equity Accounting Practices in Australia, Canada, France, Germany, Italy, Japan, The Netherlands, United Kingdom". New York, NY: Price Waterhouse.

Rosman, A. J. (1992). FASB Statement No. 94: Do lenders contract on consolidated information? *Journal of Accounting, Auditing & Finance*, Spring, 251–67.

Tosh, D. E. & Rue, J. C. (1988). The effects of unconsolidated finance subsidiary debt on market estimates of systematic risk. *Journal of Accounting Literature*, 7, 157–73.

CHARLES L. McDONALD

contingencies   The definition adopted by the US Financing Accounting Standards Board (FASB) in its standard "Accounting for Contingencies," Statement of Financial Accounting Standard No. 5 (SFAS No. 5) (1975), is: "a contingency is defined as an existing condition, situation, or set of circumstances involving uncertainty as to possible gain . . . or loss . . . to an enterprise that will eventually be resolved when one or more future events occur or fail to occur." Examples of contingencies are allowances for uncollectible accounts, estimated liabilities for warranties, estimated losses on lawsuits, and estimated losses related to pollution caused by company operations.

According to SFAS No. 5, only contingencies in which the possible future event may indicate an asset is impaired or a liability has been incurred on the balance sheet date are candidates for accrual or disclosure. For example, the risk of losses from future injuries suffered by those who interact with a company are not included in contingencies if the injuries have not yet occurred. (On the other hand, if a product is defective and customers who have used the product may take some action, a contingency exists despite the fact that no claims have been asserted.) Another example is that recording a liability for catastrophes that may occur in the future is not appropriate because the event has not occurred.

An estimated loss from a loss contingency should be charged to income if the information available prior to issuance of the financial statements indicates that it is probable that an asset had been impaired or a liability had been incurred at the date of the financial statements, and the amount can be reasonably estimated.

The FASB notes that a reasonable estimate can be established even if only a range of amounts can be estimated. In such a case the minimum amount or the better estimate in the range should be accrued and the full range disclosed in notes. An illustration of this would be a situation in which a company has lost a lawsuit but the amount of the damages remains unresolved. However, a company may be reluctant to accrue an amount because reporting of possible claims could result in changing the probability that such claims will be asserted (see Thornton, 1983, p. 82).

The FASB provided three terms to describe contingencies: *probable* – i.e., likely to occur; *reasonably possible* – a chance that is more than remote but less than probable; and *remote* – a slight chance of occurrence. If a loss contingency is both probable and reasonably estimable, it should be charged against income. If a loss is probable but cannot be estimated or if the loss is reasonably likely (whether measurable or not), it should be disclosed in a note. If the probability of loss is remote, it need not be reported at all.

Unfortunately, the term *probable*, in particular, has been interpreted in different ways by practicing accountants. In a survey of accountants average values and ranges for the three terms were: probable, average 70 percent, range 40–80 percent; reasonably possible, 60 percent, range 40–80 percent; remote: 10 percent, range 0–25 percent (Boritz, 1990 p. 24). These verbal expressions apparently mean different things to

different people and invite inconsistency in practice.

The International Accounting Standard (IAS) No. 10, "Contingencies and Events Occurring after the Balance Sheet Date," effective January 1, 1980, follows SFAS No. 5 closely. One difference between the two standards is that if a range of amounts is available, *at least* the minimum should be accrued according to the IAS standard. Recommended disclosures include the nature of the contingency, the uncertain factors that may affect the future outcome, and an estimate of the financial effect, or a statement that such an estimate cannot be made.

In practice, however, management seem to have a conservative view of the required reporting. An interesting example of contingencies is found in the Manville Corporation situation. For a number of years the company faced increasing claims in asbestos-health suits, with 9,300 suits brought by 12,800 plaintiffs at the end of 1981. Disposition costs increased rapidly as well. No liability was accrued at the end of 1981, despite an ability to calculate at least a minimum liability on claims outstanding. The company went into bankruptcy proceedings in 1982 because of the claims, but still did not record a liability. Disclosures were extensive in the 1982 report, but no liability was recorded because "the eventual disposition of the Claims cannot be predicted at this time" (p. 10). This was a consistent position maintained by the company for several years until the company emerged from bankruptcy in 1988 and recorded a $1.28 billion charge in that year.

Auditor Involvement In Contingencies

Auditor involvement with contingencies is considered in the USA by Statement on Auditing Standards (SAS) No. 58 (April, 1988), "Reports on Audited Financial Statements." The section that deals with uncertainties indicates that an explanatory paragraph in the audit report may be required unless the auditor is satisfied that the likelihood of a loss is remote.

Contingencies and Lawsuits

Disclosure of contingencies may lower stock prices and could lead to lawsuits. However, in general disclosure of contingencies should help

Figure 1. Continuum of liability items

Definite	Indefinite

Definite "hard" liabilities
        Estimated liabilities
              Recognized contingent liabilities
                Other contingent liabilities
                related to existing assets
                and liabilities
                        Contingencies that are all in the future
                        Restructuring provisions
                          Off balance sheet financing
                            Specific risks
                              General risks

to avoid lawsuits because it leads investors to form realistic expectations. When a contingent liability results in an actual loss, the largest effect on stock price should be in those cases where disclosure was insufficient or there was no disclosure.

Some companies worry that disclosing an amount will tip their hand in any lawsuit that is under way. However, the general nature of most disclosures suggests that this is not too serious a concern.

Research on Contingencies

The most extensive study on contingencies is the monograph by Daniel Thornton (1983) dealing with the conceptual issues in financial reporting of contingencies and uncertainties. The market effect of disclosure of contingencies was studied by Banks & Kinney (1982). They found that there is a negative relationship between stock price performance and initial disclosure of contingencies.

Deakin (1989), reporting on the Pennzoil-Texaco case, found no accrual until actual payment was agreed upon by the parties. In December 1985 Texaco lost a court case with a $10.5 billion jury award. The footnote disclosure for 1985 included no accrual because the amount could not be determined. After state appeals had been lost in 1986, the annual report still did not accrue any loss (now at 9.1 billion plus interest). The judgment was upheld in 1987 and Texaco filed for bankruptcy. This led to final settlement of the suit for $3 billion in early 1988. Texaco accrued the full amount of the loss in its 1987 statements. The other party,

Pennzoil, did not record the contingent gain until 1988. Deakin criticized the delay in Texaco's accrual of a loss.

Raghunandan (1993) examined the predictive ability of auditor loss contingency report modifications in terms of a later material loss. He found that modifying paragraphs in the audit opinion had predictive ability in connection with later material losses. He concluded that auditors appear to have information beyond that generally available and that they attempt to protect themselves with a qualifying paragraph if a loss is likely (p. 616).

Figure 1 shows contingent liabilities as they relate to other liabilities in terms of definiteness and measurability. As we move to the right of the chart we find more identification and measurement problems and less guidance and ability to deal with the items. Whereas users of financial reports want more disclosure of risks and contingencies, managers claim that variety of risks and uncertainties to which an entity is exposed is great, which complicates reporting, and that the information is heavily dependent on future events that may or may not occur.

Bibliography

Banks, D. W. & Kinney, W. R. Loss contingency reports and stock prices: An empirical study. *Journal of Accounting Research*, Spring, 240–54.

Boritz, J. E. (1990). *Approaches to dealing with risk and uncertainty*. CICA Research Report. Canadian Institute of Chartered Accountants.

Deakin, E. B. (1989). Accounting for contingencies: The Pennzoil-Texaco case. *Accounting Horizons*, Mar., 20–8.

Raghunandan, K. (1993). Predictive ability of audit qualifications for loss contingencies. *Contemporary Accounting Research*, **9**, 2, 612–34.

Thornton, D. (1983). *The financial reporting of contingencies and uncertainties: Theory and practice.*Canadian Certified General Accountants' Research Foundation.

R. W. SCHATTKE

convertible debt securities

General Characteristics

Convertible debt securities are debt securities that are convertible into common stock of the issuer (debtor) or an affiliated company at a specified price at the option of the holder (creditor) (e.g., a $1,000 bond that is convertible into 25 shares of the issuer's common stock). US Accounting Principles Board Opinion (APB) No. 14 (APB 14) (1969), APB 26 (1972), American Institute of Certified Public Accountants (AICPA) Interpretations of APB 26 (AIN-APB 26, 1) (1973), Financial Accounting Standards Board (FASB) Statement of Financial Accounting Standards No. 76 (FAS 76) (1983), and FAS 84 (1985) are the principal professional standards which prescribe current generally accepted accounting principles (GAAP) for convertible debt securities.

Convertible debt securities typically have the following characteristics:

(1) Sold at a price or have a value at issuance *not* significantly in excess of the *face value* of the debt.
(2) An interest rate which is lower than the issuer could establish for *nonconvertible debt.*
(3) An initial *conversion price* which is greater than the *fair market value* (FMV) of the common stock at time of issuance (e.g., a $1,000 bond sold at face value that is convertible into 20 shares of the issuer's common stock which has a FMV of $40 per share. Thus, conversion of the bond at issuance would result in the bondholder surrendering a bond with a FMV of $1,000 to obtain common stock with a FMV of $800).
(4) *Callable* at the option of the issuer and *subordinate* to nonconvertible debt. (APB 14 para. 3)

Convertible debt securities offer advantages to both the issuer and the holder. The issuer is usually able to obtain financing at a lower interest rate than would be possible with nonconvertible debt regardless of whether or not the debt is ever converted into common stock. Furthermore, if the FMV of the common stock increases sufficiently in the future, the issuer can essentially force holders to convert the debt to common stock by calling the debt for *redemption*. Thus, the issuer effectively eliminates the debt before maturity without an expenditure of assets (APB 14 para. 4).

On the other hand, the holder has a convertible debt security on which, barring default, he/she will receive interest over the life of the debt issue plus the face value of the debt at maturity if the conversion option is not exercised. Additionally, the holder has the option to convert his/her convertible debt security to common stock should he/she so desire (APB 14, para. 5).

Issuance of Convertible Debt Securities

Due to the inseparability of the debt and conversion option (as described in APB 14, para. 7), no portion of the proceeds received by the issuer from the issuance of convertible debt securities is accounted for as attributable to the conversion feature (APB 14, para. 12). Thus, the issuance of convertible debt securities is accounted for just as an issuance of a nonconvertible debt security. Additionally, any *discount* or *premium* that results from the issuance of convertible debt securities is *amortized* to interest expense for as long as the debt remains outstanding (i.e., until the debt is either converted to common stock or redeemed, either prior to or at maturity).

Conversion of Convertible Debt Securities

In a conversion pursuant to original conversion terms (i.e., the debt is extinguished in exchange for common stock pursuant to terms that were specified at the time of the initial issuance of the convertible debt) no gain or loss is recognized upon conversion (FAS 84, para. 23). In practice, the *net carrying value* of the debt is transferred from liabilities (i.e., by reducing convertible debt including any associated unamortized premium or discount) to contributed equity (i.e., by increasing common stock and paid in excess of par) upon conversion to reflect the issuance of stock and no gain or loss is recognized (AIN-APB 26, 1).

In order to induce conversion, the issuer may offer to modify the conversion terms (e.g., offer additional shares of stock and/or offer a cash payment to the holder when the debt is converted) for a limited period of time (FAS 84, para. 2). When convertible debt securities are converted pursuant to such an inducement offer, the issuer recognizes as an expense in the period of conversion an amount equal to the fair market value of all additional consideration given to the holder as a result of the inducement offer (FAS 84, para. 3).

Redemption (Extinguishment) of Convertible Debt Securities

Debt is considered extinguished when the issuer pays the holder and is relieved of all obligations with respect to the debt, or the issuer is legally released from his/her obligation either judicially or by the holder, or the issuer irrevocably places cash or other assets in a trust to be used solely to satisfy required debt interest and principal payments (FAS 76, para. 3). If the FMV of what is given up to extinguish the debt is greater (less) than the net carrying amount of the extinguished debt, then this amount is recognized in income as a loss (gain) in the period of extinguishment (APB 26, para. 20). Additionally, gains and losses from such extinguishment are classified as an *extraordinary* item in the income statement, and reported net of related tax effects (FAS 84, para. 8).

B. Michael Doran and Roger P. Murphy

corporate failure Corporate failure involves the cessation of trading or activity of a business, which is generally preceded by financial distress. Research on corporate bankruptcy prediction broadly falls into a statistically oriented or a behaviorally oriented category. Both orientations make use of published accounting data and accounting ratios.

Statistically oriented studies are devoted to developing multivariate models that capture the combination of financial ratios considered most diagnostic of failure and weighting them so as to minimize the misclassification (bankrupt as non

bankrupt and vice versa) errors. The statistical techniques most often used include multiple discriminate analysis, logit and probit.

Statistically Oriented Studies

What has emerged from statistical orientation studies is that different institutional factors render different ratios and weightings optimal across countries (Choi et al, 1983), and across industries (Platt & Platt, 1990). Several models have been developed (*see* Jones, 1987 for reviews) and the commercial demand for and success of some of these models has meant that the calculated parameter weightings are not disclosed publicly.

These models also are used to calculate relative financial distress scores (or "Z" scores as they have become known) among companies, which are of interest to users of financial statements.

Despite the proliferation of models since 1968, their classification accuracy has remained relatively stable and the original Altman model (1968, p. 594) remains robust (*see* Constable & Woodliff, 1994). It is reproduced below:

$$Z = 0.012X_1 + 0.014X_2 + 0.033X_3 + 0.006X_4 + 0.999X_5$$

where:

X_1 = working capital/total assets

X_2 = retained earnings/total assets

X_3 = earnings before interest and taxes/total assets

X_4 = market value equity/book value of total debt

X_5 = sales/total assets

Z = overall index

Altman calculated the cut-off Z score at 2.675 for the above model, below which companies were predicted as failures.

In multivariate models, ascertaining which ratio is the most stable predictor of distress depends on the time horizon of the prediction. Leverage appears to be one of the most important distinguishing characteristics up to five years prior to actual failure, with liquidity being an important predictor in the short term and turnover ratios in the long term. Interestingly, cash flow measures seldom improve model prediction significantly when added to accrual ratios. However, cash flow/total debt was found in Beaver's (1966) univariate study to be the best performing ratio followed by, in declining order of performance, net income/total assets, total debt/total assets, working capital to total assets and the current ratio.

Accuracy rates are derived by using a matched sample of both failed and nonfailed companies to derive the model (the estimation sample) and then another sample (the evaluation sample) upon which the model is tested for misclassification rates. Success in prediction increases as a function of the closeness to actual failure as reflected by financial variables. However, it is not clear that ex ante application of the models results in similarly high levels of accuracy (e.g., see Pacey & Pham, 1990; Piesse & Wood, 1992).

Behaviorally Oriented Studies

Behaviorally oriented studies on corporate failure are concerned with how well humans utilize accounting data to make predictive judgments about the failure or nonfailure of firms. The behaviorally oriented studies generally use a Brunswik (1957) Lens Model approach in which subjects are asked to use information to predict an event, "bankruptcy/non bankruptcy" or "failure/nonfailure." These cues consist usually of accounting ratios, although many studies add non accounting information such as industry norms and frequency of failure.

In order to create a viable experiment, researchers generally boost the number of bankrupt cases to between 33 percent and 50 percent, unlike the real world, and there is a possibility that the "priors" will confound the result.

The subjects used in these types of experiments have ranged from naive investors and "business" students to experienced bank loan officers and auditors.

Studies show that the choice of ratios by subjects is more important than the weightings attached to them (Abdel-Khalik & El-Sheshai, 1980) and that humans do not process model-selected ratios as well as they process self-selected ratios (Simnett & Trotman, 1989). They also show that feedback does not appear

to increase subjects' confidence in their predictions (Selling, 1993), and that humans achieve a prediction accuracy level similar to that of statistical models (e.g., Simnett & Trotman, 1989).

Bibliography

Abdel-khalik, A. & El-Sheshai, K. (1980). Information choice and utilization in an experiment on default prediction. *Journal of Accounting Research*, Autumn, 325–42.

Altman, E. (1968). Financial ratios, discriminant analysis and the prediction of corporate bankruptcy. *Journal of Finance*, Sept., 589–609.

Beaver, W. (1966). Financial ratios as predictors of failure. *Journal of Accounting Research*, supplement, 71–102.

Brunswik, E. (1952). *The conceptual framework of psychology*. Chicago: University of Chicago Press.

Choi, F., Hino, H., Min, S., Nam, S., Ujiie, J. & Stonehill, A. (1983). Analysing foreign financial statements. The use and misuse of international ratio analysis. *Journal of International Business Studies*, Spring/Summer, 113–31.

Constable, J. & Woodliff, D. (1994). Predicting corporate failure using publicly available information. *Australian Accounting Review*, May, 13–26.

Jones, F. (1987). Current techniques in bankruptcy prediction. *Journal of Accounting Literature*, 6, 131–64.

Pacey, J. & Pham, T. (1990). The predictiveness of bankruptcy models: Methodological problems and evidence. *Australian Journal of Management*, Dec., 315–37.

Piesse, J. & Wood, D. (1992). Issues in assessing MDA models of corporate failure: A research note. *British Accounting Review*, 24, 33–42.

Platt, H. & Platt, M. (1990). Developing a stable class of predictive variables in bankruptcy prediction. *Journal of Banking and Finance*, Spring, 31–51.

Selling, T. (1993). Confidence and information usage: Evidence from a bankruptcy prediction task. *Behavioral Research in Accounting*, 5, 237–64.

Simnett, R. & Trotman, K. (1989). Auditor versus model: Information choice and information processing. *The Accounting Review*, July, 514–28.

KEITH A. HOUGHTON
and CHRISTINE A. JUBB

corporate social responsibility and the accountant The way a company handles stakeholders' expectations can have varying affects on the company's bottom line. For example, in the USA Johns Manville was forced into bankruptcy by thousands of lawsuits claiming not only that John Manville had sold defective products that contained asbestos, but that the managers had known as early as the 1930s that exposure to asbestos was potentially life-threatening (Depree & Jude, 1995). On the other hand, companies, such as Ben & Jerry's and the Body Shop, which pride themselves on being socially responsible businesses have been forced by increased competition to abandon some of their social strategies (Kaufman–Rosen, 1994). Managers nowadays must predict social trends as well as financial trends to identify potentially embarrassing and costly liabilities. At the same time, managers must balance social and financial goals of a company to remain competitive, especially when expected changes seem to come from the employees, consumers, and government agencies.

While in the 1960s and 1970s considerable attention was given in the accounting literature to the issue of corporate social accounting, the recent increase in environmental regulation has forced accountants to re-evaluate their role in each of the following three areas:

Establishing Corporate Social Goals

Of the numerous issues related to corporate social responsibility (CSR), five have been dominant: community relations, employee relations, environment, product, and women/minority (Lydenburg & Kurtz, 1992. To assess what importance should be placed on the various CSR issues, a company must first identify its stakeholders. For community and employee relations, stakeholders may consider their importance to be the same across industries, while the importance of other issues may vary by industry. The way these social issues are viewed may also be related to the socioeconomic characteristics of the stakeholders. In a survey on product safety and product liability issues, consumers' perception of product issues were found to be related to their education, occupation, and income level (Darden et al., 1994). Understanding how stakeholders within each industry perceive these social issues is necessary in order to prioritize CSR goals and to ensure appropriate allocation of scarce resources to these CSR goals.

Development of Social Strategies

Since the late 17th century, CSR has been used strategically to improve employees productivity and increase market share by making investments in health, welfare, skills, and education (Hall, 1989). For example, when Julius Rosenwald took over Sear, Roebuck he recognized that he needed a healthy farm community to prosper (Drucker, 1989). Rosenwald's "farm agent" provided farmers with a means to education and modern farming methods which ultimately lead to increasing the farmers' buying power.

More recently, companies are realizing financial benefits by developing environmental compliance programs. 3M, Inc., for example, conducted an environmental compliance audit, and as a result made modifications to its processes and materials which saved the company approximately $570 million in pollution controls and operating costs (Garvin, 1993). Philanthropy is another area where companies are developing strategies to invest in causes such as education, research, the environment, and civil justice systems which will reap future financial benefits. For instance, Cray Research Corp. spends three-fourths of its donations on education with a focus in math and science (Zetlin, 1990). Developing strategies that integrate CSR goals and management goals, companies can act socially responsible without sacrificing profitability.

Measure and Audit of Social Performance

During the 1970s, numerous forms of social audits were proposed ranging widely in scope, intent, and performance measures. For instance, Abt Associates marketed a social audit that focused on "the relative costs of different equally desirable social programs, or the relative degree to which different social programs satisfy a given constituency for the same cost" (Abt, 1972, p. 41). These early social audits were focused primarily on measuring and reporting the costs and benefits of expenditures on social issues.

Recent social audits have changed in focus to evaluate corporate social performance in terms of cost reduction, enhanced product quality, liability reduction, improved operational efficiency, legal protection, and public relations.

Largely driven by the increase in environmental legislation, most of today's social audits are environmental audits. One exception is a Boston consulting firm, Smith Obrien, which is currently piloting a social audit that looks at five operating areas: environmental protection and energy reduction, manufacturing, product/service quality, employee relations, and corporate community practices. Their audit focuses on balancing the financial, social, and environmental goals of a company.

For social audits to be effective and efficient, accountants need to develop social measures that tie in with a company's stated goals and to incorporate these measures into the management information system. Currently, companies are experimenting with integrating social issues, albeit primarily environmental issues, into their cost accounting systems in order to evaluate social costs using several techniques, such as activity-based costing, total cost assessment, and life cycle assessment (Skalak et al., 1993/94).

The Accountant's Role

Although other managers will likely play a larger role in identifying social issues than the accountant, accountants are beginning to play a role in identifying environmental issues due to the increase in environmental reporting regulations. According to Rittenberg et al. (1992), "internal auditors will be increasingly called on to evaluate both (1) the entity's compliance with applicable environmental laws and regulations and (2) the entity's potential exposure to existing environmental cleanup provisions" (1992, p. 13).

The development of social strategies should be addressed by teams consisting of representatives from the various company functions, such as engineering, operations, accounting, marketing, human resource management, environmental affairs, and possibly outside experts. Kaplan & Norton's balanced scorecard, may be one technique that could be used to evaluate the successful implementation of various strategies (Kaplan & Norton, 1992). The balanced scorecard recognizes that managers need both financial and operational measures to be effective. While their model focuses solely on customers, other stakeholder groups could be included.

Social audits can identify opportunities for reducing company risk, increasing process efficiency, introducing innovative practices, and strengthening management controls. Although most large companies have implemented environmental audit programs, an increasing number of companies are relying on consulting firms to perform external audits.

Bibliography

Abt, C. (1972). Managing to save money by doing good. *Innovation*, 27, 38–47.

Darden, W. R., Babin, B. J., Griffin, M. & Coulter, R. (1994). Investigation of products, liability, attitudes, and opinions: A consumer perspective. *The Journal of Consumer Affairs*, 28 (1) 54–79.

Drucker, R. F. (1989). *The new realities: In government and politics/In economics and business/In Society and world view.* New York: Harper & Row.

Dupree, C. M. & Jude, R. K. (1995). Coping with environmental and tort claims. *Management Accounting*, Mar., 27–31.

Garvin, A. O. (1993). The 12 commandments of environmental compliance. *Industrial Engineer*, Sept., 18–22.

Hall, P. D. (1989). Business giving and social investment in the United States. In *Philanthropic giving*, R. Magat (ed.), New York: Oxford University Press.

Kaplan R. & Norton, D. (1992). Putting the balanced scorecard to work. *Harvard Business Review*, Sept./Oct., 134–49.

Kaufman-Rosen (1994). Being cruel to be kind: How social responsible businesses such as Ben & Jerry's and the Body Shop found they couldn't stay pure and make a profit. *Newsweek*, October, 7, p. 51.

Lydenberg, S. D. & Kurtz, L. (1992). Researching social performance. In P. Kinder, S. Lydenberg, A. Domini (eds), *Social investment almanac*, New York: Henry Holt & Co., 8–23.

Rittenberg, L. E., Haine, S. F. & Wegrandt, J. J. (1992). Environmental protection: The liability of the 1990s. *Internal auditing*, Fall, 13–25.

Skalak, S. L., Russell, W. G., Robinson, M., Miller, G. & Casey, D. (1993/94). Proactive environmental accounting and world/class annual reports. *Journal of Corporate Accounting and Finance*, Winter, 177–96.

Zetlin, M. (1990). Companies find profit in corporate giving. *Management Review*, Dec., 10–15.

BERNADETTE M. RUF

cost allocation Cost allocation is defined in Statements on Management Accounting, Statement No. 2: "Management Accounting Terminology," (National Association of Accountants,

June 1, 1983) as: "A process of classifying costs into categories at the time of acquisition and into their subsequent reclassification as costs of activities, products, responsibilities or other cost objectives." In the USA, the Cost Accounting Standards Board has issued four standards dealing with cost allocation. The standards specify the objective for allocation as capturing cause and effect relationships to the best extent possible and they provide a hierarchy of preferred allocation bases. Procedures for calculating cost allocations are generally mechanical and are explained in widely available cost accounting textbooks.

The early literature on cost allocation concentrated on the identification of allocation bases that seemed reasonable (usually physical attributes). In the 1950s and 1960s there were attempts to design management accounting systems to avoid allocations. At that time there was a widespread belief that allocated cost information was not relevant to any meaningful decision. More recently, it has been recognized that cost allocations are made to satisfy explicit or implicit contractual agreements.

Explicit contracts requiring cost allocations include voluntary contracts to share the cost of a resource (two people agree to share the cost of a taxi to the same destination) and those imposed by law (e.g., US environmental law requires that those who have contributed to environmental pollution must share the cost of cleaning it). In explicit contracts many of the problems with cost allocations could be avoided by being specific in advance on how cost sharing is to be determined. Unfortunately, many contracts are made only with the mutual understanding that the allocation will be "fair." When disagreements arise, it then becomes necessary to define "fair."

Game theory provides the concept of the core. In the allocation setting the core is the set of allocations that makes every participant better off by sharing the resource with others rather than by forming an alternative coalition. It is generally agreed that if a core exists a "fair" allocation must be within the core. However, there is still no agreement on how to select among competing allocations within the core. Consider two people who share a taxi for $7. Assume that if they had traveled separately the fares would have been $5 each. For this example

the core is the set of allocations in which one passenger pays between $2 and $5 and the other pays the difference to make a total of $7. If the passengers are on equal footing, an allocation of $3.50 each is usually considered the fair outcome. But "fair" changes if one passenger is entering the taxi and the second says: "I only have three dollars, may I share the taxi?" Similarly, if one passenger is travelling on business and will be reimbursed, and the second is the passenger's spouse, it is common to say it is "fair" for the spouse to only pay the additional marginal cost.

A core will not exist when marginal costs are increasing. In this case participants are better off acting independently so that voluntary coalitions should not persist. However, situations can develop where parties have a joint responsibility and a core does not exist. The responsibility for cleanup of environmental pollution is one such case. Consider two firms that unwittingly pollute a site. Assume it would cost $1,000 to clean up contaminant A if it were the only problem, and $3,000 to remove contaminant B in isolation. But the two pollutants became combined in a dangerous fashion so that it costs $5,500 to clean up the combination. Finding a way to allocate the $5,500 in a "fair" manner has proved elusive. (Conceptually it does not seem there should be a difference in splitting a gain from a coalition versus a loss from a coalition so the underlying problem may be our views on "fairness.")

Cost allocations also take on importance when implicit contracts exist to reward individuals on the profitability of activities under their control (e.g., promoting people who have "done a good job"). Accounting income usually is the performance measure used for profitability. While participants may agree at an abstract level on what "income" is, the actual measurement of income for a particular time period involves the utilization of accounting rules and the making of estimates. Many of the estimates are cost allocations.

The most frequent cost allocation in income measurement is depreciation. The cost of assets that are used for several time periods are allocated to the time periods to calculate each period's income. Another cost allocation is required when a firm incurs common costs. In this context "common cost" refers to the cost to provide a fixed capacity of service. For example, in the short run, occupancy costs (the costs of providing building space) may be fixed. These costs are usually allocated to the various occupants (departments or product lines). A third allocation arises when joint costs are incurred. Joint costs are variable costs that are incurred simultaneously to produce more than one good or service. The cost of crude oil used in a refinery to produce multiple petroleum products is an example. The cost of the crude oil as well as the processing costs are typically allocated to the products that emerge from the joint process.

Resources are typically acquired in combination because it is cheaper than the alternative. That is, it is often cheaper to buy a long-lived asset than to rent it on a month-to-month basis. It is also cheaper to put several operations in one building rather than having a separate building for each. In income measurement an attempt is made to estimate unbundled costs.

Over the years a variety of depreciation methods have been developed and several different approaches have gained acceptance for allocating common and joint costs. The existence of alternative acceptable methods for allocating costs naturally leads to criticisms of their arbitrariness. In addition, some costs are allocated instead of measured because the cost of accurate measurement cannot be justified. This adds to the perception that allocations are arbitrary. Even though practices are somewhat arbitrary, most accountants would argue that allocations attempt to capture cause-and-effect relationships.

Because most managers wish to have their performance measures look good, designers of cost systems need to be aware of the motivational effects inherent in cost allocations. How costs are allocated will affect how the underlying resource is used. This can be used to encourage desired behaviour (e.g., charging material acquisition costs to parts based on the number of unique parts instead of overall volume of parts will discourage the proliferation of unique parts). But more often the motivational aspects are not recognized and dysfunctional behaviour is unintentionally encouraged. There are many stories of firms that produced unprofitable products because their cost allocation systems erroneously made the products look profitable.

The advance of computer technology has greatly reduced the need for allocations that are made for clerical convenience. Still situations will continue to arise where coalitions of users will acquire common or joint resources for mutual economic advantage. The challenge is to either have the players agree in advance on a cost sharing arrangement or to identify the benefits received if they insist on saying "Let's allocate the cost fairly."

SHANE MORIARITY

cost behavior   *Marginal cost* is defined as the avoidable cost of an additional unit (Coase, 1968). This cost is an important one for decision-making purposes. Calculating marginal cost is problematic because of the nature of costs and their behavior pattern as production changes.

To simplify measurement of costs for decision-making, accountants classify them as either fixed or variable. Some costs do not change within a relevant range of production and are thus called fixed costs, e.g., rent and insurance. Outside of this relevant range, fixed costs may have a step-like nature: the cost will remain fixed up to a particular point of production, then it increases to a new level where it remains fixed through a new range of production. For example, if an increase in production is necessary, but the old facilities are too small, adding another plant may provide the desired capacity. With this additional plant, fixed costs will increase to a new level, but remain fixed at that level until another plant is added.

Other costs vary with output and are called *variable costs or direct costs*. Tires used in the manufacture of automobiles are a good example of a variable cost. Each time a car is manufactured, the cost per unit increases by the input price of four regular tires plus one spare tire.

A typical cost function, then, can be set out as $TC = F + vq$; where TC = total cost, F = fixed cost, v = variable cost and q = quantity produced.

Certain costs have both fixed and variable attributes; these are called *mixed costs*. Electricity consumption in a manufacturing plant may have a fixed portion, a flat service fee, and a variable portion that increases with production as machine operation increases. Estimating the fixed and variable portions of cost improves the accuracy of information for decision-making.

Methods for Separating Fixed from Variable Costs

There are three methods commonly used to separate the fixed from the variable portion of cost: the two point method (high-low), the scatter diagram method, and the regression method. All of these methods rely on the integrity of historical data. This prior data can be used for meaningful predictions if past conditions and future conditions are expected to be similar, if the data collection process is reliable, and if the data are reasonably accurate. It is important to note that costs predicted with these techniques are estimates only.

The first step in an analysis of the behavior of cost is to determine possible cost pools, a group of costs driven by a specific activity, and the associated cost drivers, i.e., those activities that cause specific costs. An example of a cost pool would be the costs of the machining department. An example of a cost driver might be number of machine hours. Developing a scatter plot of the cost (Y axis) against a possible driver (X axis) is an important step in the analysis. A plot will help to determine an appropriate cost driver and also indicate the underlying behavior of the cost. If the plot resembles a football shape around the slope (Figure 1), the cost is likely mixed and can be further analyzed. If the scatter is random (Figure 2), the cost is probably unrelated to production and can be annualized and classified as a fixed cost. If the cost appears to have a linear trend that seems to begin at the origin (Figure 3), the cost is probably completely variable.

After the data has been plotted, and if it has been determined that the cost is indeed mixed, one of the three methods for separating fixed from variable portions can be employed. The high-low method is the quickest but least accurate method. Simply choose the highest cost/quantity (TC_H, Q_H) and lowest cost/quantity (TC_L, Q_L) ordered pair of data points. Then the following formulas can be used:

$$v = (TC_H - TC_L) / (Q_H - Q_L) \quad (1)$$

$$F = TC - vq \quad (2)$$

Solve for variable cost, v, in equation (1) and then substitute v into equation (2) and choose

Figure 1: Scatter plot of maintenance costs versus output

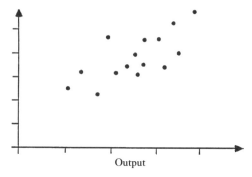

Figure 2: Scatter plot of legal fees versus output

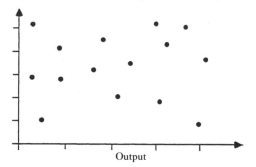

Figure 3: Scatter plot of materials costs versus output

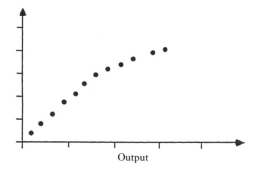

either the high cost or low cost ordered pair values for TC and q to determine the fixed portion of the cost.

The visual fit method is similar to the high-low method. Once the data has been plotted, a line is hand drawn, using a straight edge, through the data points in such a manner as to fit as many points as possible, or to visually reduce the distance between each point and the line. Any two points on this line can then be used in the formulas presented above to determine the fixed and variable portions.

This method is preferable to the high-low method because the highest and lowest observations may be outliers and introduce considerable error in the measurement of the linear function. However, this method is often subject to bias and may not be accurate.

The most precise method is regression analysis. Least squares regression selects the single straight line that minimizes the sum of the squared errors. A regression analysis application package is included with most computerized spreadsheets. The results of the regression analysis will include an intercept and a slope variable. The intercept represents the fixed portion of the cost and the slope represents the variable portion. The results include an R^2 term that indicates how much of the variation of cost (Y axis) can be explained by the cost driver (X axis). The R^2 will range in value from 0 to 1. The larger it is, the better the linear function fits the data and the more appropriate the cost driver. A value of 1 means that all of the data points fall on the regression line indicating a perfect fit. To improve the fit, unusual data points or outliers may be removed from the set of observations used in the analysis. Regression analysis packages also include correlation statistic calculations. The more highly correlated the costs and the cost driver, the higher the R^2 values. Correlation calculations can be a valuable tool when choosing an appropriate cost driver.

Underlying Assumptions

When costs are classified into fixed and variable, some implicit assumptions are made. These may or may not be typical of the data. Fixed costs are assumed to remain unchanged over a particular range of production, called the relevant range. Also, within this relevant range, the variable cost *per unit* is assumed to remain constant. These two assumptions imply that product mix and unit prices of inputs will remain constant, and the efficiency of production will not change. Economies of scale and learning curves are not accounted for in such assumptions. Thus, variable cost becomes essentially a mean around which the cost actually varies, even within the relevant range. Forecasting future costs using these cost functions will become more accurate as the data conforms more to the underlying assumptions.

Currently there has been renewed interest in cost allocation methods for overhead costs. New perspectives on aggregating costs into pools and choosing appropriate cost drivers for the pools are offered by consultants worldwide. Proponents of these new allocation systems recommend them for decision-making, and suggest that most costs are variable over time. While these systems may improve efficiency by assigning responsibility for costs in a new manner, costs that are allocated, irrespective of the method, they may not always be useful in decision-making because production decisions are often short-term decisions, especially since the advent of just-in-time inventory philosophies, and allocated costs tend to be fixed in nature over the short term.

Noreen & Soderstrom (1994) found that using average cost, which involves dividing fixed costs by volume, overstates costs by about 40 percent on average and in some cases by 100 percent. This indicates that for decision-making, costs need to be separated into fixed and variable portions for more accurate predictions because additional production in the relevant range will result in an increase in variable costs only. When data is being accumulated for analysis, the time horizon of the decision is as important as the relevant range of volume. For most product-related decisions, separating costs into fixed and variable portions, relative to time and production, increases the accuracy and predictive ability of projections.

Bibliography

Coase, R. H. (1968). Business organization and the accountant. *Studies in cost analysis.* In D. Solomon (ed.), 2nd edn, Homewood, IL: R. D. Irwin.
Noreen, E. & Soderstrom, N. (1994). Are overhead costs strictly proportional to activity? Evidence from hospital service departments. *Journal of Accounting and Economics*, 17, Jan.

LESLIE G. ELDENBURG

cost of goods sold COGS (cost of goods sold) represents the economic value of the resources consumed in manufacturing the products sold by an organization. Resources are defined as the activities performed during product production. These resources traditionally are categorized as *direct material* (DM), *direct labor* (DL), and *manufacturing overhead* (MOH). The economic value (or cost) of the resources consumed in the production process is based upon either: (1) the actual or expected cash outflows required in obtaining these resources, as in the case of material and labor, or (2) the using up of existing assets, as in the case of production equipment depreciation included in manufacturing overhead (US Statement of Financial Accounting Concept (SFAC) No. 6, 1985).

Matching the cost of producing the units sold (i.e., COGS) with the revenue generated from those sales is the cornerstone of periodic financial reporting. Financial statement users (e.g., managers, investors, and creditors) rely upon the proper matching of revenues and COGS when computing *gross profit* (sales minus COGS). Gross profit and the resulting gross profit percentage (gross profit ÷ sales) provide a basis for comparing an enterprise's current financial performance with results from prior periods or the financial performance of comparable firms.

The most difficult aspect of the matching process involves assigning the costs associated with the consumption of long-term assets (e.g., production equipment depreciation) to manufacturing overhead (Accounting Principles Board (APB) 43, Ch. 4, ¶5; Financial Accounting Standards Board 178.106). This cost allocation process represents an area of continuing debate for accounting managers, auditors, taxing authorities, and other decision-makers. No one answer exists for the allocation problem. However, the choice of allocation method directly affects net income by impacting the intermediate computations of COGS and inventory valuation. The most stringent rules have been established under the Internal Revenue Code (Section 803 of TRA 1986, Section 263A) where a broad range of costs are uniformly capitalized as part of the inventory valuation and COGS computations for tax purposes. However, the costs capitalized under these rules include additional costs not acceptable when computing COGS for financial reporting purposes. Absent any specific capitalization formula, accountants and other decision-makers must use the best approximations of how allocated costs are consumed in the production process.

SFAS No. 1 (para. 37, 1978) indicates that one of the primary objectives of financial reporting is to assist financial statement users in assessing the amounts, timing, and uncertainty of an entity's future cash receipts. Because financial statement users depend upon gross profit as an indicator of future cash receipts, the intermediate computation of COGS represents a crucial element of the reporting process. As a result, COGS must represent both a reliable measure of firm performance and a comparable measure over time (SFAC No. 2, para. 33, 1980). By specifying the costs (DM, DL, and MOH) entities must include in COGS, financial reporting guidelines have attempted to enhance the reliability and comparability of COGS across reporting periods and entities. Accordingly, when the company selects a method of allocating costs and matching revenues and expenses, these choices must be followed consistently to ensure financial statement comparability. Significant changes in cost allocation methods must be disclosed as either a change in accounting estimate or a change in accounting principle depending upon the circumstances.

Absorption Costing

Generally accepted accounting principles (GAAP) require the use of absorption costing (or full costing) when computing COGS for external financial reporting purposes. As previously discussed, including all manufacturing costs (DM, DL, MOH), fixed and variable, in the computation of COGS and per unit product costs reflects the use of absorption costing. These production costs are accumulated as products flow through the production process. Costs incurred subsequent to product completion are excluded from absorption costing product costs.

As part of the production process, typical manufacturing organizations maintain three types of inventory: (1) raw materials, (2) work in process, and (3) finished goods.

Raw materials inventory. This represents the materials going into a product's production before they are released to the shop floor. For example, the wood in desk production or the flour used in baking bread represents the materials going into the products' manufacture.

The raw materials transferred out to the shop floor represent the direct materials added into the production process.

Work in process inventory (WIP). This includes the products partially completed at any one point in time. To continue the previous example, desks without legs attached or bread waiting to enter the oven are partially complete and represent WIP inventory. Costs accumulated during the production process include the three product costs: DM (from raw materials inventory), DL, and MOH. For the units of product transferred to finished goods during any period, the corresponding total of product costs are called the *costs of goods manufactured* (COGM).

Finished goods inventory. This represents products that have completed the manufacturing process and await sale to customers. Recently completed loaves of bread and office desks would represent additions to finished goods inventory when they are transferred out of WIP. Once these products are sold to customers, the costs associated with the units sold are accumulated as the cost of goods sold and reported in the company's income statement.

Example of Cost Flows Through a Manufacturing Process

In the example below, the three inventory types are presented including the accumulation of costs within each inventory type and the flow of costs between inventories. The cost flows with raw materials inventory serves as an example of how costs flow through each of the inventory types. Inventory additions (or *purchases*) of $11,500 are made in an effort to make available a continuous flow of material as required by the production process. At any point in time, typically the end of an accounting period (e.g., one month or year), the beginning inventory and purchases are accumulated and compared to the ending inventory in an effort to determine the direct materials consumed in the production process.

This computation, known as the periodic inventory method, reflects an inventory equation that remains consistent regardless of inventory type. The equation is described as follows:

Beginning inventory	$3,000	
Plus: Additions (purchases)		11,500
Equals		14,500
Ending inventory	$4,000	
Plus: Transferred out (DM)		10,500
		14,500

WIP and finished goods inventory follow the same inventory equation in costing the units/products transferred out (see table 1).

Two additional nonfinancial performance measures are used by financial statements users when assessing the timing of future cash flows one expects from the production process: (1) inventory turnover, and (2) average days of inventory on hand. These measures provide relative measures (not distorted by inflation or volumes) of product flows through the production process. Additionally, with the continuing interest in just-in-time (JIT) inventory management systems that imply constant rates of production, managers and investors can use this information to highlight potential bottlenecks (impediments) in the production process.

Inventory turnover represents the number of times a company expects to replace their inventory during the year. In the example, inventory turnover for WIP is two times, indicating that the company must replace their WIP twice during the year to satisfy product demand (transferred out) and maintain an average WIP inventory level of $11,000.

$$[(\$12,000 + \$10,000)/2]$$

However, inventory turnover for finished goods is four times, indicating that the finished goods are moving out of the process (sold to customers) at a much faster rate than the production process can sustain. This information provides managers and investors insight into the relative strengths and weaknesses of the company's production operation. Additionally, the nonfinancial measure allows for comparison with performance in prior periods and competitors.

Average days of inventory on hand represents an alternative measure of the same basic information captured in the inventory turnover measure. For some decision-makers, the concept of inventory turnover remains abstract. However,

Table 1:   Three types of inventory

	Raw materials	Work in process	Finished goods
Beginning inventory	$3,000	$12,000	$4,000
Additions/Transferred in	11,500	(1) DM 10,500	(2) 22,000
		DL 3,500	
		MOH 6,000	
Ending inventory	4,000	10,000	6,000
Transferred out	(1) $10,500	(2) $22,000	$20,000
Technical name for transfers out of inventory	Direct materials	COGM	COGS
Inventory turnover (transferred out ÷ average inventory)	3.00 times	2.00 times	4.00 times
Avg. days of inventory on hand (360 days ÷ inventory turnover)	120 days	180 days	90 days

for some, the idea of measuring how many days the production process can continue to operate until inventory is exhausted possesses greater intuitive appeal. The results lead decision-makers to the same conclusion, WIP is moving slower than finished goods, just stated in terms of "days" instead of "times."

Financial Statement Presentation

The income statement in table 2 reflects the financial statement reporting associated with cost of goods sold.

The income statement for 19X2 reflects the link between the income statement and the flow of costs through the three inventories. The cost of units transferred out of finished goods (e.g., $20,000) represent the cost of goods sold included in the income statement. The resulting gross profit of $30,000 represents a $750 increase in gross profit from the comparable period in 19X1 (e.g., $29,250). However, the absolute increase as measured in dollars obscures the underlying decline in the relative gross profit percentage from 65.00 percent to 60.00 percent. This example demonstrates how the total dollars may indicate one result (e.g., improved performance), while relative measures

of performance, such as gross profit percentage, indicate contradictory conclusions (e.g., profit from sales are declining)..

Selling and administrative expenses represent all nonproduction expenses incurred by an

Table 2   Income statement

	For the period ended December 31	
	19X2	19X1
Sales	$50,000	$45,000
Cost of goods sold	20,000	15,750
Gross profit	30,000	29,250
Gross profit %	60.00%	65.00%
Selling & administrative expenses	17,000	14,000
Net income before interest and taxes	$13,000	$10,000

organization. These expenses include, for example, finished goods warehouse supervisor (costs incurred after production), sales and marketing expenses, and administrative expenses such as accounting.

TIM WEST

cost variances and investigation Management control in organizations involves three primary phases: planning, coordination (during plan implementation), and control. An important part of the control phase is performance feedback and evaluation that may involve both financial and nonfinancial measures. The most common financial control measure, budgetary control, involves the ex post comparison of actual financial results with the ex ante budgetary expectations. The term "cost variance" is used in accounting to denote the deviation of an actual or observed cost from the expected cost level. As such, the analysis of cost variances is a subset of budgetary control techniques used to ensure compliance of individual behavior with organizational goals. The expected cost level can be budgeted cost, standard cost, or the cost estimated from a frontier cost function.

The primary objective of cost variance analysis is to permit organizational managers to detect and correct inefficiencies wherever they exist in operations involving expenditures. Three kinds of decisions are generally necessary: (1) what kinds of variances to compute, (2) the level of disaggregation required, and (3) whether or not to investigate a particular variance once computed.

Types of Variances Computed

The types of variances computed depend on the responsibility centers and the level of management for which the review is performed. Since the objective is to determine the degree of corrective action needed, the variances computed, mostly quantitative, must relate to key performance indicators considered critical to the success of the responsibility center.

At the highest levels of the organization, the key performance indicators may consist of general concepts like product leadership, growth in market share, product innovation, cost competitiveness, and so forth. At the lower levels of the organization, at the cost centers

where cost variances are usually of primary interest, key performance indicators usually pertain to the usage and cost of materials, labor (if a key component of costs), and overhead. At revenue centers (where revenue generation is of primary interest), key performance indicators may consist of sales price variances, product mix variances, market share variances, and industry volume variances.

Recently, in manufacturing contexts, increasing interest is focusing on product cycle time. Essentially, product cycle time refers to the time it takes raw materials to be processed to the completed product stage. Holding other factors constant, the shorter the product cycle time, the lower the product unit cost.

Level of Disaggregation of Cost Variances

Budgets are established in part to provide a benchmark for evaluating performance. For cost centers, these budgets typically seek to achieve efficiency and control by specifying the expected cost levels. In discretionary and administrative cost centers, these cost budgets are typically not related to output levels (since output may be difficult to measure); instead the budgets represent the spending levels authorized for the budget period. Budget variances refer to deviations of actual spending levels from the budget. Unfavorable budget variances (i.e., spending levels above expected) would typically call for investigation from the cost center manager, while favorable variances may not require any explanation unless they are material.

The more interesting issue involving cost variances, however, arises in the case of engineered cost centers where inputs and outputs are directly measurable and can be related to each other. In such centers, the budget specification for spending levels must be a function of output levels.

In conventional accounting practice, labor standards were developed for repetitive manufacturing processes using time and motion studies, denoting the best way of performing a given operation. From these standards emerged standard costing that establishes a standard cost for each product cost element. The implementation of standard costing meant that the standards established for manufacturing operations provided the basis for establishing the budget.

Typically, standards were established for direct materials, direct labor, and manufacturing overhead. The standards specified the quantities of materials expected per unit of output and the expected price. For labor, the standards specified the number of labor hours required and the budgeted labor rates. For manufacturing overhead, the aggregate behavior of the overhead costs would be identified as a linear function of some input measures of activity such as total direct labor hours or machine hours. The budgeted overhead costs would then reflect the expected level of the input measure of activity in which budgeted overhead costs could be also related to the budgeted output level.

The ex post analysis of cost variances in such a system consists of two primary components: the flexible budget variance (FVB) and the budget adjustment variance (BAV). Algebraically, letting FBV represent the flexible budget variance and BAV the budget adjustment variance, the computations can be represented as follows:

$$FBV = AQ*AP - SQ*SP \quad (1a)$$

$$= AQ*AP - (sq*AY)*SP \quad (1b)$$

$$BAV = SQ*SP - BQ*SP \quad (2a)$$

$$= (sq*AY)*SP - (sq*BY)*SP \quad (2b)$$

where:

AQ = actual quantity of inputs used;

AP = actual price of inputs;

SP = standard price of materials;

AY = actual volume of output;

BY = budgeted volume of output;

BQ = budgeted quantity of inputs;

SQ = standard quantity of input that should have been used given the actual output level;

sq = standard quantity of input per unit of output.

Further, in a manufacturing context, the flexible budget variance is decomposed into price and efficiency or quantity variances. These variances are computed (using terms defined earlier) as follows:

For materials:

Purchase price variance
$$= AQ*AP - AQ*SP \quad (3)$$

Quantity or efficiency variance
$$= AQ*SP - SQ*SP \quad (4)$$

For labor:

Labor rate variance
$$= AH*AR - AH*SR \quad (5)$$

Labor efficiency variance
$$= AH*SR - SH*SR \quad (6)$$

where:

AQ = actual quantity of materials purchased;

AQ = actual quantity of materials used;

AH = actual hours used to produce the output of the period;

SH = sh * AY
= standard hours allowed for the output of the period;

sh = standard hours required per unit of output;

AY = actual output of the period;

and all other terms are as defined earlier.

For manufacturing overhead, the most commonly applied three-variance approach involves the identification of a manufacturing overhead spending variance and a manufacturing overhead efficiency variance (which together make up the flexible budget variance for overhead), and a denominator volume variance. Algebraically, this decomposition of the variances can be represented as:

Overhead spending variance:
$$= \text{actual MOH} - (\text{budgeted FMOH} + v*AX) \quad (7)$$

Overhead efficiency variance
= (budgeted FMOH+v*AX)
   – (budgeted FMOH+v*SX) (8a)

= (AX-SX) *v (8b)

Overhead denominator variance
= (budgeted FMOH+v*SX)
   - ([f+v] * SX) (9a)

= budgeted FMOH - f*SX (9b)

where:

MOH = total manufacturing overhead costs

(i.e., fixed plus variable manufacturing overhead);

FMOH = fixed manufacturing overhead costs;

v = variable manufacturing overhead costs per unit of the cost driver (X);

AX = Actual volume of the overhead cost driver (e.g., total labor hours)

SX = standard volume of the overhead cost driver expected given the actual volume of output (SX = sx * AY, where sx is the amount of cost driver per output unit);

f = budgeted FMOH/DX

= fixed manufacturing overhead rate per unit of the cost driver;

DX = denominator volume of the cost driver used to unitize the fixed manufacturing overhead costs.

In contexts where multiple inputs of the same type can be substituted for each other, the input efficiency variance can be further decomposed into an input mix variance and an input yield variance. The input mix variance represents the effect of the choice of mix of inputs on total costs, while the yield variance reflects the difference between the total quantities of inputs used (regardless of the type) and the total quantities expected given the output of the process.

Algebraically, this can be represented as follows:

Mix variance = Σ (AQ * SP) - Σ [(Σ; AQ) * (SM) * SP] (10a)

= Σ (AM - SM) * SP * (Σ AQ) (10b)

Yield variance = Σ [(Σ AQ) * (SM) * SP] - Σ(SQ * SP) (11a)

= Σ [(Σ AQ - Σ SQ) * SM * SP] (11b)

where:

AM = AQ / Σ AQ

= actual proportion of input j relative to the total actual input quantities used;

SM = SQ / Σ SQ

= standard proportion of input j relative to the total standard input quantities;

and all other terms are as defined earlier.

Variance Investigation

The degree to which variances are disaggregated depends on the underlying factors of causation. Material price variances, for example, are likely to be due to price forecasting errors, deficient purchasing practices, purchases of materials of a quality slightly different from original specification, or a combination of all three factors. Labor rate variances, on the other hand, may be caused by unexpected changes in the average labor mix (given different wage rates), unexpected changes in the average wage rate paid to labor of a given grade, or a combination of such factors. Similarly, input efficiency variances may be caused by significant changes in the productivity of the input factor, errors in the forecasted rate of productivity, or a combination of factors.

Under these conditions, it is apparent that nonzero variances can be caused by random errors with no control significance, or by problems in the control environment that require correction. Since there are likely to be non-zero costs of investigating the cause of any variance observed, decision rules have to be formulated on what variances should be investigated, and which ones should not be investigated. Among the decision rules used in practice are the following:

(1) Investigate all negative (unfavorable) variances.
(2) Investigate all variances exceeding budgeted (or standard) costs by a fixed percentage (e.g., 10 percent).
(3) Investigate all variances exceeding budgeted (or standard) costs by more than a given standard deviation (e.g., one standard deviation). This rule is known as the control chart rule.

Of these decision rules, the most sophisticated is the use of control charts. Essentially, the control chart rules take the following form:"Investigate if actual costs exceed X; otherwise do not investigate." The level of X is then set so that the combined costs of investigating and of not investigating are minimized when the system is out of control.

Summary of Research

Derivation of Variances. The conventional accounting method of computing variances relates manufacturing overhead costs to the volume of activity as a linear function, with some of the overhead costs fixed and others variable. This approach has not changed much. Instead, researchers have focused on refinements of direct cost variances, or on the identification of generic cost functions.

Hasseldine (1967) and Wolk & Hillman (1972) proposed refinements to the traditional approach of deriving the mix and yield variances. They pointed out an inaccuracy that stemmed from computing the conventional mix and yield variances, given changes in input prices. Using linear programing, Demski (1967) proposed a sweeping overhaul of the traditional approach. He demonstrated the feasibility of his approach with an actual application in an oil refinery. Mensah (1982) proposed that neoclassical cost functions such as the Cobb-Douglas (or linear programing, if appropriate) should be incorporated into the conventional analysis, and proposed a method of computing the yield and mix variances that linked them to the parallel concepts of allocative and technical inefficiencies so well known in the economics literature. He related these to the more commonly used

Farrell (1957) approach (which relies on proportionality of the inefficiency in the use of the inputs), although the Russell measure (which assumes non substitution technology) might be more appropriate in some circumstances (Marcinko & Petri, 1984; Callen, 1988).

One difficulty in adopting these suggestions is the identification of the efficient production frontier. In the conventional setting, it is assumed that the efficient frontier can be identified through a combination of approaches such as using industrial engineers to identify the most efficient processes and using regression to identify the best linear function for overhead.

Some researchers (Callen, 1988; Darrough, 1988) have focused on the problem of identifying the best functional form for the production possibility set. Others such as Mensah & Li (1993) have focused on identifying the production frontier by using parametric approaches, such as the translog function, as well as nonparametric approaches, such as data envelopment analysis (DEA). DEA is particularly interesting as a potential tool for evaluating performance because it does not assume any particular functional form. It is important to note, however, that these subsequent researchers are concerned with more than just the problem of identifying inefficiency for a single period. The estimation of the neoclassical production function (or the related DEA) is commonly based on cross-sectional data because time-series data is rarely available for a given cost center (and would be subject to nonstationarity even if available). Consequently, the functions identified are long-run functions, involving the identification of economies of scale present in the data, etc. In contrast, conventional standard cost systems assume short-run Leontief fixed-proportion production functions. Thus, it is an empirical question whether some of the more generalized functions can be applied in a meaningful way to identify and correct inefficiencies in practice.

Activity-based Costing. Conventional standard cost systems assume that overhead costs can be always directly related to output volume. Researchers who have re-examined that issue have concluded that the assumption is generally invalid. This has led to the emergence of activity-based costing (ABC). Essentially, ABC identifies activities as the cost drivers of over-head costs, rather than output. As a result, the diversity of output, batch size, the number of parts used in manufacturing a product, the number of setups, the number of times parts are ordered, and the number of times products are shipped can all affect the level of overhead costs incurred. Specifically, Robin Cooper, Robert Kaplan, and Peter Turney (among others) have led the cost accounting revolution that has resulted in a re-examination of the traditional unit-based allocation of overhead (see, for example, Cooper, 1988a; 1988b; 1989a; 1989b; Cooper & Kaplan, 1988; Kaplan, 1984; and Johnson & Kaplan, 1991).

One important contribution of the ABC proponents has been the recognition that the traditional distinction between fixed and variable costs may be incorrect. That is, while some costs may be fixed from the perspective of the volume of output, they are not fixed from the perspective of the activities that drive those costs. Thus, ABC proponents advocate the segregation of costs (and associated activities) into (1) unit-level costs, (2) batch-level costs, (3) product-level costs, and (4) facility-level costs. Unit-level costs are costs directly related to the volume of output for a given product (e.g., quantity of direct materials and direct labor used). Batch-level costs are incurred each time a batch of output is produced because of the related batch activities (e.g., machine setup, ordering costs for a batch of components, scheduling costs for a batch of output). Product-level costs are costs incurred at the product level relating to the product type (e.g., engineering change orders and new vendors for new components). Finally, facility-level costs are costs that relate to the entire facility (e.g., depreciation on factory buildings and nondedicated equipment).

Finally, it must be noted that ABC does not directly address the issue of variance analysis. However, it can be argued that ABC makes possible a far more sophisticated type of variance analysis for overhead than is possible under the conventional system. Since overhead costs are now better related to the cost driver activities, ex post analysis of performance can focus on two things:

(1) Given the actual volume of output, are the batch-level and product-level activities consistent with the budget?
(2) Given the actual level of the batch-level and product-level activities, are the actual costs consistent with the budgeted unit costs?

Unfortunately, much of the work to date on ABC has focussed on identifying the actual costs of production as opposed to the budgetary control implications for the more refined costing system.

Cost Variance Investigation

The identification of cost variances is designed to alert management to possible control problems in operations. However, deciding whether or not to investigate the variance is complicated. The complexity of the decision stems from the fact the variance could have been caused by a random factor, just as it could signal some problems in the environment requiring correction.

Several approaches to the cost variance investigation decision have been suggested in the literature (see Kaplan (1975) and Magee (1976) for relevant literature reviews). Among them are the Markovian approach (Dittman & Prakash, 1978), the mathematical programing approach (Kaplan, 1978; Magee, 1977), the information theory approach (LEV, 1969), and the decision theory approach (Dittman & Prakash, 1979).

Lev's (1969) information theory approach may be regarded as a sophisticated version of the basic approach which focuses on analyzing all variances above a given percentage of budgeted costs. His approach essentially requires the arrangement of all variances within the budget control system in order to compute the variances as fractions of total sales (or output). Using information theory, those variances that show the largest variance are reflected by the expected information measures.

The most widely-used of these sophisticated variance investigation techniques is the control chart approach. Essentially, the control chart approach involves comparing the value of the observed cost variance (X) against some prespecified upper and lower limits. In the basic control chart approach, the upper and lower limits are established as a fixed standard deviation based on the past observations of the variance in the process. But how does one know what is the appropriate number of standard deviations to use? The approach proposed by Dittman and Prakash (1979) seeks to minimize the total expected costs of investigation by considering the distributions of both the "in control" and "out of control" states. Since there are costs to carrying out the investigation and even higher costs in letting an "out of control" process continue unchecked, the objective is to determine what critical value of the cost variance should trigger an investigation.

Because of the uncertainties associated with estimating the probabilities of the "in control" and "out of control" states, it is conceivable that parameters estimation errors compromise the theoretical benefits of the sophisticated techniques such as Dittman and Prakash's. Magee's (1986, p. 213) suggestion that simulation may be a useful technique to try out in this context deserves serious consideration. Findings from a simulation study by Magee (1976) suggest that simple rules like "Investigate all variances exceeding 10 percent of budgeted costs" may be preferable in practice. On the other hand, statistical process control (which uses the same underlying principle) has long been used in industry and has generally been found to be useful.

Further Development

The traditional standard cost paradigm which dates back to Taylor's initial studies into scientific management and the idea that there are optimal methods of performing specific tasks which can be uncovered through time and motion studies, etc., is being challenged by a new paradigm that can be referred to broadly as the cost management paradigm. In its broad essence, cost management proponents hold to the view that continuous improvements in production operations are possible through the continual search for and elimination of non value-added activities. Thus, instead of identifying a cost frontier (or a set of standard costs) good for an indefinite period of time, efforts are directed at constantly redefining the cost frontier.

As a result, cost variances in the traditional sense are perceived to be limited in their usefulness. Instead, a series of ideas have been advanced, many of which draw from innovations first developed among Japanese world-class manufacturers. Principal among these ideas are benchmarking, total quality control/ just-in-time (TQC/JIT) philosophy, and target costing. In the benchmarking approach, the ratio of costs of performing specific functions relative to a base (such as total revenue) is computed for a given decision-making unit and compared to other units (or companies). The idea is to ensure that this ratio can be reduced to that of the most efficient unit in the industry. While this approach is frequently applied to costs incurred for overhead functions like administration, accounting, and personnel, there is no particular reason why it cannot be extended to the evaluation of functions in both upstream (basic research and product development) and manufacturing operations.

Under the total quality control/just-in-time (TQC/JIT) philosophy, conventional standard costing (where standards are established once a year or so) is regarded as obsolete. Instead, a kind of dynamic standard costing system is instituted in which the standards are continually ratcheted upwards as they are achieved. The idea is to strive for continual improvements in operations through the elimination of defects in output and the streamlining of operations such that output proceeds smoothly on a consistent basis. This objective can be related to target costing. In target costing, a company establishes a target cost for the design and manufacturing of a product and then strives to achieve that target through the continual refinement of operations.

See also **advanced manufacturing technologies**

Bibliography

Callen, J. (1988). An index number theory of accounting cost variances. *Journal of Accounting, Auditing and Finance*, (new series) 3, 2, 87–108.

Darrough, M. N. (1988). Variance analysis: A unifying cost function approach. *Contemporary Accounting Research*, 5, Fall, 199–221.

Demski, J. (1967). An accounting system structured on a linear programing model. *Accounting Review*, Oct., 701–12.

Dittman, D. & Prakash, P. (1978). Cost variance investigation: Markovian control of Markov processes. *Journal of Accounting Research*, 16, Spring, 14–25.

Dittman, D. & Prakash, P. (1979). Cost variance investigation: Markovian versus optimal control. *Accounting Review*, Apr., 358–73.

Farrell, M. J. (1957). The measurement of productive efficiency. *Journal of the Royal Statistical Society*, Series A, **120**, 3, 253–81.

Hasseldine, C. R. (1967). Mix and yield variances. *The Accounting Review*, July, 497–515.

Kaplan, R. S. (1975). The significance and investigation of cost variances: Survey and extensions. *Journal of Accounting Research*, Autumn, 311–37.

Kaplan, R. S. (1978). Optimal investigation strategies with imperfect information. *Journal of Accounting Research*, Spring, 32–43.

Lev, B. (1969). An information theory analysis of budget variances. *The Accounting Review*, Oct., 704–10.

Magee, R. P. (1976). A simulation analysis of alternative cost variance investigation models. *Accounting Review*, July, 529–44.

Magee, R. P. (1977). Cost control with imperfect parameter knowledge. *Accounting Review*, Jan., 190–9.

Magee, R. P. (1986). *Advanced management accounting*. New York: Harper & Row.

Marcinko, D. & Petri, E. (1984). Use of the production function in calculations of standard cost variances – An extension. *The Accounting Review*, July, 488–95.

Mensah, Y. M. (1982). A dynamic approach to the evaluation of input variable cost center performance. *The Accounting Review*, Oct., 681–700.

Mensah, Y. M. & Li, S-H. (1993). Measuring production efficiency in a not-for-profit setting: An extension. *The Accounting Review*, Jan., 66–88.

Wolk, H. I. & Hillman, A. D. (1972). Materials mix and yield variances: A suggested improvement. *The Accounting Review*, July, 549–55.

YAW M. MENSAH

cost-pricing relationship Marketing activity makes up the bulk of total activity of most businesses. Marketing with its focus on product, price, promotion and place (the traditional marketing mix), drives all the other activities. Price is the most elusive among these marketing mix variables in terms of making pricing decisions. Controversy is frequently engendered by disagreement between accountants and marketing personnel when deciding the appropriate price for a product or service.

In the long run the price established must be viable to remain competitive, and at a level which covers all costs, including marketing costs. Since marketing costs account for 40 to 50 percent of total costs and since pricing is a major marketing decision, understanding the cost–pricing relationship and its application to market profitability analysis is vitally important in any business situation.

Pricing: Concepts and Issues

Many different labels are subsumed under price: rent, fees, fares, etc. It is the amount of money paid in exchange for a product or service. From a marketing perspective, price must reflect the perceived value of a firm's product to a customer. If set above perceived value, the firm risks pricing its product out of the market. If below, it may not be viable to offer this product line. Price is thus a major determinant of buying behavior, as well as the source of revenue for the firm.

Different philosophies underpin the different approaches to price determination. Market-based pricing has an external focus, with a pricing strategy that is particularly responsive to customers' demand function, competitors' prices, threats from new product entries, in addition to the firm's cost structure. Understanding the impact of long-run costs is important for assessing profitability in competitive markets, but market factors are key considerations for this market-based pricing approach.

In contrast, cost-based pricing is essentially cost driven and is more prevalent in a production-oriented environment than in the more marketing-oriented environment today. Production cost sets the stage for price determination, usually a simple exercise of applying a markup on cost to yield a required gross margin or target return on investment. Hence, the term "markup pricing" is widely used to describe this approach. As Kjaer-Hansen (1967) pointed out, in the post-War marketing environment, this "old fashioned pricing system, based on a summation of ascertained costs, will not be capable of satisfying the requirements introduced by the modern trend of demand conditions" (p. 216, *Financial Dimensions of Marketing*, 1981, where he is quoted). Yet, the legal implication of the cost base used for pricing is important for marketers when there are charges of predatory pricing practices with the effect of adversely affecting competition.

Committe & Grinnell (1992) and Ursic & Helgeson (1994) point out that after 1975 the courts explicitly began to apply cost-based standards to predatory pricing cases. Various cost concepts were applied by the courts, including average-total cost and marginal cost, with one interpretation of the latter being short-run variable cost. To assist companies in answering pricing practice queries in court, Ursic & Helgeson (1994) suggest that prices be set, if possible, above marginal cost or average variable costs or even above average-total cost.

The marketing literature is replete with descriptions of pricing techniques which are usually variants of the two basic types just explained. Examples are Kotler's (1991) markup pricing, target-return pricing, perceived-value pricing, going-rate pricing, and sealed-bid pricing; price adaptations such as geographic pricing; and other pricing categories such as loss-leader pricing, image pricing, and two-part-pricing. Pricing policy is imperative for a firm with the price established at a competitive, yet reasonable, level to the customer, and which also provides an adequate return to the firm.

The pricing decision therefore is among the most important considerations in marketing, yet formulating a successful pricing strategy can prevent marketers from becoming too preoccupied with the market place, and accountants with margins, costs, and turnover ratios. The importance of a marketing–accounting interface is described in a later section.

Cost: Concepts and Issues

Costs, as perceived in conventional accounting, are monetary units paid in return for goods and services. Behind this seemingly easy definition lies a gamut of cost concepts, each delineating possibly different cost elements.

(1) Costs identified by behavior in relation to volume of activity, into variable costs, semi-variable costs, and fixed costs. An under-standing of cost behavior is necessary in cost–volume–profit analysis, which is a useful accounting tool for marketing analysis. For example, in segment profitability analysis, cost–volume–profit relationships are invoked to determine the volume at which segment revenue just covers its specific costs. Moreover, useful information

is generated about the sensitivity of segment contribution to volume fluctuations.

Another area where marketing cost analysis is based on cost behavior patterns is flexible budgeting. Flexible budgets are prepared to show costs at the different levels of sales activity, which can be used for performance evaluation purposes. Comparing the actual costs with static budgets would be misleading.

(2) Costs identified to cost objects (e.g., products, departments) such as direct costs and indirect costs. Direct costs traceable to marketing departments or sub-units of marketing departments provide reliable input for performance analysis of these departments and of their respective managers.

(3) Costs identified by differences in time horizon into short-run and long-run, and by their relevance to short-run pricing and other decisions, like using differential costs in decisions concerning acceptance of one-off orders and product abandonment.

(4) Costs identified by controllability into controllable and noncontrollable costs for a marketing department. Uncontrollable costs will be the allocated costs including those of corporate headquarters, frequently described as common costs. This classification has particular application to performance measurement of marketing departments.

These classifications of costs are not mutually exclusive. For example, depending on the situation, relevant costs can be variable and fixed, or direct and indirect.

Two principal costing methods emerge based on these cost concepts, which are relevant to marketing analysis. Direct variable costing which treats only variable costs as production costs is of significance to marketing mainly because of its emphasis on the contribution margin approach. Contribution margin represents the excess of sales over variable costs, including variable marketing costs. This contribution approach has been recommended for market segment profitability analysis (American Accounting Association, 1972) and for making marketing decisions such as product introduction, product abandonment, and pricing.

Variable costing has been specifically recommended for consideration by companies with international business activities. Since such companies are removed, both politically and geographically, from the domestic markets, and since they are likely to have different objectives in different countries, with different demand and competition, the charging of different prices in different countries is seen as having more applicability internationally than domestically. Variable costing could facilitate such differential pricing (Weekly, 1992).

In absorption (full) fixed manufacturing costs are also part of the costs of production or inventoriable costs. This method is invoked if both direct and indirect costs are assigned to the market segments.

Horngren et al. (1994) also found strong support for full product costs for pricing decisions in various cross-country studies. Mills's (1988) conclusion, therefore, that "the dysfunctional effects of full/absorption costing reliant on arbitrary allocation methods may be of less importance in practice than in theory" is probably valid.

More Recent Costing Approaches

Activity-based costing. Marketing costs can make up to 50 percent of total costs for some products (Stevenson et al., 1993). The accounting system, however, is oriented to the needs of external users, and secondarily to the needs of marketing decision-makers. Stevenson et al. (1993) discussed how activity-based costing (ABC) can be applied in an industrial marketing context. This new costing approach more appropriately identifies cost drivers related to marketing activities, such as advertising, selling, and marketing research time, so as to better allocate marketing costs to products.

Lewis (1991) also addressed the need to use ABC techniques for marketing functions, with emphasis on physical distribution: selling, warehousing, packing and shipping, and general office. Physical distribution costs "are a major factor in worldwide competition and should not be ignored in discussions of performance measurements and integrated cost systems" (Lewis, p. 34). ABC is advocated to identify, classify, and allocate the physical distribution costs using appropriately identified cost drivers.

Another application of ABC to marketing was cited by Yong et al. (1993) in the banking industry, specifically in relation to the impact on future product pricing of the allocation of mortgage department customer telephone center costs. By incorporating capacity utilization into ABC, to obtain a close approximation of long-run costs, strategic advantage in the market place could be assessed to enable decisions in relation to pricing and product entry/exit to be made more easily.

Since "developments in ABC show great promise in delivering more reliable measures of long-run incremental costs" (Committe & Grinell, 1992, p. 58), this costing technique has been recommended as a worthwhile tool for predatory pricing cases for the measurement of long-run incremental costs. This application of ABC arose from several influential court opinions which indicated the need to rely on a "causation approach to cost measurement" (Committe & Grinell, 1992, p. 58).

Target costing. In target costing cost is not used to set the price which is mainly determined by market conditions, but cost will affect a firm's decision whether to market the product at all. The procedure involves assessing the market's willingness to pay for a product which then establishes its target price. Working backwards, by subtracting the target profit, gives the target cost which the firm must hold down to through cost reduction efforts, or, if a new product, through improved product design. Drucker would call this approach "price-driven costing," as opposed to "cost-driven pricing."

Product life cycle costing. Product life cycle costing tracks and accumulates costs attributable to each product from initial research and development to final customer service and support in the market place (Horngren et al., 1994). Since marketing costs represent a major component in a product's life cycle costs, this costing technique has a useful marketing application. Understanding life cycle costing enables marketing managers to better manage marketing costs through separate identification of costs, not on an annual product-by-product basis, but over each product's life cycle. This allows a comparison of the level of marketing costs incurred by different products, and assessment of the likely impact of the inter-relationships among cost components. In relation to the latter, for example, significant reductions in the research and development and product design cost categories can lead to major increases in customer-service-related costs in later periods.

Marketing-Accounting Interface

Any discussion of costs and pricing underscores the importance of the cost–pricing relationship in marketing, already recognized by the American Accounting Association in 1972, but which still holds true today. Cost represents the "floor for price" (Kotler, 1991) and a knowledge of costs is essential for pricing decisions which, of course, are also based on other market considerations.

Market segment profitability analysis is essentially an attempt to analyse post hoc how costs and pricing decisions have resulted in specific profit outcomes. Profitability data for this purpose are normally generated by the accounting function. This emphasizes the importance of a constructive marketing–accounting interface between these two functions.

Overall, it does seem that much more needs to be done to improve the marketing–accounting interface, especially in today's global competitive environment. The view expressed by Trebuss (1978, p. 525) on the "limited attention this topic has received in business research and literature" still rings true today.

Bibliography

American Accounting Association (1972). Report of the Committee on Cost and Profitability Analyses for Marketing. *The Accounting Review*, 7, supplement, 577–615.

Committe, B. E. & Grinnell, D. J. (1992). Predatory pricing, the price–cost test, and activity-based costing. *Cost Management*, Fall, 52–8.

Horngren, C. T., Foster, G. & Datar, S. (1994). *Cost accounting*. Englewood Cliffs, NJ: Prentice-Hall.

Kjaer-Hansen, M. (1967). Marketing costs and their importance in pricing. In *Financial Dimensions of Marketing*, Richard M. S. Wilson (ed.), 1981, 214–23.

Kotler P. (1991). *Marketing Management*. Englewood Cliffs, NJ: Prentice-Hall.

Lewis, R. J. (1991). Activity-based costing for marketing. *Management Accounting*, US, Nov., 33–8.

Mills, R. W. (1988). Pricing decisions in UK manufacturing and service companies. *Management Accounting*, Nov., 38–9.

Stevenson, T. H., Barnes, F. C. & Stevenson, S. A. (1993). Activity-based costing: An emerging tool for industrial marketing decision-makers. *Journal of Business & Industrial Marketing*, 8, 2, 40–52.

Trebuss, A. S. (1978). Improving corporate effectiveness: Managing the marketing finance interface. In *Marketing Effectiveness*, S. S. Shapiro & V. H. Kirpalani, 525–36.

Ursic, M. L. & Helgeson, J. G. (1994). Using price as a weapon. *Industrial Marketing Management*, 23, 125–31.

Weekly, J. K. (1992). Pricing in foreign markets: Pitfalls and opportunities. *Industrial Marketing Management*, 21, 173–9.

Yong, G. Y. & Wu, R. C. (1993). Strategic Costing + ABC. *Management Accounting*, US, Nov., p. 33.

HERBERT P. SCHOCH and TEOH HAI YAP

current value accounting   This discussion will concentrate on those measurement bases that are currently feasible – historical cost (HC), historical cost adjusted for general price level change (GPL), current replacement cost (CRC), and current exit value (EV). The HC and GPL bases are needed for understanding the relationship of the current value accounting. The feasibility of CRC and EV is generally not considered high, but available research and experience demonstrate that certain versions of these systems are feasible today. This is in contrast to another possible valuation basis – discounted cash flow.

The discounted cash flow valuation method (also called economic value or direct valuation) consists of projecting future cash flows related to an asset, then discounting those flows to the present using an appropriate discount rate. However, the process of predicting future cash flows must be subjective, which reduces the feasibility of this choice. Further, the assumptions made and the choice of discount rate are likely to vary materially between users.

Although current value accounting discussions may appear to emphasize asset valuation, the choice of systems to be used has important effects on the values at which liabilities and owners' equity will be reported as well as the form and content of the income statement.

The USA has had one short period (1979–1983) where large companies were required to release GPL and CRC information, but no such requirements are in effect today. Other countries have current standards requiring various types of current value or GPL disclosure. And the International Accounting Standards Committee has adopted International Accounting Standard 29 requiring GPL restatement in hyper-inflationary economies (those having three-year total inflation rates over 100 percent). In essence, standard setters seem to avoid the problem of changing prices until it becomes too big to ignore.

In summary, the two systems of MC and GPL fail to provide relevant information for statement users and both suffer from the allocation problem. CRC provides somewhat more useful information, but the most commonly applied version still suffers from the allocation problem. In addition CRC may overstate the actual value of assets and the income dichotomy involved is difficult to apply and is somewhat artificial. The EV system provides information that answers important user questions and resolves the changing dollar and allocation problems. Unfortunately it suffers from the purchase loss and market saturation problems. Thus there is no perfect system, but a combination of CRC and EV seems most promising to provide information useful to decision-makers.

Historical Cost Accounting

The historical cost accounting system (HC) (without adjustment for change in general price level) is the system most often used in practice in the USA today. Since we report depreciated historical cost, the real question answered by HC would be: "How many dollars were spent to get to the current position after deducting the dollars which were assumed related to past operations?" The corresponding question answered by the income statement is: "How many dollars were received by (or promised to) the firm minus the number of dollars spent (or to be spent) to obtain those goods and services used to obtain the revenue?"

There are problems inherent in generating and interpreting the answers given by HC

statements to the above questions. First, we have very little, if any, basis for choosing depreciation methods and parameters to apply to fixed assets, which has led to some accountants calling it arbitrary. Thus, all accounting figures that depend on allocations – primarily inventory and fixed assets – must be viewed as the product of arbitrary allocations over periods. The book values of these assets, therefore, cannot be considered any more appropriate or "correct" than many other possible figures. It is *extremely* important to be aware of this allocation problem and of its potential effects on the meaning and reliability of accounting statements, especially since the statements prepared nowadays are generally based on HC. Perhaps it is equally important to recognize that alternative bases too suffer from some variation of this problem. In principle, however, the current replacement cost system does not have to be subject to the allocation problem, but its implementation does.

HC statement totals and subtotals lack meaning (because they add incompatible units), and many items lack relevance to current decisions, except for taxation. Most managerial decisions are based on some form of current value (exit value, entry value, or subjective economic value), and only at the time of acquisition does the historical cost represent the current value of an asset. Since the firm continues to hold the asset, the total benefit from the asset will be the past benefits plus estimated future benefits. Even if the past benefits can be determined based on historical cost, future benefits cannot. In summary then, a decision-maker is unlikely to consider either the original historical cost or the depreciated historical cost as relevant information.

The lack of meaning of statement totals is sometimes referred to as the "apples and oranges problem" since different book values are the net outcome of numerous judgments and assumptions. An additional serious issue is the decline in the purchasing power of money over the years. The assets might include cash measured in end-of-1995 dollars, marketable securities in 1980 dollars, accounts receivable in 1996 dollars, inventory in 1995 and earlier dollars (including some depreciation from the distant past), land in 1950 dollars, depreciable assets in 1950 to 1995 dollars, and notes receivable in 1997 or later dollars.

This is similar to saying I have 1 yard, 2 unidentified units of length, 3.5 meters, 6 groups of units of undetermined length (inventory), 4 feet (too old to identify), 3 inches, and 1/2 future centimeters. They cannot be added together *without adjustment*. Similarly in the accounting situation, we can choose an appropriate standard of measurement and convert all of our "mixed" dollars to some common scale and then add.

General-Price-Level-Adjusted Historical Cost

The general-price-level-adjusted historical cost system (GPL) is based upon the idea of adjusting HC statements for the changing amount of goods and services that can be purchased with a dollar at different points in time. Assume that we choose the purchasing power of a December 31, 1994 dollar as our measurement unit. We can then convert all of our past dollar figures to this scale by computing the ratio of purchasing power of the December 31, 1994 dollar to the purchasing power of the dollar at the time of purchase (e.g., 1958) and multiplying this ratio times the number of dollars spent at that time to get the cost in terms of purchasing power of the asset. This explicitly recognizes that the economic meaning of a dollar changes over time. Note particularly that it is still a historical cost system. The measurement of cost is based on purchasing power given up rather than number of dollars given up.

Thus, the GPL system would provide answers to user questions such as: "How much purchasing power was given up to get to the position the firm holds today?" Again we must modify the question slightly, due to depreciation, to: "How much purchasing power was given up to get to the current position after deducting the purchasing power assumed related to past operations?" The corresponding income statement question is: "How much purchasing power was received by (or promised to) the firm minus the purchasing power given up to obtain those goods and services necessary to generate the revenue?"

With inflation, GPL statements are more satisfying in answering those questions than unadjusted historical cost statements. The GPL approach also provides for the recognition of the gains and losses experienced by companies as they hold liabilities and assets through changes in the general price level. To illustrate, assume $1,000,000 from Creditor Company when the price index is 120 ($_{120}$ $1,000,000). If the loan is repaid at a time when the price index is 150, the Debtor Company will have made a GPL "gain" because it borrowed more valuable (price index 120) dollars than it repaid. In terms of purchasing power, Debtor Company repaid only the equivalent of $800,000 price index 120 dollars ($_{150}$$1,000,000 x 120/150), thereby gaining $_{120}$ $200,000 of purchasing power. We could view the situation as a repayment of $_{150}$$1,000,000 on a loan of $_{150}$$1,250,000 (= $_{120}$$1,000,000) for a gain of $_{150}$$250,000 (= $_{120}$$200,000). (Actually GPL accounting would recognize this gain at the time the price index moved from 120 to 150 whether the loan had been repaid or not.)

There are two sides to every transaction and if the Debtor Company has a GPL gain on its liability, the Creditor Company has suffered an equal GPL loss on its long-term receivable. The general result is that a creditor loses and a debtor gains during periods of inflation. Of course, no company is solely a debtor or solely a creditor so that every company has some gain and some loss during inflationary periods. The net of these gains and losses, however, will be determined by the company's *net monetary position*. The net monetary position is the balance between the company's monetary assets (primarily cash and receivables fixed in dollar terms) and monetary liabilities. The company is called a net debtor if its monetary liabilities exceed its monetary assets and it will have a net GPL gain in a period of inflation. Conversely if the company's monetary assets exceed its liabilities, it is a net creditor and will suffer a net GPL loss during inflation.

One problem with computing GPL loss (gain) in this manner and disclosing it separately is that this procedure may lead statement readers to believe that the GPL loss is a nonoperating item, which may not the case. Also the interest rates being paid will have been set after taking expected inflation into account. So the debtor's GPL gain may be offset by having to pay a higher interest rate on borrowed money.

It is important to emphasize that the adjustments from dollars of one time to dollars current at another time are just that: adjustments. They do not represent a gain any more than a conversion of 100 yards to 300 feet would mean a gain in distance. The adjustment is done only to state all items in the statements in common units so that they may be added, subtracted, etc., with each other to produce totals which are of a known "dimension" – purchasing power expressed in dollars current to a given time – rather than totals composed of dollars of indeterminate origin (and meaning).

Unfortunately the GPL system does not solve the problems of allocation and lack of relevance; knowledge of the purchasing-power-adjusted historical cost of an asset is unlikely to be much more useful in a current decision than the unadjusted dollar cost itself.

Current Replacement Cost Accounting

The current replacement cost (CRC) system measures assets at the amounts it would cost to replace them today. Thus, the CRC system would answer questions such as: "How much would it cost to set up a company in this position today?" and "How much revenue was received minus the cost *at the date of sale* necessary to generate the revenue?" (the net of which is called *current operating profit*), and "How much did the replacement cost of assets increase during the period?" (called *holding gain*). There are, unfortunately, conceptual as well as practical problems with the CRC system.

The first problem relates to the choice between measuring the replacement cost of a particular asset held by the firm in its current condition and measuring the replacement cost of the services equivalent to what the firm expects to benefit from using the asset. This is sometimes referred to as the identical asset versus equivalent services controversy. The methods of estimating CRC of the identical asset involve either estimating directly the cost of purchasing the asset in its current condition from the secondary (used) asset market or estimating the current cost of purchasing the asset new then applying some "appropriate" depreciation method to arrive at a figure that must really be defined as the "depreciated book value based on current cost of replacing the asset new" rather than the current replacement

cost of the asset held. The estimation of the current cost in new condition can be accomplished by locating the same asset for sale in the primary market if it is still being sold new, applying a specific price index for the type of asset involved to the HC, or using engineering estimates to compute a best estimate of the cost new if it were still available new. However, many assets currently held by firms are not available new. When one considers that one is choosing a depreciation method, which also involves all of the allocation problem, and that the result may bear little relationship to the CRC of the asset held by the firm, it may be that direct estimation of the cost in the used asset market is seen to be preferable when available.

Furthermore, an asset is not typically replaced by the same asset. Replacement is more often done by purchasing other assets that will provide equivalent services for the least cost. This method requires that the company estimates: (1) the type of services expected; (2) the number of units of this service remaining in the old asset; (3) the assets available for equivalent services; and (4) the cost of each alternative means of acquiring the equivalent services. Determining the CRC of equivalent services becomes much more difficult as we consider assets with various capacities, service lives, and operating costs.

The two primary US authoritative pronouncements on CRC information (Securities and Exchange Commission in its Accounting Series Release 190 and Statement of Financial Accounting Standard No. 33) required disclosure of the current cost of the asset in new condition as well as its depreciated value. This position has the practical effect of eliminating the direct reference to the used asset market method which is the only variation of the CRC system that avoids the allocation problem. However, neither requirement is currently in effect.

Another problem with CRC relates to the dichotomization of accounting income into current operating profit (COP) and holding gain (HG). COP provides a good estimate of the firm's continuing ability to earn profits because COP is revenues net of cost at current dollars. However, the assumption that best estimates of future prices are the current prices is not quite valid when related to commodity prices (even specific commodity prices). Further, the majority of sales and cost of sales are typically incurred well before the end of the period.

HG is intended to measure the gain from increase (decrease) in CRC of assets (liabilities). This calculation can get somewhat complex since the asset's CRC may be depreciating through normal use throughout the period. Unfortunately, holding gains and losses are occurring continuously, which makes the calculation difficult, especially when it is coupled with the allocation problem. It seems more reasonable to skip the disaggregation of HG and COP and consider the depreciation expense as the decrease in CRC during the period, which avoids all need to choose a depreciation method.

Drake & Dopuch (1965) point out another conceptual difficulty with the COP–HG dichotomy. They note that certain types of assets are necessary to operate a given type of business and that COP should be affected by those assets' holding gains, but that the CRC system would not allow for this adjustment. Drake & Dopuch also point out that certain costs of speculative activity (e.g., inventory carrying costs) may be charged to operations. The proper identification of COP and HG is so difficult as to reduce the usefulness of this dichotomy. However, an important feature of the CRC system is that it can include all necessary adjustments to take account of the changing purchasing power of the dollar.

In summary, the CRC system is conceptually more relevant to current decisions than historical cost and can be adjusted for changes in the purchasing power of the dollar, but in its most common implementations it still suffers from the allocation problem and computational difficulties.

Exit (Realizable) Value

The exit value (EV) accounting system reports assets at the net amount for which they *could be* sold to a willing buyer within a short period of time. A short period of time is defined as long enough to allow an orderly sale, but not long enough to allow disposal of fixed assets through ordinary use of services. Net amount is defined as the selling price less disposition costs including tax effects all discounted to the point of measurement.

The EV system generates statements that would help users to answer questions like: "What amount could be realized from the orderly disposal of the firm's assets less the amount required for the liabilities?"; and "How much has that amount increased over the accounting period?" The EV system does this by measuring assets at EV (as defined above) and liabilities at the amount for which they could be settled at the measurement date, with the net being the residual equity. No attempt is made to subdivide residual equity. Depreciation expense is typically computed as the decline in EV during the period, thereby avoiding the allocation problem.

The most prevalent misconception about the exit value system is the confusion between orderly sale and liquidation. Other misconceptions hold that EV measurements are not additive or that EV statement preparation is not feasible. In a technical sense EV measurements are not additive, but a logical criterion exists for deciding which unique sum of exit values to use (the highest sum).

Contentions that either current replacement cost (CRC) or EV statement preparation is not feasible can best be answered by referring to earlier studies. These show that a surprising number of assets can be measured by direct reference to used asset markets. Further these measurements are frequently more reliable and verifiable than similar historical cost (HC) measurements. It is also clear that EV is at least as feasible as the common versions of CRC.

Having discussed the erroneous criticisms of the EV system, it is only fair to turn to the valid criticism: EV provides a very low measurement of asset value (which causes a "loss" to be recognized at the time of purchase of an asset) and market saturation (unique asset or relatively large stock of the asset, which can in some circumstances cause difficulty in determining EV).

It is frequently true that EV is a low value for an asset, a relationship that allows use of EV statements to evaluate management decisions. If a firm is holding an asset, we can assume that the management believes that asset is worth *at least* its EV. If the asset was not expected to yield at least its EV within the firm, the management should sell it for its EV. There is no comparable presumption available relative to

CRC. The fact that a firm holds an asset does *not* imply that the management believes that asset is worth its CRC because the management knows the asset cannot be sold for the CRC. Instead the CRC can be viewed as the maximum amount the firm would lose if it lost that particular asset.

This view was best outlined by James Bonbright (1937) when he referred to "value to the owner." Very simply, value to the owner was defined as the amount of loss a firm would suffer if deprived of a particular asset. This value would be a minimum of the EV since at worst the firm could have sold the asset. The maximum value lost would be the CRC since the firm could simply replace the asset for its CRC if the firm's management believed the economic value was between the EV and the CRC, the value to the owner would be economic value. This approach to asset valuation appeals to many accountants. It is logical. It is understandable. Unfortunately it is *not* feasible since subjective economic value must be known. The value to the owner concept does, however, clearly outline the limits of asset valuation.

Bibliography

Drake, D. & Dopuch N. (1965). On the case for dichotomizing income. *Journal of Accounting Research*, Autumn, 192–205.

Bonbright, J. C. (1937). *The Valuation of Property*. New York: McGraw Hill.

JAMES C. MCKEOWN

D

database accounting Traditional accounting systems, whether manual or computerized, generally cannot provide disaggregated, multidimensional data in a form required for a diverse number of uses. The weaknesses in the conventional double-entry model have been described by a number of researchers (e.g., McCarthy (1982) and Andros, Cherrington & Denna (1992)) and are summarized as follows:

(1) Most accounting information is expressed in financial terms. Users also require nonfinancial information.
(2) Rigid classification schemes such as a chart of accounts are not always appropriate, and restrict a user to one view of the data.
(3) The level of aggregation of data often is too high to be useful.
(4) Accounting data is not easily integrated with other information systems in an organization.
(5) The number of facts recorded about each transaction is limited.
(6) The traditional processes used to record, maintain, and report information do not allow for timely information to be provided to users.
(7) Internal controls can be difficult to install and maintain.

These weaknesses are similar to those identified in traditional approaches to the design of information systems. Traditional file processing systems suffer from high levels of data redundancy, inconsistencies in the same data stored in multiple locations, limited sharing of data across applications in an organization, difficulties in responding to requests for new information or information in different formats, and inefficient programing practices. This "process approach" to information system design was replaced by the database approach as technology developed. Unfortunately, accountants have been unwilling to fully embrace the principles of database design.

Although data capture, processing, storage, and retrieval has been revolutionized by computer technology, changes in accounting have not kept up with changes in technology. There are those who believe that the problem can be attributed to a financial reporting system which, despite the significant impact of computer technology, is still based on traditional accounting conventions. The essence of the problem, as pointed out by Armitage (1985) and more recently by Geerts & McCarthy (1991), lies in a distinction made by McCrae in 1976.

McCrae states: "The clear distinction between system and technology is important since many accountants suffer from the delusion that because they have changed the accounting technology they must automatically have effected dramatic changes in the accounting system. This is not so" (p. 39). To this, Geerts & McCarthy have concluded "the major alterations called for by McCrae have, by and large, not yet materialized in the modern EDP environment" (1991, p. 160).

The Database Approach to Accounting

The objectives of the database approach include minimizing data redundancy, maintaining data integrity, allowing data to be shared among users, separating the data definition from the application programs ("data independence"), and maintaining uniform internal controls across all applications.

While different methodologies exist for developing information systems in organizations, there are common elements in data-driven approaches. Formal approaches include, "information engineering" – a top-down methodology that includes the phases of (1) planning, (2) analysis, (3) design, and (4) implementation. Less formal strategies also have similar steps for database development.

The aim of the first phase is to ensure that the planning of the information system is consistent with the strategic business plan of the organization.

In the second phase, the three main steps are (1) requirements analysis, (2) view modeling, and (3) view integration (McCarthy, 1982). The goal of requirements analysis is to identify user requirements and develop a set of "user views." These detailed specifications take into account both the data and the processes that use the data. In the "view modeling" stage, sets of user views are expressed in a form consistent with a conceptual data model such as the entity-relationship (E-R) model. The user views are then integrated into a conceptual data model. The conceptual data model is independent of database management system (DBMS) software. Also during the analysis phase, process models, which identify the flow of data between processes, are developed.

The third phase involves both (1) "logical design" and (2) "physical design." Logical

The development process described above had its origins in the work of the ANSI/X3/SPARC Study Group on Database Management Systems. The Study Group identified a three-level framework which corresponded to the external, conceptual, and internal views of the database. This three-level framework and the phases involved in database design are illustrated in Figure 1.

Data Modelling

Conceptual data modeling is usually undertaken by using a semantic data model such as the entity-relationship (E-R) or the object-oriented data model. We will concentrate on the E-R model because it is still the most common approach. The E-R model was initially suggested by Chen (1976) and has since been developed further. The E-R model is described by E-R diagrams in which entity-types and the relationships between entity-types are specified. Entity-types are entities having common characteristics such as objects, people, or events, and about which data is to be stored and maintained.

For example, one user of an organization's database may require data about customers and orders to be stored. The user's view may be specified as shown in figure 2.

Figure 2

design is a process in which the conceptual data model is mapped to specific DBMS software. The DBMS may be based on one of a number of logical database models, including hierarchical, network, relational, and object-oriented. The relational model is the most common in current database systems. Physical design is the process of specifying the physical storage structures, and methods of accessing the database.

In the final phase, the system is implemented and operationalized, which includes the input of data, programing, testing and training, and ensuring that backup, recovery, and security procedures are in place.

The entity-types are CUSTOMER and ORDER, and the diamond indicates there is a relationship (named "customer/order") between the two entity-types. The number of entity-types that are included in a relationship is known as the degree of a relationship. A binary relationship is illustrated in the above diagram since there are two entity types. Other common relationships are unary and ternary. The cardinalities of a relationship are the constraints associated with the number of instances that one entity-type may be associated with another entity-type. In the above example, the "0,N" (zero, many) indicates that a customer may exist in the database without making an order (0) and

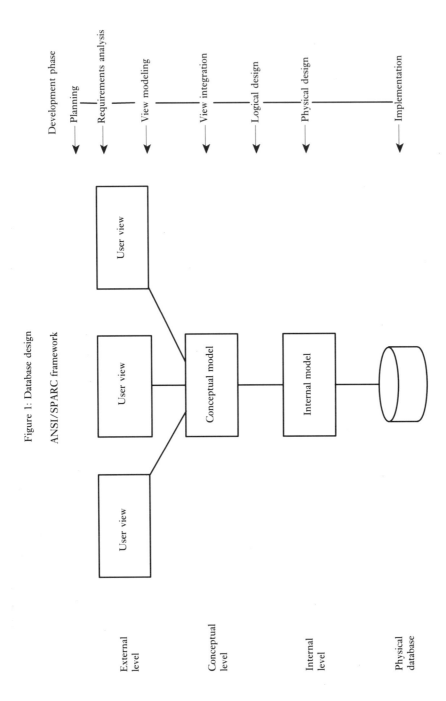

Figure 1: Database design

ANSI/SPARC framework

Figure 3

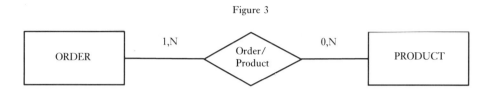

a customer may make many (N) orders. The "1,1" (one, one) indicates that an order cannot be made without a customer, and that a specific order is made to a specific customer.

A second user of the database may require data about the orders for products. The second user's view may be as shown in figure 3.

In this view, the "1,N" (one, many) indicates that an order would not exist without a product (1) and an order may contain many different products (N). The "0,N" (zero, many) indicates that a product may exist in the database if it has not been ordered (0), and a product may be listed on many different orders (N).

Once view modeling is complete, the views are integrated to form the conceptual model, as shown in figure 4.

Each entity-type has a number of attributes or characteristics. For example, the CUSTO-MER entity-type may have the following

attributes: CUST-NO, CUST-NAME, CUST-ADDRESS. Attributes associated with each entity-type may also be shown on the E-R diagram.

The conceptual model is then mapped onto the logical data model used by the DBMS software. While the hierarchical, network, and more recently the object-oriented model are used in DBMS software, the relational model is most common.

The relational model was first described by Codd (1970) and has since undergone continual extension and refinement. In simple terms, the relational model consists of two-dimensional tables ("relations"). Each table has a number of unnamed rows (the records) and named columns (the attributes). There are a number of properties to which each table or relation must conform. For example, each row must be unique; one or more attributes are nominated as a key (the primary key) that uniquely

Figure 4

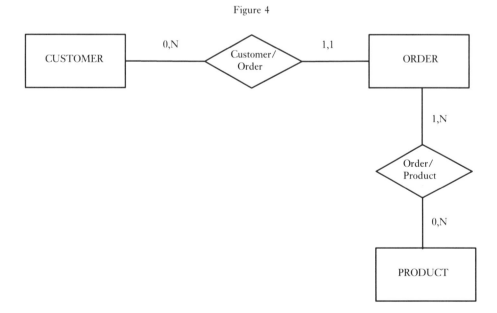

identifies a row; columns (attributes) must be single-valued; and the sequence of rows and columns is not important.

The conceptual model represented by an E-R diagram can be transformed into relations. Both entity-types and relationships need to be considered. Each entity-type in an E-R diagram becomes a relation. The relation should only contain attributes specific to that entity-type. Relationships on the E-R diagram are examined to ensure that, when needed, it is possible to link one relation to another. The way in which relationships are represented in the relational model will depend on both the degree and cardinality of the relationship. The result will either be adding the primary key of one entity-type as a foreign key in the other entity-type, or creating a separate relation. In the case of a many-to-many relationship between two entity-types, a separate relation is created.

For example, the following relations would be developed from the E-R diagram above:

CUSTOMER (CUST-NO, CUST-NAME, CUST-ADDRESS)

ORDER (ORDER-NO, ORDER-DATE, CUST-NO)

PRODUCT (PROD-NO, PROD-DESC, PRICE)

ORDER/PRODUCT (ORDER-NO, PROD-NO, QUANTITY)

The primary keys are underlined. The relationships are represented by (1) the primary key in CUSTOMER (CUST-NO) and repeating it in ORDER as a foreign key; and (2) creating a relationship table ORDER/PRODUCT because the cardinality constraint between ORDER and PRODUCT shows a many-to-many relationship in that an order may contain many different products and a product may be listed on many different orders.

It is important to ensure that the tables in a relational database contain a minimal amount of redundant data and do not cause inconsistencies when data are inserted, deleted, or modified. The process of "normalization" can be used to create tables free of such problems, or to test for redundant data and anomalies. There are a number of "normal forms" that show the state of a relation.

As an illustration, let us consider the first three normal forms. Following Weber's succinct description, a record is in first normal form if it excludes repeating groups. It is in second normal form if all non-key fields are functionally dependent on the whole key, and in third normal form if all non-key fields are not functionally dependent on any other non-key field (Weber, 1986, p. 507). The four relations (above), developed from the E-R diagram, meet the test of third normal form. However, to illustrate the normalization process, consider the following attributes of an order from a customer:

Unnormalized relation:

(ORDER-NO, ORDER-DATE, CUST-NO, CUST-NAME, CUST-ADDRESS, (PROD-NO, PROD-DESC, PRICE, QUANTITY))

First, second and third normal forms can be developed as follows:

First normal form:

ORDER (ORDER-NO, ORDER-DATE, CUST-NO, CUST-NAME, CUST-ADDRESS)

ORDER/PRODUCT (ORDER-NO, PROD-NO, PROD-DESC, PRICE, QUANTITY)

Second normal form:

ORDER (ORDER-NO, ORDER-DATE, CUST-NO, CUST-NAME, CUST-ADDRESS)

ORDER/PRODUCT (ORDER-NO, PROD-NO, QUANTITY)

PRODUCT (PROD-NO, PROD-DESC, PRICE)

Third normal form:

ORDER (ORDER-NO, ORDER-DATE, CUST-NO)

ORDER/PRODUCT (ORDER-NO, PROD-NO, QUANTITY)

Figure 5: The REA accounting model: Entities and relationships

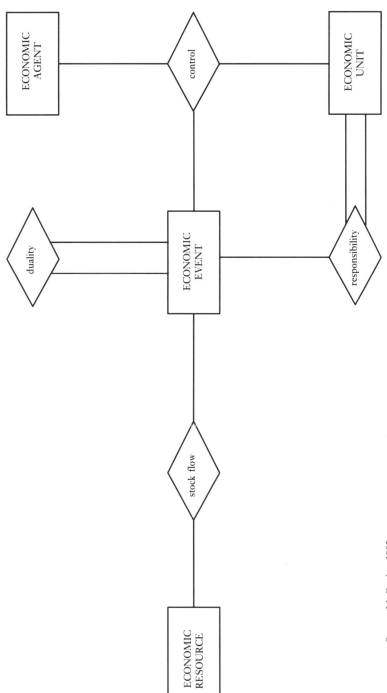

Source: McCarthy, 1982

PRODUCT (PROD-NO, PROD-DESC, PRICE)

CUSTOMER (CUST-NO, CUST-NAME, CUST-ADDRESS)

In summary, the following broad steps are undertaken to develop the conceptual and internal data models:

- identify the entity-types

- identify the relationships between the entity-types

- construct an E-R diagram

- develop relations (tables) from the E-R diagram

- ensure that the tables are normalized.

Events-based Accounting Systems

Much of the work on database accounting refers to Sorter (1969) who criticized the value approach to accounting because it is impossible to specify input values for the many and varied uses of accounting data and users employ a wide range of decision models that they cannot describe. Instead, Sorter proposed an "events approach," the aim of which "is to provide information about relevant economic events that might be useful in a variety of possible decision models" (p. 13).

Sorter was concerned with the loss of information due to aggregation and valuation, and suggested that further research could focus upon the construction of accounting reports based on the events approach. Sorter acknowledged that the events approach had been "implied by some in the past" (p. 12) and acknowledged the ideas of Vatter (1947). Although the origins of the term "event" in relation to accounting is unknown, others such as Goldberg (1965) had described the unit of activity in terms of which accounting procedures are carried out as an "event," and, at the same time, advocated that accounting should not be tied only to financial events. Ijiri (1966) also advocated the use of a system of multidimensional accounting because it "makes it possible to deal directly with physical measures without being constrained by a particular monetary valuation method" (Ijiri, 1966,

p. 163). Undoubtedly, another influence on the development of database accounting were attempts from 1957 to 1972 to represent traditional recording of accounting transactions in a new mode (*see* Leech, 1968).

Colantoni, Manes & Whinston (1971) developed a hierarchical database that incorporated multidimensional events, and described the development of a data management language for retrieving events from the database. Research on the design of hierarchical database systems in accounting continued with other studies.

In 1977, Everest & Weber criticized these previous attempts at integrating accounting and information systems primarily on the ground that hierarchical database systems do not meet the major requirement of data independence. They proposed instead that the relational approach (Codd, 1970) be used to remedy the deficiencies. This research was the first to apply the relational model, including the process of normalization, to a traditional managerial accounting model and financial accounting model. However, Everest & Weber (1977) also identify the problems in attempting to map accounting models to the data structure provided by a DBMS. A solution to these problems was proposed by McCarthy (1979).

Using Chen's (1976) methodology, McCarthy (1979) developed an entity-relationship (E-R) model of an accounting system. The model closely corresponds to the three-level architecture suggested by the ANSI/X3/SPARC Study Group and makes use of the ideas of events and multidimensional theorists. This contribution demonstrated (1) the feasibility of developing an accounting system as a conceptual model one step removed from implementing the system using any particular data structure (such as hierarchical, network, or relational) of a DBMS; (2) that the model did not need to rely on traditional accounting artifacts such as journals, ledgers, and a chart of accounts; and (3) that the mapping of the conceptual model of E-R diagrams to the relational data model in normal form is relatively straightforward.

The next major advance in database accounting was the development of a generalized framework for accounting systems known as the REA (resources, events, agents) accounting

McCarthy reviewed the process of conceptual model design (requirements analysis, view modelling, view integration), and formulated the REA accounting model as one part of a wider enterprise database system. He described the entities, and relationships between entities, as shown in Figure 5 (McCarthy, 1982, p. 564).

This generalized E-R model was then used by McCarthy (1982) to illustrate how it would work in a shared data environment. As McCarthy states: "The REA accounting framework provides a basis for what can be called the *declarative* features of a conceptual schema. These features model facts about the object system in terms of *entities, associations* of entities, and *generalizations* of entities. However, in a working data model, they must be supplemented by *procedures* that specify how the system will use those facts it has available [Wong & Mylopoulos, 1977]. In terms of concepts discussed already, the declarative features of an accounting schema consist of its *base objects* – those elements representing economic events, resources, and agents plus relationships between them – while the procedural features consist of methods for materializing conclusions about those base objects" (pp. 568–9).

The work of McCarthy (1979, 1982) has had a significant influence on the development of database accounting since the early 1980s. There has been considerable research that has tested, analyzed, or used the REA model in different settings, and other research that has made use of E-R modeling in events-based systems.

The relevance of the database approach to the design of accounting systems is now well established in the accounting literature. Conceptual modeling using semantic methods such as E-R diagrams ensures that entity-types and the relationships between entity-types are defined in such a way that it allows accounting data to be integrated with enterprise-wide information systems. At the same time, the conceptual model is independent of any particular data structure in DBMS software and is not tied to traditional accounting artifacts such as journals, ledgers, and charts of accounts. Systems implemented in this way allow for the production of accounting and other reports as required by a user. The characteristics of an event that have traditionally been of most interest to accountants may be only a very small part of all its attributes in a very large database. Potentially, there is no limit to the number or type of attributes that could be recorded about events and other phenomena. Further evidence is provided by the event-driven, database accounting system implemented by IBM (Andros et al., 1992).

Bibliography

Andros, D. P., Cherrington, J. O. & Denna, E. L. (1992). Reengineer your accounting, the IBM way. *Financial Executive*, July/August, 28–31.

Armitage, H. M. (1985). Linking management accounting systems with computer technology. *Society of Management Accountants of Canada*.

Chen, P. P. (1976). The entity relationship model – Towards a unified view of data. *ACM Transactions on Database Systems*, Mar., 9–36.

Codd, E. F. (1970). A relational model of data for large shared data banks. *Communications of the ACM*, June, 377–87.

Colantoni, C. S., Manes, R. P. & Whinston, A. (1971). A unified approach to the theory of accounting and information systems. *Accounting Review*, Jan., 90–102.

Everest, G. C. & Weber, R. (1977). A relational approach to accounting models. *Accounting Review*, Apr., 340–59.

Geerts, G. & McCarthy, W. E. (1991). Database accounting systems. B. C. Williams & B. J. Spaul *IT and accounting: The impact of information technology*. London: Chapman & Hall.

Goldberg, L. (1965). *An inquiry into the nature of accounting*. American Accounting Association.

Ijiri, Y. (1966). Physical measures and multidimensional accounting. R. K. Jaedicke, Y. Ijiri & O. Nieslen (eds), *Research in accounting measurement*. American Accounting Association.

Leech, S. A. (1986). The theory and development of a matrix-based accounting system. *Accounting and Business Research*, Autumn, 327–41.

McCarthy, W. E. (1979). An entity-relationship view of accounting models. *Accounting Review*. Oct., 667–86.

McCarthy, W. E. (1982). The REA accounting model: a generalized framework for accounting systems in a shared data environment. *Accounting Review*, July, 554–78.

McCrae, T. W. (1976). Computers and accounting. New York: John Wiley & Sons.

Sorter, G. (1969). An "events" approach to basic accounting theory. *Accounting Review*, Jan., 12–19.

Vatter, W. J. (1947). The fund theory of accounting and its implications for financial reports. Chicago: The University of Chicago Press.

Weber, R. (1986). Data models research in accounting: An evaluation of wholesale distribution software. *Accounting Review*, July, 498–518.

Wong, H. K. T. & Mylopoulos, J. (1977). Two views of data semantics: A survey of data models in artificial intelligence and database management. *INFOR*, Oct., 344–83.

STEWART A. LEECH

deferred taxes   In the USA, income taxes are paid on the basis of a taxable income determined by law and rules very much independent of generally accepted accounting principles (GAAP). Deferred taxes arise when pretax financial income differs from taxable income in the tax return. This happens when financial income, which is based on GAAP, differs from taxable income, which is based on current Internal Revenue Service (IRS) regulations. Accounting for these deferred taxes has significantly changed over the years. From 1967 to 1987, Accounting Principles Board (APB) Opinion No. 11 (1967) emphasized matching the current tax expense with current revenues. The income statement approach under APB No. 11 resulted in an accumulation of deferred taxes being reflected in the balance sheet which tended to grow as the firm's business grew. These deferred taxes reported on the balance sheet did not have real economic meaning. They did not represent a liability in the sense of having placed a claim against the firm's assets.

FASB Statement of Financial Accounting Standard (SFAS) No. 96 (1987) required a change to an asset/liability valuation approach in determining the accounting treatment of deferred taxes. SFAS No. 96 was met with considerable resistance by practitioners because of their perception of both conceptual flaws and implementation problems, which led to replacing it by SFAS No. 109, "Accounting for Income Taxes" (1992). SFAS No. 109 also requires an asset/liability valuation approach to accounting for deferred taxes, but contains a more liberal treatment of deferred tax assets than did SFAS No. 96.

Measurement of Deferred Tax Assets and Liabilities

In order to implement US Statement of Financial Accounting Standard No. 109, "Accounting for Income Taxes," the deferred tax assets and liabilities must be calculated. First, all differences between the generally accepted accounting principles (GAAP) and tax bases of assets, liabilities, and equities must be identified. The differences are then classified as either permanent or temporary differences.

A permanent difference arises when one of the two systems recognizes an event and the other does not. For example, a company would recognize goodwill in a business purchase and amortize the goodwill as an expense for financial reporting purposes, but before the Omnibus Budget Reconciliation Act of 1993 (OBRA 1993) was passed, the Internal Revenue Service did not recognize the amortization of goodwill as a deductible business expense for tax reporting purposes. The income effect arising from the treatment of goodwill purchased prior to August 10, 1993 is, therefore, a permanent difference.

A temporary difference is the difference between the tax basis of an asset or a liability and its reported amount in the financial statements that will result in taxable amounts (that will increase taxable income) or deductible amounts (that will decrease taxable income) in future years. The temporary differences exist because the timing of recognition follows a different pattern under the two systems. For example, Congress amended the law which now requires that goodwill and other intangibles purchased after August 10, 1993 be amortized over 15 years. Under GAAP, goodwill is amortized over 40 years or over the expected life of the firm, whichever is less. Under the new IRS rules, goodwill has to be amortized over '15 years. The income effect arising from the treatment of goodwill purchased after August 10, 1993 can therefore be a temporary difference if the firm amortizes goodwill over a period other than 15 years for financial reporting purposes. Some other examples of temporary differences are:

(1) different depreciation methods used for financial income and tax income, such as use of the "modified accelerated cost

recovery system" for tax reporting and straight line depreciation for financial income;

(2) expenses or losses that are deductible before they are recognized in financial income, such as prepaid expenses that are deducted from taxable income in the period paid but deferred for financial income purposes;

(3) revenues or gains that are taxable before they are recognized in financial income, such as advance payments for services not yet performed that are included in taxable income but deferred for financial income purposes;

(4) expenses or losses that are deductible for tax purposes after they are recognized in financial income, such as losses due to a reduction in the market value of the portfolio of trading securities; and

(5) revenues or gains that are taxable after they are recognized in financial income, such as revenue from investments carried under the equity method for financial reporting and under the cost method for income tax reporting.

All temporary differences are summed up to a single total, referred to as the net temporary difference. If the maximum marginal tax rate is not expected to change, this rate is multiplied by the net temporary difference to determine the net deferred tax asset or liability to be recognized on the current period's balance sheet. If a new tax rate is enacted into law for future periods, then that new rate is used for the periods to which it applies. Then the amount of the change in the net deferred tax asset or liability is determined by comparing the beginning of the period balance to the end of the period balance. This amount is then recorded (1) as an adjustment to the deferred tax asset or liability account, and (2) as the deferred tax portion of tax expense for the period. This amount can either increase (if it is a liability) or decrease (if it is an asset) income tax expense reported on the income statement.

Another event that will affect the measurement of deferred tax assets and liabilities is net operating losses (NOL). An NOL occurs when tax-deductible expenses exceed taxable revenue. The IRS allows companies to apply the amount of the loss against income generated in past and future years to provide tax relief to the company. The company may elect to carry back the loss against revenue earned three years ago (t-3) to qualify for a tax refund for taxes paid in that year (at the rate that was in effect in that year). If the amount of the loss is greater than income for year t-3, then the remainder may be applied against income earned in year t-2, with any remainder then applied to year t-1. Any loss remaining may be carried forward in future years up to 15 years in the future. Alternatively, the company may elect the loss carryforward without applying any of it to prior years. If the carryback election is chosen, then the company records a receivable for the refund and a credit to income tax expense (benefit due to loss carryback). If there is an NOL carryforward, then a deferred tax asset exists to the extent that the firm anticipates future taxable income against which the NOL may be applied. The deferred tax asset resulting from the NOL should be applied first against any existing deferred tax liability with the remainder being recognized as a deferred tax asset.

In determining the current year's deferred tax assets and liabilities, care must be taken in measuring deferred tax assets that may not be realized (actually used to offset income taxes). A deferred tax asset is the deferred tax consequences attributable to deductible temporary differences. The deferred tax asset is reduced by a valuation allowance if it is more likely than not (greater than a 50 percent chance) that some portion or all of the deferred tax asset will not be realized. The FASB requires analysis of all available evidence in determining the need for the accrual of the allowance. For example, an allowance would be accrued if "tangible, negative evidence" exists that supports the need for an allowance, such as:

(1) A history of unused NOL carryforwards expiring.

(2) The presence of expected continuing losses in the immediate future years.

(3) Unsettled circumstances (such as outstanding lawsuits) that, if unfavorably resolved, would adversely affect realization.

(4) A carryforward period so short as to limit realization under current conditions.

However, the analysis of positive evidence is also evaluated, such as:

(1) Existing contracts or firm sales backlog that will produce more than enough taxable income to realize the deferred tax asset based on existing sales prices and cost structures.

(2) An excess of appreciated asset value over the tax basis of an entity's net assets in an amount sufficient to realize the deferred tax asset.

(3) A strong earnings history exclusive of the loss that created the future deductible amount (tax loss carryforward or deductible temporary difference) coupled with evidence indicating that the loss (e.g., an unusual, infrequent, or extraordinary item) is an abberation rather than a continuing condition.

The weight given to either form of evidence should be commensurate with the extent to which it can be objectively verified. If it is more likely than not that all or a portion of the deferred tax asset will not be realized, the asset must be reduced by a valuation allowance such that the net amount reflects the expected realization. The amount of the change in the valuation allowance balance for unrealized tax benefits is calculated each year and is recorded as an adjustment to the valuation allowance for unrealized tax assets and as an adjustment to the tax expense for the period.

Balance Sheet and Income Statement Classifications

In the USA, the current deferred tax assets and deferred tax liabilities are reported net in the current section of the balance sheet; likewise, the noncurrent deferred tax assets and liabilities are reported net in the noncurrent section of the balance sheet. This determination is made by first classifying the amounts as current or noncurrent, based on the classification of the related asset or liability for financial reporting. Other deferred tax assets, such as net operating loss (NOL) carryforwards, are classified according to the expected reversal date. Next, the net current amount is determined by summing all deferred current tax assets and liabilities. Accordingly, the net noncurrent amount is determined in a similar manner. An exception to this procedure occurs when deferred tax assets and liabilities arise from different jur-

isdictions, such as state and federal income tax codes. In these cases, they cannot be netted against each other but may be combined (assets added to assets; liabilities added to liabilities) for reporting purposes.

Income tax expense is presented in the income statement by allocating income tax expense (or credit) to continuing operations, discontinued operations, extraordinary items, the cumulative effect of accounting changes, and prior period adjustments. The composition of the tax expense for the period must be disclosed either on the face of the income statement or in the notes thereto. The following components are required disclosures:

(1) Current tax expense or benefit.
(2) Deferred tax expense exclusive of No. 6 below.
(3) Investment tax credits.
(4) Government grants when recognized as a reduction of income taxes.
(5) Benefits of operating loss carryforwards.
(6) Adjustments to the deferred tax assets/liabilities arising from changes in the tax law.

US Statement of Financial Accounting Standard (SFAS) No. 109, "Accounting for Income Taxes" of 1992, also requires notes disclosures to reconcile the reported amount of tax expense attributable to income from continuing operations to the amount of tax that would result from the application of domestic federal statutory income tax rates to income from continuing operations. The amount and timing of any net operating loss carryforward, along with a description of all significant temporary differences must also be disclosed.

BARBARA BROCKIE LEONARD

depletion accounting　Depletion accounting is the rational, systemic allocation of the cost of an unextracted natural resource to the extracted units of the natural resource. Natural resources (e.g., wasting assets) include petroleum and natural gas deposits, gold, copper, silver, coal mines, and other mineral deposits that are depleted through extraction from the earth. Natural resources are recorded at the cost to a company which would normally include the purchase price plus all expenditures necessary to place the natural resource in use in the business. Additional expenditures that may be incurred to prepare a natural resource for use include site preparation costs, costs associated with building access roads, and construction costs incurred in building mine shafts, rigging platforms, etc.

On financial statements, costs associated with unextracted natural resources are considered to be noncurrent assets. Costs associated with extracted natural resources that have yet to be sold by a company are shown as inventory on the balance sheet. When the extracted natural resources are sold, the related costs are taken out of inventory and shown as expenses on the income statement.

The costs associated with unextracted natural resources are allocated to units of extracted natural resources through the process of depletion accounting. The depletion allocation is usually accomplished through the units of production depletion method. Under this method, the depletion cost associated with each unit of extracted natural resource is determined in the following way: cost of unextracted natural resource minus estimated residual value divided by estimated total units of recoverable natural resource equals the depletion cost per unit of extracted natural resource. In this formula, cost of unextracted natural resource should include all costs of the natural resource up to the date of the depletion cost computation. Estimated residual value of the natural resource is the estimated value of the natural resource property after production activity at the site has been permanently discontinued. For many natural resource sites, the residual value is nil. In other instances, land reclamation costs will be incurred by a company at a natural resource site after production has ceased. Governmental regulations may require a company to reclaim land that has been defaced through mining or other natural resource development activity. In these cases, the estimated additional costs that will be incurred by the company to reclaim land should be added to other costs in order to compute the depletion cost per extracted unit.

The estimated total units of recoverable natural resource figure included in determining depletion cost per unit would be developed through engineering studies. The units of recoverable natural resource are stated in tons, barrels, or ounces, or by the measurement method appropriate for the particular natural resource.

The estimated units of recoverable natural resource figure would include only the estimated units that will be extracted based on current or expected technology, current or expected future costs of development, and current or expected market prices for the natural resource. Units of the natural resource that will never be extracted based on current expectations should not be considered in computing the depletion cost per unit of natural resource.

Component parts of the depletion cost per extracted unit computation should be updated when new information becomes available or assumptions are changed. All changes in assumptions and estimates regarding a natural resource are used in accounting for the natural resource in the present and in the future. Changed assumptions are never used as a basis for making retroactive adjustments to the accounting records of the company.

The depletion charge per unit of natural resource is a cost of production associated with each extracted unit of natural resource. Other production costs include materials, labor, supplies, etc. All production costs associated with extracting natural resources from the earth are allocated to the extracted units of the natural resource. These extracted units are accounted for as inventory until the units are sold by the company. At that time, the costs associated with the natural resource units that are sold would be shown as an expense on the income statement in the category of cost of natural resources sold.

Equipment used on a natural resource site to extract natural resources from the earth should be depreciated over the estimated useful life of the equipment or over the estimated productive life of the natural resource, depending on the circumstances. If the estimated useful life of the equipment, such as mining rigs, is shorter than the productive life of the natural resource, the equipment is depreciated over its estimated useful life using any appropriate depreciation method (straight line, declining balance, etc.). If the estimated useful life of the equipment is longer than the productive life of the natural resource, and the equipment can be economically moved to another natural resource site, then the equipment should still be depreciated over its estimated useful life using an appropriate depreciation method. If the estimated useful life of the equipment is longer than the productive life of the natural resource, and the equipment cannot be economically moved to another natural resource site, then the equipment should be depreciated over the productive life of the natural resource. In this situation, the units of production depreciation method is often used as an appropriate depreciation method, since it would correlate depreciation recorded with units produced.

LARRY KREISER

derivatives   Financial derivatives are secondary financial instruments that are derived from underlying assets such as shares, bonds, commodities, and foreign currencies. Financial derivatives can be classified into four generic types: (1) options, (2) futures, (3) swaps, and (4) forward rate agreements (FRAs). Although there are only four generic types, the variation within each derivative type is overwhelming. Through a process of combination and repackaging, new derivatives are spawned (Lee, 1995). A derivative instrument can be tagged to a primary instrument. Examples include debt with detachable warrants or convertible bonds, wherein equity options are linked to debt instruments. Derivatives are also created through regrouping or repackaging rights of existing instruments. An example of this is the collateralized mortgage obligations (CMOs) that combine mortgages into a pool and repackage them into tranches in accordance with certain common characteristics such as interest rates, tenure, prepayment sensitivities, and final maturities.

The concept of the financial derivative is not new. Casserley & Wilson (1994) cited an early reference to a call option in Aristotle's writings. The first futures market started in Chicago in the 1800s. For several decades, farmers and agricultural traders have relied on forwards and futures to protect them from the volatility of the commodities markets.

In spite of their early entrance to the financial markets, derivatives became a force to be reckoned with only in the last decade or so.

Deregulation of currency and interest rates brought about increased volatility in financial markets and created a demand for financial instruments that enable firms to manage or even exploit those risks. Derivatives have since shed their quiet image and no longer play second fiddle to the primary instruments from which they are derived.

A financial derivative is a two-edged sword. On the one hand, companies can use derivatives to protect themselves from price and interest rate fluctuations by taking on an equal and opposite position to that of an underlying exposure. In entering a derivative contract, exposed companies are effectively transferring their risk to their counterparties. Prudent companies will thus benefit from derivatives in this manner and corporate earnings can be protected to some extent from volatility of price and interest rate changes.

Alternatively, companies can use derivatives to speculate with the intention of making profits. In such situations, derivatives do not neutralize any existing exposures but instead create new exposures for the companies concerned. Speculative use of derivatives increases the risks of contracting companies and for financial markets as a whole.

Highly publicized derivative-related losses of staggering proportions have sounded the alarm bells for corporations, banks, and regulators. The phenomenal losses from Nikkei Index futures trading caused the collapse of Barings, one of the UK's most established merchant banks. Other cases included the US$1.5 billion loss suffered by Japan's Kashima Oil resulting from the trading of foreign derivatives, the loss of US$1.5 billion on oil futures trading by Metallgesellschaft, a German industrial giant, and the loss of US$157 million by Procter & Gamble on leveraged swaps with Bankers Trust (Coonan & Dunne, 1994). Companies in developing economies are not spared from derivative-related losses. A Malaysian listed company, Berjaya Industrial Bhd, and Indonesia's conglomerate Sinar Mas were reported to have suffered losses of US$14 million and US$47.5 million respectively from derivative deals (*Singapore Business Times*, December 29, 1994).

Financial derivatives have attracted the attention of banking and securities exchange regulators across the globe. Regulators are concerned that the unrestrained use of derivatives might lead to runaway volatility and performance failures in financial markets. In July 1994, a key international panel of banking regulators issued guidelines on managing risk in derivatives. A 19-page report by the Basel Committee on Banking Supervision puts the burden on institutions to tighten internal controls on derivatives. The Committee that is comprised of senior executives of bank regulators and central banks in the USA, Canada, Japan, and Europe urges dealers and investors to observe basic principles of good risk management that include supervision by boards of directors and management, continuous monitoring of risk, and comprehensive internal controls and audit procedures. The Basel Report was issued alongside a similar report prepared by the International Organisations of Securities Commissions (*Singapore Business Times*, July 28, 1994).

As "control" is the operative word in the reports issued by the two major policy-making bodies mentioned above, there is a pressing demand to ensure proper accounting and timely disclosure of derivatives for both internal and external purposes. The provision of timely information on derivatives to external financial statement users is important to ensure that well-informed assessments of corporate risks can be made.

Professional Accounting Standards

Development of authoritative accounting standards for derivatives is still in its nascent years. Specific accounting standards that are issued to deal with derivatives in particular are rare. Any effort to regulate the accounting for derivatives is subsumed in a larger effort to regulate accounting for financial instruments as a whole.

Two major efforts to regulate the accounting for derivatives are the financial instruments project of the Financial Accounting Standards Board (FASB) in the USA and a similar project carried out by the International Accounting Standards Committee (IASC). The IASC represents professional accounting agencies worldwide. The FASB chose to carry out its financial instruments project by phases. So far, it has focused on improving disclosure of information on financial instruments. Statement of Financial Accounting Standard (SFAS) No.

105, "*Disclosure of Information about Financial Instruments with Off-Balance Sheet Risk and Financial Instruments with Concentrations of Credit Risk,*" which became effective from 1990, requires disclosure of financial instruments with off balance sheet risk and credit risk. SFAS No. 107, "Disclosures about Fair Value of Financial Instruments" was issued in 1991, and requires firms to disclose market values of all financial instruments, regardless of whether these instruments are on balance sheet or off-balance sheet items.

Unlike the FASB that broke its financial instruments project up into constituent standards, the IASC, working with the Canadian Institute of Chartered Accountants, tackled its financial instruments project by means of one comprehensive accounting standard. It issued Exposure Draft 48 (E48) on "Financial Instruments" in January 1994. The approach in E48 is to provide a conceptual framework that guides accountants and managers in their decisions relating to the recognition, measurement, and disclosures of financial instruments. It provides some illustrations with respect to specific financial instruments in an appendix. As its thrust is one of establishing principles as opposed to prescribing detailed procedures, there is a fair amount of judgment involved in the application of E48.

Characteristics and Implications for Financial Reporting

Since derivatives endow their owners with rights to underlying financial assets, the main accounting question pertains to the timing and manner in which these rights and their attendant obligations, as well as the gains or losses arising therefrom, are recognized in the financial statements of derivative holders. Derivatives have frequently been accounted for as off balance sheet financing and disclosure of their existence in financial statements is voluntary. Because the instruments are hived off the balance sheet, the magnitude of losses and the extent of total commitments are not revealed until maturity date, giving rise to the fear that companies may be sitting on undisclosed "time bombs" that can wipe out their assets and reserves.

There is also confusion as to whether a derivative is an asset in its own right or merely a commitment that leads to a "real" asset. If it is indeed true that a derivative is not an asset (or a liability), no recognition need be made in the financial statements prior to realization or maturity date. It is thus important to establish the principles that determine a financial asset or a financial liability.

Derivatives as off balance sheet items? Financial derivatives are often seen as off balance sheet financial instruments because of their executory nature. Performance of a derivative contract is at some future date when the unconditional right to an underlying asset is exercised. This characteristic makes the derivative an attractive form of leveraged investment since the initial outlay is only a fraction of the purchase price of the actual asset. There is also the commonly-held perception that off balance sheet financing improves solvency ratios by hiving financial liabilities off the balance sheet. Traditionally, executory contracts are not recognized in the financial statements at inception date. However, the case of finance leases has set a precedent for the recognition of executory contracts even though they are partially or wholly unperformed (Lee, 1995).

Although derivative contracts are executory in nature, the International Accounting Standards Committee's Exposure Draft 48 (E48) deems them to be financial assets. According to E48, a financial asset includes a contractual right to receive cash or another financial asset from another enterprise. Thus, following the guidelines of E48, the right that a derivative holder has to an underlying asset is a benefit to the holder and has an economic value which should be recognized at inception date. The common perception of derivatives as being "off balance sheet" instruments is therefore not supported by E48. Conversely, a derivative holder is exposed to a financial liability that is defined by E48 as a contractual obligation to exchange financial instruments with another enterprise under conditions that are potentially unfavorable.

So, as to the nature of derivatives – it can be said that they are financial assets and liabilities in their own right and are on balance sheet and not off balance sheet items. As to the timing of their recognition, E48 provides two overriding criteria:

(1) substantially all of the risks and rewards associated with the asset or liability must be transferred to the reporting enterprise; and
(2) the cost or fair value of the asset to the enterprise or the amount of the obligation

Table 1: Measurement standards of E48

Classification of financial instruments	Benchmark measurement standard	Alternative measurement standard
Instruments held to maturity or for the long term		
(1) Where the instrument is to be settled through scheduled payments of fixed or determinable amounts	(1) Value of scheduled future payments and/or receipts discounted at an initially recognized effective rate of interest	(1) Fair value
(2) Others	(2) Cost, less provision of impairment	(2) Fair value
Hedging instrument	Same basis as that used for measuring underlying exposure	Fair value
Purposes other than hedging or investment	Fair value	Fair value

Source: International Accounting Standards Committee, Exposure Draft 48, 1994

assumed must be capable of being measured reliably.

As most derivatives are contractual in nature, there is no doubt that risks and rewards transfer to the contracting enterprise on the date of the derivative contract. As to the second criterion, the cost of the derivative is objectively determined by way of any premiums paid on the derivative. The fair value of the derivative is more difficult, but not impossible, to determine. In most cases, there would not be any significant problems that would prevent the recognition of derivatives in the financial statements.

Presentation of derivatives in the balance sheet
If derivative instruments are on-balance sheet items, at what amounts and on what bases should they be carried in the balance sheet? Only the rights and obligations inherent in derivatives are to be recognized and not those of the underlying assets that are to be exchanged at maturity. A case in point is the stock option whose value, while dependent in part on the value of the underlying stock, is different from that of the underlying stock.

Another issue to consider is the manner in which financial derivatives should be presented in the balance sheet. In the case of futures, swaps, and forward rate agreements (FRAs), derivative instruments vest in their owners both contractual rights to future assets and the attendant contractual obligations. Where there is a legally enforceable right of set-off, the financial asset and the financial liability can be offset against each other and only the net amount need be shown in the balance sheet.

The case of an option is more complicated in view of its one-sided risk-reward attribute. The payment of the option premium endows the holder with a contractual right to an underlying asset. The holder does not, however, have the obligation to exercise the right if the conditions are unfavorable to him/her. Similarly, the option writer has a clearly established obligation to exchange the underlying asset under conditions that are potentially unfavorable to him/her but does not have a clearly established right to receive future benefits. The option holder will show a financial asset in the balance sheet, while the writer will show a financial liability.

Hedging versus speculative derivative contracts
The measurement of derivatives is complicated by the fact that in various reporting regimes there is more than one basis of measuring an instrument (e.g., at historical cost or at fair value). The measurement of a derivative depends on whether it is a hedge of an underlying exposure or whether it is entered into for speculative reasons. The test for a hedge in International Accounting Standards Committee Exposure Draft 48 (E48) is three-pronged:

(1) the underlying exposure can be specifically identified (e.g., a foreign currency payable);

(2) the derivative contract is specifically entered into to hedge the underlying exposure (e.g., a foreign currency forward purchase contract is taken up to hedge a foreign currency payable); and

(3) the derivative is an effective hedge, i.e., it is highly probable that value changes in the derivative have a high correlation with negative value changes in the underlying exposure (e.g., an increase in foreign currency payable arising from an exchange rate change is offset by an increase to the foreign currency amount to which the derivative holder is contractually entitled).

The determination of whether a derivative is a hedging instrument or not is understandably subjective. Other difficulties exist and these are discussed by Lee & Tan (1994). Complications include the level at which hedge effectiveness is determined (i.e., enterprise, divisional, or transaction level) and the special situations involving partial and rollover hedges and the hedge of anticipated transactions.

The measurement principles governing derivative instruments are:

(1) Derivatives that qualify as hedge instruments are to be measured on the same basis as the underlying exposure. The basis would be typically one of these – historical cost, fair value, lower of cost and market value or present value of future cash flows. Where a derivative contract is entered into for speculation, they should be always carried at fair value or "marked-to-market."

(2) Gains or losses from a hedge instrument are to be accounted for in a manner that is symmetrical to the treatment of gains or

Table 2

Date	Floating rate	Floating rate receipt	Fixed rate payment	Net receipt/(payment)
31.12.1994	7.0% p.a.	$350,000 (receivable)	$375,000 (payable)	$(25,000) (net swap amount payable)
30.6.1995	8.0% p.a.	$400,000	$375,000	$25,000 (net cash receipt)
31.12.1995	9.0% p.a.	$450,000 (receivable)	$375,000 (payable)	$75,000 (net swap amount receivable)

The effects of the above swap arrangement will be reflected in Company A's financial statements as follows:

Company A
Income statement for the year ended 31 December 1994 (an extract)

Interest expense	$350,000
Net swap payment	$25,000
Financing Cost	$375,000

Balance sheet as at 31 December 1994 (an extract)
Liabilities

Net swap amount payable	$25,000

Company A
Income statement for the year ended 31 December 1995 (an extract)

Interest expense	$850,000
Net swap received	$(100,000)
Financing cost	$750,000

losses arising from the underlying exposure. Gains or losses from hedging derivatives may be deferred to future periods if the underlying exposure relates to a future transaction. Gains or losses from speculative derivatives on the other hand are one-sided and are always accounted for in the income statement in the year in which the gains or losses arise.

Table 1 summarizes the relatively complex measurement rules of E48.

Disclosure
The perception that derivatives are off balance sheet items could be dangerous if it leads companies to believe that information about derivatives need not be disclosed until such time when they mature or are realised. Without mandatory disclosures, a derivative is aptly

described as the invisible "iceberg" or "time bomb," which may reveal itself under horrifying circumstances to the unsuspecting investor.

Given the rapid rate at which new financial instruments are spawned and their increasing complexity, it is not surprising that standard setters around the globe are placing so much emphasis on disclosures of derivatives. The first accounting standards that arose from the US Financial Accounting Standards Board (FASB) financial instruments project dealt with disclosures. Disclosure is also an important elements in the International Accounting Standards Committee's IASC's Exposure Draft 48 (E48), in which the following types of disclosures must accompany financial statement recognition of derivatives:

(1) *General disclosures.* These include the extent and nature of the financial instruments,

whether recognized or unrecognized, including significant terms and conditions that may affect the amount, timing, and uncertainty of future cash flows; and the accounting policies and methods adopted in recognizing, measuring, and presenting the instruments.

(2) *Disclosures concerning interest rate risk.* These include interest rate risk, including contractual repricing or maturity dates and effective interest rates.

(3) *Disclosures concerning credit risk.* Disclosures should include information on maximum credit risk exposure, without taking account of the fair value of any collateral, the enterprise's policy with respect to obtaining collateral, and significant concentrations of credit risk.

(4) *Disclosures concerning fair value.* If this information is not practicably determinable, this fact should be disclosed, together with information that is pertinent to the instrument's fair value.

Example Interest Rate Swaps

Company A has floating rate obligations totaling $10 million and wants to hedge its interest rate risk by entering into an interest rate swap arrangement with Company B on 30 June 1994. Under the arrangement, Company A will pay a fixed interest rate of 7.5 percent per annum on a notional principal of $10 million to Company B over a two-year period in exchange for receipt of floating rate interest, based on prime lending rate. Floating rate receipt is to be exchanged with fixed rate payment annually on 30 June.

As the swap was entered into for hedging purposes, the interest will be accrued for in the basis of time in the same manner as the interest expense on the underlying exposure. Company A's financial year-end is 31 December. The information in Table 2 is relevant.

The above illustration shows that the swap acts as a hedge for the exposed floating rate obligations. The swap effectively transforms the floating rate interest streams into one which is fixed at 7.5 percent p.a.

If the company enters into a swap deal in anticipation of making profits from rising interest rates (and not for purposes of hedging), the swap should be revalued at the end of each year and the gain or loss on revaluation

recognized in income statement. This treatment is in keeping with the International Accounting Standards Committee's Exposure Draft 48 (E48) which requires financial instruments to be stated at fair values in non-hedging situations.

Bibliography

Associated Press and Reuters (1994). Global panel issues Guidelines on Managing Risk in Derivatives. *Singapore Business Times.* 28 July.

Balan, A. (1994). Berjaya Industrial denies Liability for Derivatives Loss. *Singapore Business Times.* 29 December.

Casserly, D. & Wilson, G. (1994). Demystifying derivatives. *Bank Management*, May/June, 40–7.

Coonan, C. & Dunne, M. (1994). Derivatives: The banking time-bomb. *Business & Finance*, November, 11–14.

Lee, P. (1995). Accounting for Financial Instruments: An Overview of Issues and Standards Development.Pang Yang Hoong (ed.) *Contemporary Issues in Accounting.* Addison-Wesley.

Lee, P. & Tan, P. (1994). Hedge accounting: An evaluation and illustration of the guidelines of Exposure Draft 48. *Accounting and Business Review*, 1–2, 357–90.

Stewart, J. E. (1989). The challenges of hedge accounting. *Journal of Accountancy*, **168**, 6, 42–6.

PEARL TAN and PETER LEE

discontinued operations Discontinued operations involves the disposition of a major segment of a business through sale or abandonment. A segment consists of a major line of business, a major class of customer, or a subsidiary. To qualify for accounting purposes as a discontinued operation, the assets and related activities of the segment must be clearly distinguishable from other assets of the company, both physically and operationally. For example, closing down one of three plants making the same product, eliminating part of a business line, or shifting management functions from one location to another would not qualify as a discontinued operations. The management of a company may decide to dispose of a business segment because of profitability, geographic location, need for funds, and strategic issues such as avoiding a takeover.

Since management's decision to dispose of a business segment is a significant financial decision, information about this discontinued operation is explicitly presented to readers of the financial statements. The financial results of discontinued operations are disclosed on the income statement, net of tax, after income from continual operations, and a footnote disclosing the event is included in the financial statements.

Reporting   Requirements   for   Discontinued Operations

US Accounting Principles Board (APB) Opinion No. 30 (1973), "Reporting the Results of Operations," discusses the reporting of discontinued operations. This Opinion requires that discontinued operations be presented on the financial statements as a below the line item (below income from continuing operations) preceding extraordinary gains and losses.

Like extraordinary items and other below the line items, discontinued operations are shown net of tax. If the discontinued item is a gain, it is reduced by the tax on the gain. If the item is a loss, it is deductible against other income for tax purposes and its existence saves income taxes.

The gain or loss resulting from the discontinued operations are presented on the income statement in two categories. These categories are (1) the current year income/loss from operating the discontinued segment, and (2) disclosure of the gain or loss on the actual disposal of the business segment.

APB 30 also provides guidelines to determine what amounts are recorded as (1) gain/loss from operations of a discontinued business segment versus (2) gain/loss on disposal of the business segment. To arrive at these two amounts, a company decides on a particular date (measurement date) to dispose of a business segment, but realizes a phase-out period between that date and the date the segment is actually sold (disposal date). The gain or loss on disposal includes any income or loss from operating the segment during the phase-out period.

For example, assume a company decided on July 1, 19x6 to phase out a segment of its operation. This date is the measurement date and marks the beginning of the phase-out period. Now assume the segment is disposed of on November 15, 19x6. All operating gains or losses before July 1, 19x6 would be reported as a gain/loss on discontinued *operations*, and this gain/loss would be reported net of tax. Then, all operating gains or losses from July 1, 19x6 until November 15, 19x6 (the actual disposal date) are included with gains and losses on the *disposal* of the assets associated with this business segment.

The scenario presented above considers the most basic possibility for accounting for discontinued operations since all of the events relating to the disposal occurred within one accounting year. That is, the decision to dispose of the business segment as well as the actual disposal of the business segment occurred in the same year. In reality, the phase-out period can often extends several years beyond the measurement date, or the date that management decides to discontinue the operation.

Referring to phase-out periods that extend beyond one reporting year, APB 30 states that if a loss is expected on disposal, the estimated loss should be reported in the current period's financial statements. If a gain on disposal is expected, it should be recognized when realized, which is ordinarily the disposal date.

For example, in September 1991, Winnebago decided to discontinue its commercial vehicle division after its fiscal year (ending August 31, 1991), but before it issued its 1991 financial statements. Thus, management decided to show the discontinued operations of this division on the 1991 financial statements to provide more information to the user. Winnebago incurred a loss (net of tax) in fiscal year 1991 of $4,992,000 from operating the commercial vehicle division. For the phase-out period, which was expected be completed in the 1992 fiscal year, Winnebago estimated operating losses of $1,042,000 and a loss on disposal of division assets of $7,076,000. Therefore, the total loss on disposal was $1,042,000+$7,076,000 = $8,118,000.

Another requirement of APB 30 is that the prior year income statements be presented in a comparable manner if presented with current year financial statements. To accomplish this objective, management must revise prior year income statements by removing all revenues, expenses, gains, and losses from continuing operations (those accounts above income from continuing operations) and summarize them below the line net of tax.

In the Winnebago income statement, a loss is shown from discontinued commercial vehicles division operations for 1990 and 1989 of $3,269,000 and $1,497,000 respectively. To arrive at these figures, Winnebago has removed prior year revenues, expenses, gains, losses, and taxes related to the discontinued operation from related components of continuing operations and has aggregated this accounting data below the line. This aggregated data is then presented under the heading gain/(loss) from operations of discontinued segment to make the financial statements comparable with the current year. This comparability adds to the usefulness of the income statement as now a user could examine the statement and notice that the discontinued segment realized a loss in the two previous years. Now, a financial statement user could review the three years' worth of financial figures relating only to operations that will be continuing in the future. The user can then evaluate whether or not to invest in Winnebago based only on its continuing operations.

In addition to this financial disclosure on the income statement, APB 30 requires a footnote explaining discontinued operations. This footnote should contain the following:

(1) The business segment being discontinued.
(2) Description of assets and liabilities relating to the disposed segment that have not yet been disposed of at the balance-sheet date.
(3) Expected disposal date and method of disposal.
(4) The income/loss from operations that occurred between the measurement date and the balance-sheet date.

These components as well as the estimated loss on disposal for the time up until and including the phase-out period are to be included.

JAMES D. STICE

E

earnings forecasts

The Time Series Properties of Earnings

Research has shown that annual earnings numbers are well described by a random walk with drift process, meaning that next year's annual earnings are expected to equal this year's annual earnings plus a trend. However, there are ways to improve the accuracy of the expected annual earnings number by using publicly available data other than past annual earnings, such as past values of the firm's quarterly earnings, its stock price, or its book rate of return.

Corporations' quarterly earnings numbers are well described by a seasonal random walk with drift process, meaning that a particular quarter's earnings number (e.g., *second quarter* of 1996) is expected to equal the most recent earnings number reported for that particular quarter (i.e., the *second quarter* of 1995) plus a trend. There are ways to improve the accuracy of the expected quarterly earnings number by exploiting other information in the quarterly earnings time series, such as autoregressive and moving average terms. Moreover, for the approximately 15 percent of firms which are not in a seasonal business, a model which uses a seasonal factor is inappropriate. For these firms, the next quarter's earnings number can be modeled as this quarter's earnings number plus a trend.

Analysts' Earnings Forecasts

Analysts' earnings forecasts generally are more accurate than forecasts generated by time series models. A principal reason for this is that analysts have both a timing advantage and a contemporaneous information advantage. Their timing advantage is due to the fact that a time series model makes a forecast only once a quarter, because it lacks access to information other than quarterly earnings that become available between consecutive earnings announcements. In contrast, analysts continually update their forecasts when new information arrives. The principal sources of their contemporaneous information advantage are managers, published financial information, macroeconomic data, and industry statistics.

Analysts' earnings forecasts often are managers' earnings forecasts in disguise. Managers are reluctant to make their earnings forecasts publicly available to investors because they do not want to bear the potentially large legal costs of providing forecasts that, ex post, are quite inaccurate.

The evidence is mixed regarding whether or not stock prices are better described as being based on analysts' earnings forecasts than on forecasts of time series models. There also is evidence that a composite earnings forecast based on both analysts' and time series model predictions yields a higher association of "earnings surprises" with stock price movements than is obtained by using either analysts or time series model forecasts individually. The last result suggests that the stock market incorporates forecasts by both analysts and time series models, and that analysts ignore information embedded in the earnings time series.

Improving the Accuracy of Analysts' Earnings Forecasts

It has been shown that analysts ignore information in the earnings time series and in stock prices. Thus, the way to improve forecast accuracy is to combine analysts' forecasts with earnings time series and stock prices. Additionally, there is evidence that analysts can improve forecast accuracy by combining analysts' forecasts with other information from financial statements.

Bias in Analysts' Earnings Forecasts

Analysts generally are overly optimistic in predicting earnings in that they expect earnings to exceed those that are subsequently reported. There is evidence that some of the analysts' optimistic bias is unintentional, attributable to human nature rather than a deliberate attempt to mislead investors. However, analysts are overly pessimistic for some firms, overly optimistic for most others, and their degree of pessimism or optimism persists over time. Thus, the bias in their forecasts appears to be systematic, not random.

The evidence regarding whether there are differences in analyst forecast ability is mixed.

Dispersion Among Analysts In Their Earnings Forecasts

Dispersion among analysts in their earnings forecasts has often been used to proxy for the precision of investors' earnings estimates (Ajinkya & Gift, 1985). It has been shown that, in general, earnings announcements reduce the dispersion among analysts in their forecasts of future earnings, hence increasing the precision of their estimates. However, when "earnings surprises" are very large, the dispersion among analysts' forecasts actually increases, thus reducing the precision of investors' estimates of future earnings.

Managers' Earnings Forecasts

Managers' own published forecasts generally are more accurate than forecasts by analysts (Patell, 1976). There are at least three reasons for this phenomenon. First, managers choose when to make forecasts. Thus, they are more likely to make forecasts when they are confident of the forecast's accuracy. Second, managers have access to private information regarding the firm and possibly the industry which is unavailable to analysts. This asymmetric information is likely to improve the accuracy of managers' forecasts. Third, managers are able to manipulate earnings within generally accepted accounting principles (GAAP). Thus, they have the ability to "create" an actual earnings number that conforms to their predictions. Moreover, they are more likely to "create" the numbers

when they have difficulty attaining the numbers they forecast.

The stock market typically reacts to managers' earnings forecasts, and the direction of the stock price reaction depends upon whether the forecast is greater or less than the market's expectation. Using analysts' earnings forecasts to proxy for the unobservable market expectation, it has been shown that stock prices typically rise if the manager's forecast exceeds the consensus of analysts' expectations. In contrast, if the manager's forecast falls short of the consensus analyst expectation, the stock price typically drops. If the manager's forecast equals the consensus analyst expectation, the stock price generally rises slightly if the managers' forecasts are considered to be more precise than the analysts' forecasts.

LAWRENCE D. BROWN

earnings per share   Earnings per share (EPS) is widely used by analysts and investors to assess the profitability of firms, and changes in firm profitability, over time. EPS statistics are widely published in financial statements and frequently quoted in the financial press. However, as a summary measure of firm performance, EPS is subject to some important limitations.

EPS is a ratio of earnings available to common shareholders (after claims of preferred stocks) divided by the weighted average number of shares of common stock outstanding for the period. The EPS denominator uses shares outstanding on a weighted average basis for the year. EPS calculated in this way is called *basic* EPS.

EPS calculations are more complex for firms that have significant amounts of outstanding convertible securities, warrants, options, or other agreements by which common shares are contingently issuable – the *complex capital structure* firms. The holders of these complex capital structure securities have the opportunity to convert or exercise an option to obtain common stock. If such conversion or exercise occurs, there is the potential to dilute the ownership interest of the previously outstanding common stock. Accounting policy-makers have decided that it is important to reflect the effects of potential dilution in EPS calculations. For complex capital structure firms, two EPS numbers must be reported: (1) *primary EPS*, which reflects dilution for some potentially dilutive securities, called common stock equivalents, and (2) *fully-diluted EPS*, which reflects dilution from all potentially dilutive securities.

This, however, has created some problems. In the first place, for complex capital structure firms, there is no reported EPS statistic that is comparable to basic EPS for simple capital structure firms. Secondly, the US standard is not compatible with international standards.

The international standards require reporting of: (1) basic EPS for simple capital structure firms, and (2) basic EPS *and* diluted EPS for complex capital structure firms, where diluted EPS reflects maximum potential dilution. The following example illustrates the calculation of basic and fully diluted EPS for a typical firm:

Example company: Earnings per share calculations

Assumptions:

Net income	$2,000,000
Preferred stock dividend	$320,000

Common stock options outstanding:
  300,000 options to purchase 1 share each at $12 per share

Common shares outstanding:

January 1	800,000
Additional shares issued on July 1	400,000

Convertible debt, 6%, $1,000,000 face amount, convertible into 100,000 shares

Convertible preferred stock, 8%, $4,000,000 face amount, convertible into 250,000 shares

Average market price of common stock	$15 per share
Income tax rate,	40%

Calculation of basic EPS:

Basic EPS = (net income − preferred dividends)
            / weighted average common shares
Numerator = $2,000,000 − $320,000
          = $1,680,000
          = net income available for common shareholders
Denominator = 0.5(800,000) + 0.5(1,200,000)
            = 1,000,000
            = weighted Average common shares outstanding for the year
Basic EPS = $1,680,000/1,000,000 = $1.68
Calculation of diluted EPS:

The diluted calculation starts with basic EPS and then adjusts both the numerator and the denominator for the assumed conversion or exercise of dilutive securities. Results are summarized and explained in table 1.

Treatment of stock options. (a) Stock options are assumed to be dilutive if the option price, in this case $12, is less than the average market price of the common stock, in this case $15. A "treasury stock" method is used, which assumes that expected proceeds from exercising options will be used to buy back for the company common shares (treasury stock) at the average

Table 1:   Diluted calculation of EPS

	Income (numerator)	Shares (demoninator)	Per share amount
Net income	$2,000,000		
Preferred dividend	(320,000)		
Basic EPS	$1,680,000	1,000,000	$1.68
Stock options		60,000 (a)	
Convertible debt	36,000 (b)	100,000 (b)	
Convertible preferred stock	320,000 (c)	250,000 (c)	
Fully diluted EPS	$2,036,000	1,410,000	$1.44

common stock price. In this example, the proceeds from the exercise of 300,000 options at $12 is $3,600,000. At a market price of $15, the proceeds could repurchase 240,000 shares of common stock, so the incremental shares outstanding would be 60,000 (300,000–240,000).

Treatment of convertible debt. (b) Convertible debt is handled using the "if converted" method. If the convertible debt were converted into common stock, interest, on an after-tax basis, would no longer be paid, and net income would be higher. However, additional shares of stock then would be outstanding.

In this example, interest on the convertible debt is 6% x $1,000,000, or $60,000. However, the tax rate is 40%, so, on an after-tax basis, the interest savings is $60,0001.4 = $36,000. The assumed increase in net income is offset by the additional 100,000 shares of common stock outstanding if conversion occurs.

Treatment of convertible preferred stock.   (c) The "if converted" method also is used for convertible preferred stock. In this case, if conversion occurs, the preferred dividends would no longer be paid. They need to be added back (reverse the deduction in the basic EPS calculation) to reflect additional income that would be available for common shareholders. Here, this additional income is offset by the additional 250,000 shares of common stock that would be outstanding if conversion occurred.

Disclosure

EPS disclosures usually are required as part of the overall income statement disclosures. Per share disclosures for income from continuing operations and net income are required on the face of the income statement and per share disclosures for other income statement components such as discontinued operations, extraordinary items, and cumulative effect accounting changes are found in footnotes.

The Uses of EPS

Although it is difficult to capture the performance of the firm in a single number, EPS frequently is used for that purpose. From the investor's standpoint, the firm's earnings performance is related to the share(s) of stock that

he/she owns. Further, changes in EPS reflect changes in earnings performance.

An additional advantage of EPS is the ease of relating it to the market price of stock using a price/EPS (P/E) ratio. P/E ratios are summary measures of the market's assessment of earning power for different firms. To the extent that earnings prospects differ among firms, so too should their P/E ratios differ. There is widespread evidence of such cross-sectional diversity in firm P/E ratios. At least three factors are hypothesized to explain differences in P/E ratios across firms – growth rate differences, risk differences, and differences in accounting methods.

High-growth firms tend to have high P/E ratios. For high-growth firms, share price will depend greatly on expected higher future earnings, and price will be high relative to current earnings. At various times P/E ratios may be as high as 25, 40, or even higher for expected high growth rate firms. For low growth rate firms, P/E ratios may be in the more modest range of 8 to 10. In addition, risk differences and accounting method differences should explain part of the P/E diversity across firms.

Limitations of EPS

As a measure of firm profitability, EPS has some important limitations. First, profitability in general should be measured relative to the amount of investment that generated the profit. For example, return on assets (ROA) = net income/total assets measures profitability relative to the asset base of the firm. The shares denominator of EPS is a poor proxy for shareholder investment. Further, EPS is not comparable across firms. Firms with the same capital would report different EPS merely for having issued different numbers of shares.

EPS has the additional limitation that it is subject to management manipulation. For example, if earnings is not expected to be as high as management desires, EPS can be increased by repurchasing common shares and reducing the EPS denominator. Finally, like all performance measures based on earnings, the quality of EPS is subject to the quality of the earnings number itself. To the extent the accounting methods and estimates used to estimate earnings are misleading, so too will the EPS measure be misleading.

THOMAS J. FRECKA

environmental accounting and reporting
Industrial pollution has long been recognized as the classic example of a production externality, where the production function of a firm is affected directly by the actions of another agent. The existence of externalities directly leads to socially inefficient outcomes (Varian, 1984, p. 260). To counter this social inefficiency in the USA, regulations specifically limiting certain types of emissions have been promulgated by both the federal and state governments. The impetus for these regulations is twofold. First, improved technology has made it possible to more accurately monitor the release and adverse consequences of emissions into the air, water, and soil. Second, public pressure for responsible corporate environmental stewardship has led to political pressure for greater environmental regulation.

The costs of compliance with environmental laws, as well as the costs of pollution prevention, are considerable. Sikich (1991) reports that the environmental expenditures of the utilities industry in the USA are an average of $340 million (6.1 percent of revenue), $430 million annually (1.9 percent of revenue) for the oil industry, and $56 million annually (1.3 percent of revenue) for the chemical industry. However, a 1992 Price Waterhouse survey indicates that 62 percent of their industrial respondents carry unrecorded potential environmental liabilities (Surma, 1992).

As environmental costs become more significant, disclosure standards are beginning to emerge. Mandatory guidelines have been promulgated through federal institutions such as the Securities and Exchange Commission (SEC) and the Environmental Protection Agency (EPA), as well the Financial Accounting Standards Board (FASB), and many state agencies. In addition, the Institute of Management Accountants (IMA), the Global Environmental Management Institute (GEMI), and the Chemical Manufacturers Association have implemented or are in the process of implementing voluntary guidelines for the measure-

ment and reporting of environmental performance.

FASB Standards

To date, the FASB has provided little direction for corporate disclosure of environmental issues. The only rules addressing environmental disclosure deal with the issues of contingent liabilities, and whether outlays for environmental costs should be capitalized or expensed:

Contingent liabilities. Rules for accounting for contingencies are contained in FASB Statement No. 5, "Accounting for Contingencies" (SFAS 5). According to SFAS 5, loss contingencies should be recognized as losses if (1) it is probable that a liability has been incurred or an asset impaired, and (2) the amount of the liability or the impairment can be reasonably estimated. With regard to the measurement of contingent losses, FASB Interpretation No. 14, "Reasonable Estimation of the Amount of a Loss," states that when the reasonable estimate of a loss is a range and no amount within the range is a better estimate than another, the minimum amount should be accrued. Issue No. 93–5, "Accounting for Environmental Liabilities" states that environmental liabilities should be determined independent of potential claims for recovery. Potential claims should reduce the amount of the liability only when the claim is probable of realization. Furthermore, discounting environmental liabilities for a cleanup site is appropriate only if the cash flow parameters are fixed or reliably determinable.

Capitalization. The FASB's Emerging Issues Task Force (EITF) has released two Issue Statements on the treatment of costs incurred for environmental purposes. Issue No. 90–8, "Capitalization of Costs to Treat Environmental Contamination," primarily recommends expensing the cost of contamination treatment. However, capitalization is permitted if the costs: (1) extend the asset's life, increase its capacity, or improve its efficiency relative to the property's condition when originally constructed or acquired, (2) mitigate or prevent future contamination, or (3) are incurred in preparing the property for sale. Further, costs are capitalized to the extent of recoverability. Issue No. 89-13, "Accounting for the Cost of Asbestos Removal," recommends the capitalization of costs incurred to treat asbestos as long as they are experienced within a reasonable time frame after the acquisition of property with a known asbestos problem.

SEC Standards

While environmental reporting in corporate annual reports remains primarily voluntary, the SEC requires greater levels of disclosure in the annual filing with the SEC (Form 10-K and proxy statements). SEC disclosure requirements are intended to ensure that securities purchasers and sellers have access to vital information about a company's environmental liabilities:

Regulation S-K, Item 101 requires a general description of the business and specific disclosure of the effects that compliance with environmental laws may have on the capital expenditures, earnings, and competitive position, when material. The estimated amount disclosed for capital expenditures should represent the current and succeeding fiscal years and any future periods in which those expenditures may be material.

Regulation S-K, Item 103 requires disclosure of pending or contemplated administrative or judicial proceedings if: (1) such proceedings are material to the business or financial condition of the registrant, (2) such proceedings involve a claim which exceeds 10 percent of the registrant's current assets, or (3) a government authority is a party to such proceedings where sanctions will be greater than $100,000.

Regulation S-K Item 303 requires disclosure of material events and uncertainties known to management that would cause reported financial information to be unrepresentative of future operating results or financial conditions.

Staff Accounting Bulletin No. 92, "Accounting and Disclosures Relating to Loss Contingencies," addresses a number of issues. These include: (1) using a probable claim for recovery to offset a probable contingent liability in the financial statements (it generally cannot); (2) discounting environmental liabilities to their present value to reflect the time value of money (they may, if amounts and timing of cash flows are fixed or reliably determined, using an "arm's length" discount rate); (3) using estimates and assumptions in measuring environmental liability (costs should be estimated using currently

available costs and technologies); and (4) recognizing joint and several liability where there is a reasonable basis for apportioning cleanup costs among potentially responsible parties (a company may recognize only its fair share, unless it becomes probable that other potentially responsible parties will not fully pay their allocated share).

The SEC requirements have not been carried over into annual report disclosure. A Price Waterhouse survey found that SEC filings were the most popular forum for disclosure of potential or acknowledged environmental liabilities (Surma, 1992). This is probably due to the differential reporting requirements between the FASB and the SEC.

Research on Environmental Disclosure

The significance of environmental disclosure has been addressed in previous literature. In addition to surveys by stakeholder organizations, such as Price Waterhouse and the United Nations, the literature has addressed the relevance of environmental disclosure through both market studies and association studies.

Market studies: Disclosure and market reaction

There is evidence that the market uses environmental information in firm valuation. Belkaoui (1976) found that the market reacted differentially to firms that disclosed pollution control information than to those that did not. On the date of disclosure, the stock market performance was positively associated with pollution control expenditure disclosure. This advantage over market persisted for a period of four months after disclosure.

Anderson & Frankle (1980) examined the market reaction to firms making social disclosures, including investments in environmental controls. Those firms outperformed nondisclosing firms. Further analysis revealed that portfolios that disclosed social information for two contiguous years outperformed portfolios that disclosed social information only in one year.

Shane & Spicer (1983) investigated whether security price movements were associated with the release of company-specific pollution control performance information. This information was produced by the Council of Economic Priorities (CEP). The results indicated that the firms being reported upon had, on average, relatively large negative abnormal returns on the two days immediately prior to newspaper reports covering the release of the CEP report.

Several other studies have attempted relating firm performance to the disclosure of environmental information. The results, however, are mixed and vary by type of industry.

Bibliography

Belkaoui, A. (1976). The impact of the disclosure of the environmental effects of organizational behavior on the market. *Financial Management*, Winter, 26–31.

Sikich, G. W. (1991). Reducing environmental vulnerability. *New Accountant*, Mar., 8–10, 42.

Surma, J. (1992). A survey of how corporate America is accounting for environmental costs. *Understanding Environmental Accounting & Disclosure Today*, 85–94.

Varian, H. R. (1984). *Microeconomic analysis.* 2nd edn, New York: W. W. Norton.

DEVAUN KITE and DAVID SHIELDS

ethics in the accounting information system
Ethics is an important consideration in the development of accounting information systems. The policies and procedures for dealing with ethics-related issues are essential elements of any well-designed internal control system. This is true because breaches of ethics generate loss exposures that can result in severe penalties to both the officers of the company and the company itself. For example, A. H. Robbins was a large, successful company that failed in the face of a deluge of lawsuits relating to the safety of its IUD product. Some have argued that the managers of this company did not give enough attention to the ethical issues relating to marketing of an unsafe product, and that with a better focus on ethics the entire debacle could have been avoided.

The importance of ethical standards to accounting information systems was emphasized by the report of the Committee of Sponsoring Organizations (COSO) of the Treadway Commission. The committee stated that the internal control structure consists of five components: (1) the control environment, (2) the practice of risk assessment, (3) control activities, (4) information and communication, and (5) monitoring. Further, the COSO report stated that important to the control environment is management's demonstration of a strong commitment to ethical standards through words and actions. This commitment should include the implementation of a corporate code of conduct, as well as the means to monitor compliance with the prescribed ethical guidelines.

It should be emphasized, however, that corporate codes of conduct and related monitoring mechanisms are often legal-like documents that do little to affect employee behavior. Rather, the core problem that often must be addressed is the corporate culture. If the basic corporate culture is not conducive to ethical conduct, then even the best conduct codes and controls are likely to fail. Some warning signs of problems with the corporate culture are as follows:

(1) *Excessive internal focus.* A company that focuses too much internally and not enough on the outside world (customers and suppliers) is more likely to get into trouble. Examples of excessive internal focus would include overemphasis on sales quotas, making unreasonable deadlines, pleasing the boss, and so on. For example, if construction employees were told to either complete a building by a certain date or be fired, they might be tempted to cut corners and compromise safety.

(2) *Excessive short-run focus.* A company that focuses too much on the short run might be more inclined not to worry about the long-term consequences of its actions. In the case of Manville Company, the long-run health hazards of asbestos was overlooked to the point that it led the company into bankruptcy.

(3) *Morale problems.* Unhappy employees can be dangerous. One such case involved a disgruntled employee of a company that produced an accounting software package. The employee made changes to the software that scrambled up the records of those companies which used the accounting system.

(4) *Infighting and disarray.* These problems can lead to unpredictable behavior.

(5) *An excessively autocratic organizational structure.* Highly autocratic managers are relatively unlikely to accept criticism, and the employees of such managers may fear the consequences of pointing out ethics problems.

Studies have shown that it can take several years to completely change a company's corporate culture. The usual place to begin is with a cultural audit, which needs to be followed up with specific programs for education, training, and compliance monitoring. General Dynamics, for example, dealt with its problems in part through a series of educational and training seminars.

Good ethics education, training, and compliance are best achieved by giving these activities a formal place in the organization chart. Each division should have its own ethics director, and employees should be trained and encouraged on how to contact this person, not only for problems involving ethical violations but also for routine questions. Further, mechanisms (such as a hotline telephone number) should be in place to allow employees to anonymously or confidentially contact the ethics director.

Finally, the company needs to give special attention to certain high-risk issues such as safety, equal opportunity employment, sexual harassment, product and service quality, privacy, honesty in business dealings, conflicts of interest, and respect for intellectual property. For all these and other high-risk issues, the company must take a pro-active stance in avoiding problems. The internal auditor can also play an important role by monitoring the overall operation of the ethics control system. Weaknesses should be reported directly to the board of directors.

Bibliography

Bodnar, G. & Hopwood, W. S. (1995). *Accounting and Information Systems*. 6th edn, Englewood Cliffs: Prentice-Hall, Inc.

Committee of Sponsoring Organizations of the Treadway Commission (COSO) (1992). *Internal control–integrated framework*. Vols 1–4, Coopers & Lybrand.

Rezaee, Z. (1994). Implementing the COSO Report. *Management Accounting*, **76**, July, 35–37.

Robin, D. P. & Reidenbach, R. (1989). *Busines ethics*. Englewood Cliffs: Prentice-Hall.

WILLIAM S. HOPWOOD

F

financial accounting theory and research
Financial accounting has emerged in response to the need of managers to communicate to owners (principal) regarding whether the principal's capital entrusted to them is preserved intact, whether investment yielded income, and how much. This is the traditional role of an agent accounting to a principal, cloaked in modern attire.

But with multiplicity of participants in the market place and with increased specialization, owners of capital had to delegate the conduct of business to professional managers. It is this development that has made accounting a tool for guaranteeing that management fulfill its stewardship function toward stockholders: management accounts for how it safeguards and manages the owners' resources. Seen from this perspective, accounting is a monitoring mechanism either demanded by stockholders or volunteered by management to minimize diversion of resources to activities that do not serve the purpose of owners. An unresolved issue is whether the resulting accounting intelligence is socially optimal, but accounting has evolved to provide information for resource allocation in the economy – and consumption and investment decisions.

Nature of Accounting Theory and Its Environment

Unlike the finance discipline, we do not yet have anything approximating an accounting theory.

An accounting theory must accomplish two objectives: (1) describe, document, and explain accounting practices as an equilibrium phenomenon within a market with diverse constituencies; and (2) pave the way for the normative improvement upon what currently exists.

The fact that constituencies (investors, financial statement preparers, financial analysts, auditors, investment bankers) exert pressure on accounting rule-making bodies (e.g., the Financial Accounting Standards Board (FASB) in the USA) to establish accounting standards that would further their own self-intent implies that a formulation of an accounting theory is not feasible.

The role of accounting rule-making bodies (such as the FASB) in an environment of conflicting interests also should be to gain an understanding as to what corporations would voluntarily wish to disclose. For example, would self-interested, corporate managers have incentives either to withhold information that is important for resource allocation or to disclose misleading information? Given the conflicts between owners and managers (and divergences of preferences), managers have an incentive to misrepresent. In fact, there is evidence of managers delaying the disclosure of negative information until such time when the auditor "flushes out" the news. This possibility of misrepresentation gives explicit recognition to the asymmetry of information: managers possess private information gained from their intimate involvement in the operational activities, and can signal expectations of future cash flows contingent on their own actions when given incentives to do so. By "accounting" to owners for their actions and the assets under their custody, managers fulfill a stewardship function and an informativeness function. Stockholders require reporting not only as means for providing an agreed-upon measure of performance, but also to obtain information on the basis of which they can make future decisions. This can also be referred to as the role of signaling.

In the USA, class action suits brought under the Securities and Exchange Act of 1934 create disincentives not to report truthfully or in a timely fashion, and may deter managers from disclosing relevant information which they have no duty to disclose under present rules. Indeed, the optimal amount of misrepresentation induced by the intricate web of existing incentives and disincentives (compensation schemes, legal liability, and ethical rules of conduct) is above zero.

The role of the FASB (or other regulatory bodies), were they to identify the deficiencies in existing disclosure due to the lack of sufficient incentives, would then be to provide the proper incentives (including penalties) for the generation and provision of useful information. To minimize expected costs of misrepresentations, it would then be in the managers' best interest to deviate from the guidelines only for the sake of truth-saying.

Accounting Standards, Uniformity versus Flexibility

Should management be afforded flexibility among alternative treatments that would fit the different circumstances in ways that satisfy accounting objectives?

Increasing the uniformity of accounting standards (reducing the flexibility of management in choosing among different accounting treatments) could reduce audit (monitoring) costs and the ambiguity of the resulting signal. The greater the ambiguity of the signal, the lesser the reliability of the resulting inferences.

But the more confining the generally accepted accounting principles and the methods of their application, the lesser the flexibility that management can use to convey its expectations of the firm's prospects. This reduction in the ability of management to signal counteracts the reduction in monitoring cost produced by the enforcement of uniform standards. I conclude, not surprisingly, that there is an optimal amount of uniformity of accounting standards that balances the costs of limiting management flexibility and signaling against the benefits inherent in the reduction of monitoring costs due to uniformity.

The Descriptive Role of Accounting

The informativeness role of accounting has both descriptive and normative implications. A descriptive finding that accounting information is used in decision-making by market transactors is a necessary, but not sufficient, condition for the claim that the manifested effects should guide the selection among accounting alternatives.

A large body of empirical evidence suggests that accounting information is used but that it explains only a small proportion of the variations in stock returns. But the suggestion that earning should be the sole criterion by which to judge the usage of accounting reports is fraught with hazard. The problem of jointness of factors influencing returns is a severe one and cannot be addressed adequately by empirical studies. Earnings is but one, albeit important, output of the financial accounting process. However, producing earnings requires generating contemporaneously available accounting information other than earnings that also contribute to explanation of returns. From this perspective, the cumulative effects of balance sheet items as well as other accounting variables can be viewed as the informational outputs of the "earnings" generating process. An emphasis on the earnings generating process as the informative source also implies that the earnings measurement process is designed more to reveal a firm's economic structure than simply to release each period's data. That is, the earnings process may be viewed as building an archival history to facilitate predictions of how a company will respond to new external developments.

Inference of usage, however, does not imply usefulness. Usage does not address the desirability of the resulting resource allocation and the social utility derived from risk sharing induced by the "used" accounting information. Securities' prices would reflect the net benefits of accounting information if such information were sold at a competitive market price. But accounting information does not constitute a "private" good in the sense that it is exchanged in the market place. It cannot be sold to consumers (users of accounting information) because of the difficulty of guaranteeing exclusive access to the information if it were sold. As a result, they cannot be used to assess the net benefits of different accounting alternatives.

Interpretation of the evidence: Pitfalls. Aside from the impossibility of inferring desirability, assessing the "effects" of accounting and auditing methods is fraught with hazards. Observing an effect (e.g., an association of an accounting number, change in method, or regulation, with a price movement) need not be attributable to the accounting "event." Consider the two cases: (1) when an association is observed, and (2) when no association is observed.

The *first instance* is consistent with one or more of the following:

(a) The observed price change is *induced* incrementally by the accounting event reflecting a change in the fundamental value of the firm that would not have occurred in the absence of the accounting event.

(b) Publicly known nonaccounting events would have induced the same price change in the absence of the accounting manifestation.

(c) The accounting manifestation was not a cash flow event, but it induced a price change because it was perceived as a credible signal of management's expectations about the future prospects of the firm.

(d) Without the accounting information traders will have engaged in the acquisition of substitute private information which will have resulted in similar (or different) equilibrium price changes. That is, the observed associated (with the accounting event) price changes need not reflect the incremental impact of the accounting event.

(e) Managers misrepresent and traders rely on the misrepresentation as if it were truth – in light of high costs of private information acquisition and/or the promise of recovery under legal statutes and the case law, so that the price change coincident with the accounting misrepresentation is a distorted reflection of changes in the fundamental value of the firm.

(f) The price change associated with the accounting event, by itself, does not fully reflect the information content implied in the event. Other measures must be incorpo-

rated, some observable (such as trading volume reaction) and some possibly not easily observable (dispersion of traders' beliefs).

(g) The price change associated with the accounting event does not fully capture the information content of the publicly announced accounting event because in a noisy rational expectations capital market equilibrium prices do not fully reflect *publicly available* information, i.e., the capital market is not semi-strong efficient. (*see* Dontoh et al., 1994).

Thus, independently of the magnitude of the explained variation (R^2 values, which were observed by Lev (1989) to be very small), the observation of an association between the two does not tell us much about the "usage" of accounting information.

And, symmetrically, in the *second instance*, the observation of "no effect" need not imply that accounting information is not used:

(1) First, even if there is no observed effect on market prices, the accounting event may have an effect on utility transfers among individuals as manifested in trading activity – clearly a relevant factor if wealth distribution is considered important.

(2) Secondly, the effect of an accounting manifestation may become visible subsequent to the issue of the accounting report. Thus, a disclosure that management took a particular action (or a financial statement manifestation of such action) may have little or no effect at the time of disclosure. But later, the occurrence of an unexpected event significantly altering cash flow expectations *given* that management had taken the said prior action, would affect stock prices.

One cannot argue that the effect observed on the security prices contingent on the disclosure of the information about the event's occurrence is solely attributable to the information on the event. The effect is a joint result of (1) the occurrence of that particular event, and (2) the action taken by management that had previously been disclosed in the accounting reports. However, the disclosure of the action may have an "effect" that is conditional on additional information which becomes available only later. In this circumstance it is wrong to claim that the disclosure of the action in the annual report had no effect. In other words, the observation of security market prices cannot be used definitively to assess whether the accounting information has an effect on market equilibrium.

Thus, event studies that focus on the association between market returns and accounting numbers do not shed much light on the question as to whether accounting numbers are used. Even if they did, we would still be in the dark as to whether any accounting numbers, used or not used, are useful. Existing empirical evidence, as well as evidence expected to be yielded by future empirical studies of the type conducted in the past, provides us (or will provide us) with little, if any, guidance as to how to structure the accounting model, how to report, and how to formulate the objective, scope, or procedures of accounting and auditing.

We are left with what may be the only promising path of research toward construction of a financial accounting theory: normative research (including empirical or experimental tests of the assumptions underlying the normative analysis). And this should not exclude consideration of social welfare implications of generally accepted accounting principles (GAAP) alternatives. To the extent that such implications are best flushed out in the political process, the aim of research should be to provide valuable inputs to the political debate. This research should certainly allow for well-reasoned, well-thought-out, hypotheses as to which accounting models would best serve society's needs.

Bibliography

Dontoh, A., Ronen, J. & Sarath, B. (1994). Post-announcement drift in rational expectations models. (May). Vincent C. Ross Institute of Accounting Research. Working papers series.

Lev, B. (1989). On the usefulness of earnings and earnings research: Lessons and directions from two decades of empirical research. *Journal of Accounting Research*, (supplement), 153–92.

Ou, J. A. & Penman, S. H. (1989). Financial statement analysis and the prediction of stock returns. *Journal of Accounting and Economics*, Nov., 295–329.

Patell, J. N. (1989). Discussion on the usefulness of earnings and earnings research: Lessons and directions from two decades of empirical research. *Journal of Accounting Research*, (Supplement), 27.

Ronen, J. (1979). The dual role of accounting: A financial economic perspective. *Handbook of Financial Economics*, James L. Bicksler (ed.), 415–54. New York: North-Holland Publishing Company.

Simmonds, A., Sagat, K. A. & Ronen, J. (1992). Dealing with anomalies, confusion, and contradiction in fraud on the market securities class actions. *Kentucky Law Journal*, 81, 123–86.

JOSHUA RONEN

financial ratios and statement analysis

Profitability Ratios

Profitability is the usual measure of financial performance. It is related to the ability to pay dividends, service loans, and invest in new assets. This entry presents key indicators of profitability. The first two measures are concerned with components of income.

Gross profit on sales. Gross profit or gross margin is measured as sales less the cost of goods sold. The gross profit on sales compares gross profit to sales.

$$\text{gross profit on sales} = \frac{\text{gross profit}}{\text{sales}}$$

This ratio provides an indication of income before subtracting selling and administrative costs, interest, income taxes, and other items. As such, it provides a useful starting point in the analysis of profitability.

Profit margin. The profit margin measures income as a percentage of sales.

$$\text{profit margin} = \frac{\text{net income}}{\text{sales}}$$

Analysts often estimate future profit margins and incorporate these estimates in the prediction of future income. For example, an analyst may read that future sales are expected to be $10,000,000 per year. If the profit margin is estimated at 9 percent, this implies future profits of $900,000.

Return on equity. Return on equity is a widely used measure of return on invested capital. The return on equity is measured as net income divided by owners' equity.

$$\text{return on equity} = \frac{\text{net income}}{\text{average equity}}$$

One deficiency of the usual return on equity measure is the use of book (accounting) carrying values. Since shares usually trade at a premium to book value, this measure does not reflect the shareholder's opportunity cost. Consequently, some analysts substitute the market value of equity for book value.

Earnings per share. Investors and potential investors are interested in the earnings attributable to each common share.

$$\text{earnings per share} = \frac{\text{net income}}{\text{common shares outstanding}}$$

If preferred stock is outstanding, dividends paid or accumulated on the preferred are subtracted from income to obtain earnings for common shareholders. Special adjustments apply when options, warrants, or other potentially dilutive securities are outstanding.

While earnings per share comparisons over time can be useful, the measure cannot compare two or more businesses because the number of outstanding shares is not a function of financial performance. Stock splits, for example, cause the outstanding shares to change. When reporting comparative earnings per share data, companies adjust for stock splits and dividends to facilitate meaningful trend analysis.

Conclusion. The ratios presented here, while only a subset of available profitability measures, are selected because they are widely referred to in the literature. There are no formal guidelines for developing ratios and no single ratio is considered best for all purposes. The appropriate ratio for a given situation depends upon the particular decision purpose, the availability of data, and the time available for analysis. Consequently, some analysts modify the ratios shown here.

Risk Analysis Ratios

Investors, lenders, and most users of financial information are interested in the risks associated with short-term liquidity and long-term solvency. Short-term liquidity addresses the possibility of financial difficulty in the near future.

Two widely used measures of short-term liquidity are the current and quick ratios.

Current ratio. Current assets include cash, receivables due within one year, inventory, and prepayments. Liabilities are current if due within one year. The current ratio relates the carrying values of current assets to the carrying values of current liabilities:

$$\text{current ratio} = \frac{\text{current assets}}{\text{current liabilities}}$$

One interpretation is that an excess of current assets over current liabilities provides a safety cushion against the possibility of insolvency. However, high current ratios are not always optimal. For example, a high ratio could also indicate an undesirable increase in receivables or inventory. Similarly, low current ratios do not necessarily indicate financial difficulty. Many of the more successful airlines and other businesses which sell goods or services for cash and operate without inventories have low current ratios.

Some firms seem to engage in "window dressing" to improve reported ratios. For example, when the current ratio exceeds one, equal reductions of current assets and current liabilities will improve the ratio. One way to dress up the current ratio is to pay bills before year-end.

Quick ratio. The current ratio includes all current assets including inventories and prepayments. Businesses rarely obtain returns of prepayments and it may take months to sell inventories. Thus, analysts also calculate the quick ratio, a short-term liquidity ratio which ignores inventories and prepayments.

$$\text{quick ratio} =$$

$$\frac{\text{current assets - inventories - prepayments}}{\text{current liabilities}}$$

The quick ratio is always less than the current ratio.

Debt-to-equity. The debt-to-equity (financial leverage) ratio is a longer run risk measure. Debt-to-equity compares debt to the owner's investment in the business.

$$\text{total debt to equity} = \frac{\text{total debt}}{\text{total owner's equity}}$$

Some analysts include only long-term debt or only interest-bearing debt in the debt-to-equity calculation. One rationale is that borrowers tend to replace accounts receivable, wages payable, and other short-term debt as it matures and due to a rollover effect, this debt is not actually paid. Other statement users believe that the market values of debt and equity provide more relevant information and substitute these measures for book values.

Times-interest-earned. The times-interest-earned ratio considers the ability to cover interest charges if earnings decrease. It is calculated by comparing earnings before interest and taxes to interest expense as follows:

$$\text{times-interest-earned} = $$

$$\frac{\text{earnings before interest and taxes}}{\text{interest expense}}$$

One limitation of this coverage ratio is that interest is not the only fixed charge. Alternative measures of coverage consider all fixed charges (including lease and rental payments) and compare cash from operating activities to interest payments.

Efficiency and Other Ratios

The accounts receivable and inventory turnover ratios provide rough measures of efficiency in the use of assets. These ratios also provide measures of liquidity.

Accounts receivable turnover. Accounts receivable turnover measures efficiency in the collection of these receivables. This calculation is only meaningful when companies disclose accounts receivable (separate from interest-bearing notes receivable).

$$\text{accounts receivable} = $$

$$\frac{\text{credit sales}}{\text{turnover average accounts receivable}}$$

Low turnover (long collection periods) generally indicates low efficiency and low liquidity and may reflect difficulty collecting receivables. Low ratios imply low liquidity in the sense that

delays in the conversion of receivables to cash reduce cash flow.

Inventory turnover. Inventory turnover measures the efficiency and risk associated with the investment in inventory. Speed in converting inventory to cash implies high efficiency and low risk.

$$\text{inventory turnover} = \frac{\text{cost of goods sold}}{\text{average inventory}}$$

For seasonal businesses, balance sheets report the year-end rather than average investment in receivables and inventory. In this case, analysts can use average quarterly asset balances to calculate turnover ratios.

Two popular, additional ratios are the dividend payout and price-to-earnings ratio.

Dividend payout ratio
Dividends are important to investors because these distributions provide tangible increases in shareholder's wealth and to lenders because they represent funds not available for loan payment. Dividend payout relates dividends and earnings.

$$\text{dividend payout ratio} = \frac{\text{dividends}}{\text{earnings}}$$

Some firms attempt to achieve specified long-run dividend payout ratios such as 40 percent. With these firms, increases in earnings imply proportional increases in dividends.

Price-to-earnings ratio
The price-to-earnings ratio relates earnings to stock prices. Some investors feel that stocks with low price earnings ratios are underpriced. Others realize that the ratio is based on past earnings. They look for firms with high expected future earnings and cash flows.

$$\text{price to earnings} = \frac{\text{market price per share}}{\text{ratio earnings per share}}$$

Comparison of Financial Ratios

Ratio analysis is based on comparisons. Analysts typically compare ratios both over time for a given business and cross-sectionally between businesses.

Importance of accounting alternatives. Meaningful statement analysis requires comparability in accounting. For example, two companiesmay have similar financial situations, but use different methods of accounting for inventories (such as FIFO and LIFO). Thus, in theory, analysts need to be aware of material accounting differences when comparing ratios. However, Dawson, Neupert & Stickney (1980) adjusted ratios to compensate for differences in accounting for inventory, depreciation, and other items and concluded that in most cases, the adjustment process was hardly worth the effort.

Industry comparisons.   Since each industry has unique opportunities, problems, and financial structures, analysts usually compare the firm under analysis to other firms in the same industry. One widely used source of comparative information is *Annual Statement Studies* published by Robert Morris Associates, the association of commercial loan officers, based in Philadelphia, USA. This document summarizes key financial ratios for each major industry. It compares average ratios over time and also partitions each industry according to business size. When comparing their own ratios to data obtained from sources such as *Annual Statement Studies*, analysts should be sure that the ratios are computed the same way.

A problem that bears on industry comparisons and industry analysis is that many diversified firms do not fit clearly into a single industry. For example, food is more important to PepsiCo's profits than the soft drink segment. Similarly, some large manufacturing companies engage in financial services through their credit subsidiaries. In some cases, the loan receivables exceed the values of manufacturing assets.

Distributions of ratios.   The distribution of financial ratios is another consideration in analysis. The analyst may find, for example, that a particular company's current ratio has a value of 1.7 compared to the industry average of 2.0. One determinant of the importance of the company and industry difference is the standard deviation of the industry average. If the standard deviation is large, the analyst may determine that the company's current ratio is approximately equal to that of the industry. Conversely, a small standard deviation may well imply that the company's ratio falls significantly below the industry average.

Key Empirical Research

Considerable research effort has been directed toward determining the ability of past financial relationships to predict financial distress, loan default risk, and stock prices. The general characteristics of financial ratios have also been the subject of considerable research.

Financial distress.   In a comparison of financially distressed firms and healthy firms, Beaver (1966) found that three years prior to financial distress, the ratios of cash flow to total debt and net income to total assets help to distinguish between many of the firms in each group. Later research including Altman (1968) worked with multivariate models for bankruptcy prediction. Altman's model located a critical "z score." It showed that firms with combinations of selected ratios scoring below this critical value were more likely to fail than firms with higher z scores. Although the original z score is based on data from the 1960s and considers only selected industries, the model with many later refinements seems to have some use in practice.

Loan risk.   A related group of studies has examined the assignment of bond ratings. Research studies show that financial ratios can formulate bond ratings that are similar to those developed by Moodys and that ratios classify loan risk in a manner similar to bankers.

Stock returns.   Researchers have tested the ability of financial ratios to predict stock returns. In one such study, Ou & Penman (1989) combined a set of financial ratios and reported that the combined measure successfully predicts stock returns.

Ratios over time.   A number of studies examined the relationship between individual company ratios and industry average ratios. These studies found that over time, individual firm ratios tend to converge toward the industry average. This finding may result from managers' efforts to target their ratios toward industry averages or the tendency of overall economic circumstances to act on the industry in similar ways.

Another issue of concern to analysts is whether a given ratio's departure from the norm is expected to be permanent or just temporary. Davis & Peles (1993) examined the behavior of selected ratios over time for a large sample of firms. They found that particularly for liquidity ratios, changes in ratio values generally tend to move quickly back toward their initial values. However, relatively slow adjustments were observed, on average, for the profit margin, gross margin, and debt to equity ratios.

Bibliography

Altman, E. I. (1968). Financial ratios, discriminant analysis and the prediction of corporate bankruptcy. *The Journal of Finance*, **23**, Sept., 589–609.

Beaver, W. H. (1966). Financial ratios as predictors of failure. *Journal of Accounting Research*, **4**, (supplement), 71–111.

Dawson, J. P., Neupert, P. M. & Stickney, C. P. (1980). Restating financial statements for alternative GAAPs: is it worth the effort? *Financial Analysts Journal*, **36**, Nov.–Dec., 38–46.

Davis, H. Z. & Peles, Y. C. (1993). Measuring equilibrium forces of financial ratios. *The Accounting Review*, **68**, Oct., 725–47.

Ou, J. & Penman, S. (1989). Financial statement analysis and the prediction of stock returns. *Journal of Accounting and Economics*, **11**, Nov., 295–329.

Robert Morris Associates (1995). *Annual Statement Studies*. Philadelphia, PA: Robert Morris Associates.

WILLIAM RULAND

flexible budgeting

Flexible Budgets As A Planning Tool

For planning, a *static* budget is prepared only for the forecasted volume level of activity. In contrast, when a *flexible* budget is used for planning, a series of static budgets are prepared at various volume levels of activity. An analysis of the sensitivity of the firm's net operating income to changes in volume permits managers to prepare contingent plans should sales volume differ from the most likely estimate. The *"FLEX"* in flexible budgeting comes from its ability to project revenues and costs at different volumes of activity by segregating costs into their fixed and variable components. Thus, in order to develop a flexible budget, some knowledge of cost behavior is important. This enables managers to express the budget in the form of a budget equation (which is equivalent to the cost-volume-profit equation). That is, a

flexible budget equation is a "recipe" of what inputs are necessary to produce a certain level of output. Consider the following example:

$$\text{Revenues} - \text{variable costs} - \text{fixed costs} = \text{net income}$$

$$SP(X) - VC(X) - FC = \text{net income}$$

$$\$20(X) - \$8(X) - \$60{,}000 = \text{net income}$$

where:

$SP = \$20$ is the estimated selling price per unit

$VC = \$8$ is the estimated variable cost per unit

$FC = \$60{,}000$ is the estimated total annual fixed cost

$X =$ is the estimated volume of activity, such as direct labor hours, machine hours, units, etc.; this is subject to change (i.e., it is the flexible part of the budget)

As the volume of activity (X) changes, the estimated total revenue, total costs, and net income change. For example, if the volume is estimated to be 6,000 units, total revenue would be $120,000, total costs would be $108,000, and net income would be $12,000. If the volume is estimated to be 8,000 units, total revenue would be $160,000, total costs would be $124,000, and net income would be $36,000. Additionally, managers are not limited to using only one variable in the flexible budgeting equation. If different costs vary with different variables (i.e., there is a variety of relevant cost drivers for a particular firm), managers can model the flexible budgeting equation using multiple inputs.

Flexible Budgets As A Control Tool

Flexible budgeting is an important management control tool because significant variations from planned volume are almost certain to occur. In the performance evaluation function, the static budget is used to measure effectiveness or how close the firm came to meeting its particular goals. Effectiveness is measured by comparing the static budget activity level (unit sales or production) to the actual level of output achieved. In contrast, the flexible budget is used to measure efficiency. Measuring efficiency involves comparing the actual amount of inputs (resources) the firm used with the amount of inputs allowed by the flexible budget to produce the actual level of output the firm achieved this past period. In order to do this, the flexible budget is adjusted, at the end of the period, to the actual level of output so as to compute what the cost *should have been*. The flexible budget shows the amount of inputs allowed for the actual level of output achieved. This makes the comparisons more useful since both the budgeted and the actual costs are compared using the same volume. Thus, the manager's boss plays a FAIR GAME when evaluating the manager or his/her department. A manager's performance is judged given the output level actually achieved (i.e., if more output was produced than what was forecasted in the static budget, the flexible budget is adjusted to the actual output level so that management is evaluated against the budget adjusted to the actual output achieved).

Flexible budgets are an integral part of variance analysis. Resources measured by the accounting system (i.e., raw materials, direct labor, and manufacturing overhead) are consumed in the production process to produce an actual level of output. This actual level of output is translated, through the standard relationships used in the budgeting process, to determine what resources *should have been used* to achieve that output. Variances are computed as the difference between the budgeted cost and the actual cost at the same volume of output. This can be accomplished by restating the flexible budget, *after the fact*, to see what the *cost should have been* for the *actual volume achieved*. The flexible budget variances are calculated as:

Actual costs − (standard quantity) (standard price)

where:

standard quantity = the standard quantity of input allowed for the actual level of output produced

standard price = price per unit of input which should be paid

The input quantity allowed is expressed in quantities of raw materials (such as pounds, cubic yards, board feet, etc.), hours of labor, or any of a number of cost drivers (such as direct labor hours, machine hours, number of machine setups, number of engineering change orders, etc.) which are used for allocating manufacturing overhead to the product.

ROBERT CAPETTINI

foreign currency   Accounting regulations for foreign currency vary internationally. Foreign currency accounting regulations are contained in Statement of Financial Accounting Standard No. 52, "Foreign Currency Translation", (1981) (SFAS 52) in the USA; Statement of Standard Accounting Practice No. 20 (SSAP 20) in the UK; CICA 1650, "Foreign Currency Translation," in Canada; AASB 1012 and AAS 20, "Foreign Currency Translation" in Australia; International Accounting Standard IAS 21, "The Effects of Changes in Foreign Exchange Rates"; standards issued by the Business Accounting Deliberation Council in Japan; recommendations issued by Sweden's Authorized Accountant Association; the Plan Comptable Général in France, and other forms of regulation in various countries. Not all countries' regulations regulate all foreign currency accounting issues; nor do all countries' regulations concur. It is noteworthy that the European Community's (EC's) Fourth and Seventh Directives are both silent concerning foreign currency accounting, requiring merely the disclosure of exchange rates used to translate foreign currency balances.

Offshore investments

To incorporate a firm's equity investment in operations with foreign–currency denominated accounts into the firm's own group accounts, it is necessary to translate the foreign operation's accounts into the investor's reporting currency. Of the following translation methods the current rate and temporal methods are those most frequently adopted.

The *current rate method* was used by British accountants in the 19th century and has been followed by UK, European, Asian, Australian, and New Zealand firms. It is currently permitted for self-sustaining operations under international, US, Canadian, UK, European, Australian, and Asian accounting standards. All the foreign operation's assets and liabilities are translated at the exchange rate ruling on balance date. Profit and loss statement items are translated using exchange rates ruling at the times of the transactions or approximations thereto. Because a self-sustaining operation operates independently of the investor, the investor's currency risk is limited to its "net investment." Most international standards therefore require that the net investment in self-sustaining operations, i.e., assets less liabilities, be translated using the current rate method.

A claimed advantage of the current rate method is that it preserves the relativity of measures in the foreign operation's accounts. A claimed disadvantage is that when assets valued at other than current values are translated using a current exchange rate, the resultant measure is devoid of economic meaning.

The *temporal method* is sometimes required by international, US, Canadian, UK, European, and Australasian countries' accounting standards, and generally is to be applied only where the foreign investment is "integrated," i.e., where the overseas firm frequently exposes the reporting firm to currency risk because of financial and/or operating interdependencies. Under the temporal method, assets and liabilities are translated using exchange rates corresponding to their valuation: historical-cost-valued items are translated using historical exchange rates; items at current or revalued amounts are translated using exchange rates ruling at their (re)valuation. Revenues and expenses are translated using exchange rates at the time of the transactions.

The current rate and temporal methods often produce translation differences of the opposite sign. Because all assets and liabilities are translated at current rates under the current rate method, and assets generally exceed liabilities, the accounting exchange rate exposure arises from net assets. In contrast, the temporal method generally yields an exposure from net liabilities since liabilities are more frequently measured at current values than are assets. While the temporal method retains the subsidiary's measurement system, the current

rate method yields exchange rate gains or losses consistent with the parent entity's economic currency exposure from the subsidiary's net assets and does not distort the relationships of items in the offshore operation's accounts.

The *monetary–non-monetary method* translates monetary items using balance-date exchange rates and non-monetary items using historic exchange rates, yielding effects similar to the temporal method if assets are not revalued. Where revaluations are common, as in some European and most Australasian countries, the differences can be material.

The *current–non current method* entails translating current assets and liabilities at balance-date exchange rates; non current items are translated at historic rates. The method was common when rates moved gently, as within a stabilization system like the European Monetary System. It was advocated on the grounds that current items were likely to be settled at rates approximating the current rate. In contrast, exchange rates might have returned to prior levels by the time long-term items were settled.

Translation policies under hyperinflation

For subsidiaries in countries with high inflation, a particular problem arises due to two economic relationships:

(1) Purchasing power parity, whereby an inverse relation between currency strength and inflation rates ensures that asset values in countries with different exchange rates remain relatively constant in terms of either currency.

(2) The "Fisher effect," where there is an inverse relation between interest rates and currency movements so that as a currency strengthens relative to another, the interest rate weakens.

Over extended periods, both effects tend to operate. Translating the accounts of an operation in a hyperinflationary country can therefore distort the accounts relative to the parent's. US and UK standards respond differently to the problem: US Statement of Financial Accounting Standard (SFAS) 52 requires temporal translation if prices more than double in three years; while Statement of Standard Accounting Practice (UK) (SSAP) 20 requires inflation adjustments to the foreign operation's accounts before using the current rate method. International Accounting Standard (IAS) 21 permits either method.

Treatment of Translation Gains and Losses

Translation gains or losses (differences) can pass through earnings or go directly to reserves such as a foreign currency translation reserve. Internationally, regulations require different practices for different translation methods. In turn, the extent of integration of the investor and investee operations determines the translation method. The current rate method is required for self-sustaining operations and combines with taking translation gains and losses to reserves; the temporal method combines with taking translation differences to earnings for integrated operations.

Foreign currency transactions of the reporting firm

Foreign currency transactions are recorded at exchange rates ruling when the transactions occur. When resultant debts or receivables are settled before balance date, realized gains or losses are recorded in earnings: there appears to be no international or national accounting regulation requiring that they be taken directly to reserves.

At balance date, any unsettled monetary assets or liabilities are translated using the balance-date exchange rate. Most countries' accounting standards require the unrealized gains or losses to be taken to earnings if the item is short term (current). For long-term monetary items there has been greater diversity. IAS 21 and US, UK, Australian, and New Zealand standards require unrealized gains or losses on long-term monetary items that are not hedges to be recognized as income or expenses of the period when the exchange rate moves. The Canadian accounting standard recently adopted this practice. Previously, it required them to be deferred to a balance sheet account and amortized the related items' lives. Deferral and amortization policy was once required under Australian regulations also.

Foreign currency hedges

Countries vary considerably in their treatment of foreign currency hedges, and many countries' standards do not cover hedge accounting. International Accounting Standard (IAS) 21 does not deal with hedge accounting except to require equity classification of exchange differences from monetary items forming part of an enterprise's net investment in a foreign subsidiary or hedging a net investment until the investment is disposed. Then, these differences are recognized as income or expenses (IAS 21, para. 17). US Statement of Financial Accounting Standard (SFAS) 52, requires identical treatment, as do UK Statement of Standard Accounting Practice (SSAP) 20, paras 51, 57, AASB 1012, para. 31 (Australia) in AASB 1012, para. 31 and CICA 1650.50 (Canada).

Where foreign currency transactions such as forward contracts hedge an identifiable, specific foreign currency commitment such as a purchase or sale commitment, Australian, New Zealand, and US accounting standards require the unrealized gains or losses on the hedge transaction to be deferred and included in measuring the hedged commitment (AASB 1012 (XXV); as in New Zealand; SFAS 52, para. 21). The Canadian approach defers the gain or loss until monetary item settlement (CICA 1650.54).

The treatment of premiums or discounts on forward contracts can depend upon the purpose of the contracts. Under Australian, New Zealand, and US regulations, if the purpose is not to hedge a specific identifiable foreign currency commitment, the premiums or discounts are deferred to the balance sheet and amortized over the lives of the contracts. If a contract hedges a specific identifiable commitment, the portion related to the commitment may be included in measuring of the commitment (AASB 1012, Commentary; SSAP 21, para. 5.5; SFAS 52, para. 19). International, UK, and Canadian standards are silent on the treatment.

Disclosure

Almost all countries with foreign currency accounting standards require disclosure of the amount of exchange rate differences included in the period's net profit or loss; net exchange differences classified as a separate component of equity; and a reconciliation of amounts at the start and end of the period. Additional disclosures sometimes required include details of changes in the classification of significant foreign operations and the financial impact of the changes (IAS 21, para. 44); and the amounts and currencies of payables and receivables (AASB 1012, para. 60).

Reactions to Proposed and Actual Accounting Standards

Most research investigating reactions to proposed and actual foreign currency accounting standards emanates from the USA. Research indicates that firms increased foreign exchange risk management to reduce exposure to earnings variability subsequent to the introduction of Statement of Financial Accounting Standard, the predecessor to SFAS 52 (SFAS) 8. Further studies of lobbying and changes in financing or operating activities in response to SFAS 8 indicate managerial risk aversion to increased reported income variability and that managers adopted the new standard when it had the potential to most reduce their contracting and political costs.

While their results have been mixed, researchers have generally found negative stock price reactions to SFAS 8 and positive reactions to SFAS 52 and that the share price effects are associated with the extent to which the SFAS-induced earnings variability affected firms' earnings-based contracts and political vulnerability.

Foreign Currency Accounting Policy Choices

In one of the few publications to examine firms' voluntary foreign currency accounting policies, Taylor, Tress & Johnson (1990) note that most Australian firms prefer current rate translation. They investigate why firms varied in taking the consequential translation differences to reserves, operating earnings, or extraordinary earnings and find that the selected policies facilitated risk sharing between shareholders and managers. Godfrey (1992) finds evidence that voluntary policies were optimal in sharing risk between Australian lenders, shareholders, and managers. She finds that Australian companies' policies for translating accounts of overseas subsidiaries and for foreign currency long-term debt combined to yield an accounting hedge if the firm hedged its economic exchange rate risk, and did not give an accounting hedge if the firm did not hedge the economic risk.

Godfrey (1994) investigates whether, prior to regulation of accounting for foreign currency

long-term debt, Australian managers used accounting policies to reflect firms' underlying exchange rate risk exposure, or whether the policies were used opportunistically to influence reported earnings levels. Policies included taking all currency differences to current earnings; deferring and amortizing them over the life of the debt; or recognizing them in earnings only when the debt was repaid. She finds that managers chose methods that reflected the firms' underlying economic exposures to currency risk. In particular, when foreign debt hedged currency exposure for foreign currency-export-earning assets, managers selected the method that best reflected the results of the hedging objective.

Generally, research indicates that Australian firms' voluntary reporting practices reflected the underlying nature of the firms' foreign currency exposures and that alternative practices imposed costs on the firms and their shareholders.

Bibliography

Financial Accounting Standards Board (1995). *Original Pronouncements–Accounting Standards as of June 1995*, Vol. 1. New York: John Wiley & Sons, Inc.

Godfrey, J. M. (1992). Foreign Currency Accounting Molicies: Reporting the exchange rate/asset value correlation. *Accounting and Finance*.

Godfrey, J. M. (1994). Foreign currency accounting policies: The impact of asset specificity. *Contemporary Accounting Research*, Spring.

Taylor, S., Tress, R. B. & Johnson, L. W. (1990). Explaining intraperiod accounting choices: The reporting of currency translation gains and losses. *Accounting and Finance*.

Jayne M. Godfrey

foreign currency accounting

Introduction

In the USA, accounting for foreign currency transactions and translation of foreign denominated financial statements is covered in Financial Accounting Standards Board (FASB) Statement of Financial Accounting Standards No. 52 (1981) (SFAS 52). Foreign currency accounting issues affect the financial reporting for companies that operate in foreign countries.

Transaction gains and losses occur when a transaction is denominated in a currency other

Table 1   Functional currency selection criteria

Functional currency = parent currency	*Functional currency = local currency*
(translation gains and losses flow through earnings)	*(translation gains and losses are reflected in equity and bypass earnings)*
1. Cash flows related to the foreign entity directly impact parent's cash flows on a current basis.	1. Cash flows related to the foreign entity do not impact parent's current cash flows.
2. Sales prices for foreign entity's products aare determined by worldwide competition and vary with changes in exchange rates.	2. Sales prices are locally determined.
3. The sales market is the parent company market.	3. The sales market is primaarily the local market.
4. Labor, material, and other expenses are obtained from the parent entity.	4. Labor, material, and other expenses are locally incurred.
5. Financing depends on the parent company or is denominated in the currency of the parent.	5. Financing is in local currency.
6. There is a high volume of intercompany transactions.	6. The volume of intercompany transactions is low.

Source: SFAS 52 ¶ 42 (1981)

than the functional currency of the business entity. As an example, a US company may purchase merchandise from a Swiss company and incur a payable or liability denominated in Swiss francs. Transaction gains and losses occur due to changes in exchange rates between the time the transaction occurs and the time payment is made. These transaction gains and losses are usually included in the income of the US company because they represent a real economic gain or loss. Exceptions include (1) foreign currency transactions intended to hedge specific purchase commitments, and (2) transactions that are part of a long-term investment in a foreign country.

Reporting Issues

Translation gains and losses occur as a result of companies acquiring subsidiaries based in foreign countries. Such subsidiaries may maintain a set of books denominated in the foreign

currency. However, when companies prepare periodic financial statements of a consolidated entity it is necessary that all financial statements are denominated in the same currency (for US based multinationals this would be the dollar). SFAS 52 seeks to report the effect of translation gains and losses in a way that assures that the reported gains and losses which flow through the income statement correspond to the underlying economic reality of the transaction. SFAS 52 is based on the concept of an entity's functional currency. The functional currency is defined in SFAS 52 (¶5) as "the currency of the primary economic environment in which the entity operates; normally that is the currency of the environment in which an entity primarily generates and expends cash."

To illustrate, suppose a US clothing manufacturer establishes a foreign subsidiary. The subsidiary operates a manufacturing plant to manufacture clothing that is shipped primarily to US markets for resale. The employees of the company are located in the foreign country, but the operation is financed using US debt and the raw materials used are shipped from the USA. Sales prices for the final products are determined primarily based on current prices for competitive goods in US markets. Here the functional currency would be the US dollar. Translation gains and losses that occur because of translating from the subsidiary's financial statements (expressed in foreign currency) to the parent's (expressed in dollars) are recognized in the parent's income statement each year. This is because the expectation is that when the functional currency is the dollar, any gains and losses are real gains and losses to the parent entity and should be recognized as such. In contrast, consider the same situation but assume the clothing manufactured uses textiles from the foreign country and is primarily resold in that country. The foreign subsidiary's debt is financed at a bank in that country and the employees are almost entirely from the foreign country. The foreign subsidiary essentially operates as a self-contained entity. Here the functional currency would be the local currency and any gains and losses occurring from translating from the foreign currency to the US dollar would not be recognized in earnings but would instead be carried to a separate stockholders' equity account, "Cumulative Translation Adjustments." The rationale here is that any gains and losses accruing as a result of translation from the subsidiary to the parent are not expected to be realized and as a result forcing such translation gains and losses to flow through the parent company's earnings is misleading.

Accounting Requirements

Statement of Financial Accounting Standards No. 52 replaced Statement of Financial Accounting Standards No. 8 (1975) that required that all gains and losses from transactions and translation flow through earnings. This was viewed by management and many analysts as misleading and causing excessive earnings volatility or costly hedging designed to protect the appearance of the income statement, without being necessarily based on sound management practice.

The effectiveness of Statement of Financial Accounting Standards No. 52 (SFAS 52) hinges on the extent to which it leads to reporting which reflects the underlying cash flows of the consolidated entity, which is critically dependent on the selection of the functional currency. Table 1 summarizes the major determinants of functional currency as stipulated by SFAS 52. It is important that the financial statement user and corporate management realize that the functional currency choice reflects a significant degree of management interpretation of the SFAS 52 guidelines and that alternative interpretations may lead to significantly different reported earnings. Another important point to note is that for tax purposes foreign currency gains and losses are recognized on a transactions basis (as dividends are transmitted from the foreign subsidiary to the parent). Thus, managements' choice for financial reporting purposes is independent of any direct cash flow effects.

Research on the Effects

Research in foreign currency accounting has focussed on three primary areas: (1) theoretical analyses of the role of translation in valuation and interpretation of financial statements; (2) empirical tests of the impact of foreign currency reporting methods on analysts' forecasting ability; and (3) managements' incentives to manage earnings through foreign currency reporting.

Theoretical analyses of translation methods Beaver & Wolfson (1982) identify two desirable properties for financial statement translation. These are "economic interpretability" and "symmetry." Economic interpretability implies that book values on the balance sheet equal market values. Symmetry requires that economically equivalent investments result in the same financial statement numbers upon translation into a common currency. Beaver & Wolfson demonstrate that under certain conditions market value accounting with translation at market value is necessary to achieve both economic interpretability and symmetry. Goldberg & Godwin (1994) extend this analysis to isolated economies and reach a similar conclusion.

*The impact of foreign currency on analysts'
forecasts.* Griffin & Castanias (1987) and
Ayres & Rodgers (1994) report that analysts'
forecast errors decreased following Statement of
Financial Accounting Standards No. 52 (SFAS
52) adoption. This finding is consistent with the
contention of analysts that SFAS 8 made
forecasting earnings more difficult due to the
volatility in earnings induced by exchange rate
fluctuations.

Management's incentives to manage earnings.
Several studies report findings consistent with
the hypothesis that management uses foreign
currency reporting to "manage" earnings. Ayres
(1986) reported that early adopters of SFAS 52
had lower earnings prior to SFAS 52 adoption
and were closer to debt and dividend constraints
than were firms that deferred adoption. The
impact of SFAS 52 adoption on earnings was
generally positive (about 11 percent of earnings), allowing management to use SFAS 52 to
boost earnings in a poor performance year. In
addition Elliott & Philbrick (1990) and Ayres &
Rodgers (1994) both find evidence consistent
with managers adopting SFAS 52 with an
income – smoothing motivation.

Bibliography

Ayres, F. L. (1986). Characteristics of firms electing
early adoption of SFAS 52. *Journal of Accounting
and Economics*, 8, June, 143–58.
Ayres, F. L. & Rodgers, J. (1994). Further evidence
on the impact of SFAS 52 on analysts' earnings
forecasts. *Journal of International Financial Management and Accounting*, June, 120–41.
Beaver, W. & Wolfson, M. (1982). Foreign currency
translation and changing prices in perfect and
complete markets. *Journal of Accounting Research*,
Autumn, 528–50.
Elliott, J. A. & Philbrick, D. R. (1990). Accounting
changes and earnings predictability. *The Accounting
Review*, Jan., 157–74.
Goldberg, S. R. & Godwin, J. H. (1994). Foreign
currency translation under two cases – integrated
and isolated economies. *Journal of International
Financial Management and Accounting*, June,
97–119.
Griffin, P. A. & Castanias, R. P. (1987). *Accounting for
the translation of foreign currencies: The effects of
Statement 52 on equity analysts.* Research Report
Stamford, CT: Financial Accounting Standards
Board.

FRANCES L. AYRES

G

goodwill accounting Goodwill accounting is a complex and controversial reporting issue. Being an intangible asset, the degree of uncertainty associated with its measurable benefits tends to be higher than for tangibles. Goodwill has a value only in relation to a given firm. Unlike patents or brand names that could be sold or exchanged individually in the market place, goodwill is inseparable from the business as a whole. It is often described as the most "intangible" of intangibles.

Box 1: Factors generating goodwill

- Superior management team
- Weakness in a competitor's management
- Effective advertising
- Secret manufacturing process
- Good labor relations
- Excellent credit rating
- Top-flight training program for employees
- Favorable association with another company
- Favorable tax conditions
- Favorable government relations
- Production economies
- Low-cost funds
- Cash reserves
- Assurance of supply
- Good public relations
- Unfavorable developments in a competitor's operations
- Access to technology

Source: Catlett & Olsen (1968)

Goodwill can be thought of as the ability of a firm to generate "above average" earnings. Box 1 highlights additional factors that are thought to generate goodwill.

A characteristic of these factors, however, is that they give rise to goodwill as a result of their interaction with other assets of the firm. Thus high-quality products (inventory) coupled with a favorable location enables the firm to achieve a higher volume of sales than would be possible had the firm's location been less accessible to the consuming public. However, location is not an asset that can be valued separately. This interaction or dependence gives rise to a significant measurement problem.

Goodwill can be developed internally and/or externally. As an example of the former, expenditures on advertising, employee training, or patent development incurred to benefit current operations often generate goodwill (i.e., increased future earning power) as a byproduct. Goodwill can also be developed externally. Assume that a company acquires another company and pays more for the target company than the sum of the fair market values of the target's net assets. In this instance, the premium paid acknowledges the existence of goodwill; i.e., above-average future earnings expectations on the part of the acquirer.

Measurement issues associated with goodwill are:

(1) Should goodwill, whether internally- or externally-developed, be recognized (i.e., measured and recorded) in the accounts?
(2) If goodwill is recognized, should it be charged directly to shareholders' equity? Should it be treated as a permanent asset and written down only when there is evidence that its value has been impaired?

Or, should it be amortized to income in some systematic fashion?

Goodwill Recognition

An asset may be defined as a probable future economic benefit that is obtained or controlled by a particular entity as a result of a past transaction or event. Since goodwill is associated with a stream of above-average earnings, most would agree that it is an asset. The question is whether it should be recognized as such in the accounts.

Internally developed goodwill is often a byproduct of transactions such as advertising and employee development activities. In these instances it is extremely difficult, if not impossible, to determine which portion of the actual expenditure is associated with normal operating benefits and which is associated with producing a future stream of above-average earnings. Since these expenditures work in concert in generating goodwill, it is impossible to reliably identify the transactions that give rise to this intangible asset. Owing to difficulties of measurement, expensing or non-recognition of internally-developed goodwill is common.

External-developed goodwill, in contrast, is more amenable to measurement albeit with differing degrees of reliability, especially using the *excess earnings* approach. This measure draws on the theory that an asset's value is equal to the discounted present value of the future earnings stream that it generates. Since goodwill generates above-average or excess earnings (i.e., earnings in excess of the industry average), the present value of this excess earnings stream is a measure of the value of this intangible asset.

This measurement approach is not without its drawbacks, however. Issues relate to (1) determining what constitutes a representative rate of return as a measure of normal earnings, (2) choosing an appropriate discount rate, (3) obtaining reliable estimates of excess earnings, and (4) determining the relevant time horizon for discounting purposes.

A measurement approach that is considered to be more objective is the *excess cost* approach. Under this measurement scheme, goodwill is recognized when a business is acquired. The difference between the purchase price and the fair market value of the identifiable net assets acquired represents the value of goodwill. *Negative goodwill* is said to arise whenever the purchase price is less than the fair market value of net assets acquired.

Of the two measurement approaches described above, the excess cost approach is most popular in practice because it is based on a past transaction. It is also relatively more objective.

Asset versus Expense

Should goodwill, once recognized, be treated as a permanent asset and written off only when there is evidence that its value has been impaired? Should it be amortized instead to income on a periodic basis? Or, should goodwill immediately be charged to shareholders' equity without taking it through the income statement?

Treating goodwill as a permanent asset is rationalized on several grounds. First, as purchased goodwill is being used up, some would argue that it is constantly being replaced by internally-developed goodwill. Thus, goodwill in total does not deteriorate. Periodic goodwill amortization under these circumstances understates asset values. Moreover, being an arbitrary process, goodwill amortization adds a random element to reported earnings, destroying the usefulness of past earnings as a predictive device.

Those favoring periodic amortization of capitalized goodwill argue that goodwill has a finite life. Favorable circumstances that make possible an above-average earnings stream, such as a unique product design or a conscientious sales team, do not last forever. Hence, keeping goodwill on the books indefinitely causes assets to be overstated. Amortization of purchased goodwill is also consistent with the treatment accorded internally-developed goodwill. All funds expended to generate future earnings are therefore charged to earnings. Also, amortization is consistent with the matching principle as expenditures for goodwill are made with the intention of generating future benefits.

Periodic amortization, however, raises yet another issue; namely, over what time period should goodwill be amortized? While a logical tack would be to amortize goodwill "over the periods expected to be benefitted," the latter has proven difficult to operationalize in practice. Factors which need to be considered in determining a relevant amortization horizon include:

(1) Legal, regulatory or contractual provisions that may limit the maximum useful life.
(2) Effects of obsolescence, demand, competition, and other economic factors that may reduce useful life.
(3) The service life expectations of individuals or groups of employees.
(4) Expected actions of competitors and others that may restrict present competitive advantages.
(5) The fact that goodwill may be a composite of many individual factors with varying effective lives.

The effects of goodwill amortization on accounting rates of return and profitability statistics have led some to conclude that amortization periods are likely to be chosen more for pragmatic reasons than pure matching considerations.

The immediate write-off of acquired goodwill is yet another reporting option for purchased goodwill. Proponents of this alternative argue that immediate write-off treats both internally- and externally-developed goodwill in similar fashion. Since internally-generated goodwill is expensed, so too should purchased goodwill be, especially since goodwill is an integral part of the business as a whole. As such there is no predictable relationship to the costs paid on acquisition to justify its continued existence. Concomitantly, determining the future periods likely to benefit from goodwill is so difficult that immediate write-off to shareholders' equity is justified.

Diversity in National Practice Treatments

In the USA, goodwill accounting is prescribed by two authoritative accounting pronouncements, Accounting Principles Board (APB) Opinions Nos. 16 and 17. APB Opinion No. 16 states that an acquisition by purchase is the only objective means of measuring goodwill. Accordingly, it requires that the excess of purchase price over the sum of the amount assigned to identifiable net assets acquired be recorded as goodwill. Negative goodwill must first be allocated proportionately to reduce the carrying values assigned to noncurrent assets to their fair market values with any remaining negative goodwill classified as a deferred credit (a liability). The latter would be amortized over a period similar to that for positive goodwill. APB Opinion No. 17, in turn, requires that goodwill be amortized to income over its estimated useful life, but not over a period to exceed 40 years.

Table 1 illustrates the wide diversity of

Table 1:   International comparison of goodwill accounting

	Aus	Can	Fra	Ger	HK	Jpn	Itl	Ndl	Swz	US	UK	EC	IASC
Purchased goodwill													
Permanent asset recognition	U	U	U	A	A	U	U	U	U	U	U	U	U
Asset recognition & amortized	R	R	R	A	A	A	A	A	A	R	R	A	R
Charged to equity	U	U	A	A	A	U	A	A	U	U	A	A	A
Internally-developed goodwill													
Asset recognition	U	U	U	U	U	U	U	U	U	U	U	U	U
Max. amortization period	20	40	20	15	NS	5	10	10	NS	40	20	5	20

Country/institutional codes:
Aus: Australia; Can: Canada; Fra: France; Ger: Germany; HK: Hong Kong; Jpn: Japan; Itl: Italy; Ndl: Netherlands; Swz: Switzerland; US: United State; UK: United Kingdom; EC: European Community; IASC: International Accounting Standards Committee;
Table entries:
U: Unauthorized treatment; R: Required treatment; A: Allowed treatment

international practice.

In this discussion of goodwill accounting differences, the differences in national tax treatments for goodwill have not been addressed. Thus, the reporting differences under discussion relate primarily to financial reporting differences. On this score numerous studies have shown that the securities markets are not misled by differences in accounting rules. Despite the academic evidence, however, business concern over the differential impact of national goodwill accounting treatments has failed to die. In a recent survey of US chief financial officers, one of the most frequently voiced complaints was that differences in accounting for purchased goodwill give non-US companies a competitive advantage in acquiring foreign target companies.

Differences in accounting treatments for purchased goodwill are perhaps most pronounced between the UK and the USA. Unlike the US practice, the accounting treatment preferred by UK managers is to write-off goodwill immediately against reserves. While goodwill is not deductible for taxes in either the USA or the UK, differences in accounting treatment for goodwill provide an incentive for UK companies to offer more than US acquirers for common acquisition targets, in the knowledge that their future earnings need not be penalized by the higher price paid. To ascertain whether this is indeed the case, Choi & Lee (1991) found merger premiums associated with UK acquisitions to be consistently higher than those for US acquisitions. Moreover, higher premiums offered by UK acquirers were in part associated with not having to amortize goodwill against earnings. A follow-up study including German and Japanese acquirers again finds higher merger premiums offered by firms that enjoy favorable accounting treatments relative to US acquirers. Tax considerations were even more important, however, owing to the tax deductibility of goodwill charges in these countries. This evidence suggests that diversity in goodwill accounting does impact market behavior.

Bibliography

Catlett, G. R. & Olsen, N. O. (1968). Accounting for goodwill. *AICPA Accounting Research Study No. 10.* New York.

Choi, F. D. S. & Lee, C. (1991). Merger premia and national differences in accounting for goodwill. *Journal of International Financial Management and Accounting*, Autumn, 219–40.

Choi, F. D. S. & Mueller, G. G. (1993). *Globalization of Financial Accounting and Reporting.* New Jersey: Financial Executives Research Foundation.

Duvall, L. et al. (1992). Can investors unravel the effects of goodwill accounting. *Accounting Horizons*, June, 1–14.

Lee, C. & Choi, F. D. S. Effects of alternative goodwill treatments on merger premia: Further empirical evidence. *Journal of International Financial Management and Accounting.*

Riley, Jr. V. J. (1988). The U.S. on sale. *Chief Executive*, Nov.–Dec., 46–51.

Russell, A., et al. (1989). *Accounting for Goodwill.* London: Chartered Association of Certified Accountants.

Weetman, P. & Gray, S. (1990). International financial analysis and comparative corporate performance: The impact of UK versus US accounting principles on earnings. *Journal of International Financial Management and Accounting*, Summer & Autumn, 111–30.

FREDERICK D. S. CHOI

impairment of asset values

Impairment of Long-lived Asset Values

Long-lived assets such as plant and equipment generally are recorded at their acquisition cost, which is usually the fair value at the date of acquisition. The value that an enterprise pays for a plant asset is based on estimates of future use, of future demand for products and services, and of other considerations of future events. When circumstances dramatically change, plant assets may experience an impairment in value.

Asset impairments are caused by casualty, obsolescence, lack of demand for a company's products, negligence, or mismanagement. Other reasons for writing down assets include decisions to close a plant or sell a product line, edicts by regulators that a product must be taken off the market, and expropriation of assets by a foreign government. The impairment in value may be partial or total. In some cases, the asset will continue in use at a greatly reduced carrying value; in other cases, the asset, valueless for its original intent, is worth only its salvage value.

From a conceptual viewpoint, write-downs to reflect significant declines in the value of long-lived assets should be recognized as soon as they are objectively determinable because the write-downs reflect information regarding the decreased future cash flow potential, which should be reported to the extent it is reliable and objective.

In the USA the Financial Accounting Standards Board (FASB) has recently (1995) issued a statement (No. 121) that would provide standards for accounting for impairment of long-lived assets. (Statement of Financial Accounting Standard No. 121, "Accounting for the Impairment of Long-Lived Assets, and for Long-Lived Assets to be Disposed of," March 1995). The statement is summarized later in this entry.

Determining whether impairment exists requires comparing the historical cost carrying amount of an asset or group of assets with some measure of value of the asset or group of assets. The amount of the impairment is the excess of the carrying amount over that measure of value. Thus, the major accounting issue is what measure of value is to be compared to the carrying amount to determine the amount and existence of impairment.

FASB Concepts Statement No. 5, "Recognition and Measurement in Financial Statements of Business Enterprises," (1994), describes five different measurement attributes that are used in present practice: historical cost, current costs, current market value, net realizable value, and discounted value of future cash flows.

In two separate occasions, the FASB addressed the issue of impairment. According to FASB Statement No. 90, "Regulated Enterprises – Accounting for Abandonment and Disallowances of Plant Costs," (1986), a company computes the present value of the future revenue that is expected to result from the inclusion by a regulator (e.g., a state regulatory commission) of the cost of an abandoned plant in allowable costs for rate-making purposes. This present value is recorded as a separate asset, and if the book value of the abandoned plant exceeds that present value, a loss is recognized. Also, any cost of a recently completed plant that are disallowed by a regulator are recognized as a loss.

In FASB Statement No. 86, "Accounting for the Costs of Computer Software to Be Sold, Leased, or Otherwise Marketed," (1985), the FASB required that at each balance sheet date, unamortized computer software costs must be compared with the estimated net realizable value of the product. If net realizable value is below unamortized cost, the asset should be written down to its net realizable value and a loss equal to the write-down should be recorded. The reduced amount of capitalized cost is considered cost for subsequent accounting purposes, and write-downs cannot be subsequently restored.

In dealing with the general rules, the FASB took a different direction. In its Statement No. 121, the FASB concluded that assets expected to be held or used by an entity should be reviewed for impairment whenever events or circumstances indicate that the carrying amount may not be recoverable. The assessment of recoverability should be made by comparing the *undiscounted expected future cash flows* with the carrying amount of the asset. If the undiscounted expected future cash flows are less than the carrying amount, an impairment loss should be recognized. FASB Statement No. 121 identifies significant decrease in the market value of an asset, a significant change in the extent or manner in which an asset is used, and offers other examples as evidence of impairment.

However, the decision to base recognition on *undiscounted* future cash flows, with measurement based on fair value discounted cash flows, lacks logic and consistency. In its deliberation, the FASB favored adopting the economic criterion for impairment recognition that calls for the immediate recognition of a loss whenever the carrying amount of an asset or group of assets exceeds the fair value of the same asset or group of assets.

Assuming that fair values can be reasonably measured, impairment might be recognized for assets when it is probable that their carrying values cannot be fully recovered. Impairment may be disclosed for assets when it is reasonably possible that their carrying amounts cannot be fully recovered, and there might be neither recognition nor disclosure of assets when only remote possibility exists that the carrying amounts cannot be recovered fully (*see* Figure 1)

Restoration of Previously Impaired Values

A critical issue is whether an entity should reverse an impairment write-down if the fair value subsequently increases and exceeds the carrying amount after the write-off.

In a survey by the Financial Executive Institute, entitled "Survey on Unusual Charges: Summary of Responses" September 26, 1986, 63 percent of the respondents stated that it is inappropriate to restore all or part of the write-off. There were three major arguments supporting this alternative. First, the reduced asset carrying amount is considered the asset's cost for subsequent periods, therefore no write-up above cost would be appropriate. Second, the future upward adjustments might cause users to question the credibility of the initial measures. Third, restoration would violate the historical cost concept, create inconsistency with lower of cost or market principle and lead to abuses in practice. The US Financial Accounting Standards Board has supported this argument and has decided that restoration of the write-downs is not appropriate.

Reporting and Disclosure

The impairment loss for assets to be held and used is to be reported as a component of income from continuing operations (before income taxes) under a separate caption. In addition, the firm should disclose a description of the impaired asset, the facts and circumstances leading to the impairment, the amount of the impairment loss, how fair value was determined, and for public companies, the business segment(s) affected.

Write-Down of Land

Land, although not depreciated, is subject to impairment loss. Land can be written down to market value due to permanent erosion, because natural or man-made pollutants have made it unusable, and for other, similar reasons.

International Practices

In a study of accounting for asset impairment in nine countries (Australia, Canada, France, Germany, Italy, Japan, Mexico, New Zealand, and the UK), the US Financial Accounting Standards Board (FASB) found variation across accounting issues in practice. (FASB's Discussion Memorandum, 1990, p. 55). For example, the accounting principles in eight countries required recognition of asset write-downs. There were seven countries that require a loss

Figure 1: Asset impairment

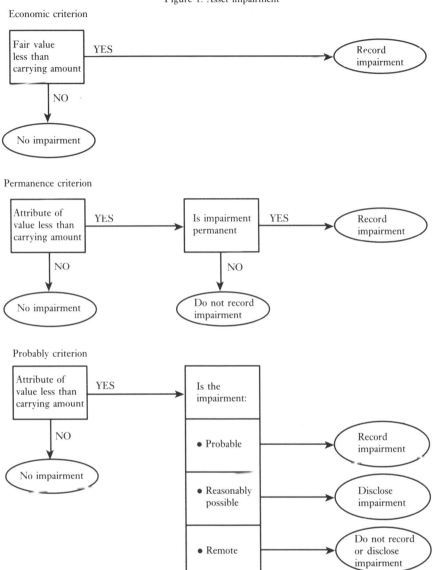

Source: Adapted from the FASB's Discussion Memorandum, December 1990

Table 1: Requirements of the International Accounting Standards Committee, and nine selected countries for accounting for impairment.

	Long-lived assets are written down (other than by depreciation) if their measurement attribute is lower than book value	Concept of impairment for recognition purpose	Treatment of recovery value
IAS 16	Yes	Permanent	Reversal of previous write-downs
EC directives	Yes	Permanent	Reversal
Australia	Yes	Permanent	Reversal
Canada	Yes	Permanent	No reversal
France	Yes	Permanent	Reversal
Germany	Yes	Permanent	Reversal
Italy	No	N/A	N/A
Japan	Yes	Permanent	N/A
Mexico	Yes	Economic	Reversal
New Zealand	Yes	Economic	No reversal
United Kingdom	Yes	Permanent	Reversal

Source: FASR Discussion Memorandum, December 1990.

to be permanent for recognition and of those seven allowed restoration of book value when market value increased (see table 1). Furthermore, countries allow upward revaluation of assets.

Bibliography

FASB (1990). "Accounting for the Impairment of Long-Lived Assets and Identifiable Intangibles," A Discussion Memorandum.Dec. Financial Accounting Standards Boards.

MARC F. MASSOUD

income classification and reporting Income is the change in a firm's net worth over a period of time. The income statement has two primary purposes: to report this change, and to provide information useful for predicting future income. The "all-inclusive" or "comprehensive income" requires that all adjustments to net worth, other than from transactions with the owners, flow through the income statement. An alternative definition is the "current operating performance." This permits irregular events to bypass the income statement and to be entered directly as adjustments to owners' equity.

Accounting standard setters in the USA have increasingly moved toward a "comprehensive" definition of income. They have also increasingly constrained firms' flexibility in the aggregation and classification of income statement components.

Accounting Principles Board Opinion (APB) No. 9, "Reporting the Results of Operations," (1966) required firms to follow the all-inclusive concept of income, with a few exceptions. The promulgation of this opinion decreased the number of adjustments to owners' equity. In the American Insititute of Certified Public Accountants (AICPA) "Accounting Trends and Techniques" in 1955, there were 153 adjustments to owners' equity, while in 1969 the number of adjustments was 8 for an equal number of firms sampled.

Current US accounting standards permit three departures from the all-inclusive concept of income. These relate to the reporting of errors from prior periods (prior period adjust-

Table 1:   Components of a Multiple Step Income Statement

Components and subtotals	Definitions
Net sales	Total sales to customers less any discounts or returns and allowances
Cost of goods sold	The cost of the goods that were sold to produce the sales
Gross margin on sales	Net sales less cost of goods sold
Operating expenses	Selling, general and administrative expenses necessary to generate sales
Operating income	Gross margin less operating expenses
Other revenue gains and expenses/ losses	Revenues or gains earned and expenses or losses incurred from peripheral and unusual or infrequent (but not both) activities
Income from continuing operations before taxes	Operating income + other revenues/gains − other expenses/losses
Income tax expense	Federal and state taxes related to income from continuing operations
Income before discontinued operations, extraordinary items and cumulative effect of change in accounting principle	Income from continuing operations less income taxes
Discontinued operations (net of tax)	Material gains and losses from dispositions of segments
Extraordinary items (net of tax)	Material gains and losses from unusual and infrequent activities
Cumulative effect of change in accounting principle (net of tax)	Cumulative effect of changes from one generally accepted principle to another
Net income	Income after discontinued operations, extraordinary items and cumulative effect of change in accounting principle

ments), unrealized gains or losses on marketable securities, and foreign currency translation.

The Classification of Income

There are two income statement formats used by companies. The single step format classifies all revenues together and all expenses together; no intermediate balances are reported. The multiple step income statement includes logical intermediate balances such as net sales or operating income. Frequently used components of a multiple step income statement are described in Table 1.

Current accounting standards are very specific regarding the definition and classification of income taxes, discontinued operations, extraordinary items, and cumulative effect of changes in accounting principles. Statement of Financial Accounting Standard (SFAS) No. 109 issued February 1992, entitled "Accounting for Income Taxes," covers the reporting of income tax expense. Income tax expense must be reported separately on the income statement after income from continuing operations. Any taxes applicable to discontinued operations, extraordinary items, or changes in accounting principle are to be netted against the corresponding item on the income statement.

APB No. 30, "Reporting the Results of Operations – Reporting the Effects of Disposal of a Segment of a Business, and Extraordinary, Unusual, and Infrequently Occurring Events and Transactions," (June 1973) requires that gain or loss from disposal of a segment of a business be reported net of tax as a separate component between income from continuing operations and extraordinary items. Gains and losses from disposals that are not identified as business segments are to be reported in income from continuing operations.

This pronouncement also requires that a material event be both unusual in nature *and* infrequent in occurrence to qualify as extraordinary. Other pronouncements, business combinations, extinguishment of debt, and intangible assets of motor carriers identify additional events or transactions that may be classified as extraordinary items. Additionally, unusual *or* infrequent events or transactions are reported as a separate component of income from continuing operations.

Current Reporting Practice

Of the 600 firms included in the AICPA "Accounting Trends and Techniques" ten percent report gains or losses on discontinued operations, and another ten percent report extraordinary items. The latter arises mostly from early retirement of debt, and tax loss carryforwards.

Approximately two-thirds of the firms use the multi-step income statement format, providing subtotals for "gross margin" and/or "operating income." About 25 percent of the firms report gross margin; the others deduct all operating expenses from sales revenues to arrive at operating income. Most of the survey companies report single figures for each of (1) cost of goods sold, and (2) selling and/or general and administrative expense. Interest expense is reported by. 97 percent, and about half report research and development expense.

Among the other gains and losses commonly identified on the face of the income statement by firms are those shown in Table 2.

Table 2: Gains and losses identified on Income Statements

Transaction	Percentage of firms reporting data
Sales of assets	28%
Asset write-downs	10%
Investment income (loss)	34%
Restructuring costs	20%
Foreign currency transactions	25%
Amortization of intangibles	14%
Minority interest	5%
Litigation settlements	5%

Research on Income Statement Classification

Prior to the 1990s, there was surprisingly little empirical research on the usefulness of income statement classification. In a review of contemporary research on the informativeness of accounting earnings, Brennan (1991) states: "the careful consideration given by practicing accountants to the manner in which earnings are reported, and to which items are included in earnings, stands in marked contrast to the casual attitude of most researchers toward the definition of the variable under investigation."

Rapaccioli & Schiff (1991) find that the discretion allowed firms in identifying business segments led firms to classify disposal gains as income from continuing operations and losses as discontinued operations. They conclude that the discretion allowed under Accounting Principles Board (APB) No. 30 permitted firms to manipulate income from continuing operations.

A number of authors have shown that stock price movements can be better explained using income statement components rather than bottom-line earnings. Lipe (1986) reports that different stock market reactions to earnings components for a firm can be associated with the estimated persistence of the component. Swaminathan & Weintrop (1991) show small but statistically significant market reactions to unexpected revenues and unexpected earnings, after controlling for unexpected earnings. Strong & Walker (1993) use data on UK firms to show that stock market returns are more highly correlated with pre-exceptional earnings (corresponding to earnings before unusual and extraordinary items) than with bottom line earnings. Ohlson & Penman (1992) find that, for one-year intervals, some components (e.g., depreciation and taxes) have weaker association with stock price movements than others, but for ten-year intervals, the magnitudes of the associations are similar across components. They conclude that the components are economically equivalent but that some earnings components are harder to measure over short horizons.

Fairfield, Sweeney, & Yohn (1994) show that income statement classifications can be used to improve predictions of future profitability. They conclude that a forecasting model should disaggregate income items into four components: operating income before unusual items and taxes, nonoperating income and income taxes, unusual items, and extraordinary items and discontinued operations. The operating income component should be weighted most heavily in predicting next period's earnings, followed by nonoperating income and taxes, and then by unusual items. Extraordinary items and discontinued operations have no predictive power with respect to next period's earnings.

Bibliography

Brennan, M. (1991). A perspective on accounting and stock prices. *The Accounting Review*, Jan., 67–79.

Fairfield, P., Sweeney, R. & Yohn, T. (1994). The contribution of earnings components to forecasts of future profitability. Georgetown University, working paper.

Lipe, R. C. (1986). The information contained in the components of earnings. *Journal of Accounting Research* (supplement), 37–64.

Ohlson, J. A. & Penman, S. H. (1992). Disaggregated accounting data as explanatory variables for returns. *Journal of Accounting, Auditing and Finance*, Fall, 553–73.

Rapaccioli, D. & Schiff, A. (1991). Reporting sales of segments under APB Opinion No. 30. *Accounting Horizons*, Dec., 53–9.

Strong, N. & Walker, M. (1993). The explanatory power of earnings for stock returns. *The Accounting Review*, Apr., 385–99.

Swaminathan, S. & Weintrop, J. (1991). The information content of earnings, revenues and expenses. *Journal of Accounting Research*, Autumn, 418–27.

PATRICIA FAIRFIELD and TERI L. YOHN

income taxation based on financial statements At one extreme, the calculation of taxable business income may be completely isolated from income that is measured for financial reporting. At the other extreme, taxable income can be simply defined as the equivalent of reported financial income. The former case may not refer to financial statements in tax laws, and therefore a complete set of income tax rules would be promulgated for every taxable transaction and event. In contrast, the latter case need not require any specific income tax rules at all; it is the case of conformity in a strict sense or perfect alignment between tax and financial accounts. In practice neither of these two extremes exist, and there are considerable differences among countries – from applying a fairly integrated to applying an almost completely separated system for financial reporting and calculation of taxable income.

In the Anglo-American tradition, measured financial income is typically not recognized as a suitable basis for taxation of business income, but there are cases of a partial conformity between tax and financial accounts, e.g., in the USA where the inventory accounting method LIFO (last-in, first-out) must be used in the financial reporting if it is to be used for tax purposes. However, in the Anglo-American tradition the measurement of financial income and taxable income are predominantly based on two sets of separate and independent rules. The tax effects of measurement differences are recognized in the financial reports as deferred taxes. On the other hand, many small businesses (e.g., in the USA) do only prepare accounts for tax purposes. Further, income tax rules are often believed to have had adverse effects on accounting theory and principles in many areas (Hendriksen & van Breda, 1992).

In other countries, following the continental European tradition, the financial statements have also served the interest of the tax authority in addition to other prime users such as stockholders and creditors. Generally, within the continental European tradition, financial reporting is regulated by legislation. In some countries, closely following the so-called German approach, detailed prescriptions regulate the reporting of a large number of accountable events. In contrast, in the four Nordic European countries, Denmark, Finland, Sweden, and

Norway, the accounting legislation is more modest and refers to concepts such as "generally accepted accounting principles" (GAAP) or "good accounting practice" as a basic principle for financial reporting, the interpretation of which is left to accounting practice. Also, the German accounting acts do not give prescriptions for every accountable transaction and event, and reference is made to the German version of GAAP if no legal regulations are in existence (Baetge et al., 1995). The national GAAPs are all dynamic concepts allowing accounting practice to develop, and are influenced and interpreted by the accounting profession, the administration of justice, and academics. However, the de facto status and influence of the interpretations vary considerably among countries. Accounting regulations within the continental European tradition normally require most businesses to prepare financial statements. Further, the accounting regulations and the interpretations of GAAP do not rely or refer to income tax rules or tax practice, and are not motivated for income taxation purposes.

In general, national income tax acts define the taxable and deductible items and also include a more or less complete set of specific rules for revenue and expense recognition in the corporate tax returns, e.g., if received dividends are taxable, tax-based valuation of inventory and tax-based depreciation. However, in most of the countries under the influence of the legalistic continental European accounting tradition, the national tax act states that the financial statements form the basis for computing taxable income. Additionally, in line with the German interpretation, the tax authority usually requires that the specific tax rules should be utilized in the preparation of the individual business entity's financial statements. For example, in Germany if a firm wants to use accelerated depreciation in its tax balance sheet in line with the specific tax regulations, then it must show the same value in the financial statements (Busse von Colbe, 1992). Further, in German accounting practice, when there is no prescription in the accounting legislation, companies rely on the tax laws and tax court rulings (Harris et al., 1994).

Thus, outside the Anglo-American tradition, financial statements are to a large extent relevant as a tax base. Further, due to the widespread general requirement in the accounting regulation, even for most small businesses, to prepare financial statements, a cost-saving argument is made in favor of the use of one set of books and the preparation of a single set of financial statements.

However, under this system of partial alignment of financial and tax accounts, the financial reporting of transaction and events becomes sensitive to the specific national tax rules. Although disclosure of the impact of applying tax rules in the financial statements is often mandated, and, as in Germany, theories of financial accounting have had some influence on legal judgment in the area of taxation, tax-induced financial reporting has caused considerable concern. It is widely held that the mandatory interdependence between tax and financial accounts has adverse effects on the accounting practice both in terms of the application of accounting principles and in making accounting estimates, and has therefore limited the informational content of the financial statements to users, other than the tax authority (e.g., Baetge et al., 1995, p. 98).

The interplay between tax and financial accounting varies greatly between countries and is frequently subjected to change, as a result of development in the accounting regulations and income tax policy. For example, in some countries, such as Norway, financial income forms the basis for computation of taxable income, but only if specific rules do not exist in the tax code. Thus, financial and taxable income become less aligned by the promulgation of specific and standardized tax rules. Further, as the individual company in general is the taxable entity, in several countries such as France and Sweden, accounting principles applied in the consolidated financial statements may differ from those used in the tax-influenced individual company's reporting (Alexander & Archer, 1995). Therefore, care should be exercised when evaluating the scope and extent of influence of taxation policy on financial reporting in various countries.

Bibliography

Alexander, D. & Archer, S. (1995). *Miller European accounting guide*. San Diego CA: Harcourt Brace.

Baetge, J. Berndt, H. et al. (1995). German accounting principles: An institutionalized framework. Working Group on External Financial Reporting of the Schmalenbach-Gesellschaft-Deutsche Gesellschaft für Betriebswirtschaft. *Accounting Horizons*, Sept., 92–9.

Busse von Colbe, W. (1992). Relationship between financial accounting research, standards setting and practice in Germany. *European Accounting Review*, May, 27–38.

Elling, J. O. (1993). Financial reporting in the Nordic countries. *European Accounting Review*, Dec., 581–4.

Harris, T. S., Lang, M. & Möller, H. P. (1994). The value relevance of German accounting measures: An empirical analysis. *Journal of Accounting Research*, Autumn, 187–209.

Hendriksen, E. S. & van Breda, M. F. (1992). *Accounting Theory*. Homewood, IL: Irwin.

AASMUND EILIFSEN

independent auditing   The American Accounting Association Committee on Basic Auditing Concepts defined auditing as follows:

> A systematic process of objectively obtaining and evaluating evidence regarding assertions about economic actions and events to ascertain the degree of correspondence between those assertions and established criteria and communicating the results to interested users.

In layman's term, auditors are financial detectives. Auditors pore over financial records to ascertain whether the financial statements prepared from those records faithfully portray what they are intended or designed to portray.

Auditing is a field of accounting, and most auditors think of themselves as accountants first, auditors second. The two primary segments of the auditing profession are internal auditing and external auditing, the latter being more commonly known in the business world as "independent auditing." Regardless of the actual job title of auditors, their principal responsibility, like all accountants, is to facilitate the economic judgments of decision-makers. An internal auditor accomplishes this objective by, among other things, "auditing" the compliance of an organization's employees with its operating policies and procedures. Such monitoring is important if top management is to maintain effective control over an organization and keep its employees focused on the entity's goals and objectives.

The independent audits performed by public accounting firms are quite different from the services provided by internal auditors. The principal objective of an independent audit is to determine whether an entity's financial statements have been prepared in accordance with generally accepted accounting principles (GAAP), which are the fundamental rules, guidelines, and concepts that accountants follow in recording and reporting financial information. This determination is made following the performance of a series of audit procedures or tests. For example, a common type of audit procedure is "test-counting" portions of a client's inventory to ensure that the inventory records are correct in all material respects. If a company's accountants have used GAAP in preparing its financial statements, those statements are presumed to fairly reflect the financial affairs of the company.

Literally all investors, creditors, and other financial decision-makers worldwide rely directly or indirectly on independent auditors to determine whether published financial statements have been prepared in accordance with GAAP. In the absence of an independent audit function, individual financial statement users would be much less likely to assume that published financial statements are honest representations of given entities' financial affairs. Why? Because business owners and nonowner company executives have an economic incentive to "window dress" their financial statements i.e., make their entities appear more profitable and financially stable than they actually are.

By independently examining the financial statements and accounting records of business entities, and not for profit entities as well, public accounting firms bolster the confidence that third parties have in the accuracy of those statements. This higher level of confidence in financial statements makes it more likely that investors and creditors will provide the capital needed by these entities for operating, expansion, and other purposes. Thus, by providing this service, independent auditors (hereafter referred to simply as auditors) greatly facilitate the flow of investment funds in the capital markets.

On a technical level, an independent audit consists of four primary components or phases: planning, internal control assessment, substantive tests, and "wrap-up" procedures. During the planning phase, the team of auditors assigned to an audit engagement obtains a general understanding of the client, including its principal lines of business, key personnel, industry trends, and related issues. The product of this initial phase of an audit is an overall strategy to use in approaching the remainder of the audit as well as a preliminary audit program, which is a listing of specific tasks to be performed in subsequent phases of the engagement. In the second phase of an audit, the engagement team evaluates the client's internal control structure. An internal control structure consists of the accounting journals and ledgers, procedures, and policies established by an entity to safeguard its assets and provide for reliable financial records. Based upon their assessment of a client's internal controls, auditors finalize their audit program. If a client has a strong system of internal controls that appears to be functioning effectively, auditors will diminish the amount of audit tests performed in the following phase of the audit.

In the substantive testing phase of an audit, a variety of detailed tests are performed on each major financial item included in a client's accounting records. Although there are other objectives as well, the central purpose of these tests is to determine whether the recorded dollar (in the USA) figure for each major financial item is "materially" correct. For instance, auditors will attempt to determine whether the cash balance reflected by an entity's accounting records is materially accurate. (Notice the qualifier "materially.") Auditors are not required to determine that a reported dollar figure for a financial item is precisely correct but rather that the given figure is not misstated by a material amount. An error is considered "material" if it is large enough to change or at least influence the decision of a third party that will be relying on the given entity's financial statements to make an economic decision of some type. An example of an audit procedure or audit test for a cash balance would be the mailing of a confirmation to the client's bank. This confirmation would simply ask the client's bank to report the entity's cash balance on the date of the financial statements being prepared by the client.

In the final phase of an audit, the audit engagement team performs a number of "wrap-up" procedures. The most time-consuming of these procedures is a detailed review of the "audit workpapers" prepared during the course of the engagement. Audit workpapers document for each major financial item the procedures performed during the course of an audit, the purpose of those procedures, the primary results of those procedures, and the individual who performed those procedures. During this review process, the senior members of the audit engagement team write review comments concerning unaddressed or insufficiently addressed issues. Subsequently, these comments are considered and then "cleared" in some manner, typically by the performance of additional audit procedures, by the junior members of the engagement team.

The most important product of the fourth and final phase of an audit is an audit opinion. This opinion summarizes clearly and concisely the overall results of the audit. If the audit results suggest that the client's financial statements are materially accurate in all respects, then the audit opinion will be "unqualified." When major omissions, errors, inconsistencies, or other problems are discovered during the course of an audit, a "qualified," "adverse," or "disclaimer" audit opinion will be issued.

Several large, international public accounting firms dominate the auditing profession. Collectively referred to as the "Big Six," these firms audit a large majority of all major private and public companies worldwide. Ernst & Young, one of the largest of these firms, has several hundred offices scattered across the world and generates annual revenues approaching three billion dollars. At the other end of the spectrum are literally thousands of small public accounting firms. These firms typically provide independent audits, or related engagements known as compilations and reviews, as ancillary services to their clients which tend to be small businesses, not for profit agencies, and individuals.

M. CHRIS KNAPP

information content of accounting numbers A key function of financial markets is to filter information and coordinate the allocation of economic resources. In this setting, information is anything that causes economic agents to revise their beliefs about the future returns from the assets traded in financial markets. In well-functioning markets, economic agents condition their demands for financial markets. In well-functioning markets, economic agents condition their demands for financial assets on their available information (which will include asset prices). Equilibrium prices, through a process of balancing demands with supplies, impound this information. If asset prices change to reflect the latest information, they will direct resources to their most efficient use.

Participants in financial markets gather information about the value of firms from various sources. Some information comes from the activities of individual investors and financial analysts generating private information. Other information comes from public releases by firms themselves. Firms communicate with financial markets through a complex set of formal and informal channels. When management have information about the firm that outside investors do not have, any action by management, e.g., to raise new capital, can signal information about firm value to the market. However, the most visible and regular form of communication by firms to financial markets is the public disclosure of accounting numbers contained in financial statements.

Studies of the information content of accounting numbers investigate the relation between accounting numbers and asset prices or returns. This area of largely empirical research has formed a major part of the agenda of market-based accounting research, otherwise known as capital market research in accounting, over the last thirty years.

We can define a formal test of information content of some accounting number(s), Y_i, from a financial reporting system or generally accepted accounting principles (GAAP) regime, , in the general form of null and alternative hypotheses. In the following definition, $f(\tilde{R}_j | y_i)$ is the distribution of asset j's return conditional on available information that includes the accounting number(s) of interest. The corresponding marginal distribution, $f(\tilde{R}_j)$, is conditional on available information excluding the accounting number(s) of interest.

H_N: $f(\tilde{R}_j | y_i) - f(\tilde{R}_j) = 0$ for all $y_i [Z$,

H_A: $f(\tilde{R}_j | y_i) - f(\tilde{R}_j) \, \dot{\iota} \, 0$ for at least one $y_i [Z$.

This definition accommodates the effect on any parameter of the return distribution, including mean, volatility, skewness, etc. It also accommodates any potentially affected financial asset, from the equity stock of the disclosing firm itself, the firm's bonds or other securities, options written on the firm's securities, through to stocks of other firms. However, because the focus is on traded securities and market prices, traditional tests have not examined the information content of accounting numbers for stakeholders with a nontraded claim on the firm.

Most information content studies have examined the effect of an accounting disclosure by a firm on the mean of the firm's return distribution. Here, the alternative hypothesis would state that for the firm's accounting number y_i to possess information content, the firm's unexpected return conditional on y_i must be non-zero. In some studies this requires separate classification of "good news" and "bad news" information signals, y_i. There are also several studies that have investigated the effect on return volatility or variance of announcements of accounting numbers. If accounting numbers have information content, asset price changes, and therefore returns, should be greater in announcement periods than nonannouncement periods. Tests based on return variability may avoid the need for classifying news.

One of the first and most famous pieces of published academic research on the information content of accounting numbers was Ball & Brown (1968). This study offered a rigorous examination of the relation between accounting earnings and stock returns. The study was motivated as a response to accusations that accounting numbers, and earnings in particular, were worthless to investors trying to value firms and were ignored by financial markets. Contrary to popular belief, Ball & Brown found that the information content of earnings numbers, given by the contemporaneous association between earnings changes and a measure of firm-specific stock price change over the period, was considerable. They also found strong evidence of the market anticipating the accounting numbers to be released, suggesting the public disclosure date is not timely, and weaker evidence of a delayed response to at least part of the public disclosure. For a personal account of the story of Ball & Brown (1968) and subsequent developments (see Ball, 1989).

Many studies following Ball & Brown, using increasingly sophisticated research designs, have confirmed the link between earnings and stock returns. Researchers have consistently found statistically significant *earnings response coefficients* – measuring the effect on stock returns of one unit of unexpected earnings – across alternate samples, periods, research designs, and countries. Subsequent landmarks in this literature are Beaver et al. (1980) and Kormendi & Lipe (1987). Lev (1989) caused a brief pause in this research in suggesting that the explanatory power of earnings for stock returns, and therefore the usefulness of earnings disclosures, was embarrassingly low. Active research areas now include more detailed examination of market anticipation of accounting numbers, their value-relevance, and whether the market responds rationally to accounting numbers. Work of Ohlson (*see*, for example, Ohlson, 1995), which provides a clearer theoretical link between value and accounting numbers, has stimulated further research.

Research has also investigated the information content of accounting numbers besides historic cost earnings. Much of this has examined the *incremental information content* (IIC) of accounting numbers – their additional information content after controlling for the information in other accounting numbers. The IIC of components of earnings over the bottom line earnings figure would be an example. Evidence on the IIC of cash flows and accruals over earnings is mixed. Similar mixed evidence comes from studies on the IIC of current cost disclosures over historic cost earnings. A major problem in tests of IIC is in hypothesizing the effect of the information. Are higher accruals good news or bad news, or good for some firms bad for others? Later, more sophisticated research designs, specifically addressing this issue, have found IIC that earlier studies failed to detect (*see*, for example, Ali, 1994).

Future work on information content of accounting numbers is likely to require more detailed theoretical work on *fundamental analysis* – the link between firm value and accounting numbers – and on the time-series properties of accounting numbers. To test and interpret information content of accounting numbers, researchers will need to understand better the context of individual firms' operating and reporting environments. Comparative international studies offer the challenge of examining alternative dimensions of the issue.

Bibliography

Ali, A. (1994). The incremental information content of earnings, working capital from operations, and cash flows. *Journal of Accounting Research*, **32**, Spring, 61–74.

Ball, R. (1989). [Ball & Brown, 1968] *Journal of Accounting Research*, **27**, (supplement), 202–17.

Ball, R. & Brown, P. (1968). An empirical evaluation of accounting income numbers. *Journal of Accounting Research*, **6**, Autumn, 159–78.

Beaver, W. H., Lambert, R. A. & Morse, D. (1980). The information content of security prices. *Journal of Accounting and Economics*, **2**, June, 3–28.

Kormendi, R. C. & Lipe, R. (1987). Earnings innovations, earnings persistence, and stock returns. *Journal of Business*, **60**, July, 323–46.

Lev, B. (1989). On the usefulness of earnings and earnings research: Lessons and directions from two decades of empirical research. *Journal of Accounting Research*, **27**, (supplement), 153–92.

Ohlson, J. (1995). Earnings, book value, and dividends in security valuation. *Contemporary Accounting Research*, Spring.

NORMAN C. STRONG

information cues   The information set on which any accounting or auditing judgment is made is one of the most important determinants of the quality of that judgment. However, very little guidance is provided within the accounting or auditing standards as to what are the appropriate components of these information sets. The major reason for this is that the uniqueness of the decision context makes it very difficult to define or suggest an appropriate information set. The only general guidance is in the audit evidence standards (International Auditing Standard 500, AUS 502 in Australia, AU 326 in the USA, Auditing Standard 400 in the UK, Auditing and Related Services Standard 5300 in Canada, AS501 in New Zealand). This gives the following guidance on the reliability of information cues:

- External information cues (e.g., confirmation received from a third party) are generally more reliable than information cues generated within an organization.

- Information cues generated within an organization are more reliable when the related internal controls of the organization are satisfactory.

- Information cues obtained by decision-makers themselves are generally more reliable than those obtained from entities.

- Information cues in the form of documents and written representations are generally more reliable than oral information cues.

Where the decision-maker has to choose a set of information cues from a population in order to make a choice between competing options, there are various strategies that can be undertaken.

These are (Shaklee & Fischhoff, 1982):

(1) *parallel cue choice* – where the decision-maker selects information about all competing options before making any judgments. This approach has the advantage of allowing the decision-maker to concentrate on one choice strategy at a time;

(2) *serial cue choice* – where the decision-maker seeks information about one option. Having secured the relevant evidence for this option, the evidence for the next possible option is collected, and so on. This approach has the advantage of allowing the decision-maker to concentrate on one option at a time; and

(3) *truncated cue choice* – where the decision-maker seeks information about one option, and, if satisfied that choice can be made on the basis of this information, does not seek further information.

Parallel and *serial* search would normally lead to similar options being chosen, if all possible options are investigated. *Truncated* search may mean that the "best" option is not explored, if a satisfactory option is selected first.

It is not necessary that any one strategy is superior to others in all instances. Because of potential problems with information overload, or because information acquisition is not costless, it may be that the truncated search may prove superior in complex tasks (especially those where there are a large number of options), while serial or parallel search may be more appropriate when the range of options and/or number of cues are small or have been sufficiently narrowed down.

Two potential biases relevant to information cue choice have been identified in the literature:

The first is *confirmatory bias* (Klayman & Ha, 1987). The decision-maker tends to select (or rely on) information that could confirm the rule or option to be tested, ignoring potentially disconfirmatory information. If only a subset of the relevant data is collected, such a decision-maker risks prematurely accepting an option. To the extent that such a bias exists, care must be taken in the framing of questions or statements that are to guide information choice. Confirmatory bias suggests that if questions are framed in particular ways, the information seeker will tend to choose cues to support such frames.

The second type of potential bias is the *conservatism bias* (Kida, 1984; Smith & Kida, 1991). Accountants and auditors are trained to be conservative, and to the extent that this reflects particular loss functions, such conservatism may be appropriate. However, conservatism may also mean that other relevant information is ignored. For example, if an auditor selects information more likely to suggest misstatement compared with non-misstatement, or failure compared with viability, relevant information may be overlooked.

Relevant Characteristics of Information Cue Choice

There are a number of factors which will affect information cue choice. These factors can be categorized under decision-maker, cue, task, and environmental characteristics:

Decision-maker characteristics

(1) Cue familiarity/recognition-decision-makers will tend to choose that information with which they are more familiar.

(2) Expertise (Bedard & Chi, 1993; Bonner & Pennington, 1991; Libby, 1985; Davis & Solomon, 1989). This may be related to cue familiarity, as decision-makers who are experts in the particular task may understand more about the characteristics of the available information set; may be aware of a broader set of relevant information for the decision at hand; may be better able to differentiate between relevant and irrelevant information; may recognize patterns in cue collection; may be able to generate further competing hypotheses; or may have the steps needed to effectively undertake the task ordered in their mind in a different way. Any or all of these factors may influence information cue choice.

(3) Other factors that may need to be considered include the motivation, preferences, and personality of the decision-maker.

Characteristics of Information Cues

(1) *Cue cost* – the cost of obtaining a specific information item may determine whether it is chosen. Such costs will take into account the availability of the cue and the use of resources to acquire the cue.

(2) *Cue diagnosticity* – this refers to the ability of the cue to distinguish between competing hypotheses. Cet. par., information cues which are the more diagnostic should be preferred by the decision-maker.

(3) *Cue redundancy* – this is one aspect of cue diagnosticity and refers to the fact that the specific cue contains no information content beyond that which is contained in the already chosen information cue set. However, it may be that in certain instances, decision-makers do choose and make use of redundant cues. For example, the auditor is interested in ensuring consistency of information, even though the additional information cues contain no further explanatory power. Also, the confirmation bias may lead the decision-maker to choose redundant information, e.g., information consistent with the content of other confirmatory cues. The conservatism bias may also lead the decision-maker to seek more information cues for a particular alternative, irrespective of whether those cues have information value.

(4) *Source reliability* – the assessment of source reliability may also affect information cue choice. For example, in seeking audit evidence, auditors are provided with general rules on source reliability, including the view that evidence from external sources is generally more reliable than evidence generated internally.

Task Characteristics Affecting Information Cue Choice

It has been frequently argued that seemingly minor changes in the task can affect performance (Bonner, 1994). These changes may occur either through different strategies for choice of information cues or information processing. Task characteristics that may affect information cue choice include:

(1) *Task complexity* – including increases in number of alternatives and/or number of cues per alternative, and the structure or stability of the relationship between the cues.

(2) *Information cue order* – depending on the order in which cues are presented and the selection strategy, this may change the cues which are selected.

(3) *The framing of the task* – this can be important, especially given the possibility of the existence of a confirmation bias.

(4) *The response mode* – the output that is required and the form in which it is required may influence cue choice.

(5) *Base rates* – perceptions of the underlying population rates, or the frequency or infrequency of event occurrence, may influence cue choice. For example, auditors may be influenced in their search for explanations of unexpected fluctuations in an account balance by their perceived frequency of errors.

Environmental Factors Influencing Information Cue Choice

Environmental considerations which may influence information cue choice include:

(1) *Group decision process including the review process* – knowledge as to whether decisions will be reviewed and by whom may influence information cue selection.

(2) *Incentives* – the extent to which the environment provides incentives and the ways in which this influences the decision-maker may also influence information cue choice.

(3) *Justification* – the extent to which decisions require justification may influence the choice of cues.

(4) *Pressure* – time or budget pressures, e.g., in audit, may influence choice of cues.

(5) *Decision aids* – the availability of decision aids may also influence information cue choices, or may even suggest which cues are to be chosen.

Research Including Information Choice in Research Design

Research that has included information choice in its research design has allowed a greater understanding of the decision process. However, the conclusions arising from the literature on the comparative ability of people to choose and process information are mixed. The early findings from cognitive psychology on the comparative abilities of people in choosing and processing information is summarized in the following quote from Dawes (1979, p. 573) "people – especially the experts in a field – are much better at selecting and coding information than they are at integrating it."

This general conclusion, however, has not been strongly supported by the limited number of accounting studies that have specifically studied the relative contribution of information selection and information processing. In fact, the four principal accounting studies in this area have all concluded differently. Abdel-khalik & El-Sheshei (1980) concluded that information choice was the major reason for inferior prediction achievement, while Chalos & Pickard (1985) found that information processing was a major factor for such inferior achievement. Lewis et al. (1988) concluded that subjects given model-selected data do not perform any better than those given self-selected data, and that lower performance of subjects given model-selected data when compared with a statistical model can in part be attributed to some overfitting of the statistical model. Simnett & Trotman (1989) concluded that information choice was a limiting factor on decision accuracy for two levels of task predictability, and while

information processing was not a limiting factor when auditors selected their own ratios, it did become a limiting factor when they were provided with model-selected ratios. Thus, further evidence on the relative contributions that information selection and information processing by decision-makers make toward determining the quality of their decision outputs is required.

The other group of studies that have examined the effect of information choice are the protocol and process tracing studies. The studies in accounting have tended to emphasize differences between experts and novices. The general findings are that the better decision-makers are able to better identify the more relevant information cues and have a more directed, potentially higher order, choice strategy for the decision at hand (Bedard & Biggs, 1991; Bedard & Chi, 1993).

Bibliography

Abdel-khalik, A. R. & El-Sheshai, K. M. (1980). Information choice and utilization in an experiment on default prediction. *Journal of Accounting Research*, 18, Autumn, 325–42.

Bedard, J. C. & Biggs, S. F. (1991). Pattern recognition, hypotheses generation and auditor performance in an analytical task. *The Accounting Review*, 66, July, 622–42.

Bedard, J. C. & Chi, M. T. H. (1993). Expertise in auditing.. *Auditing: A Journal of Practice and Theory*, 12, (Supplement), 21–45.

Bonner, S. E. & Pennington, N. (1991). Cognitive processes and knowledge as determinants of auditor expertise. *Journal of Accounting Literature*, 10, 1–50.

Bonner, S. E. (1994). A model of the effects of audit task complexity. *Accounting, Organizations and Society*, 19, 213–34.

Chalos, P. & Pickard, S. (1985). Information choice and cue use: An experiment in group information processing. *Journal of Applied Psychology*, 70, 634–41.

Davis, J. S. & Solomon, I. (1989). Experience, expertise and expert-performance research in public accounting. *Journal of Accounting Literature*, 7, Fall, 150–64.

Dawes, R. M. (1979). The robust beauty of improper linear models in decision-making. *American Psychologist*, 34, 571–82.

Kida, T. (1984). The impact of hypothesis-testing strategies on auditors' use of judgment data. *Journal of Accounting Research*, 22, Autumn,

332–40.

Klayman, J. & Ha Y. W. (1987). Confirmation disconfirmation and information in hypothesis testing. *Psychological Review*, **94**, 211–28.

Lewis, B. L., Patton J. M. & Green, S. L. (1988). The effects of information choice and information use on analysts' predictions of municipal bond rating changes. *The Accounting Review*, **63**, Apr., 270–82.

Libby, R. (1985). Availability and the generation of hypotheses in analytical review. *Journal of Accounting Research*, **23**, Autumn, 648–67.

Shaklee, H. & Fischhoff, B. (1982). Strategies of information search in causal analysis. *Memory & Cognition*, **10**, 520–30.

Simnett, R. & Trotman, K. (1989). Auditor versus model: Information choice and information processing. *The Accounting Review*, **64**, July, 514–28.

Smith, J. E. & Kida, T. (1991). Heuristics and biases: Expertise and task realism in auditing. *Psychological Bulletin*, **109**, 472–89.

ROGER SIMNETT

intangible assets Intangible assets other than goodwill are separately identifiable long-lived, nonphysical rights or resources that possess a determinable future use and are specifically developed or acquired for the production or distribution of external goods or services. Examples of allowable intangible assets include patents, copyrights, trade names, trademarks, franchises, licensing agreements, leaseholds, organizational costs, and some software development costs. In the USA, all intangible assets acquired or developed after October 31, 1970 must be initially capitalized at historical cost (fair value exchanged at the time of acquisition or cost incurrence) and must be periodically amortized over the expected life of the future benefit according to Accounting Principles Board (APB) Opinion No. 17 (1973), "Intangible Assets." If any one of the qualifying conditions does not hold, then the expenditures cannot be capitalized and must be expensed as incurred. Judgments concerning the capitalization of intangible costs should be governed by the accounting concepts of asset and liability measurements, matching, consistency, and conservatism (Financial Accounting Standards Board (FASB) Statement of Financial Accounting Concept No. 1, 1978, "Objectives of Financial Reporting by Business Enterprises";

FASB Statement of Financial Accounting Concept No. 2, 1980, "Quantitative Characteristics of Accounting Information").

Capitalization of research and development costs is not allowed as a general rule due to the difficulty in the determination of the association of those costs with particular future benefit activities, the magnitude of the future benefits, and/or the length of time over which such benefits may be realized. However, if the research and development activities can be uniquely identified with particular assets that have determinable future alternative uses, then they may be capitalized as intangible assets and are periodically amortized as research and development expense (FASB Statement of Financial Accounting Standard (SFAS) No. 2, 1974, "Accounting for Research and Development Costs"; FASB Interpretation No. 5, 1975, "Applicability of FASB Statement No. 2 to Development Stage Enterprises;" FASB Interpretation No. 6, 1975, "Applicability of FASB Statement No. 2 to Computer Software;" FASB SFAS No. 68, 1982; FASB Technical Bulletin No. 84–1, 1984 "Accounting for Stock Issued to Acquire the Results of a Research and Development Arrangement"; FASB SFAS No. 86, 1985 "Accounting for the Costs of Computer Software to be Sold, leased or Otherwise Marketed").

Intangible assets should be separately identified on the balance sheet as "intangible assets." Required disclosures in the notes to the financial statements include specific explanations of each intangible asset's value, amortization method, and useful life determination. Presenting the detailed intangible information in the body of the balance sheet or in a separate intangibles policy statement rather than an intangibles note is also allowed. In the USA, management has the option of not amortizing intangibles acquired before October 31, 1970 if a determinable useful life cannot be ascertained (APB Opinion No. 17).

All intangible assets must be completely amortized within the maximum allowable of 40 years. If the useful life of an intangible asset is restricted due to legal, regulatory, or contractual provisions, obsolescence, competition, or other economic factors, the shorter of the restricted life or 40 years must be used. The straight line depreciation method is recommended unless a better method can be documented. The periodic amortization of the intangible asset should be presented as an operating expense on the income statement and directly reduces the asset balance on the balance sheet (a contra account for accumulated amortization is allowed but is rarely utilized). At sale or disposal of an intangible asset, the periodic amortization is recorded for the expired portion of the accounting period, the asset is removed, and the gain or loss is calculated and recognized. Significant write-offs due to loss of value must be presented as an extraordinary item on the income statement (APB Opinion No. 17; Williams, Stanga & Holder, 1992).

The value and/or the useful life of an intangible asset may change over time due to new circumstances and therefore should be periodically reassessed. For example, expenditures incurred during the life of the asset that are clearly related to future use of the intangible asset may be added to the value of the intangible asset. If the useful life of the intangible asset is reassessed, however, the maximum life limit of 40 years still holds and is calculated from the date of the original intangible asset recognition (APB Opinion No. 17).

Patents are transferable rights that exclude others from making, using, or selling the original work without contractual permission. Their value stems from creating competitive advantage. The maximum legal life of a patent in the USA is 17 years and is not renewable. Practically speaking, however, the useful life of a patent may be extended by successfully filing for another closely related patent before the original patent expires and adding any remaining original patent value to the cost of the new patent. Factors that may reduce a patent's economic life include new and more efficient inventions by the same enterprise or by competitors, new substitute products for current products, and/or changes in customer demands. Costs available for capitalization as patents typically include legal fees, registration fees, and the cost of models and drawings that accompany registration applications. All related research and development costs must be expensed as incurred. During the life of a patent, any costs associated with successful legal defenses of claims related to an infringement on a patent may be added to the patent account.

Costs related to unsuccessful legal defenses must be expensed, an event that is usually accompanied by a write-off of the unamortized portion of the remaining patent as a loss (APB Opinion No. 17).

Copyrights are transferable exclusive rights to the publication, production or reproduction, and sale of literary, dramatic, musical, or artistic work. Prior to 1978, the US Copyright Office (a department of the US Library of Congress) granted copyrights for 28 years with a right to renew for another 28 years. Since 1978, copyrights are valid for the length of the author's life plus 50 years (APB Opinion No. 17).

Trade names and trademarks are legally protected and renewable symbols, designs, or phrases used by an enterprise to encourage public identification with the product or company. Capitalizable costs include legal fees, registration costs, design costs, acquisition costs, successful legal defense, and other expenditures directly related to the acquisition of the right to use the trade name or trademark (APB Opinion No. 17; Williams, Stanga & Holder, 1992).

Franchises and licensing agreements are contractual agreements allowing performance of certain functions in exchange for specific payments or the fulfillment of other obligations. If the contract can be terminated at the will of the entity granting the franchise, the cost should be amortized over a relatively short period of time. Periodic payments made under a franchise agreement are expensed as incurred. While unamortized costs of interstate operating rights must now be written off, the costs of intrastate operating rights in non deregulated states may still be carried as intangible assets (FASB SFAS No. 44, 1980, "Accounting for Intangible Assets of Motor Carriers;" Reilly, 1992).

Leaseholds are lessee's capital expenditures that improve the quality of a leased property that would revert back to the lessor at the end of the lease. Leaseholds are accumulated in a separate "leasehold improvement" account and can be presented within the classification of intangible assets or the property, plant and equipment sections of the balance sheet, regardless of whether the lease is recorded as an operating or a capital leases (APB Opinion No. 17).

Organizational Cost

Organizational costs include the legal fees of drafting the corporate charter and bylaws and of corporate registration, promotion expenditures, initial stock-issuance costs, and other miscellaneous costs of organization. These costs are usually capitalized and amortized over a relatively short period in the early years of the enterprise's life. Since the USA tax laws require a period of five years for the amortization, many companies use this same time period for financial reporting purposes. Special additional disclosure requirements exist for development stage companies that have not yet generated significant revenue (Financial Accounting Standards Board (FASB) Interpretation No. 5, 1975, "Applicability of FASB Statement No. 2 to Development Stage Enterprises").

Software development costs are allowed to be capitalized as intangible assets if they pass the technological feasibility tests set forth by FASB's Statement of Financial Accounting Standard (SFAS) No. 86 (1985), "Accounting for the Costs of Computer Software to be Sold, Leased, or Otherwise Marketed," relate to future products, are intended to be externally marketed, and are not considered research and development (FASB SFAS No. 2, 1974, "Accounting for Research and Development Costs;" FASB Interpretation No. 6, 1975, "Applicability of FASB Statement No. 2 to Software;" Fields, Waters & Thompson, 1986). Technological feasibility is established upon either (1) the completion of a detailed program design that ensures that the company has the necessary skills, hardware and software technology, and product specifications and has resolved all high-risk development issues, or (2) the presentation of a tested working model. Before the technological feasibility point is reached, all costs must be charged to research and development expense. All costs after the product is ready for release must be capitalized as inventory and charged to cost of sales. If the software is to be part of another product or process, then all of the research and development activities for the entire product or process must be completed before any costs are capitalized. If purchased software has a clearly documented alternative future use, then that portion of the purchase cost can also be capitalized.

Amortization should begin when the final product is ready for general external release. The asset balance should be the lower of the capitalized costs or the current net realizable value. The greater of (1) the remaining asset balance multiplied by the ratio of current revenues to anticipated future revenues, or (2) the ratio of the current asset balance to the remaining useful life (straight line method) should be used as the basis for amortization, with the straight line amount establishing the minimum required periodic amortization. If later enhancement costs extend the life or improve marketability, they must be capitalized and added to the asset balance (FASB SFAS No. 86). Disclosures required for capitalized software production costs include: the unamortized computer software costs included in each balance sheet presented and the total amount of non research and development software costs that were charged to expense in each income statement presented, detailing the amounts amortized, written down, written off, or not capitalized. Directly expensed software development costs must conform with the research and development costs disclosure requirements (FASB SFAS No. 2).

The USA standards on accounting for intangible assets generally favor conservatism and objectivity – some critics argue at the expense of proper valuation, relevance, and matching. These debates demonstrate a need for a unified conceptual framework. Challenges to the accounting standards for intangible assets often arise from marketing, human resources, research and development costs, air pollution emission, and computer software development cost.

For example, the future benefits of direct-response advertising are both quantifiable and expected when an enterprise has had previous direct-advertising experiences. Accordingly, proponents argue that they should be recorded as intangible assets until their associated revenue is realized (American Institute of Certified Public Accountants (AICPA) Statement of Position No. 93–7, 1993, "Reporting on Advertising Costs;" Tannenbaum, 1993; Tannenbaum & Finger, 1994). Other marketing issues often argued to receive intangible assets treatment include measuring and recording the value of brand names, customer lists, contract-related favorable supplier contracts, product image, and product reputation (Guilding & Pike, 1990; Kay & Cook, 1990). With similar arguments, the value of specific human resources could be measured, as the increased patient trust in medical abilities, closer relationships with suppliers, customers, or government, or superior ability to innovate and adapt as needed to maximize wealth creation (James, 1993). Proponents argue that there is at least the same if not more subjectivity allowed in US pronouncements relating to pensions or stock options, and request an explanation for the argument that omitting these intangibles is more informative than a possibly biased estimation of their values.

Most critics argue for more flexibility in capitalization of research and development costs to improve matching, since no rational decision-maker would expend these costs if there were not probable beliefs in future benefits. The international accounting standards allow more flexibility than do the US standards: see International Accounting Standards Committee (IASC) of the International Accounting Standards Board, International Accounting Standard No. 9, 1993, "Accounting for Research and Development Activities".

The US Clean Air Act of 1990 grants transferable units, called "allowances," of air-pollution emission rights to companies. The allowances can be used in their appropriate year or saved for future years. Proponents argue that these allowances should be accounted for as intangible assets similar to franchises or other contractual licenses and suggest using current market value for the asset valuation method and the units-of-production method for the amortization method (Ewer, Nance & Hamilton, 1992).

The definition of technological feasibility for software development cost capitalization has been attacked repeatedly. Enterprises consider the definition ambiguous, creating inconsistency in its application, stating that the point as defined occurs too late in the development process, fails to optimize the matching of expenses to related revenues, forces some production costs into research and development expenses, and confuses product risk with steps in the production cycle that may be are

unrealistic for smaller, younger enterprises. Japan, for example, allows for capitalization of software development costs at an earlier point, during the systems analysis and design phases, in addition to the coding and testing stages that are only allowed by the US standards (Fox & Ramsower, 1989; Kirsch & Sakthivel, 1993; Scarborough, McGee & Sakurai, 1993).

Explicit guidance for the accounting treatment of development costs of software for internal enterprise use does not exist and these costs are currently expensed with other research and development costs. Critics argue that these costs are not research and development expenses, that the immediate expensing creates incorrect matching of internal operating revenues and costs, and, finally, that these costs should be capitalized and allocated to the departments that will be consuming the future benefits of the new management information system.

Bibliography

Ewer, S. R., Nance, J. R. & Hamilton, S. J. (1992). Accounting for tomorrow's pollution control. *Journal of Accountancy*, July, 69–74.

Fields, K. T., Waters, G. L. & Thompson, J. H. (1986). Accounting for the costs of certain computer software. *CPA Journal*, January, 32–7.

Fox, T. L. & Ramsower, R. M. (1989). Why FASB 86 needs revision. *Journal of Accountancy*, June, 93–100.

Guilding, C. & Pike, R. (1990). Intangible marketing assets. A managerial accounting perspective. *Accounting and Business Research*, Winter, 41–9.

James, D. (1993). Why human capital can't be an asset on the books. *Business Review*, May, 166–7.

King, A. M. & Cook, J. (1990). Brand names: The invisible assets. *Management Accounting*, Nov., 41–5.

Kirsch, R. J. & Sakthivel, S. (1993). Capitalize or expense?: Accountants need guidance on software developed for internal use. *Management Accounting*, Jan., 38–43.

Reilly, R. (1992). Interstate intangible asset transfer programs. *The CPA Journal*, Aug., 34–40.

Scarbrough, P., McGee, R. & Sakurai, M. (1993). Accounting for software costs in the United States and Japan: Lessons from differing standards and practices. *The International Journal of Accounting*, June, 308–24.

Tannenbaum, J. (1993). Financial accounting: Reporting on advertising costs. *Journal of Accountancy*, June, 79–80.

Tannenbaum, J. & Finger, A. D. (1994). Reporting on intangibles. *The CPA Journal*, May, 36–40.

Williams, J. R., Stanga, K. & Holder, W. (1992). Intangible assets. *Intermediate Accounting*. San Diego, CA: Harcourt Brace Jovanovich College Publishers.

MARGARITA MARIA LENK

interim reporting

Reporting Requirements and Concerns

In paragraph 6 of US Accounting Principles Board (APB) Opinion 28, "Interim Financial Reporting," the APB asserted that "periodic and timely financial information during a fiscal year is useful to investors and others." Based on this assumption, the APB issued guidance on accounting and disclosure issues peculiar to interim reporting and set minimum disclosure requirements for interim financial reports of publicly traded companies.

The APB recognized that many reporting and disclosure issues faced in compiling interim reports are also faced in construction of the annual report. For this reason, the APB asserted that most accounting policies related to revenue and expense reporting should be consistent with policies used in full year reports. While most policies adapt easily to the shorter interim periods, the APB cited several areas of interim reporting that might require special attention to assure the usefulness of the interim reports. These include (1) the allocation of frequent year-end adjustments to interim periods; (2) the estimate of the applicable tax rate; (3) the disclosure of extraordinary items; (4) the disclosure of accounting changes; and (5) the reporting of seasonal trends.

The concerns expressed relating to the first two items are based on the fact that the actual amount of year-end adjustments and the firm's tax rate are not known until year-end. This occurs in part because complete analysis of many income and expense accounts, such as inventory shrinkage or the allowance for doubtful accounts, may not be conducted until after year-end, commensurate with the outside, independent audit. However, the APB asserted that estimates of these adjustments should be made in each of the interim periods to the extent to which they can be reasonably approximated.

The remaining three issues address concerns of distortions brought about by the fact that interim reports cover smaller time periods. The APB suggested that any accounting policy changes, large write-offs, or seasonal trends should be highlighted to ensure that results reported are not misleading. It also stressed a need for consistency with and comparability to the results reported in the previous year annual report.

Academic Research on Interim Reporting

The concern over the timeliness of reported expense adjustments was the focus of much of the early research on interim disclosures. For example, Penman (1984; 1987) and Kross & Schroeder (1984) both demonstrate that earnings numbers containing "bad news" are generally reported later than expected. McNichols (1988) also reports that security returns around earnings announcement dates are less positively skewed than what is found in non-announcement periods. Elliott & Shaw (1988) demonstrate an apparent difference in the timing of asset write-off announcements by documenting that 151 (62.9 percent) of 240 announcements between 1982 and 1985 occurred in the fourth quarter of the year. Finally, Pastena & Ronen (1979) find that managers tend to delay the disclosure of bad nonearnings news until the fiscal year-end to correspond with the time of the firm's audit.

While these studies seem to indicate that firms do defer earnings reducing disclosures, early studies of the investors' reactions to interim earnings did not document a significant difference in how the disclosures were interpreted. For example, Brown & Kennelly (1972) find no differential stock price reaction to interim earnings when compared to annual earnings releases.

Recent studies have, however, documented that differences do exist. For example, Cornell & Landsman (1989) report greater coefficients on fourth quarter earnings forecast errors than those found for interim earnings errors. These findings lead them to conclude that audited annual earnings announcements are uniquely informative. In contrast, Mendenhall & Nichols (1988) argue that managers have greater discretion over interim reported earnings. They, therefore, claim that disclosures of bad news in interim reports will be more informative leading to greater earnings response coefficients. While their results seem to support this hypotheses, Palepu (1988) points out that fourth quarter earnings coefficients are smaller for both good and bad news. Such a finding might suggest that fourth quarter earnings numbers are simply more noisy. A variety of explanations could explain that result.

One confounding factor in the Mendenhall & Nichols's (1988) study is that they limited the study to relatively large firms. Kross & Schroeder (1991) address this issue by broadening their sample to include a set of smaller firms. Their results suggest that the hypothesis of greater noise in fourth quarter earnings is supported only for small firms. Such noise would be consistent with fourth quarter earnings numbers for small firms containing greater amounts of year-end settling up of errors from the interim periods. However, it does not explain the result found by Mendenhall & Nichols (1988) for larger firms. The noise hypothesis for small firms is confirmed by Kinney & McDaniel (1989) who document that firms that correct previously reported earnings generally make reductions and are generally smaller firms.

Another purported cause of cross-quarter differences in the response to earnings has been seasonal effects on interim earnings numbers. Salamon & Stober (1992) find that earnings response coefficients are greater in quarters containing the largest share of a seasonal firm's annual sales. These results suggest that the greatest amount of uncertainty is resolved in the peak sales quarters. They also find that both smaller and larger firms have smaller fourth quarter earnings coefficients.

Bibliography

Brown, P. & Kennelly, J. (1972). The informational content of quarterly earnings: An extension and some further evidence. *Journal of Business*, July, 403–15.

Cornell, B. & Landsman, W. (1989). Security price response to quarterly earnings announcements and analysts forecast revisions. *The Accounting Review*, Oct., 680–92.

Elliott, J. & Shaw, W. (1988). Write-offs as accounting procedures to manage perceptions. *Journal of Accounting Research*, (supplement), 91–126.

Kinney, W. & McDaniel, L. (1989). Characteristics of firms correcting previously reported quarterly earnings. *Journal of Accounting and Economics*, Feb., 71–93.

Kross, W. & Schroeder, D. (1984). An empirical investigation of the effect of quarterly earnings announcement timing on stock returns. *Journal of Accounting Research*, Spring, 153–76.

Kross, W. & Schroeder, D. (1991). The differential market response to interim versus annual earnings reports: An empirical investigation. Working paper. Purdue University.

McNichols, M. (1988). A comparison of the skewness of stock return distributions in earnings announcement and non-announcement periods. *Journal of Accounting and Economics*, July, 239–73.

Mendenhall, R. & Nichols, W. (1988). Bad news and differential market reactions to announcements of earlier-quarters versus fourth-quarter earnings. *Journal of Accounting Research*, supplement, 63–86.

Palepu, K. (1988). Discussion of bad news and differential market reactions to announcements of earlier-quarters versus fourth-quarters earnings. *Journal of Accounting Research*, (supplement), 87–9.

Pastena, V. & Ronen, J. (1979). Some hypotheses on the pattern of management's informal disclosures. *Journal of Accounting Research*, Autumn, 550–64.

Penman, S. (1984). Abnormal returns to investment strategies based on the timing of earnings reports. *Journal of Accounting and Economics*, Dec., 165–84.

Penman, S. (1987). The distribution of earnings news over time and seasonalities in aggregate stock returns. *Journal of Financial Economics*, June, 199–228.

Salamon, G. & Stober, T. (1992). Cross-quarter differences in stock price responses to earnings announcements: Fourth-quarter and seasonality influences. Working paper. Indiana University.

Wayne H. Shaw

internal control in auditing

The words "internal controls" act like catnip on accountants: they produce a frenzy of enthusiasm, sometimes for reasons not entirely clear to the outside world. (*Financial Times*, October 5, 1993, p. 19)

Internal control constitutes part of the *client's* system that governs the nature, timing, and extent of *audit* procedures. The definition bears on two interrelated audit tasks: (1) the nature of the actions that need to be taken by the auditor as a result of control conditions, and (2) the identification of controls that should be considered by the auditor in determining those actions. The latter subject, controls coverage, has given rise to either a "broad" or a "narrow" view of the universe of controls.

The public's expectations of auditing have been increasing, perchance suggesting that a relatively broad interpretation of controls would be appropriate. Contrariwise, auditors have resisted the broad interpretation, fearing an expansion of legal liability. Corollary issues involve the desirability of having publicly-held company managements reporting on the state of their internal control, as well as whether, and to what extent, external auditors should participate in such reporting. Moreover, technology has brought about great advances in the tools available to auditors.

Professional, Regulatory, and Legal Standards

The Second Standard of Field Work (study and evaluation of internal control) was included in the American Institute of CPAs' (certified public accountants') (AICPA's) 1972 omnibus Statement on Auditing Standards (SAS) 1. It instructed the auditor to decide how much reliance to place on the internal control system in determining the scope of audits. In 1988, the AICPA Auditing Standards Board revised the Second Standard of Field Work; auditors now are enjoined to obtain a sufficient understanding of internal control to plan the audit and determine the nature, timing, and extent of tests to be performed.

An unresolved question is whether operational controls are to be included in the auditor's considerations, and, if so, which controls. Until the issuance of the so-called "expectation gap" Statements on Auditing Standards, the professional literature had guided auditors to evaluate "internal accounting controls," to the de facto exclusion of "operational controls."

In 1988 the broader view of controls appeared to be in the ascendancy. Statement on Auditing Standards 55 required the auditor to document his or her understanding of the internal control structure (i.e., of the control environment, accounting systems, and control procedures) to identify types of potential misstatements, to consider factors that bear on the risk of material misstatements, and to design substantive tests.

In the aftermath of the savings and loan crisis, the US General Accounting Office (GAO), an arm of the US Congress, placed a spotlight on breakdowns in internal controls, seeking to link such breakdowns with collapses of the entities and with audit failures. However, the GAO's reports did not address the specifics that caused losses or how the accounting profession might have prevented the losses. In any event, the US Congress was persuaded to pass the Federal Deposit Insurance Corporation Improvement Act (FDICIA).

Thus, the need for guidance on internal control assumed crisis dimensions. For fiscal years starting 1993, insured depository institutions with more than $150 million in assets were required by law to prepare a management report on internal control over financial reporting, together with management's assessment of how effectively the internal control mission had been discharged. External auditors were to report on management's assertions.

Also the sponsors of the National Commission on Fraudulent Financial Reporting, who are called the Committee of Sponsoring Organizations (COSO) and include the AICPA, had commissioned a study involving guidance on internal control. The end product of this study, referred to as the COSO report, averred that the *broad* definition of internal control would meet the needs of the numerous interested parties. The COSO report created standardized criteria to help companies measure the adequacy of their own controls. Inconsistently, the COSO report suggested that management's *public* reporting ought to be limited to controls over financial reporting which were seen as affecting the reliability of data and the safeguarding of assets and records. Similarly, COSO sought to restrict the auditor's participation.

The COSO report, which was published in 1992, received an influential negative review from the GAO that saw the report as a retreat from the public interest (Chapin, 1993). GAO had long favored public reporting on internal controls beyond financial reporting matters and had endeavored to bring certain operational and compliance controls within the purview of reporting. The GAO's stance in support of the *broad* view was juxtaposed to the initiatives of the AICPA in seeking wider application of the *narrow* view; the AICPA's Public Oversight Board (POB) endorsed the FDICIA approach and recommended its mandatory extension to all public companies (Sullivan, 1994).

In the same vein, the AICPA's Auditing Standards Board issued Statement of Standards for Attestation Engagements (SSAE) No. 2, "Reporting on an Entity's Internal Control Structure over Financial Reporting" (1993). This statement outlines the conditions that must exist before a practitioner can examine and report on management's assertions: the conditions include management's preparation of a written assertion concerning its evaluation of the effectiveness of the internal control structure, presumably on the basis of reasonable criteria. In the case of a report intended for general distribution, such criteria will have been issued by the AICPA, regulatory agencies, and other bodies composed of experts that follow due process procedures. (In 1995 the SAS 55 definition and description of internal control were synchronized with the COSO report.)

Mention should be made of a federal agency, the US Sentencing Commission, a body created by Congress in 1984, which exerts enormous influence on the maintenance of anti-fraud controls in US companies. In 1988 the Commission recommended to judges that the introduction of corporate codes of ethics be viewed as a mitigating circumstance in sentencing corporate offenders. And the Commission is introducing new topical coverage (of environmental matters) and is also updating prior recommendations. Among other things, the sentencing guidelines allow companies to accrue credits against potential penalties by showing due diligence in seeking to prevent and seeking to detect criminal conduct. Stated differently, a credible internal control compliance program could strengthen a company's hand with judges.

Research

Auditors have subscribed to the custom which asserts that the nature, timing, and extent of substantive tests depend upon the auditor's reliance on the functioning of the client's internal controls. No systematic research or vetting has ever been conducted relating to this postulate which appears to have been published first in *Dicksee's Auditing* in 1905. However, some believe that Dicksee assumed that management would display reasonable integrity and would, in effect, be found on the same side as the auditor.

Eventually researchers studied the model of the audit *process* as described in the professional literature. For example, in 1983 Cushing & Loebbecke compared auditing methodologies of 12 large firms; they observed a trend toward more structured and systematic approaches. However, my experience shows that the differences detected as existing from firm to firm were softened, at least to some extent, by firm "corporate cultures" and by non technical means available to the firms to impose discipline, via directives of supervisors and administrators. Interestingly, one relatively important area of inter-firm differences involved applications of the AICPA's audit risk model, which had been described in the American Institute of Certified Public Accountants' Statement on Auditing Standards No. 47 (1983); the differences largely related to the extent to which a particular firm had introduced quantitative methods. Very little research was performed on the audit risk model itself: in general, researchers in the USA tended to support the model, and those in the UK, Canada, and Australia dissented, usually by questioning the mathematics of the model.

The auditor's assessment of the strength of the internal control system and, consequently, of the extent to which substantive testing could be restricted involve practical considerations of great importance to public accountants. Accordingly, considerable research has been conducted to inquire into the consistency of audit planning decisions; most of these studies involve a case study/questionnaire approach.

As in the case of research relating to models of the audit process and the risk management model, results were mixed. For example, in 1981 Mock & Turner utilized a case study that sought to identify actions that would be taken by auditors based on changing and differing internal control scenarios. The decisions of the subjects varied; meaningful explanations were not obtained for the variances.

The inexplicable results of experiments structured in several ways can possibly be attributed to differences between the rules taught to auditors (and built into the experiments) vis-a-vis what may be done in the "real world" in light of conditions obtaining at a particular firm. For example, when tests fail to confirm the functioning of a control, the rules preclude the auditor from restricting his or her substantive tests. In other words, more auditing will have to be done, with negative consequences for the time budget and even for engagement profitability. Therefore, auditors may make a concerted effort, possibly with firm encouragement, to explain away test results that point to a control malfunction.

Some foresee a rapprochement of academic and practice research prompted by technological advances. The *Deloitte & Touche Professor's Handbook* suggests: "Professional research by academic and practicing accountants is essential to solving the many complex problems faced by corporations... For both academic and practicing professionals, the information explosion will necessitate much more use of sophisticated research tools, data bases, and methodologies" (Kay & Searfoss, 1992).

Direction of Internal Controls

In essence, internal control has an uncertain provenance, as well as an uncertain future. Although internal control may deter certain fraudulent acts, opinions on its efficacy differ. For example, Jensen (1994) uttered a blanket condemnation of internal control: "By nature, organizations abhor control systems, and ineffective governance is a major part of the problem with internal control mechanisms. They seldom respond in the absence of a crisis . . . The infrequency with which large corporate organizations restructure or redirect themselves solely on the basis of the internal control mechanisms . . . is strong testimony to the inadequacy of these control mechanisms."

Still others recognize that an auditor's special utilization of internal control may become progressively less important in the future, given computer-based capabilities for auditing voluminous detail and for more rigorous testing. However, some perceive that internal control has actually increased in *social* significance: internal control may have become a surrogate for measuring an entity's commitment to accountability. Antonio Sanchez DeLozada, former Comptroller of Bolivia, believes that accountability and democracy go hand in hand; his comments were made at a 1993 meeting of the International Consortium on Governmental Financial Management.

Those who hold middle ground views believe that nurturing of internal control can strengthen control effectiveness and improve operating results. Periodic attention to systems adequacy has always been necessary, because existing practices may be rendered obsolete by growth in the volume of activity and by the emergence of transactions not foreseen when the systems were developed. Moreover, when too many changes take place in the economy, industry, or within a company, controls may break down. Thus, Schiff suggests that internal controls warrant reexamination every time a business process is shifted (Schiff, 1994).

These diverse views point to the conclusion that internal control systems represent a priority target for improvement and an opportunity for audit researchers. In any event, it seems unreasonable to expect that a focus on low-level controls will deter management fraud. Improvement is most likely to come about from rethinking control objectives, development of standards of internal control, and introduction of innovative controls designed to mitigate and manage particular threats. Companies may find top-level environmental controls, rather than individual transaction controls, an effective means of protection from management fraud.

Expectations for the Future Across Some Countries

There seems to be little or no information content to management reports on internal control. Walter Schuetze, the former Chief Accountant of the US Securities and Exchange Commission, stated that he has not heard of *any* user group arguing for such management reports (Schuetze, 1994). The Chief Accountant's views were echoed by a panel composed of members of the bar experienced in shareholder litigation. The panelists thought that management reporting would not contribute to better financial reporting or to improved public confidence. Concerning auditors' failure to detect fraud, there is no known relationship between that failure to detect fraud and the proposed reporting. Beyond this concern, however, there appears to be no organized high-level endeavor to attack fraud detection problems.

In the UK, Sir Adrian Cadbury directed a working group which sought management reporting on internal controls and auditor involvement in such reporting; in certain respects, Cadbury's initiatives covered ground similar to the Committee of Sponsoring Organizations (COSO) report in the USA. As in the USA, the focus was on low-level controls, that are unlikely to affect high-level conduct (Cowe & Buckingham, 1994). The Cadbury proposals drew opposition from many quarters, including individuals who thought that insufficient attention had been given to the costs of reporting. Regarding auditors' attestations of management reports, Sir Ron Dearing, the Chairman of the Financial Reporting Council, thought that auditors should not be drawn into opinions "on the edge of their professional competence" (*The Times*, January 13, 1994).

The UK Accounting Principles Board recommended that internal control should be redefined to mean high-level financial controls, reportable weaknesses should be defined in terms of materiality, and the wording of the proposed report should be revised to become more descriptive (Accounting Principles Board, 1994). And UK internal auditors appear to have become concerned with the potential assignment of internal-control-related tasks to external auditors. The internal auditors were worried that the external auditors were likely to concentrate on financial aspects, rather than on operational issues. Internal auditors saw themselves as making a larger contribution in the evaluation of internal control, a premise which appears to be losing support with the profession and its clients. On the other hand, the internal auditors were not alone in voicing concern; the UK Chartered Institute of Management Accountants issued its own broad guidelines on internal control (Trapp, 1993).

In most cases, assuming an automated system and use of computer-assisted audit techniques, the auditor of the future will find it cost-effective to choose unrestricted substantive tests. If he/she follows this approach, substantive tests will become dual purpose – i.e., they will serve to validate individual transactions and account balances, and also to establish that controls are, in effect, appropriately designed, and functioning as planned. Of course, the extent to which the client or a regulatory agency expects the auditor to target all or a select number of internal controls for review may require separate testing of certain controls, regardless of the auditor's reliance thereon.

Bibliography

Accounting Principles Board. (1994). Response on internal controls. In Finance/Business Section. *World Accounting Report*, March.

Chapin, D. H. (1993). Quoted in Robert L. May, Letter. *Management Accounting*, 74, 9, 60–3.

Cowe, R. & Buckingham, L. (1994). Cadbury lobby fighting rearguard action. In Guardian City Page, *The Guardian*, February 21, 1994, p. 10.

Cushing, B. E. & Loebbecke, J. K. (1983). *Comparison of audit methodologies of large accounting firms*. University of Utah, July.

Jensen, M. C. (1994). The modern industrial revolution, exit, and the failure of internal control systems. *Continental Bank Journal of Applied Corporate Finance*, 6, 4, 4–23.

Kay, R. S. & Searfoss D. G. (1992). *Deloitte & Touche Professor's Handbook*. Boston: Warren, Gorham & Lamont, (1992 update), p. 35.

Mock, T. J. & Turner, J. L. (1981). Internal accounting control evaluation and auditor judgment. *Audit Research Monograph No. 3*, AICPA.

Schiff, J. B. (1994). quoted by L. Calabro in All eyes on internal controls. *CFO*, 9, 8, 51–2.

Schuetze, W. P. (1994). Reporting by independent auditors on internal controls. *CPA Journal*, 63, 10, 40–3.

Sullivan, J. D. (1994). The POB tackles internal control reporting: Boundaries, thresholds, and auditor involvement. *Journal of Corporate Accounting & Finance*, 5, 2, 231–42.

Trapp, R. (1993). Campaigning for internal controls. In Accountancy and Management Page. *The Independent*, January 12, 1993.

FELIX POMERANZ

international accounting   According to statistics compiled in *The Economist* (Crook, 1992, pp. 6, 9), the volume of cross-border transactions in equity securities has expanded more than tenfold in the course of a decade, increasing from (US) $120 billion in 1980 to (US) $1.4 trillion in 1990. The increase in international bank lending has been even more staggering, from $324 billion in 1980 to $7.5 trillion in 1991. International business has moved in a very few years from the specialty of a few to the mainstream. Accompanying this trend has been an expanded interest in international accounting. Although there is much diversity in international accounting practice, recent years have been marked by a movement toward international accounting harmonization. This movement has been led by the efforts of the International Accounting Standards Committee and, in Europe, by the accounting directives of the European Union.

Comprehensive reviews of international accounting issues and research are provided by Wallace & Gernon (1991) and Meek & Saudagaran (1990). In recent years, a more rigorous vintage of international accounting research has accompanied the growing volume of international transactions. At a more practical level, several comprehensive international accounting references now exist, such as a handbook edited by Choi (1991), a thorough guide to international practices compiled by Coopers & Lybrand (1993), and a guide to European accounting practices edited by Alexander & Archer (1991).

International Accounting Diversity

The process of comparing financial reports from different countries might seem only to require translating to a common language and a common currency. Although the currency translation process can itself be quite complex, translation alone is a small part of the exercise. There are vast differences in accounting practices that hinder direct comparison among international financial reports – differences that can seem subtle and inconspicuous to the casual user. For example, the requirement to depreciate long-lived assets is common. However, countries' traditions differ widely in assumed useful lives of assets, which leads Bavishi (1993, p. 225) to conclude that "depreciation is probably the most inconsistently applied accounting standard in the world." Moreover, some countries (e.g., the USA and Japan) restrict asset bases to historical cost, with downward adjustments in cases of asset impairment. By contrast, other countries (e.g., the UK, the Netherlands, and Australia) permit upward revaluations to reflect changing market conditions. Research indicates that such revaluations can be employed strategically by managers, and are reflected in the prices of firms' equity securities.

A comprehensive analysis of international accounting differences is compiled by Bavishi (1993), while a more concise review of key differences is provided by Peller & Schwitter (1991). Such differences are not arbitrary, but rather have evolved from unique economic and societal forces in different countries. Some of the more important forces are considered below:

Securities markets

Financial reporting serves various constituencies, and the relative importance of these constituencies molds the framework of the reporting process. In countries where investors provide the principal source of capital through securities markets, the accounting standard setting process espouses the objective of providing a "fair view" of financial operations. The USA and the UK are prime examples. It is no coincidence that the securities markets in these two countries together account for 63 percent of the world's total equity capitalization (including both domestic and foreign listings), with the USA having by far the largest domestic capitalization, while the UK dominates in foreign listings (*see* tabulation by the Organisation for Economic Cooperation and Development (1994, p. 27)). A comparison and analysis of US and UK accounting disclosure practices is provided by Frost & Pownall (1994).

Some recent research has compared stock market reactions to accounting reports in different countries (Alford et al., 1993), although Pownall (1993) has cautioned that it is difficult to separate the informativeness of different accounting systems (as reflected in different security price reactions) from more fundamental differences in shareholder clienteles and stock market characteristics. Choi & Levich (1990) (as summarized in Choi & Levich (1991)) conducted a comprehensive survey of securities market participants in various countries, reporting that one-half of the respondents felt that international accounting diversity affected them adversely. Accounting practices in Japan, Germany, and Switzerland were most frequently mentioned as a cause of concern. In these countries, restrictive regulatory accounting standards prevail to varying degrees over the "fair view" model.

Credit markets. The alternative to the "fair view" model of accounting can be labeled a "stewardship" model. This alternative is characteristic of accounting practices in Japan and Germany, where accounting adopts a more rigid and conservative focus, consistent with creditors' demands for a conservative estimate of the assets underlying their loans. It is noteworthy that the historical focus on conservatism in US financial reporting has waned over the years, while conservatism (also known as "prudence") continues to be considered a desirable quality of accounting in several other countries. In fact, one conspicuous difference between the otherwise similar conceptual frameworks of the International Accounting Standards Committee (IASC) and the US Financial Accounting Standards Board (FASB) is that the IASC includes "prudence" in its list of qualitative characteristics of accounting (IASC, 1994, pp. 44–45), but neither conservatism nor prudence appear in the FASB chart of desirable accounting qualities (FASB, 1980, figure 1). In Japan, which has a traditional heavy reliance on credit financing as well as a large domestic stock market, a dual reporting system has evolved. One report is typical of the conservative, stewardship view of accounting, while the other is intended to be more useful to equity investors. For a discussion of Japanese accounting conservatism in general, *see* Aron (1991).

Taxation. The importance of the interrelationship between a country's system of taxation and its system of financial reporting cannot be overemphasized. In many countries, the two systems are structurally linked, such that a company pays tax on the same net income that is reported in general purpose financial statements. To varying degrees, alignment between tax and financial accounting is common in continental Europe and Scandinavia (*see* table 1 of Alford et al. (1993) for a listing by country). This linkage imposes a natural discipline on accounting choice; managers may be hesitant to choose income-increasing accounting methods if those methods also increase taxes. In the USA, taxes and financial reporting are linked by regulation only for inventory costing, which partially explains why there are so many accounting standards in the USA designed to prevent managers from overstating income. Research and development expenditures, to offer one example, must be charged to current

expense. This requirement is rare internationally, but the freedom to account for research costs as an asset is not nearly so appealing if this election results in a higher tax liability.

Another consequence of the requirement to report the same net income for tax and financial accounting purposes is the use of *reserves*, a bookkeeping technique that provides an exception to the general rule that equates operating changes in net assets with net income. In effect, reserve accounting involves a reclassification of owners' equity from net income (and hence retained earnings) to various alternative designations. Reserves have typically dominated the owners' equity sections of financial statements in European countries that have a high degree of alignment between tax and financial reporting. Although some owners' equity designations similar to reserves have been introduced for selected items in the USA, the use of reserves in the USA is not nearly as prevalent as it is in Europe.

Taxes also impact intercompany transfer prices for multinational firms. Firms may distribute profits among their various foreign and domestic operations in such a manner as to minimize their global tax liability. Leitch & Barrett (1992) provide a comprehensive review of multinational transfer pricing and related research.

Economic stability. The stability of the monetary unit on which accounting values are based exerts an important influence on accounting systems. The most vivid example is in several countries in South America, where inflation has long been rampant. Accordingly, mandated inflation adjustments are common in the financial reports of South American and Mexican companies, in contrast to the historical cost standard prevalent elsewhere. Germany provides an interesting counterexample to illustrate this contrast. German experiences with hyperinflation earlier in the 20th century have elevated the perceived importance in Germany of monetary stability. This has resulted in a strict German adherence to the historical cost postulate as an accounting manifestation of that stability.

Emphasis on Social Responsibility. In a capitalist economy, the primary mandate of the business firm is to maximize profit, providing a return to the firm's investors. In addition to the profit motive, however, different countries have different expectations regarding the firm's broader, societal objectives. These differing expectations give rise to different accounting disclosures. In some countries, for example, information regarding the number of employees (addressing the full employment objective) may be considered just as important as disclosure of product lines. Mueller, Gernon & Meek (1994, p. 83) provide the interesting example of the French firm Pernod Ricard's 1991 disclosure of a new air conditioning system, reflecting the company's "concern for constant improvement of working conditions." Another example on a broader scale is the *value-added statement*, a supplement to the traditional income statement that focuses on the applications of "sources of value" to various constituencies, including employees, the government, and investors. International examples of social responsibility accounting are provided by Gray & Roberts (1991) and Gray, Owen & Maunders (1987). As a counterexample, Lynn (1992) documents the virtual absence of social responsibility disclosures in Hong Kong, where a powerful capitalist ethic predominates.

Culture. Differing cultural values in different societies may influence acceptable accounting values, although researchers are only now beginning to systematically investigate such influences (Gray, 1988). Some recent research has applied the cultural typology of Hofstede (1980; 1991) to accounting and auditing issues. Schultz et al. (1993) (considering France, Norway, and the USA) and Kachelmeier & Shehata (1995) (considering China, Hong Kong, and Canada) are two accounting research applications.

International Accounting Harmonization

Given the economic and social forces that have conditioned international accounting differences, the task of replacing such differences with a harmonized set of comparable accounting standards is quite daunting. Yet, the need for comparability resulting from the surge in international finance has made harmonization a priority that cannot be ignored.

International Accounting Standards Committee. The prominent force in the quest for harmonization is the International Accounting Standards Committee (IASC), an organization that has been in existence for over twenty years. Founded in 1973 as an outgrowth of the efforts of accounting bodies in Canada, the UK, and the USA to foster international comparability, the IASC has grown considerably, and now boasts 109 member bodies in 80 countries. The volume of accounting pronouncements issued by the IASC has grown at a commensurate rate, now published in an annual compilation. The IASC standards comprise an invaluable resource to anyone in business who deals with international accounting.

Notwithstanding this growth, it is important to recognize that the IASC has little if any enforcement power, and that its pronouncements have often been more descriptive than proscriptive. For example, the original wording of International Accounting Standard No. 9 (1978) on research and development provided that such costs "should be charged as an expense of the period in which they are incurred except to the extent that development costs are deferred..." Standards such as this can essentially be read to permit anything, which has led to the criticism that the IASC is more of a figurehead than a substantive harmonizing agent (Purvis, Gernon & Diamond, 1991). In recent years, however, the IASC has proposed more restrictive standards, most notably its comparability project (Draft E32, as modified and finalized in November 1993). This explains why Purvis, Gernon & Diamond (1991) find a lower degree of national conformity with later IASC standards than with earlier standards.

It is likely that the IASC will continue to grow in stature and influence as international trade continues to escalate. An increasingly frequent international practice is the reconciliation of financial statements prepared under local accounting standards to statements prepared under IASC standards. Research has shown that reconciliations such as these can be of significant importance to securities markets. Amir, Harris & Venuti (1993) provide a US example, where regulations for foreign listings require a reconciliation to US standards. Also, developing countries with little accounting infrastructure may find it both cost-effective and internationally beneficial to adopt the IASC model.

The European Union.   In Europe, the European Union (EU) has complemented and to some extent competed with the IASC's harmonization efforts. The most pervasive of EU accounting directives have been its Fourth Directive (issued in 1978), dealing with various accounting issues, and its Seventh Directive (issued in 1983), dealing with consolidated financial reporting for affiliated enterprises. In sum, the spirit of the EU accounting directives has been to shift toward the "fair view" model of the UK and away from the more conservative and rigid models typical of continental Europe. Another objective has been to relax regulatory requirements linking tax generation to general purpose financial reporting (Joos & Lang, 1994).

Despite (or perhaps due to) the ambition of these objectives, countries have been slow to adopt the directives (Mueller, 1991). Even after adoption, evidence suggests that the effect of the EU directives has been more form than substance. For example, Nobes (1993) describes subtle but important differences in how the English words "true" and "fair" were translated in country-specific versions of the Fourth Directive. Emenyonu & Gray (1992) assert that significant accounting differences persist among France, Germany, and the UK in spite of the EU directives. Joos & Lang (1994) provide some market evidence corroborating these assertions. Using a capital markets methodology (i.e., research based upon security prices), they show that the EU directives did not result in any measurable convergence of the valuation relevance of French, German, and UK financial statements.

Other harmonization efforts also exist or may arise. For example, it is possible that the North American Free Trade Agreement may result in accounting pressures among Canada, the USA, and Mexico similar to those present in the European Union. Another region of rapid accounting change is in the former socialist countries of Eastern Europe (Gray & Roberts, 1991) and Russia (Enthoven, 1992), where market-oriented accounting models are just now beginning to emerge. Even in the People's Republic of China, which remains under socialist rule, accounting changes have been rapid and profound (Winkle, Huss & Xi-Zhu, 1994).

Whether harmonization will gain an edge over diversity remains an open question. The growing pressures of international markets strengthen calls for accounting harmonization, while nationalistic pressures from both economic and social sources are likely to resist change.

Bibliography

Alexander, D. & Archer, S.; Eds. (1991). *European accounting guide.* London: Academic Press.

Alford, A., Jones, J., Leftwich, R. & Zmijewski, M. (1993). The relative informativeness of accounting disclosures in different countries. *Journal of Accounting Research*, **31**, supplement, 183–223.

Amir, E., Harris T. S. & Venuti, E. K. (1993). A comparison of the value-relevance of US versus non-US GAAP accounting measures using Form 20-F reconciliations. *Journal of Accounting Research*, **31**, supplement, 230–64.

Aron, P. (1991). Japanese P/E ratios in an environment of increasing uncertainty. *Handbook of international accounting*, F. D. S. Choi, (ed.), Chapter eight, New York: John Willey & Sons.

Bavishi, V. B. (Ed.). (1993). *International accounting and auditing trends.* 1, 3rd edn, Princeton, NJ: Center for International Financial Analysis and Research.

Choi, F. D. S. (Ed.). (1991). *Handbook of international Accounting.* New York: John Wiley & Sons.

Choi, F. D. S. & Levich, R. M. (1990). *The capital market effects of international accounting diversity.* Homewood: Dow Jones-Irwin.

Choi, F. D. S. & Levich, R. M. (1991). Behavioral effects of international accounting diversity. *Accounting Horizons*, **5**, June, 1–13.

Coopers & Lybrand (1993). *International accounting summaries: A guide for interpretation and comparison.* 2nd edn, New York: John Wiley & Sons.

Crook, C. (1992). Fear of finance: The world economy. *The Economist*, **324**, 19 Sept. (supplement), 1–48.

Emenyonu, E. N. & Gray, S. J. (1992). EC accounting harmonisation: An empirical study of measurement practices in France, Germany and the UK. *Accounting and Business Research*, **23**, Winter, 49–58.

Enthoven, A. J. H. (1992). Accounting in Russia: From perestroika to profits. *Management Accounting*, **74**, Oct., 27–31.

FASB (1980). *Statement of Financial Accounting Concepts No.2: Qualitative Characteristics of Accounting Information.* Stamford, CT: Financial Accounting Standards Board.

Frost, C. A. & Pownall, G. (1994). Accounting disclosure practices in the United States and the

United Kingdom. *Journal of Accounting Research*, **32**, Spring, 75–102.

Gray, R., Owen, D. & Maunders, K. (1987). *Corporate social reporting: Accounting and accountability*. London: Prentice-Hall.

Gray, S. J. (1988). Toward a theory of cultural influence on the development of accounting systems internationally. *Abacus*, **24**, Apr., 1–15.

Gray, S. J. & Roberts, C. B. (1991). Corporate social and nonfinancial disclosures. *Handbook of international accounting*, (Ed.), F. D. S. Choi, (Ed.), Chapter 24. New York: John Wiley & Sons.

Gray, S. J. & Roberts, C. B. (1991). East–West accounting issues: A new agenda. *Accounting Horizons*, **5**, Mar., 42–50.

Hofstede, G. (1980). *Culture's consequences: International differences in work-related values*. Beverly Hills: Sage Publications.

Hosfstede, G. (1991). *Cultures and organizations: Software of the mind*. London: McGraw-Hill.

IASC (1994). *International Accounting Standards*. London: International Accounting Standards Committee.

Joos, P. & Lang, M. (1994). The effects of accounting diversity: Evidence from the European Union. *Journal of Accounting Research*, **32**, (supplement), 141–68.

Kachelmeier, S. J. & Shehata, M. (1995). Internal auditing and voluntary cooperation in multinational firms: A cross-cultural laboratory experiment.- Working paper University of Texas at Austin and McMaster University.

Leitch, R. A. & Barrett, K. S. (1992). Multinational transfer pricing: Objectives and constraints. *Journal of Accounting Literature*, **11**, 47–92.

Lynn, M. (1992). A note on corporate social disclosure in Hong Kong. *British Accounting Review*, **24**, June, 105–10.

Meek, G. K. & Saudagaran, S. M. (1990). A survey of research on financial reporting in a transnational context. *Journal of Accounting Literature*, **9**, 145–82.

Mueller, G. G. (1991). 1992 and harmonization efforts in the EC. *Handbook of international accounting*, Ed. F. D. S. Choi, ed., Chapter 12, New York: John Wiley & Sons.

Mueller, G. G., Gernon, H. & Meek, G. K. (1994). *Accounting: An international perspective*. Burr Ridge, IL: Business One Irwin.

Nobes, C. W. (1993). The true and fair view requirement: Impact on and of the Fourth Directive. *Accounting and Business Research*, **24**, Winter, 35–48.

Organisation for Economic Cooperation and Development (1994). *Financial statistics monthly*. Section 2, October.

Peller, P. R. & Schwitter, F. J. (1991). A summary of accounting principle differences around the world. *Handbook of international accounting*, Ed. F. D. S. Choi ed., Chapter 4, New York: John Wiley & Sons.

Pownall, G. (1993). Discussion of the relative informativeness of accounting disclosures in different countries.. *Journal of Accounting Research*, **31**, supplement, 224–9.

Purvis, S. E. C., Gernon, H. & Diamond, M. A. (1991). The IASC and its comparability project: Prerequisites for success. *Accounting Horizons*, **5**, June, 25–44.

Schultz, J. J., Jr,, Johnson, D. A., Morris, D. & Dyrnes, S. (1993). An investigation of the reporting of questionable acts in an international setting. *Journal of Accounting Research*, **31**, supplement, 75–103.

Wallace, R. S. O. & Gernon, H. (1991). Frameworks for international comparative financial reporting. *Journal of Accounting Literature*, **10**, 209–64.

Winkle, G. M., Huss, H. F. & Xi-Zhu, C. (1994). Accounting standards in the People's Republic of China: Responding to economic reforms. *Accounting Horizons*, **8**, Sept., 48–57.

STEVEN J. KACHELMEIER

international accounting standards This entry discusses the International Accounting Standards (IAS) issued by the International Accounting Standards Committee (IASC) which are in effect as of 1 January 1995 and the corresponding national accounting standards in the USA, UK, Australia, and Singapore.

The IASC was established in 1973 to achieve the goal of harmonization of international financial reporting. The IASs issued by the IASC are, however, not mandatory unless and until they are adopted by the accounting profession in the country concerned.

The professional accounting bodies in the USA, UK, Australia, and Singapore are members of IASC. However, with the exception of Singapore, the other three countries had their own accounting standard setting bodies long before the establishment of the IASC and, therefore, have been setting their own national accounting standards.

Sources of Accounting Standards

In the USA, accounting standards consist mainly of the Statements of Financial Accounting Standards (SFAS) issued by the Financial

Accounting Standards Board (FASB), and the pronouncements of its predecessors (a subset of the American Institute of Certified Public Accountants (AICPA)), principally the Opinions issued by the Accounting Principles Board (APB). Accounting practices are also influenced by the Financial Reporting Releases issued by the Securities and Exchange Commission (SEC) and the Statements of Position (SOP) issued by the Accounting Standards Executive Committee of the AICPA.

In the UK, accounting standards are derived basically from the Financial Reporting Standards (FRS) issued by an independent Accounting Standards Board (ASB) and the Statements of Standard Accounting Practices (SSAP) issued by the ASB's predecessor body, the Accounting Standards Committee (ASC). The Companies Act (1989) and the UK's International Stock Exchange's Continuing Obligations (the Yellow Book) contain provisions relating to accounting disclosure requirements.

In Australia, accounting standards consist of Australian Accounting Standards (AAS) issued by the Australian Accounting Research Foundation on behalf of the two Australian accounting bodies, the Institute of Chartered Accountants and the Australian Society of Certified Practicing Accountants, and the standards issued by the Australian Accounting Standards Board (AASB). The AASB standards are applicable to companies, while the AASs are applicable to all types of organizations except companies. The Corporations Law (1990) also provides for detailed disclosure requirements for corporate entities.

In Singapore, the accounting standard setting body is the Institute of Certified Public Accountants of Singapore (ICPAS). The standards issued by ICPAS, Statements of Accounting Standard (SAS) are basically based on the IAS issued by the IASC. The SASs are often preceded by a foreword dealing with relevant local issues.

IAS and Corresponding National Accounting Standards

The IAS issued by the IASC that came into effect on 1 January 1995 cover the following topics:

(a) consolidation accounting
(b) property, plant and equipment
(c) intangible assets
(d) investments
(e) inventories
(f) borrowing costs
(g) revenue recognition
(h) government grants and assistance
(i) deferred income taxes
(j) extraordinary items
(k) construction contracts
(l) leases
(m) foreign currency financial statements
(n) accounting changes
(o) correction of error
(p) post balance sheet events
(q) contingencies
(r) related party transactions
(s) segmental information

Each is discussed below.

(a) Consolidation accounting

The IAS that deal with consolidation accounting are IAS 22 (1993), IAS 27 (1989), and IAS 28 (1989).

IAS 27 requires a parent (defined as an enterprise that controls, i.e., having power to govern the financial and operating policies of, another enterprise) to present consolidated financial statements.

The accounting treatment for goodwill is provided for in IAS 22. For positive goodwill, IAS 22 provides that the goodwill should be capitalised and amortized over a period not exceeding five years (unless a longer period, not exceeding 20 years, can be justified). For negative goodwill, the benchmark treatment is to allocate the deficit over the non-monetary assets acquired, and the allowed alternative treatment is to treat it as deferred income to be amortized on a systematic basis over a period not exceeding five years (unless a longer period, not exceeding 20 years, can be justified).

IAS 27 also provides that minority interest in the consolidated income statement should be presented as an adjustment against the income of the group in order to arrive at the net income attributable to the owners of the parent, and the minority interest in the consolidated balance sheet should be presented separately from the liabilities and the parent shareholders' equity.

IAS 28 provides that an investment in an associated company should be accounted for in consolidated financial statements using the equity method. (For the USA see CONSOLI-DATED FINANCIAL STATEMENTS)

In the UK, the Companies Act (1989); SSAP 22 (1989) and FRS 2 (1992) require the parent undertaking of a group to prepare consolidated accounts that include all subsidiary undertakings, including unincorporated entities. Control rather than legal ownership determines whether an undertaking is a subsidiary. For recording goodwill in consolidation, the UK standards provide for two methods, namely, the "immediate write-off to reserves" method (which is preferred) and the "amortization" method. Under the amortization method, the period over which the goodwill is to be amortized is not specified. Negative goodwill should be accounted for as an adjustment to reserves.

The standards require full consolidation and the presentation of minority interest in the consolidated income statement and consolidated balance sheet. All associated undertakings are to be accounted for using the equity method in the consolidated financial statements.

In Australia, the Corporations Law (1990) and accounting standards (AASB 1016 (1989), AASB 1018 (1992) and AASB 1024 (1992)) require the parent in an economic entity to present consolidated financial statements. The notion of control rather than ownership is the criterion for identifying the existence of parent-subsidiary relationship. Goodwill should be capitalized at acquisition as an asset and amortized by systematic charge to income over its useful life, which in any event should not exceed 20 years. Negative goodwill should be accounted for by reducing proportionately the fair values of the non-monetary assets acquired.

The minority interest in the profit of the subsidiary should be presented in the same manner as provided in IAS 27. The minority interest in the net assets of the subsidiary is, however, presented in the shareholders' equity section of the consolidated balance sheet, identifying separately the capital, retained profits (or accumulated losses), and reserves of that component.

The use of equity method in accounting for investment in an associated company is not permitted. Consequently, the investment in an associated company must be accounted for under the cost method. However, footnote disclosures are required to show the equity accounting information in relation to the associated company.

In Singapore, IAS 27 and IAS 28 are adopted as SAS 26 (1990) and SAS 27 (1991) respectively. Thus, the provisions of IAS 27 and IAS 28 discussed above are equally applicable in Singapore. However, SAS 22 (1987) is based on the now-superseded IAS 22 (1985), under which goodwill may either be written off against shareholders equity or be capitalized and amortised. The Companies Act (1967) also requires a company to present consolidated financial statements if it becomes a holding company by virtue of the fact that it (1) controls the board of directors of another company, (2) controls more than half of the voting power of another company, or (3) holds more than half of the issued share capital of another company.

(b) Property, plant and equipment
IAS 16 (1993) provides that an item of property, plant, and equipment should initially be measured at its cost. Subsequent to its initial measurement, the item should be carried at its cost less any accumulated depreciation. However as an allowed alternative treatment, the item may be carried at a revalued amount, being its fair value at the date of revaluation less any subsequent accumulated depreciation. The depreciable amount of an item of property, plant, and equipment with limited useful life should be allocated on a systematic basis over its useful life. The depreciation method used should reflect the pattern in which the asset is used. The depreciation charge for each period should be recognized as an expense unless it is included in the carrying amount of another asset.

In the USA (APB Opinion 6 (1965) and APB Opinion 12 (1967)), revaluation of property, plant, and equipment is not allowed, except for serious asset impairment. Items of property, plant, and equipment are carried at cost. The depreciable amount (cost less residue value) of items of property, plant, and equipment is to be allocated systematically over their useful lives.

In the UK (SSAP 12 (1987) and FRS 3 (1992)), items of property, plant, and equipment (referred to as fixed assets) may be carried at cost or revalued amount. The depreciable amount (cost or valuation less residue value) of items of property, plant, and equipment is to be allocated systematically over their useful lives.

In Australia (AASB 1001 (1985), AASB 1010 (1991), and AASB 1021 (1989)), accounting treatments for property, plant, and equipment (fixed assets) are similar to those in the UK. Singapore SAS 14 (1996)), however, follows IAS 16.

(c) Intangible assets

The only intangible assets dealt with by the IAS are goodwill, and research and development. IAS 9 (1993) provides that all research costs (i.e., costs associated with original and planned investigation undertaken to gain new scientific or technical knowledge) should be recognized as an expense in the period in which they are incurred. As for development costs (i.e., costs associated with the translation of research findings into a plan for production of new product, process, or services prior to the commencement of commercial production), if they meet the criteria for capitalization, they should be recognized as an asset and amortized; otherwise, they should be written off as expense when incurred.

In the USA, SFAS 2 (1974) requires all research and development costs to be written off as expenses when incurred (*see* RESEARCH AND DEVELOPMENT).

In the UK (SSAP 13 (1989)), accounting treatments for research and development costs are the same as those provided in IAS 9, except that development costs that meet the capitalization criteria (as those in IAS 9) may either be expensed or capitalized and amortized.

In Australia (AASB 1001 (1985), AASB 1010 (1991), AASB 1013 (1988), and AASB 1021 (1989)), the general rule is that all research and development costs must be expensed as incurred unless they satisfy the criterion for deferral. If they are capitalized, the research and development costs must be amortized so that they are matched with related benefits.

Singapore follows IAS 9 (SAS 9 (1996)).

(d) Investments in Marketable Securities

IAS 25 (1986) deals with accounting for investments, other than investments in subsidiary and associated companies. It provides that investments classified as current assets should be carried in the balance sheet at either market value or the lower cost or market value;

investment classified as long-term assets should be carried in the balance sheet at either cost, or revalued amount, or in the case of marketable equity securities, the lower of cost or market. IAS 25 further provides that the carrying amount of all long-term investments should be reduced to recognize a decline other than temporary in the value of the investments.

For the USA *see* MARKETABLE SECURITIES.

In the UK, FRS 3 (1992) requires current investments to be carried at the lower of cost or market value, and noncurrent investments to be carried at cost or at revalued amount, adjusted for any provision for permanent diminution in value.

In Australia (AASB 1001 (1985), AASB 1010 (1991), and AASB 1018 (1992)), current investments are to be carried at the lower of cost or net realizable value. Noncurrent investments are stated at cost, adjusted for any provision for permanent diminution in value. Noncurrent investment may also be revalued to reflect increases in market value above cost.

In Singapore (SAS 25 (1988)), accounting treatments for investments are the same as those provided in IAS 25.

(e) Inventories

IAS 2 (1993) provides that the closing balance of inventories should be measured at the lower of cost and net realizable value.

The cost of inventories comprises of all cost incurred in bringing the inventories to their present location and condition. In assigning the cost to individual item of inventories, IAS 2 provides that the first-in, first-out (FIFO) or weighted average formulas should be used as the benchmark treatment. The last-in, first-out (LIFO) method is an allowed alternative treatment. However, for inventories that are not ordinarily interchangeable, the cost should be assigned by using specific identification basis.

The net realizable value is the estimated selling price in the ordinary course of business less the estimated costs of completion and the estimated costs necessary to make the sale.

For the USA *see* INVENTORY VALUATION.

In the UK, SSAP 9 (1988) requires inventories (referred to as stocks) to be carried at the lower of cost or net realizable value, and the costs of items of stock that are indistinguishable from one another may be assigned using a cost flow method such as FIFO, weighted average, or any similar methods. LIFO is, however, not commonly used. Similar rules are adopted in Australia (AASB 1001 (1985) and AASB 1019 (1989)), although LIFO is not permitted.

Singapore follows IAS 2 (SAS 2 (1996)).

(f) Borrowing costs

IAS 23 (1993) provides for a benchmark treatment: all borrowing costs should be recognized as an expense in the period in which they are incurred. An alternative treatment allows borrowing costs to be recognized as an expense when incurred except for those that are directly attributable to the acquisition, construction, or production of a qualifying asset, which is an asset that necessarily takes a substantial period of time to get ready for its intended use or sale. These costs should be capitalized as part of the cost of the related asset.

In the USA, SFAS 34 (1979) provides that borrowing costs may be capitalized for assets that require long period of time to be prepared for their intended use, but not assets routinely manufactured or produced in large quantities on a repetitive basis.

In the UK, the Companies Act (1989) allows interest on any fund borrowed to finance the production of an asset to be included in the production cost of the asset.

In Australia (AASB 1001 (1985) and AASB 1009 (1986)), it is an accepted practice to capitalize interest that is incurred in bringing the asset to the condition and location of its intended use as part of the cost of an asset.

In Singapore, SAS 9 (1996) follows IAS 23.

(g) Revenue recognition

IAS 18 (1993) deals with accounting for revenue arising from (1) sale of goods, (2) rendering of services, and (3) the use by others of reporting entity's resources yielding interest, royalties, and dividends. IAS 18 provides that revenue from sale of goods should be recognized when the enterprise has transferred to the buyer the significant risks and rewards of ownership of the goods, and there is no significant uncertainty as to the amount of the revenue and the costs incurred or to be incurred and the collectibility of the consideration.

For rendering services, IAS 18 provides that the revenue therefrom should be recognized by reference to the stage of completion of the transaction at the balance sheet date if the outcome of the transaction can be reliably estimated.

IAS 18 also specifically provides that interest should be recognized on a time proportion basis, royalties should be recognized on an accrual basis in accordance with the substance of the relevant agreement, and dividends should be recognized when the shareholder's right to receive payment is established.

For the USA, see REVENUE RECOGNITION, EXPENSES, GAINS AND LOSSES.

In the UK, there is no specific standard dealing with revenue recognition. However, in accordance with the prudence concept, it is a generally accepted practice that revenue and profit should not be anticipated and should be recognized only when realized.

In Australia, the provisions of accounting standards (AASB 1001 (1985), AASB 1004 (1986), and AASB 1009 (1986)) for revenue recognition is similar to those of IAS 18. In Singapore, SAS 16 (1996) has the same provisions as IAS 18.

(h) Government grants and assistance

IAS 20 (1984) provides that government grants should be recognized in income, and not credited directly to shareholders' equity. Government grants should be recognized only when there is reasonable assurance that the enterprise will comply with the conditions attached to the grants and that the grants will be received. The same treatment is used in Singapore (SAS 18 (1985)).

In the USA, the AICPA Issues Paper, "Accounting for Grants Received from Governments" (1979), recommends that government grants be recognized in income, and that the period of recognition depends on the type of grant.

In the UK, SSAP 4 (1990) provides that government grants and assistance should be recognized when the expenditure that they are intended to finance is recognized.

In Australia, SAC 4 (1992) requires that government grants and assistance be recognized as revenue.

(i) Deferred income taxes

IAS 12 (1981) requires that the tax expense for the period be determined on the basis of tax-effect accounting. It, however, allows the use of either the deferral method or the liability method. It also allows the adoption of either comprehensive or partial allocation basis. IAS 12 provides that deferred tax should not be carried in the balance sheet with a debit balance (i.e., as an asset) unless there is a reasonable expectation of realization. This is similar to SAS 12 (1983) adopted in Singapore.

IAS 12 also provides that taxes relating to a previous period which are recovered as a result of tax loss carried back should be included in net income in the period of the loss. However, the potential tax saving relating to a tax loss that is available to be carried forward for the determination of taxable income in future periods should not be included in the net income until the period of realization, unless there is assurance beyond any reasonable doubt that future taxable income will be sufficient to allow the benefit to be realized.

For the USA, see DEFERRED TAXES.

In the UK (SSAP 15 (1992)) and Australia (AASB 1020 (1989)), the accounting standards require the use of the liability method with partial allocation in tax effect accounting. The UK, Australian, and Singapore tax laws do not allow tax losses to be carried back. For the tax effect of losses carried forward, the accounting standards in the UK, Australia, and Singapore contain similar provisions as those of IAS 12.

(j) Extraordinary items

IAS 8 (1993) defines extraordinary items as income or expenses that arise from events or transactions that are clearly distinct from the ordinary activities of the enterprise and there fore are not expected to recur frequently or regularly. Two examples are provided for events or transactions that generally give rise to extraordinary items, namely, expropriation of assets and natural disaster.

In the USA (APB Opinion 9 (1966) and APB Opinion 30 (1973)), extraordinary items are defined as those items that are unrelated to the typical activities of the entity and would not be expected to recur in the foreseeable future. In addition, early extinguishing of debt gives rise to an extraordinary item.

In the UK (FRS 3 (1992)) and Australia (AASB 1018 (1992)), extraordinary items are defined as those items possessing a high degree of abnormality that arise from events or transactions that fall outside the ordinary activities of the reporting entity and that are not expected to recur.

In Singapore, SAS 8 (1981) is based on the now-superseded IAS 8 (1979), where the scope of extraordinary items is broader than IAS 8 (1993).

(k) Construction contracts

The now superseded IAS 11 (1980) acknowledged two methods of accounting for construction contracts: (1) the percentage of completion method which recognizes profit periodically based on the stage of completion of the contract at each accounting year-end, and (2) the completed contract method which recognizes profit only in the year in which the contract is completed. The revised IAS 11 (1993), however, requires the use of the percentage of completion method. This is the same treatment in the UK (SSAP 9 (1988)), Australia AASB 1001 (1985), AASB 1004 (1986), and AASB 1009 (1986). Singapore (SAS 11 (1983)), however, retains the provisions of IAS 11 (1980).

For the USA, see LONG-TERM CONSTRUCTION CONTRACTS.

(l) Leases see LEASES

(m) Foreign currency financial statements see FOREIGN CURRENCY.

(n) Accounting changes

IAS 8 (1993) deals with two types of accounting changes, namely, changes in accounting policies and changes in accounting estimates.

IAS 8 provides that a change in accounting policy should, as a benchmark treatment, be applied retrospectively. Any resulting adjustment should be reported as an adjustment to the opening balance of retained earnings, and comparative information should be restated. As an allowed alternative treatment, the resulting adjustment may be included in the determination of the net profit or loss for the current period; comparative information should not be restated, but instead additional pro forma comparative information should be presented.

IAS 8 requires a change in accounting estimate to be accounted for prospectively. The effects of the change should be accounted for as part of income in the period of change and future periods.

The corresponding standards in the UK (FRS 3 (1992)), Australia (AASB 1001 (1985) and AASB 1018 (1992)), and Singapore (SAS 8 (1995)) have essentially the same provisions as IAS 8.

For the USA, *see* PRIOR PERIOD ADJUST-MENTS.

(o) Correction of errors

Under IAS 8 (1993), the accounting treatments for correction of errors are the same as those for changes in accounting policies, as discussed above. In general, the same approach is used in the USA (SAFS 16 (1977)), the UK (FRS 3 (1992)), Australia (AASB 1018 (1992)), and Singapore (SAS 8 (1981)).

(p) Post balance sheet events

Post balance sheet events are those events that occur between the balance sheet date and the date on which the financial statements are authorized for issue.

IAS 10 (1980) classifies post balance sheet events into two categories: (1) for post balance sheet events that provide additional evidence of conditions that existed at the balance sheet date, the related assets and liabilities should be adjusted; and (2) for those indicative of conditions that rose subsequent to the balance sheet date, no adjustment will be required, but disclosure in the notes may be necessary. This is essentially the same treatment followed in the USA (SAFS 5 (1975)), the UK (SSAP 17 (1980)), Australia (AASB 1002 (1986)), and Singapore (SAS 10 (1980)).

(q) Contingencies

A contingency is a condition or situation, the ultimate outcome of which, gain or loss, will be confirmed only on the occurrence, or non-occurrence, of one or more uncertain future events.

IAS 10 (1980) provides that contingent loss should be accrued by a charge to the income statement if (1) it is probable that future events will confirm that an asset has been impaired or a liability incurred at the balance-sheet date, and (2) a reasonable estimate of the amount of the resulting loss can be made. The existence of a contingent loss should be disclosed in the notes to financial statements if either condition is not met, unless the possibility of a loss is remote. For contingent gains, they should not be accrued in financial statements, but should be disclosed in the notes to the financial statements only if it is probable· that the gain will be realized.

For the USA, *see* CONTINGENCIES.

In Australia, AASB 1002 (1986) requires the same treatment for both contingent gain and contingent loss and are accounted for in the same manner as provided in IAS 10 for treatment of contingent loss.

(r) Related party transactions

For accounting purposes, parties are considered related if one entity has control or significant influence over the other.

IAS 24 (1986), which is adopted by Singapore as SAS 21 (1987), requires disclosure of related party relationships where control exists irrespective of whether there have been transactions between the related parties. For transactions between related parties, disclosures should be made of the nature of the related party relationships as well as the type and elements of these transactions.

In the USA (SFAS 57 (1982)), disclosure of "material" related party transactions includes in addition the dollar amount of the transactions. Adding to this, Australia (AASB 1017 (1992)) requires director-related disclosures regardless of the amounts involved.

In UK, the Companies Act (1989) requires disclosures of transactions between the reporting entity and its directors and persons connected with directors.

(s) Segmental information

IAS 14 (1983) requires disclosure of information relating to both industrial segments and geographical segments. The disclosure should include segment turnover, segment results, and segment assets. Australia (AASB 1005 (1986)), and Singapore (SAS 23 (1987)) follow IAS 14. In the UK, SSAP 25 (1990) requires similar information, but provides that, if presenting the information would seriously prejudice the interest of the company, it need not be disclosed; however, the omission has to be disclosed.

In the USA FAS 14 (1976) and SFAS 21 (1978), certain financial segment information regarding different industries and foreign operations and sales to major customers is required. For each industry segment, information relating to revenue, profitability, assets, depreciation, and amortization should be disclosed. If the reporting entity has operations outside the USA, it should also disclose information relating to revenue, profitability, and identifiable assets, by geographical areas. In addition, export sales and major customer sales should also be disclosed, if significant.

addition, export sales and major customer sales should also be disclosed, if significant.

MENG HYE LEE and ENG JUAN NG

inventory valuation To match revenues recognized in an accounting period with the costs of generating these revenues, it may be necessary to divide the period's expenditures into current period expenses and capitalized expenditures to be expensed in later periods. In the case of expenditures on acquisition and production of sellable goods and services, the capitalized portion of a period's expenditures are called inventories. Inventory is tangible property that

- is held for sale in the ordinary course of business (termed finished goods),

- is in the process of production for such sale (termed work in process), or

- is consumed (directly or indirectly) in the production of goods or services for sale (termed raw material and supplies).

Inventories are current assets since, by definition, they are consumed within a single business cycle (albeit not necessarily within a year).

When inventory is comprised of large or high-valued identifiable units, as is the case in the production of airplanes, buildings, movies, etc., its cost can be determined by tracing the specific costs incurred in the production of each unit. Often, however, inventories are comprised of many identical items. In such cases, the cost of each unit is not directly traced. Rather, an *assumption* about the way costs flow is used in determining inventory costs, which need not match the *actual* flow of physical units. Rather, *the objective in selecting an appropriate assumption about the flow of costs is to accurately measure periodical income*.

Methods of Costing Inventories

These are:

first-in-first-out (FIFO) under which it is assumed that the cost of the units sold during the period is the cost of the units bought or produced *first*.

last-in-first-out (LIFO) under which it is assumed that the cost of the units sold during

the period is the cost of the units bought or produced *last*.

average cost under which it is assumed that the cost of the unit sold during the period is the *average cost of the units bought during the period*.

Under the FIFO method, the cost of units in the closing inventory is the cost of the units acquired or produced most recently. The LIFO method, on the other hand, charges the cost of the most recently acquired or produced units to the cost of sales. Thus, when unit costs rise over time (e.g., in inflationary periods), the cost of goods sold reported under FIFO would be lower than the cost of goods sold reported under LIFO and the reverse for profits.

The tracing of inventory costs can be updated with each transaction (perpetual inventory system) or only at the end of each accounting period (periodic inventory system). In some cases it is permissible to use the *retail* or *gross margin* approximations under which it is assumed that markups on all units held in inventory are the same.

The general rule in US accounting is that inventories are reported at the *lower of cost or market (LCM)* where "market" refers to the cost of replacing the inventories. The major qualifications to the LCM rule are:

- If the replacement value of inventories exceeds their net realizable value – selling price less additional costs needed to complete the sale – inventories will be reported at their net realizable value.

- If the net realizable value of inventories less normal gross profits exceeds their replacement cost, inventories will be reported at the net realizable value less normal gross profits even if replacement value is less than cost.

- The LCM rule does not apply when LIFO is used.

The LCM rule is applied to homogeneous categories of goods rather than to individual items. The adjustment of inventory's value from cost to the lower market value is included in the cost of goods sold, unless the adjustment is material, in which case it is reported as a separate item in the income statement.

The 1993 US publication *Accounting Trends and Techniques* reports that, of a sample of 600

US firms, 41 percent use FIFO, 35 percent use LIFO, and 19 percent use average cost. Cross-industry patterns differ. The industries with the lowest rate of LIFO usage are aircraft and aerospace equipment, electronic equipment, and business equipment. The food and beverage, department stores, and mail order stores are the industries with the highest rate of LIFO usage.

The US Internal Revenue Code (Section 472 and Regulations § 1.472-1 through 1.472-8) allows the use of LIFO for inventory costing for tax purposes only if it is also used for financial reporting.

The requirement that LIFO be used in financial reports when it is used for tax reporting purposes ties the firm's cash flows to its financial reporting. In particular, in inflationary periods income reported under LIFO is lower than the income reported under FIFO. Therefore, firms that value inventories using LIFO pay less taxes than they would pay had they used FIFO. To enjoy these tax savings, the firm has to use LIFO also for financial reporting.

Comparing LIFO and FIFO

Absent any other effects of "last-in-first-out" (LIFO) reporting, LIFO is the preferred inventory valuation method in inflationary times because of entailing tax savings proportional to the *LIFO reserves* – the excess of the inventory's current replacement cost over its historic LIFO value – and to the firm's tax rate. (LIFO involves charging the cost of the most recently acquired or produced units to the cost of sales.)

The tax savings associated with LIFO reporting imply that only LIFO should be used in inflationary periods, a counter-factual prediction. Other theories suggest nontax effects of LIFO reporting that may explain the observed use of "first-in-first-out" (FIFO) even in the face of long inflationary periods. (FIFO assumes that the cost of the units sold during the period is the cost of the units bought or produced first.) These explanations include:

- LIFO reporting may require higher administrative costs than FIFO.

- Management compensation contracts are often tied to reported earnings via bonus

plans, etc., which induce managers to choose FIFO over LIFO.

- Covenants included in many debt contracts are based on reported income or on shareholders, equity, which favors use of FIFO.

- When managers are more informed about their firm's prospects than shareholders, use of FIFO may signal that the firm is more valuable than is perceived externally.

- Firms that fear competition may use FIFO to signal that they expect their production costs to decline as they become more efficient producers.

Some of the empirical regularities that have been documented by these studies are:

- LIFO is chosen primarily because of LIFO's tax advantages.

- Two-thirds of the managers who use FIFO justify their decision by LIFO's adverse effects while roughly one-third do so because they believe FIFO to be a better accounting method.

- Firms using FIFO tend to have effective tax rates that are lower than the effective tax rates of firms that use LIFO for inventory valuation.

- Managers of firms using LIFO for inventory valuation could have their bonus based on "as-if" FIFO-based income. LIFO users are less restricted by debt covenants than FIFO users.

- There is evidence that LIFO users increase inventory purchases prior to fiscal year-end to avoid liquidating LIFO reserves and paying tax on such liquidations.

- Liquidation of LIFO reserves is primarily by firms that have experienced low profitability.

- Firms using FIFO tend to be smaller than firms using LIFO for inventory valuation. Perhaps only large firms gain enough LIFO tax savings to warrant expanding the associated higher administrative costs.

- Firms using FIFO tend to be in industries with higher innovation rate (as measured by the intensity of R&D expenditures).

● There is no conclusive evidence on whether the investors value a switch from FIFO accounting to LIFO accounting.

SASSON BAR YOSEF and ODED SARIG

J

Judgment in financial statement audits
The best-known form of an audit is a financial
statement audit. In such audits, generally
accepted accounting principles (GAAP) are the
criteria against which assertions about the
organization's transactions are evaluated, the
reports are issued by independent certified
public accountants (CPAs), and the interested
users include prospective and current owners,
creditors, regulators, and employees.

Early in an engagement, the auditor must
determine the level of scrutiny to attach to each
financial statement assertion (e.g., existence,
valuation). This determination will be based on
judgments of the significance of the balance and
assertion as well as the degree of risk of
misstatement. Subsequently, when focussed on
a specific financial statement assertion and
account balance (e.g., valuation of fixed assets),
the auditor must judge the method and amount
of evidence to confirm or disconfirm the
assertion and the timing of each during the
audit. Then, the auditor must evaluate the
evidence produced and form a judgment about

its meaning. At the end, the auditor must
integrate all findings and determine what to
communicate to financial statement users.

In the US, generally accepted auditing
standards are set forth by the Auditing
Standards Board (ASB) of the American
Institute of Certified Public Accountants
(AICPA). The ASB issues Statements on
Auditing Standards (SASs), which are authoritative in that an auditor must comply with them
or be prepared to justify non-compliance. As of
March 1995, 74 SASs had been issued, although
some have been superseded by subsequently-
issued SASs.

As a measure of the importance of judgment,
we searched the SASs in effect as of June 1991
using three categories of "key words". The
"Direct References to Judgment" category has
13 words, including seven versions of the word,
"judgment." The word "assess" in various
forms, which often is used as a synonym for
the word judge, comprises the remaining six
entries in this category. About 65 percent (40/
62) of the individual sections in the database

Table 1: The most "judgment-laden" of the statements on auditing standards

Rank	Ratio	SAS Sec No.	Title
1	0.0219	313	Substantive tests prior to the balance-sheet date
2	0.0175	390	Consideration of omitted procedures after the report date
3	0.0158	550	Other information in documents containing audited financial statements
4	0.0156	350	Audit sampling
5	0.0144	341	The auditor's consideration of an entity's ability to continue as a going concern
6	0.0136	312	Audit risk and materiality in conducting an audit
7	0.0124	342	Auditing accounting estimates
8	0.0118	339	Working papers
9	0.0118	380	Communications with audit committees

contain at least one direct reference to judgment. When the scope is expanded to include direct and indirect references to judgment (e.g., considers, determines), the percentage rises to about 94 percent (58/62).

We also computed ratios of the word counts, for both direct and indirect categories, to the total number of words contained in a section. These results, suggesting the relative importance of judgment in each SAS, are presented in Table 1 for the SASs with the highest ratios.

Judgment Research

Audit sampling. "How much testing is enough?" is one of the oldest audit questions. It has led to both development and testing of quantitative tools for sampling as well as research on the sampling process (which is judgment-laden to a surprising extent).

When an auditor employs nonstatistical sampling, planning judgments must be made about matters such as the audit objective of the test, the scope of the population from which the sample will be drawn, the sampling technique to be employed, the definition of what constitutes an error, the acceptable level of risk, the amount of error expected, and the amount of the error to be tolerated. The auditor also must determine how much error to expect in a specific sampling context. Such a judgment may be based on prior year's sampling results, changes in the current year such as business operations or controls, or a combination of both types of matters. In addition, the auditor must judgmentally determine which sampling technique to employ. As conditions change, different sampling techniques may perform better or worse. Thus, there is an inevitable interrelationship between error expectations and sampling technique selection. Planning considerations such as these are antecedents to the auditor's judgments about the size of the sample to be drawn and later the evaluation of the sample results.

Although statistical sampling imposes structure, judgment remains integral to planning and executing the sampling process. For example, the auditor still must make judgments about the objective of the sampling plan, the scope of the population from which the sample will be drawn, the definition of an error, the expected error rate, and the risk of compromising audit

effectiveness (and, perhaps, efficiency). The sample size, however, is determined by combining judgmental inputs in accordance with theories of mathematical statistics and probability, such that target risk thresholds are not violated. Further, sample results are evaluated in the same manner.

The foci of judgment research on sampling largely have been threefold: (1) factors affecting and the extent of variability of sample size judgments, (2) decision aids for reducing sample size variability, and (3) judgmental evaluation of sample results. Little, if any, research, however, has been published on how and how well auditors assess many of the judgmental inputs to statistical sampling plans.

In the early 1970s, it was reported that, when left to their own devices, auditors facing the same set of facts often specified substantially different sample sizes (Aly & Duboff, 1971). Much of the early research shows that auditors' judgments exhibit moderate levels of consensus. Because any significant judgment variability can be problematic, recent research has examined ways of reducing judgment variability. In the sampling arena, this research is exemplified by studies like Kachelmeier & Messier (1990) which focussed on improving auditor judgmental consensus via a structured decision aid. They reported that the structured decision aid for determining sample size, specified in the AICPA's (1983) *Audit and Accounting Guide, Audit Sampling*, can produce the opposite of the intended result – auditors who used the decision aid specified sample sizes with greater variability than auditors using unaided judgment.

The research on judgmental evaluation of sample results is exemplified by Uecker & Kinney's (1977) study reporting that a high proportion of the judgments made reflected correct identification of the stronger of two sample results, but that about half of the auditors made at least one sample evaluation error.

Audit risk and materiality. Materiality and risk are two of the most pervasive audit constructs. Materiality is a recognition that not all matters are of equal import. Accounting materiality deals with reporting precision, while audit planning materiality deals with the precision of audit tests. Focusing on the former, an auditor might ask the question – is a matter, like a related-party relationship, of great enough significance that it should be reported? Although rules of thumb exist, accounting materiality generally is a matter of professional judgment. Focusing on planning materiality, the auditor would ask the question – how small a misstatement do I wish to be able to detect via the procedures I will perform? While some algorithms have been devised (see Elliot, 1993), the norm is that planning materiality is determined on the basis of professional judgment.

Auditors assess risk across an entity's financial statements and within financial statements at the level of individual accounts, transaction classes, and assertions (e.g., existence, valuation). Further, when focussed on accounts and transaction cycles, auditors consider the inherent risk and control risk.

Most of the audit research on materiality has focused on reporting materiality. These studies have shed light on factors associated with and rules of thumb that explain auditors' reporting materiality judgements (e.g., if a matter is > x % of net income, it should be reported). Studies such as these are exemplified by Bates et al. (1982) in which the impact on reporting materiality judgments of audit partner rotation and the length of the auditor–client relationship were investigated. In many respects, the findings of these studies have confirmed conventional wisdom. For the Bates et al. (1982) study, therefore, greater audit partner "involvement" with the client was shown to lead to higher disclosure thresholds for a loss contingency.

Research related to risk assessment in auditing has been fairly extensive. In some experimental studies, the focus was on inherent risk assessments and, in particular, on the factors which influence such assessments (e.g., financing pressure, key employee turnover; see Colbert, 1988). In other studies, both inherent and control risk were investigated using archival research methods (Waller, 1993). No association between inherent and control risk assessments and between these assessments and detected misstatements was identified. These findings were attributed to strategic auditor behavior. That is, because of a desire to *not* rely on controls, auditors assessed control risk at a high enough level, irrespective of their actual beliefs, that reliance would not be possible.

Still other studies are exemplified by Pincus (1989) in which a more macro focus was taken and the issue was the process used by auditors to assess the potential for fraud. Using a red flag questionnaire, she reported that enhanced levels of comprehensiveness and uniformity in data gathering were achieved but unexpected negative consequences arose, under some conditions, for the actual fraud assessments.

Bibliography

Aly, H. F. & Duboff, J. I. (1971). Statistical vs. judgmental sampling: An empirical study of auditing and accounts receivable of a small retail store. *The Accounting Review*, 119–28.

AICPA (1983). *Audit and Accounting Guide: Audit Sampling*. New York: American Institute of Certified Public Accountants.

Bates, H. L., Ingram, R. W. & Reckers, P. M. J. (1982). Auditor–client affiliation: The impact on materiality. *Journal of Accountancy*, Apr., 60–3.

Colbert, J. L. (1988). Inherent risk: An investigation of auditors' judgments. *Accounting Organizations and Society*, 111–21.

Elliott, R. K. (1983). Unique audit methods: Peat Marwick International. *Auditing: A Journal of Practice and Theory*, 1–12.

Kachelmeier, S. J. & Messier W. F. Jr. (1990). An investigation of the influence of a nonstatistical decision aid on auditor sample size decisions. *The Accounting Review*, Jan., 209–26.

Pincus, K. V. (1989). The efficacy of a red flags questionnaire for assessing the possibility of fraud. *Accounting, Organizations and Society*, 153–63.

Uecker, W. C. & Kinney Jr, W. R. (1977). Judgmental evaluation of sample results: A study of the type and severity of errors made by practicing CPAs. *Accounting, Organizations and Society*, 269–75.

Waller, W. S. (1993). Auditors' assessments of inherent and control risk in field settings. *The Accounting Review*, Oct., 783–803.

TOM CLAUSEN and IRA SOLOMON

L

leases Leasing versus buying has been a common choice in obtaining the right to use many productive assets (or licenses). Along with some economic advantages, leasing brings many accounting problems for both the lessee and the lessor. The US Financial Accounting Standards Board (FASB) provides the bases for the accounting measurement and recognition of leases in Statement of Financial Accounting Standard No. 13, "Accounting for Leases." (SFAS No. 13 as amended by numerous changes).

Leases vary significantly in characteristics. A lease can be cancelable or noncancelable without significant penalty. Some leases provide the lessee with the option to buy the asset at the end of the lease term. Still others transfer the ownership of the leased asset to the lessee at the conclusion of the lease period. Also, some leases are for very short period while others may extend for the entire economic life of the leased asset. The common feature of all leases is that a lease represents the right to use an asset and the obligation to pay rents at future dates. The question is whether such a right and the related obligation constitute an asset and a liability to afford recognition in the balance sheet.

There are two competing perspectives in accounting for leases. The first reflects the contractual (legal) aspect of the lease. This perspective states that the lease represents a mutual executory contract that is dependent on passage of time. Accordingly, current lease payment is only recognized as a liability, while future payments are disclosed in footnotes to the financial statements. The other view argues that leasing constitutes a financing of the acquisition of an asset, where the lease payments represent installments of the purchase price. Therefore, an asset and a corresponding liability should be recognized and measured at the present value of the future minimum lease payments (hereafter lease payments).

SFAS No. 13

In resolving the lease accounting problem, the FASB took the position that when a lease substantially transfers to the lessee both the benefits and the risks associated with the ownership of an asset, the lease is to be accounted for as a capital lease. SFAS No. 13 lists four specific conditions, meeting any of which is considered an indicator of conveying the benefits and risks of the asset's ownership. These conditions are: (1) transfer of ownership of the leased asset to the lessee at the end of the lease term; (2) provision of a bargain purchase option; (3) the lease term is for 75 percent or more of the estimated economic life of the asset; and (4) the present value of the lease future payments equals 90 percent or more of the fair market value of the asset on the date of the lease inception. If the lease terms do not satisfy any of the above conditions, the lease is treated as an operating lease.

Under a capital lease, the lessee recognizes an asset and a corresponding liability measured at the present value of the future lease payments discounted at the assumed interest rate. Consequently, an interest expense on the lease liability and a depreciation expense for the asset are charged as operating expenses each year.

For the lessor, the lease should satisfy the following two conditions besides any one of the four criteria stated above to be accounted for as a capital lease: (i) the collectibility of the minimum lease payments is assured; and (ii) no important uncertainties for nonreimbursable costs are to be incurred by the lessor.

Under a capital lease, the lessor removes the leased asset from the corporate books and recognizes long-term lease receivables. Depending on the structure of the lease transaction, the lessor may classify the capital lease as "direct financing" or "sales type" lease. In the direct financing lease, the lessor buys an asset and leases it to the lessee. The role of the lessor here is merely to finance the acquisition of the asset for the lessee. In exchange, the lessor earns interest income on the long-term lease receivables. According to SFAS No. 13, an indicator of direct financing lease is the equality between the cost of the asset and the present value of future lease payments.

In a sales-type lease, the lessor structures the lease transaction to earn one lump sum profit (or loss) in the year of the lease inception only, but the interest income on the long-term lease receivables is to be earned during the lease term. The profits (losses) represent the difference between the present value of lease payments and the cost of the asset to the lessor. Technically, this is achieved by recognizing a lease sales revenue for the present value of the lease payments and a cost of sales for the cost of the leased asset.

Under the operating lease treatment, an annual rent expense is recognized by the lessee, while future commitments on the lease are disclosed in footnotes. The lessor keeps the leased asset on the books and recognizes both rent income and depreciation expense.

Sale-Leaseback Transactions

A sale-leaseback transaction refers to the case where an owner sells an asset to another party and then leases it back. For the seller-lessee, the sale-leaseback transactions are financing devices that often are kept off the balance sheet. If the lease terms meet any of the capital lease criteria, the seller-lessee should account for the lease as capital lease, otherwise it would be an operating lease. However, any profits or losses on the sale should be deferred and amortized in proportion to the amortization of the leased asset if treated as a capital lease, or in proportion to rental payments during the period of time the asset is expected to be used if treated as an operating lease (SFAS No. 13, p. 32). For the lessor, a sale-leaseback transaction is accounted for either as direct financing lease or as operating lease, depending on the lease terms.

Off-Balance Sheet Financing

Off balance sheet financing refers to the case where a firm obtains the right to use/acquire an asset for a long period but does not recognize the acquisition liability as a balance sheet debt. Leasing assets and accounting for them as operating leases achieves this goal. Lessees believe that operating lease accounting helps them preserve their borrowing capacity, and enhances their accounting-based performance (Abdel-khalik, 1981). In fact, empirical studies show that firms with high leverage ratios and compensation plans that are based on accounting income are likely to use operating lease accounting (El-Gazzar et al., 1986, 1989).

The findings of the above-mentioned research do not necessarily imply that users of financial statements (especially lenders) are informationally inefficient. In structuring debt contracts, lenders and borrowers tend to maximize their own respective interests. They involve a set of tradeoffs including available accounting contracting technology. A borrower may be willing to pay higher interest or bond discount for obtaining more flexibility and base debt restrictions on generally accepted accounting principles (GAAP) (Thornton & Bryant, 1986; El-Gazzar & Pastena, 1990). When US Statement of Financial Accounting Standard (SFAS) No. 13 tightened the flexibility of keeping leases off the balance sheet, lessees expressed concern that capitalizing off balance sheet leases may bring them closer to violation of debt covenants and reduces their ability to finance growth opportunities at a favorable cost of capital. El-Gazzar (1993) provides results indicating that the market reacted negatively in response to SFAS No. 13 for firms that were required to capitalize material off balance sheet leases.

Bibliography

Abdel-khalik, A. R. (1981). *The economic effects on lessees of FASB Statement No. 13, Accounting for Leases*. Research report. Stamford, (CT): FASB.
El-Gazzar, S., Lilien, S. & Pastena, V. (1986). Accounting for leases by lessees. *Journal of Accounting and Economics*, 8, Oct., 217–37.

El-Gazzar, S., Lilien, S. & Pastena, V. (1989). The use of off-balance sheet financing to circumvent financial covenant restrictions. *The Journal of Accounting, Auditing, and Finance*, Spring, 217–31.

El-Gazzar, S. & Pastena, V. (1990). Negotiated accounting rules in private financial contracts. *Journal of Accounting and Economics*, **12**, Dec., 381–96.

El-Gazzar, S. (1993). Stock market effects of the closeness to debt covenant restrictions resulting from capitalization of leases. *The Accounting Review*, **68**, Apr., 258–72.

Thornton, D. & Bryant, M. (1986). *GAAP (generally accepted accounting principles) vs. TAP (tailored accounting principles) in lending agreements: Canadian evidence*. Toronto: The Canadian Academic Accounting Association.

SAMIR M. EL-GAZZAR

liquidation accounting Liquidation accounting involves the development of financial statements for companies on the verge or in the midst of bankruptcy proceedings. Liquidation accounting suspends the normal rules for valuation of assets and liabilities, namely, historical or acquisition cost (or, in some jurisdictions, price level adjusted or current replacement cost values), in favor of assessing the balance sheet items at their "sell off" value. Thus financial statements prepared under the liquidation assumption would show the balance sheet at wind up and any proceeds to be distributed to creditors and equity holders from the sell off of the balance sheet items. (The manner and priority of distribution of proceeds to holders of the entity's debt and equity is defined by the Bankruptcy Laws and statutes of the jurisdiction in which the entity has operated.)

One of the basic assumptions underlying all accounting activities is that entities are presumed to be *going concerns*, i.e., accountants assume that entities intend to continue operations into the future. The *going concern* assumption provides the basis for the definition of *assets* as

> Probable future economic benefits obtained or controlled by a particular entity as a result of past transactions or events (Statement of Financial Accounting Concept (SFAC) 6, para. 25.)

and *liabilities* as

> Probable future sacrifices of economic benefits arising from present obligations of a particular entity to transfer assets or provide sources to other entities in the future as a result of past transactions or events (SFAC 6, para. 35).

Under liquidation accounting the going concern concept is abandoned and, hence, assets and liabilities have no probable future economic existence. In fact, the underlying economic concept of liquidation accounting valuation is that of distress prices or break up value. Entities which are not going concerns have lost organizational synergy, which effectively eliminates any subjective goodwill that might be present and results in a major decline in the value of the equity held by common shareholders. (Edwards & Bell (1961) provide definitions of both subjective and objective goodwill: The subjective value of, at least, the selected asset structure must equal or exceed the market value of the assets involved or it would pay to liquidate the firm by selling its assets and to invest the proceeds at the market rate of interest. . . . The excess of the market value of the firm as a whole over the market value of its assets is *objective goodwill*. The excess of subjective value over the total market value of individual assets we shall call *subjective goodwill* (p.37)). With no "probable future" value assets and liabilities can only be measured at their current break up price. This valuation is similar to that recommended by Chambers (1975; 1977) and described as *exit values*.

What Chambers (1975; 1977) argued was that entities on an ongoing basis needed balance sheet values that would help them to determine whether they should stay in business, i.e., remain going concerns. By restating balance sheet information on the basis of exit prices and comparing this with probable future value, entities could make rational economic decisions about continuing or winding up operations, and about holding or selling off assets or investments (Sterling, 1981). Liquidation accounting uses exit value accounting, but whereas a value in the Chambers model assumed a fair, free market value, the liquidation model, because of time pressures imposed by creditors to realize whatever values remain in assets, may be forced to use distress prices. Hence the actual value of an entity under liquidation accounting may be less than its historical cost book value and also less than replacement cost or fair market value as normally determined (Newton, 1989).

Liquidation Accounting in Canadian and US Accounting Standards

The generally accepted accounting principles (GAAP) of preparing accounts and financial statements for entities in the process of winding up are found as part of various pronouncements of standard setting bodies. For example, the determination of liquidation wind up value is analogous to the permanent write-down of impaired assets and the adjustment of liabilities under a reorganization or debt restructuring. *See,* for example, Statement of Financial Accounting Standard (SFAS) 118 (1994) provides a discussion of loan impairment and the 1993 Exposure Draft on long-lived assets (still outstanding at February, 1995) outlines the US treatment. In Canada, Section 3060 of the *CICA Handbook* (paragraphs 42 to 50) treat impairment of capital assets.

The revaluation of assets under liquidation accounting can also be related to the adjustment of assets and liabilities to fair market values when accounting for a merger or acquisition under the purchase method *(CICA Handbook,* (Canada), Section 3050; US Statement of Financial Accounting Standard (SFAS) 12; SFAS 94). Thus the GAAP of liquidation accounting derives from a variety of areas, ranging from recommendations on the way in which to treat individual balance sheet items to the overall valuation of entities (long-term investments). Other than statements on impairment of debt (SFAS 118, 1994) and various discussions on impairments of assets, no specific, integrated standard of valuation and disclosure for liquidating companies exists.

Determination of Breakup Values in Liquidation

When an entity is declared a bankrupt and loses its status as a going concern, it becomes necessary to determine in an orderly fashion the inventory of the entity's assets and liabilities and their liquidation value. Such estimation usually falls within the ambit of business valuation experts and receivers or trustees in bankruptcy. The receiver or trustee in bankruptcy physically takes charge of the entity and

determines by direct observation and investigation the present status of assets and liabilities of the entity. The business valuator provides estimates of the value of the entity's physical assets individually or as a basket purchase and the value of any intangibles such as trademarks, patents, etc. These liquidation values are used to determine the amount available for distribution to creditors (first to secured and then to unsecured). If the amount to be realized on the sell off of assets exceeds the liabilities of the liquidating entities, any residual is distributed to the holders of equity. The receiver or trustee in bankruptcy is normally charged with the orderly sell off of assets and the settlement of obligations in a liquidation.

Accountants are normally involved in the liquidation of entities serving both as business valuators and as receivers. In neither case, however, would the auditors of record act as receivers or valuators for companies in bankruptcy proceedings. Such an action would represent a conflict of interest for an audit firm since the entity's auditors were presumably operating under the going concern assumption, and acting as an agent of the shareholders, whereas the receiver is primarily an agent of the court acting for the creditors.

Liquidation accounting thus represents an amalgam of accounting principles and practices designed to measure and report on the economic outcome of planning for and execution of a sell off of a bankrupt entity.

Bibliography

Chambers, R. J. (1975). Accounting for inflation. *Accounting theory and policy: A reader*, R. Bloom & P. T. Elgers, (eds), 382–97. Orlando, Fl.: Harcourt Brace Jovanovich, 1987, 2nd edn,

Chambers, R. J. (1977). Current value accounting – COCOA or REPCO. *Accounting for inflation stating a true financial position*, R. W. McGee, (Ed.), 118–36. Englewood Cliffs, NJ: Prentice-Hall. 1981

Edwards, E. O. & Bell, P. W. (1961). *The theory and measurement of business income*. Berkeley: University of California Press.

Newton, G. W. (1989). *Bankruptcy and insolvency accounting*. New York: John Wiley & Sons.

Sterling, R. R. (1981). Costs (historical versus current) versus exit values. *ABACUS*, 17, 93–129.

BERNADETTE E. LYNN

long-term construction contracts In the construction industry the production of goods to be sold extends over several accounting periods. For example, bridges and highways require several years to complete. A finished project's acceptance by the purchaser signals the completion of the earnings process, the point when revenue is ordinarily recognized. However, accounting measurement of revenue-generating activities are performed during each year of construction in order to provide periodic information.

Accounting standards for long-term construction contracts provide some flexibility regarding the timing and extent of revenue to be recognized and the treatment of costs incurred in the productive process. In 1955, the US Committee on Accounting Procedures issued Accounting Research Bulletin (ARB) 45, "Long-Term Construction Type Contracts" basic generally accepted principles. In 1981, Statement of Position (SOP) 81–1, "Accounting for Performance of Construction-Type and Certain Production-Type Contracts" and the "Audit and Accounting Guide for Construction Contractors," were issued by the American Institute of Certified Public Accountants (AICPA). In 1982, Statement of Financial Accounting Standards (SFAS) No. 56 designated the latter two as preferable principles.

The two generally accepted accounting methods for long-term construction contracts are: (1) the percentage of completion method, and (2) the completed contract method. In a 1993 survey, of the 600 sample companies, 129 of 133 companies involved in long-term construction used the percentage-of-completion method.

Selection of Method

The percentage of completion method is required when all of the following conditions exist: (1) reasonably determinable estimates of contract revenues, contract costs, and the extent of progress toward completion can be made; (2) contracts clearly specify the enforceable rights regarding goods or services to be provided and received by the parties, the consideration to be exchanged, and the manner and terms of settlement; (3) the buyer can be expected to satisfy his or her obligations under the contract, i.e., collection by the contractor must be

reasonably assured; and (4) the contractor can be expected to perform his or her contractual obligations.

The completed contract method should be used (1) if any of the above conditions are not met, (2) when a contractor has numerous, relatively short-term, contracts, or (3) when the inherent risks associated with a contract are greater than normal business risks. The method used must be disclosed in the financial statements. Costs incurred and total revenue recognized over the life of a contract are identical under both methods; thus the total profit or loss on a contract is unaffected by method choice. Timing of the recognition of revenue and profit during the contract's life differs between the methods. The two methods are summarized in table 1.

The Percentage of Completion Method

The recognition of revenues and profits is generally related to costs incurred in providing the services required under the contract (ARB 45, para. 4). This matching of the revenues to costs incurred provides a determination of the profit or loss arising from the contract while work is in progress. The application of this method necessitates use of estimates.

Measuring the percentage of completion. Various methods are currently used in practice. The commonly used measures can be grouped into input measures and output measures:

(1) *Input measures.* Input measures are computed in terms of effort devoted to a contract, such as costs incurred or labor hours worked. The degree of completion is determined by the ratio of costs already incurred to expected total costs to complete the project. The revenue to be recognized to date is the corresponding percentage of the contract price.

Any change in the estimated total costs to complete the contract is accounted for in the period the change is determined, and is not applied retroactively to prior years. If in any year of the contract it is apparent that the total costs to complete the project exceed the contract price, or revenue, then the entire loss must be included in the year of making such a determination.

(2) *Output measures.* Output measures are determined in terms of physical results. The

Table 1: Accounting methods for long-term construction contracts

	Percentage of completion method	Completed contract methods
Definition	Recognizes income on a contract prior to delivery of goods. Recognition is based on either an input or an output measure of the earning process.	Recognizes income only after the contract is complete or substantially completed.
Criteria for use	● Reasonably dependable estimates can be made. ● Contract provisions clearly specify the enforceable rights by the parties, the consideration, and the manner and terms of settlement. ● The buyer expected to satisfy his/her obligations. ● The contractor expected to perform his/her contractual obligations.	● Any of the necessary conditions of using the percentage of completion method do not exist. ● Has numerous relatively short-term contracts. ● The financial statement presentation does not vary materially from using the percentage of completion method.
Balance sheet		
Current assets		
Account receivable	Same.	Same.
Inventories		
Construction in progress	Costs of construction and gross profit recognized from long-term contracts.	Costs of construction.
Less: billings	Same.	Same.
Current liabilities	Billings in excess of contract costs and recognized profit.	Billings in excess of contract costs.
Income statement		
Revenue	Recognized each year based on the completion percentage toward the total completion.	Recognized only when the contract is completed.
Costs of construction	Actual cost of construction incurred in that year.	Recognized only when the contract is completed.
Gross profit	Recognized each year as the difference between revenue and costs of construction.	Recognized only when the contract is completed.
Tax purpose	Large contractors have to use.	Small contractors are allowed to use.

measures used are specific to the item under construction such as stories of a building completed or miles of a highway completed. The ratio is computed by dividing the amount of the physical measure completed by the total physical measure for the contract. Normally when output measures are used architects and engineers are asked to estimate what percentage of a job is complete based on the physical progress made on a contract.

The Completed Contract Method

Under this method no income is recognized until the contract is complete, or substantially complete. Although estimates are not used, if a loss is anticipated on a contract prior to its completion, the entire loss must be recorded in the year of discovery, regardless of completion.

The International Accounting Standards Committee issued an exposure draft, "Contraction Contracts" (E-42), in May, 1992. While percentage of completion is most commonly used in the USA, the Netherlands and Germany require the completed contract method to be used. The percentage of completion is required in Australia, Brazil, Mexico, and the UK.

Financial Statement Presentation and Contract Price

Balance sheet disclosure. Construction in progress, an inventory account is used to accumulate actual construction costs. In the completed contract method this account reflects only costs, but in the percentage of completion method it also includes the gross profit earned to date. A contra inventory account, billings on long-term contracts, is used to accumulate billings during the construction and is the same amount under both methods. Balance sheet presentation for each year is determined by subtracting billings on long-term contracts from construction in progress. If the net is positive, it is presented as a current asset; otherwise, it is a current liability.

Cash Flow in Long-term Contracts

Cash flow and accounts receivables balances are independent of the revenue recognition method and are the same under both the completed contract and the percentage of completion method. As the production process spreads over multiple accounting periods, contractors make partial billings as various milestones are reached in the performance of the contract. Ordinarily, formal acceptance by the purchaser does not occur until inspection of the project has been performed. Often there is a retention of a percentage of the contract price by the purchaser until all terms of the contract have been completed to the purchaser's satisfaction.

Cost-plus Contracts

In this type of contract, the final price of a contract is the cost plus a predetermined profit. The "plus" is either a stated percentage of the cost, a lump sum dollar amount (in the USA) or an amount or percentage that varies based upon the timeliness of the project's completion. For these contracts, the total dollar amount of the revenue is often not known until the contract's completion, so an estimated revenue amount may be recognized each year. This estimated revenue is computed so that the proportion of cost to revenue is as stipulated by the terms of the contract.

Determination of the cost to be reimbursed and used as the base for computation of the "plus" is a central issue in cost-plus contracts. Direct costs such as labor and materials incurred for a specific contract are easily identifiable with an individual project. Allocation of indirect contractor's costs, or overhead, to individual contracts requires judgment and sound business ethics to be appropriate. Cost-plus contracts in the USA are commonly used in governmental projects, particularly defense contracting. The US Cost Accounting Standards Board (CASB) operated as a governmental agency from 1970 to 1980 and was reinstated in 1988. The CASB formulates standards for the determination costs that may be allocated for reimbursement for any US government agency contracts in excess of $500,000 (Sourwine, 1994).

Bibliography

American Institute of Certified Public Accountants (1981). *Audit and Accounting guide for construction contractors.* New York.

American Institute of Certified Public Accountants (1981). *Statement of position (SOP) 81–1, accounting for performance of construction-type and certain production-type contract.* New York.

American Institute of Certified Public Accountants (1994). *Accounting trends and techniques.* New York.

Committee on Accounting Procedures (1955). *Accounting Research Bulletin (ARB) 45, Long term construction-type contracts.*

Financial Accounting Standards Board (1982). Financial accounting standards (FAS) 56. *Designation of AICPA Guide*, and SOP 81–1 on Contractor Accounting and SOP 81–2 on Hospital-Related Organizations as Preferable for Applying APB Opinion 20.

Sourwine, D. A. (1994). CASB: Is it doing the job? *Management Accounting*, Jan., 39–43.

JOANNA L. HO and DIANE H. ROBERTS

M

management accounting in hospitals - Cost accounting information systems and the standards applied under those systems in US hospitals have been influenced by various sources, including the accounting profession, the hospital accrediting agencies (i.e., the Joint Commission of the Accreditation of Hospitals), the American Hospital Association, state agencies (e.g., those which administer all payer systems and Medicaid), federal regulatory agencies (i.e., those which regulate Medicare), and third party insurance payers such as Blue Cross. The main professional accounting and auditing standards for hospitals are contained in the guide *The Audits of Providers of Health Care Services*, published by the American Institute of Certified Public Accountants in 1993. Government hospitals generally are required to follow this guide except where Government Accounting Standards Board statements override it.

The Economic Environment of Hospitals in the USA

The unique managerial accounting problems in hospitals can be traced to the fundamental uncertainty in the practice of health care. The nature of demand is irregular and unpredictable. Also, medical services are generally associated with a considerable risk of death or impairment of the patient. The customer in a hospital cannot test the product before consuming it, and there is an element of trust in the relation between customer and health care provider.

The uncertainty surrounding the practice of health care has created many problems for hospitals in planning and controlling their operations. The general system of checks and balances normally found in businesses is often not found in hospitals. A hospital is typically organized as a not for profit organization – i.e., a charity, where the monitoring function is more complicated than is the case in usual businesses.

Cost Reimbursement in the USA

The early payment systems in the USA under which hospitals were reimbursed by its two major revenue sources – Medicare (which is a federal program that pays the hospital costs of individuals 65 or older) and Blue Cross (which is a private insurance program that pays the hospital costs of most privately insured patients) have contributed to the poor planning and control mechanisms found in hospitals. Until the 1950s, most hospitals did not maintain detailed accounting records. Blue Cross changed its payment scheme to a retrospective cost reimbursement scheme (Preston, 1992) similar to Medicare's. Under this system hospitals were able to shift their costs of inefficiency to the third party payer, which removed the incentive to be efficient. Most hospitals had developed "top-down" departmental cost accounting approaches to meet the reimbursement informational requirements. Under departmental cost accounting, hospitals did not determine the costs of individual procedures, products, and services, except through a gross averaging method (e.g., departmental costs per patient).

The insurance reimbursement schemes have played a large role in the hospital's capital expenditures decisions by fostering excess consumer demand for unnecessary treatments and high technology. In 1950, for example, approximately one-half of the cost of hospital care was paid directly by the consumer and one-half was paid by third parties. By 1991, however, the consumer only paid about 16 percent (Eastaugh, 1992, Chapter 2). Since the 1970s there has been a major change in the health care environment. The cost has increased dramatically and new institutional arrangements have evolved, such as the health maintenance organizations that provide health care services to individuals or groups in exchange for a predetermind monthly payment, and the personal provider organizations, health care provider organizations that offer the insurer or employer discounts.

The Accounting Environment for Hospitals

What effects have these environmental factors had on the management information and control systems of hospitals? Some studies have suggested that hospitals have not become more efficient under prospective payment systems (PPS) – which are based on grouping homogeneous categories into diagnostic related groups (DRG). Borden (1988), for example, reports that DRGs had no apparent impact on hospital efficiency in New Jersey and that any pre-DRG inefficiency differences among hospitals still exist. Hadley, Zuckerman & Feder (1989) find that after the first year of PPS/DRGs there was a resurgence of rising costs per case. Despite the tighter reimbursement climate in the 1980s, community hospitals continued to purchase more and more expensive technology (Eastaugh, 1992). Hospitals were still experiencing problems in product line planning, unbundling of services, cost accounting, and explaining new developments to their medical staffs.

However, other evidence exists that suggests that hospitals are responding appropriately to the fundamental changes in the reimbursement system. For example, hospitals are shifting health care activities from inpatient to outpatient care (Carey & Stefos, 1992), as admission rates and length of stay are dropping. This reflects the intended consequence by Medicare to encourage less expensive outpatient care as a substitute for inpatient care (without compromise of quality). The inpatient/outpatient cost ratio remained stable during the same period, suggesting possible economies of scale in outpatient care. There have been many changes to more sophisticated cost accounting approaches by hospitals following PPS/DRGs. Eastaugh (1992) describes six potential types of cost accounting from less to more sophisticated:

(1) The ratio of costs to charges (RCC), which is a very aggregate "top-down" costing approach.
(2) RCC with job order costing in a few departments. Job order costing is a "bottom-up" costing approach which treats patients as separate "jobs" whose costs need to be separately tabulated (e.g., by DRG).
(3) Job order for a wide variety of departments.
(4) Process costing procedures in departments using relative value units (RVUs). Under this bottom-up approach, the hospital first determines the costs of the individual inputs (materials, labour, and indirect costs), and then allocates a share of the costs to a procedure based on the relative amount of time needed to perform the procedure.
(5) RVUs in most departments using standard costing, which involves assigning a budgeted cost for each procedure in order to determine variances for responsibility accounting.
(6) Standard costing using microcosting. Microcosting is the most precise method of determining costs which uses time and motion studies and sampling techniques to identify individual activities that make up the patient's care.

Factors to Improve Accounting

What approaches can be effective in improving the hospital's management accounting systems? One approach that has been shown to be effective is to provide comparison information to doctors on individual case costs or on the average practice patterns within a hospital. Also, hospitals can use more sophisticated methods in developing their budgets. Mensah & Li (1993) suggest, for example, that line-item (i.e., detailed) budgeting is an essential part of any effective budgeting system in not for profit organizations and that data envelopment analysis (DEA) is more suitable than, say, a linear translog budget model for estimating the appropriate line item budgets. DEA enables hospitals to estimate a cost frontier based on the performance of other hospitals with a similar case mix and scale of outputs, under which the cost standards for each hospital would represent an "efficient and attainable" target. Standards are set at the highest (rather than the average) level of performance that is justifiable by the available evidence.

It has also been suggested that activity-based costing can be effective in helping hospitals attain more accurate overhead allocations. Rotch (1992), for example describes the successful activity-based approach used by the Alexandria Hospital, which relies on a nursing acuity scale (i.e., severity of illness) as the primary cost driver. Noreen & Soderstrom (1994) suggest that hospitals must be careful, however, when using activity-based costing, as the costs from activities are not generally proportional. Thus, the average costs derived from cost driver analysis cannot be used to estimate marginal costs for various economic decisions. In determining the appropriate procedures for analyzing costs, hospitals often use the 80/20 rule, where departments concentrate on only the 20 percent of procedures which account for 80 percent of its revenue (Mahlen, 1994). The question is whether the hospital should determine the costs for the approximately other 80 percent of its departmental procedures.

In their discussion of managing the stages of an effective hospital cost accounting system, Young & Pearlman (1994) describe several attainable objectives of a good hospital cost information system. It should be able to determine DRG winners and losers, to determine the fixed and variable costs for making profitable bids on health maintenance organization and preferred provider organization jobs, and to determine the costs attributed to managers in different departments. The authors mention four evolutionary stages to achieve these goals. In stage 1, the hospital is able to track each patient through the hospital by recording all tests, procedures, and other resources (e.g., special meals), and supply a full cost figure for each test, procedure, and other resource provided to the patient, which requires identification of costs for each item. The goal is to eliminate cross-subsidization of different outputs. In stage 2, the hospital determines the incremental cost behavior from different decisions. In stage 3, the hospital identifies factors that drive costs at the individual patient level. Six factors which can influence a hospital's costs are case mix, volume, resources per case, input unit prices, input efficiency, and fixed facility costs. Stage 1

focuses primarily on case mix and volume; stage 3 on resources per case, input unit prices and input efficiency; and stage 4 on fixed facility costs. In stage 3 clinical patient protocols are developed; in these protocols, procedures for different illnesses are standardized. (Changes in technology, however, can make planning and controlling for protocols more difficult.) The primary objective in stage 3 is to develop budgets and responsibility centers. For example, hospitals can probably treat professional and support service departments (e.g., dietary, laundry, housekeeping, radiology, lab, anesthesiology, intensive care unit, and pharmacy) as "standard expense centers," where flexible budgets are based on actual volume and case mix. Hospitals can treat administrative and overhead departments (e.g., billing, legal and records) as "discretionary expense centers," where financial controls should not be used. Finally, clinical care departments (e.g., surgery, medicine, pediatrics, and emergency) can be treated as "profit centers" to motivate managers to increase the number of DRG winners and decrease the number of DRG losers and eliminate cross-subsidization of DRGs (i.e., winning DRGs subsidizing losing DRGs). In stage 4, the cost control effort must extend beyond traditional departmental boundaries in order to prevent departmental managers from taking actions which help their units but hurt the hospital. Under an administrative system, senior management considers each department to be part of a larger whole, which results in reorganizing the hospital. Some hospitals include a set of nonfinancial indicators to monitor the activities of each administrative system, e.g., waiting times at various intervals. Also, transfer prices can be used to encourage managers to take actions based on an appropriate pricing system. A problem, however, is that market prices may not be available for many hospital services.

Bibliography

Borden, J. (1988). An assessment of the impact of diagnostic related group (DRG)-based reimbursement of the technical efficiency of New Jersey hospitals using data envelopment analysis. *Journal of Accounting and Public Policy*, 7, 77–96.

Carey, K. & Stefos, T. (1992). Measuring inpatient and outpatient costs: A cost-function approach. *Health Care Financing Review*, **14**, 155–24.

Eastaugh, S. (1992). *Health care finance: Economic incentives and productivity enhancement*. Westport, CT: Auburn House.

Hadley, J., Zuckerman, S. & Feder, J. (1989). Profits and fiscal pressure in the prospective payment system: Their impact on hospitals. *Inquiry*, **26**, 354–65.

Mahlen, K. (1994). Improving hospital cost accounting with activity-based accounting. *Issues in cost accounting for health care organizations*. S. Finkler, ed., Gaithersburg, Md: Aspen Publishers.

Mensah, Y. & Li, S. (1993). Measuring production efficiency in a not for profit setting: An extension. *The Accounting Review*, **68**, 66–88.

Noreen, E. & Soderstrom, N. (1994). Are overhead costs strictly proportional to activity? *The Journal of Accounting and Economics*, **17**, 225–78.

Preston, A. (1992). The birth of clinical accounting: A study of the emergence and transformations of discourses on costs and practices of accounting in US hospitals. *Accounting, Organizations, and Society*, **17**, 63–100.

Rotch, W. (1992). Activity-based costing in service industries. *Emerging practices in cost management*. B. Brinker, (Ed.), Boston, MA: Warren, Gorham & Lamont.

Young, D. & Pearlman, L. (1994). Managing the stages of hospital cost accounting. *Healthcare Financial Management*, **47**, 58–80.

JOSEPH KERSTEIN

managing accounting earnings   This refers to the purposeful manipulation that results in altering reported accounting numbers. This definition includes the notion of smoothing income around some "normal" level as well as managers' accounting choices that benefit themselves or stockholders at the expense of other claimants. However, it excludes "fraudulent" reporting and is restricted to the latitude provided by generally accepted accounting principles (GAAP). Incentives for managing earnings differ by assumed goal.

Incentives for Earnings Management

Opportunistic incentives.   Managers are assumed to have incentives to use accounting choices to maximize their current and future compensation (*see* Watts & Zimmerman, 1986). In these situations, auditors, compensation committees and other monitors also are assumed to be unable to undo these opportunistic effects on earnings. A second potential benefit for managers is to increase their own job security. They might increase earnings in periods of poor performance using alternative accounting choices in order to enhance the likelihood of remaining on the job.

Income smoothing.   Ever since Hepworth (1953) suggested that income smoothing increases the confidence of investors in the firm, several studies attempted to examine that hypothesis. Others have argued that reducing income volatility increases managers' job security, while recent researchers have suggested that smoothing reduces perception of systematic risk.

There are three types of income smoothing accounting choices: (1) "classificatory" smoothing, (2) intertemporal smoothing, and (3) real smoothing. An example of classificatory smoothing is classifying a huge loss as extraordinary rather than ordinary (e.g., arising from operations). Intertemporal smoothing involves using accounting methods and choices to shift income or expenses between periods. For example, increasing the provision for doubtful debt in good times so that in bad times underprovision can be used to increase income. Real smoothing involves using real transactions to alter income. Examples are realization of gains on investment securities to boost income or deferring research and development (R&D) expenditures to subsequent periods.

Earnings management in the interest of other parties.   One incentive for earnings management that could benefit shareholders is to avoid violation of debt covenants by using income-increasing accruals and accounting changes. Such attempts may help the firm avoid or delay bankruptcy, which in turn could benefit shareholders. A second incentive for earnings management arises from the political and regulatory environment in which the firm operates. For instance, in the 1970s oil companies attracted a lot of attention for making abnormally high profits. Managers can potentially avoid adverse political scrutiny by using income-decreasing accounting choices. Nowadays, profits of pharmaceutical companies are attracting increasing attention when healthcare costs are thought to be out of control. Such companies have incentives to understate their performance to deter price controls or other kinds of regulations on their industry. In addition, several studies hypothesize earnings management in specific settings.

Methods of Earnings Management

Changes in accounting methods. Generally accepted accounting principles (GAAP) permit managers to choose accounting methods from within an acceptable set. These methods typically differ in terms of their effect on income measurement. For example, firms can switch from straight line to accelerated depreciation, or change inventory flow assumption from FIFO (first-in, first-out) to LIFO (last-in, first-out) for inventory valuation. However, changing accounting methods from year to year is not feasible because each change has to be justified and agreed to by the auditors. Also, GAAP often allow flexibility in adoption of new accounting standards. The choice of adopting a new accounting standard earlier than the required effective date can also offer opportunities for earnings management.

Changing accounting estimates or assumptions. - Such changes are more subtle than accounting *method* changes. Examples of these changes include increasing the estimate of useful life of an asset, changing the assumed rate of return on pension investments, or other allowed accrual choices. Since many of these estimates do not require justification by the auditor as "preferable" to the old estimates, managers may find it easier to adopt such changes. However, an important feature of managing accruals is their reversibility. For example, lower depreciation expense today implies higher depreciation of the underlying assets at some point in the future.

Real transactions. Perhaps the most costly way of managing earnings is through real transactions. For example, managers may selectively sell investment securities that have appreciated in value to realize gains while reporting securities on hand that have declined in value at historic cost. Real earnings management can also be achieved by changing R&D or advertising expenditures, as well as increasing production when overheads are allocated based on some normal level of production, thereby shifting more of the overheads into inventory rather than treating them as expenses. Such transactions have real costs such as taxes on realized gains or commissions to brokers.

Empirical Findings on Managing Earnings

Compensation related to reported earnings (bonus). Healy (1985) examines whether managers manipulated reported earnings (or discretionary accruals) for the purposes of improving their own bonus awards. When earnings before bonus is above the upper limit of the bonus plan, more discretionary net accruals would be charged to income. Also, when earnings before bonus is below the lower limit, management would again choose income-decreasing accruals. Healy's results support the bonus maximization hypothesis for total accruals.

Gaver et al. (1995) replicate Healy's bonus compensation study using different data, and correctly employ *discretionary* accruals in their tests. Their results show that when earnings before discretionary accruals falls below the lower bound, managers choose income-increasing discretionary accruals (as opposed to Healy's results that indicate income-decreasing *total* accruals). Gaver et al. interpret their results as being consistent with the income smoothing hypothesis rather than the bonus maximization hypothesis.

Different studies offer different inferences possibly because *non*-discretionary accruals are likely to vary with economic conditions and because the various incentives for earnings management are not mutually exclusive. When two incentives clash, the stronger incentive for *that* particular sample may mask the weaker, even though both incentives may apply.

Income smoothing. Beidleman (1973) uses regression analysis to normalize both the object of smoothing (reported net income) as well as potential smoothing variables (pension and retirement cost, incentive compensation, R&D costs, remitted earnings, sales and advertising, and plant retirements). It is the abnormal portion of income that is susceptible to manipulation. Beidleman interpreted his results as consistent with smoothing.

Before the US Accounting Principles Board Opinion No. 30 (Reporting the Results of

Operations) became effective in 1973, there were a host of irregular items – nonrecurring or extraordinary – that the accounting profession did not treat consistently. For a transaction that has already occurred, the only incentive is to classify it in a certain manner: e.g., irregular or nonrecurring revenues or expenses can be *classified* either as ordinary or as extraordinary to impart a smoother appearance to the object of smoothing, ordinary income (the component that is apparently used by financial analysts for predictive purposes).

Ronen & Sadan (1975) report results suggesting that potential extraordinary items were classified by managers so as to *diminish* the fluctuations of ordinary income. Recently, Hand (1989) examines the capacity of undertaking a real financing transaction as motivation for earnings management. He questions why certain firms undertook debt–equity swaps in the early to mid–1980s and reported large accounting gains. The results indicated that swapping debt for equity results in smoother earnings.

Additionally, Hand examines whether "swaps enabled firms to relax potentially binding sinking-fund constraints in the cheapest feasible manner, thereby providing a true financial gain." However, his results are weakly consistent with the incentive of relaxing debt constraints. The capricious timing of the swap gain would *not* have been possible if liabilities are valued at market.

Relaxing debt constraints and enhancing performance. Research evidence suggests that financial leverage (measured by some form of debt/equity ratio) is a proxy for the existence and tightness of accounting-based debt constraints. Also, managers of firms with higher debt/equity ratios have greater incentive to select income-increasing procedures. Bartov's (1993) findings suggest that managers time the gains and losses for disposals of long-lived assets and investments to both smooth income and loosen debt covenant restrictions.

In a recent study, Defond & Jiambalvo (1994) show that accrued expenses are unexpectedly income-decreasing in the year of violation for firms that are *known* to have violated debt covenants in their annual report footnote disclosure. However, auditors had issued going concern qualifications for 24 of the 94 firms and

it is reasonable that auditors expected relatively more conservative (or income-decreasing) choices. Also, 27 firms changed management and were expected to "take a bath," leading to income-decreasing accruals in order to have a fresh start.

Other studies suggest that adoption of new standards *earlier* than the effective date might be with the intention of managing earnings. This was observed for standards on foreign currency translation and accounting for income taxes.

Regulation-related and situation-specific earnings management. One of the functions of the US International Trade Commission (ITC) is to protect US domestic firms from injurious actions such as foreign dumping, etc. To counteract such injuries, the ITC issues so-called "import relief" decrees that increase tariffs (or reduce the quota) on particular foreign goods. Jones (1991) examines earnings management during the ITC's import relief investigations. Management's best interests would be served by decreasing earnings (accruals) during such investigations. The empirical results support the contention that managers manipulate earnings downwards during import relief investigations.

Bibliography

Bartov, E. (1993). The timing of asset sales and earnings manipulations. *The Accounting Review*, Oct., 840–56.

Beidleman, C. (1973). Income smoothing: The role of management. *The Accounting Review*, Oct., 653–67.

Defond, M. & Jiambalvo J. (1994). Debt covenant violation and manipulation of accruals. *Journal of Accounting and Economics*, Jan., 145–76.

Gaver, J., Gaver K. & Austin J. (1995). Additional evidence on bonus plans and income management. *Journal of Accounting and Economics*, Feb., 3–28.

Hand, J. (1989). Did firms undertake debt–equity swaps for an accounting paper profit or true financial gain? *The Accounting Review*, Oct., 587–623.

Healy, P. (1985). The effect of bonus schemes on accounting decisions. *Journal of Accounting and Economics*, Apr., 85–107.

Hepworth, S. (1953). Periodic income smoothing. *The Accounting Review*, Jan., 16–34.

Jones, J. (1991). Earnings management during import relief investigations. *Journal of Accounting Research*, Autumn, 193–228.

Ronen, J. & Sadan, S. (1975). Classificatory smooth-ing: Alternate income models. *Journal of Accounting Research*, Spring, 133–49.

Watts, R. & Zimmerman, J. (1986). *Positive accounting theory*. Englewood Cliffs, NJ: Prentice-Hall.

ANWER AHMED and BIPIN B. AJINKYA

marketable securities Marketable securi-ties, consisting primarily of short-term invest-ments, are categorized as current assets on a classified balance sheet. Marketable securities include such temporary investments as short-term paper (e.g., commercial paper), debt securities (e.g., corporate and government bonds), and equity securities (e.g., preferred and common stock). In addition to securities representing ownership shares, this classification also includes instruments representing the right to acquire such shares (such as warrants and call options), or instruments to dispose of such shares (such as put options). Finally, short-term derivative financial instruments (e.g., futures, forward, swap, or option contracts) and financial instruments used to hedge other investments are also considered marketable securities. Market-able securities should include, however, only those securities held for liquidity or temporary investment purposes. This classification is usually ranked after cash on the balance sheet in terms of liquidity. The generally accepted method of accounting for short-term invest-ments is promulgated in US Statement of Financial Accounting Standard (SFAS) No. 115, "Accounting for Certain Investments in Debt and Equity Securities" (1993). Other standards referring to short-term investments are SFAS No. 105, "Disclosure of Information about Financial Instruments with Off-Balance-Sheet Risk and Financial Instruments with Concentrations of Credit Risk" (1990); SFAS No. 107, "Disclosure about Fair Value of Financial Instruments" (1991); and SFAS No. 119,"Disclosure about Derivative Financial Instruments and Fair Value of Financial Instru-ments" (1994).

Classification as Marketable Securities

In order for a firm to classify a short-term investment as a marketable security, generally accepted accounting principles (GAAP) require the following, according to US Statement of Financial Accounting Standards (SFAS) No. 115, "Accounting for Certain Investments in Debt and Equity Securities" (1993): First, the instrument must be readily convertible into cash. For equity securities, for example, this means that the security is traded on a national securities exchange or a comparable foreign exchange and that sales prices or bid and ask prices are readily available. Secondly, the company must have the intention of converting the investment into cash when needed, usually within one year of the balance-sheet date.

Valuation of Marketable Securities at Acquisition

Marketable securities are recorded at acquisition cost. This includes the purchase price of the security plus any commissions, taxes, or addi-tional costs involved in the acquisition.

Valuation of Marketable Securities Subsequent to Acquisition

Valuing the security subsequent to acquisition, however, must comply with SFAS No. 115 which represents a departure from historical or acquisition cost accounting. GAAP requires that firms classify marketable securities into three categories: (1) debt securities held to maturity; (2) debt and equity securities held as trading securities; (3) debt and equity securities held as securities available for sale.

Debt securities held to maturity. Included in the held-to-maturity category are those debt secu-rities that an enterprise has the *intent* and *ability* to hold to maturity. This determination must be made at acquisition. As noted in SFAS No. 115, paragraph 59, the intent to hold the security to maturity "is distinct from the mere absence of an intent to sell." For these debt instruments, the difference between acquisition cost and maturity value is amortized. Debt securities are thus held at amortized acquisition cost.

Debt and equity securities held as trading securities. This category contains both debt and equity securities intended to be held by an enterprise for a short period of time. These securities are purchased primarily with the objective of generating profits on short-term differences in price. For this category, as well as for available-for-sale securities (*see below*), SFAS No. 115 requires that these securities have readily determinable fair values.

Subsequent to acquisition, securities included in this classification are listed at fair value. Other common terms for fair value are market value, current value, or mark-to-market. For financial instruments, SFAS No. 107, "Disclosure about Fair Value of Financial Instruments" (1991), considers quoted market prices, if available, as the best evidence of fair value. If unavailable, management's best estimate of fair value based upon the quoted market price of similar financial instruments is recommended.

Any changes in the fair value of trading securities appear on the income statement as an unrealized gain or loss on the valuation of trading securities. An offset valuation account to marketable securities also reflects the unrealized gain or loss. In this manner, trading securities are reported on the balance sheet at fair value.

Debt and equity securities held as securities available for sale.   Securities that do not qualify as held-to-maturity or trading securities are classified as available-for-sale securities. Unlike trading securities, which are generally held for profit, this group of securities is primarily for operating purposes. As with trading securities, available-for-sale securities are reported at fair value. Unlike trading securities, however, the unrealized holding gain or loss appears as a separate stockholders' equity account until realized, rather than as an adjustment to net income. Available-for-sale securities appear on the balance sheet at fair value.

Transfers of Securities Between Categories of Investments

SFAS No. 115 (1993) requires that any transfer of a security between categories of investments be accounted for at fair value. Paragraph 15 establishes the following treatment for any unrealized holding gain or loss at the date of transfer:

(1) For a security transferred from the trading category, the unrealized holding gain or loss at the date of the transfer will have already been recognized in earnings and shall not be reversed.

(2) For a security transferred into the trading category, the unrealized holding gain or loss at the date of the transfer

shall be recognized in earnings immediately.

(3) For a debt security transferred into the available-for-sale category from the held-to-maturity category, the unrealized holding gain or loss at the date of the transfer shall be recognized in a separate component of shareholders' equity.

(4) For a debt security transferred into the held-to-maturity category from the available-for-sale category, the unrealized holding gain or loss at the date of transfer shall continue to be reported in a separate component of shareholders' equity but shall be amortized over the remaining life of the security.

Disclosures

The following disclosures regarding securities are required according to US Statement of Financial Accounting Standard (SFAS) No. 115, "Accounting for Certain Investments in Debt and Equity Securities" (1993):

(1) For securities classified as available-for-sale or held-to-maturity, the aggregate fair value, gross unrealized holding gains and losses and contractual maturities.

(2) The proceeds from sales of available-for-sale securities and the gross realized gains and losses on those sales including the basis on which cost was determined (i.e., specific identification, average cost or FIFO).

(3) The gross gains and losses included in earnings from transfers of securities from the available-for-sale category into the trading category.

(4) The change in net unrealized holding gain or loss on available-for-sale securities included in the separate component of shareholders' equity during the period.

(5) The change in net unrealized holding gain or loss on trading securities included in earnings during the period (paragraph 19).

Gains and Losses on Financial Instruments Used to Hedge Marketable Securities

Gains and losses on financial instruments using to hedge securities would be classified according to the instrument hedged. Gains and losses on instruments hedging securities classified as trading would be reported in earnings, while those classified as available for sale would be reported in a separate component of stockholders' equity.

Marketable Securities and the Historical Versus Current Cost Controversy

Prior to SFAS No. 115, marketable securities were carried on the balance sheet at the lower of cost or market value. By requiring that trading and available for sale securities be recognized at fair value, the historical versus current cost accounting controversy has resurfaced.

Supporters of fair value argue that this form of valuation assists investors, creditors, and other users of financial information to evaluate a company's investment strategies. In addition, as concerns financial institutions, the market value of investment securities provides an indicator of the solvency of the institution.

Opponents of fair value question the relevance of reporting unrealized gains and losses due to the focus on events and transactions that do not truly involve the company. A second criticism relates to the subjectivity involved in valuing those securities for which market quotes are unavailable. Finally, opponents argue that it is uncertain whether the costs incurred by a company in satisfying the necessary reporting and disclosure requirements are justified by the additional information provided. To resolve this last issue, studies need to determine whether the incremental information provided by accounting for certain marketable securities at fair value is useful. If so, it is necessary to establish that this information is not already provided elsewhere to investors, creditors, and other users of financial information. Prior studies that address the issue of current versus historical costs provide some answers to this controversy even though the focus is not specifically on marketable securities.

Valuation of Marketable Securities and the ASR 190 and SFAS No. 33 Studies

In response to the criticism that historical cost income numbers do not reflect changing price levels for inventories and plant and equipment, reflected in cost of goods sold and depreciation expense on the income statement, the US Securities and Exchange Commission (SEC) issued Accounting Series Release (ASR) Number 190. According to this release, from 1976 certain large US firms were required to make supplemental disclosures regarding replacement costs for inventories and plant and depreciation. Studies by Gheyara & Boatsman (1980), Beaver et al. (1980) and Ro (1980) found no share price effects from the SEC requirement of replacement cost disclosures. In addition the studies suggest that replacement cost data provides no new information to the capital market that was not already available from competing information sources.

In 1979, SFAS No. 33 required firms with gross fixed assets exceeding $125 million or total assets exceeding $1 billion to report supplemental current cost and general price level based income numbers. Several studies conclude that SFAS No. 33 earnings provide no explanatory power with respect to differences in annual security returns over that provided by historical cost earnings. A number of studies, such as those by Bublitz et al. (1985), Murdoch (1986), and Haw & Lustgarten (1988), however, produced conflicting results. The different findings were attributed to measurement errors, cross-sectional correlation, and limited time periods in the above-cited studies. Although Bublitz et al. find little incremental explanatory power above and beyond that provided by historical cost income measures using the ASR No. 190 variables, SFAS No. 33 variables are found to provide significant explanatory power. Bublitz et al. attribute any differences with prior findings to having based their tests on two additional years of data and having controlled for industry effects.

Murdoch (1986) controls for the cross-sectional correlation effect by using a matched-pair design. The study indicates that historical cost returns on equity do not possess information content incremental to current cost returns. Haw & Lustgarten (1988) also examine the association between security returns and current cost accounting data as reported under both ASR 190 and SFAS No. 33, but with several extensions. First, variables are defined in terms of realized returns, income, and holding gains instead of the unexpected changes in these variables as in prior studies. This eliminates possible measurement error involved with estimations of investors' expectations. Secondly, the regression equation is specified so as to equal economic income. A third extension involves the use of standard econometric procedures to eliminate heteroscedasticity. Unlike many prior studies, Haw & Lustgarten found the ASR 190/SFAS 33 variables to be statistically significant with their signs consistent with predictions of income measurement theory.

Fair Value Accounting and Market Valuation of Banks

Several recent studies have investigated banks and thrifts in a continued effort to resolve the fair value accounting controversy. As with the studies examining ASR 190 and FAS No. 33, however, these studies report mixed findings as to the incremental information of disclosures purportedly providing indications of fair value. Beaver et al. (1989) find that supplemental disclosures with respect to default risk (non-performing loan data) and interest rate risk (loan maturity data) do provide incremental explanatory power beyond that already available. In examining similar disclosures for thrifts, Barth et al. (1991) find that only scheduled items, an indicator of default risk, are incrementally informative. Findings in a more recent study by Barth (1994), however, indicate that fair value estimates of investment securities do provide significant explanatory power beyond that provided by historical costs.

Marketable Securities and the Issues of Intent and Gains Trading

Although SFAS No. 115 addresses several problems concerning the reporting practices for debt and equity securities, it does not resolve two important problems. These are accounting based on intent and the issue of gains trading. Additional effort is currently under way to improve financial instrument disclosure.

Bibliography

Barth, M. E. (1994,). Fair value accounting: Evidence from investment securities and the market valuation of banks. *The Accounting Review*, **69**, Jan., 1–25.

Barth, M. E., Beaver, W. H. & Stinson, C. H. (1991). Supplemental data and the structure of thrift share prices. *The Accounting Review*, **66**, Jan, 56–66..

Beaver, W. H., Eger, C., Ryan, S. & Wolfson, M. A. (1989). Financial reporting, supplemental disclosures, and bank share prices. *Journal of Accounting Research*, **27**, Autumn, 157–78.

Beaver, W. H., Griffin, P. A. & Landsman, W. R. (1980). The information content of SEC accounting series release No. 190. *Journal of Accounting and Economics*, Aug., 127–58.

Beaver, W. H. & Landsman, W. R. (1983). The incremental information content of replacement cost earnings. *Journal of Accounting and Economics*, July, 15–39.

Beaver, W. H. & Ryan, S. C. (1985). How well do Statement No. 33 earnings explain stock returns? *Financial Analyst Journal*, Sept.–Oct., 66–71.

Bernard, V. & Ruland, R. (1987). The incremental information content of historical cost and current cost numbers: Time series analysis. *The Accounting Review*, **62**, Oct., 701–22.

Bublitz, B., Frecka, T. J. & McKeown, J. C. (1985). Market association tests and FASB Statement No. 33 disclosures: A reexamination. *Journal of Accounting Research*, (Supplement), 1–23.

Gheyara, K. & Boatsman, J. (1980). Market reaction to the 1976 replacement cost disclosures. *Journal of Accounting and Economics*, Aug., 107–26.

Haw, I. M. & Lustgarten, S. (1988). Evidence on income measurement Properties of ASR No. 190 and SFAS No. 33 data. *Journal of Accounting Research*, **26**, Autumn, 331–52.

Murdoch, B. (1986). The information content of FAS 33 returns on equity. *The Accounting Review*, **61**, Apr., 273–87.

Ro, B. T. (1980). The adjustment of security returns to the disclosures of replacement cost accounting. *Journal of Accounting and Economics*, Aug., 159–89.

PATRICIA A. WILLIAMS

N

not for profit organizations A not for profit organization (NFPO) is characterized by: (1) not having intentional surplus from activities; and (2) absence of indicia of ownership that gives owners or resource providers a simultaneous share in profit and control. Most NFPOs receive a significant amount of resources from providers who do not expect repayment or economic benefits proportionate to the resource provided. It is assessed that, in the USA, NFPOs' activities account for about 3.5 percent of the gross national product. Many NFPOs are tax exempt. Of the approximately 1,600,000 tax-exempt NFPOs, 60 percent are religious, educational, scientific, and charitable organizations.

In the USA, many NFPOs are members of national umbrella organizations that promulgated accounting guidance for their members. Such organizations include the National Committee of the American Council of Higher Education, the National Assembly of National Voluntary Health and Social Welfare Organizations, the American Hospital Association, the National Conference of Catholic Bishops, the United Way, and others. The accounting practices vary among the various pronouncements. In addition, two major private sector organizations set accounting standards for NFPOs: the Financial Accounting Standards Board (FASB), and the Government Accounting Standards Board (GASB). The GASB founding agreement provides that the GASB is responsible for establishing accounting standards for activities and transactions of state and local government entities. The FASB is responsible for activities and transactions of all other entities. In general, if the GASB has not issued a pronouncement on a particular matter, then governmental entities are to be guided by the FASB pronouncements. This provision, however, does not apply to FASB standards, concerning colleges and universities, that have been promulgated after November 30, 1990. Following a 1988 jurisdictional dispute between the two standard setters, the FAF resolved that, regardless of ownership status, colleges and universities, health facilities, and gas and electric utilities are subject to FASB pronouncements. However, governmental entities could select the GASB as their standard setter, providing the choice was made by December 1990. Unless specifically stated otherwise, the FASB and the GASB pronouncements supersede all applicable pronouncements or recognized practices by other bodies.

FASB/NFPO constituencies must follow the specific NFPO standards and unless explicitly exempted, are also subject to all information disclosures required by generally accepted accounting principles (GAAP) The FASB has issued three NFPO specific standards. Statement No. 93 "Recognition of depreciation by Not-For-Profit Organizations" (1987) requires depreciation of all tangible long-lived assets, except for certain art work and historical treasures, and the disclosure of the periodic and accumulated depreciation expense clustered by the nature or function of the assets. The choice of depreciation method is left to the reporting entity and must also be disclosed in the financial statements.

FASB Standard No. 116, "Accounting for Contributions Received and Contributions Made," (1993), applies to all contributions in the form of gifts, donations, and promises to give. To be recognized as contribution the non-reciprocal transfer must be legally enforceable. Contributions in the form of services shall be recognized only if they create or enhance nonfinancial assets or require specialized skills.

All nonmonetary contributions are valued at their "fair value." The standard distinguishes between unconditional and donor-imposed conditional contributions. Unconditional contributions must be recognized as revenue when received. Donor-imposed conditional contributions are subject to the occurrence or lack of occurrence of a future event, and must be recognized when the condition is met. In addition the standard distinguishes between contributions whose uses are subject to restrictions imposed by donors and those whose uses are unrestricted. Restrictions may be permanent or temporary and contributions must be grouped in the financial statements accordingly. When a restriction on the use of a particular contribution has lapsed, the latter is reclassified as unrestricted. Unconditional promises to give must be grouped on the balance sheet by maturity, i.e., one year or less, more than one year but less than five, and more than five years.

FASB Standard No. 117, "Financial Statements of Not-For-Profit Organizations," (also of 1993, which requires the application of fund accrual accounting, applies to all NFPOs except voluntary health and welfare organizations. The latter are permitted to follow the American Institute of Certified Accountants' Standard "Audit of Voluntary Health and Welfare Organizations" (1974). The statement requires the annual preparation of a set of three financial statements: Statement of Financial Position (SOFP), Statement of Activities (SOA), and Statement of Cash Flows (SOCF).

In the SOFP, assets and liabilities must be grouped into current and noncurrent net asset categories. Within each category assets and liabilities must be clustered by the nature of restriction on their use. Changes in net assets and equity are reported in the SOA. Increases in net assets – gains and revenues – and decreases in net assets – expenses and losses – should articulate to the net assets or equity reported in the SOFP. The SOA must also provide information on expenses reported by their functional classification such as major programs or services. The required SOCF is essentially the same as prescribed in FASB Standard No. 95, "Statement of Cash Flows" (1993), except for the terminology, which is adjusted to that of NFPOs.

The GASB issued two major standards concerning NFPOs: Standard No. 8, "Applicability of FASB Statement No. 93, Recognition of Depreciation by Not-For-Profit Organizations to Certain State and Local Governmental Entities," (1988) and Standard No. 15, "Governmental College and University Accounting and Financial Reporting Models," (1991). Standard No. 8 prescribes that NFPOs that follow the applicable American Institute of Certified Public Accountants (AICPA) pronouncements should continue doing so and should not follow the depreciation requirements of FASB Standard No. 93. All the relevant AICPA pronouncements require that tangible assets be capitalized at cost, when purchased, or at their fair market value, when received as donation. The recognition of depreciation is required for all NFPOs except colleges and universities.

Statement No. 15 gives colleges and universities a choice of following the requirements of the applicable AICPA pronouncements or the National Council on Governmental Accounting's (NCGA's) Statement No. 1, "Governmental Accounting and Financial Reporting Principles." Neither of these pronouncements require the recognition of depreciation. Whereas the AICPA pronouncements generally adopt the accrual accounting model, the NCGA pronouncements generally recognize assets, expenses and revenues on a cash basis. Most colleges and universities follow the AICPA requirements. The colleges that adopted the NCGA standard generally operate in a manner similar to government or a governmental department or agency. Some such colleges and universities have taxation authority.

Entities with tax exemption status may be liable for tax on their income from unrelated operation activities (UOA). These activities are defined as those which are categorized as a trade or business, carried out regularly, and are unrelated to the organization's tax exempted purpose. Thus, although the Internal Revenue Service (IRS) does not specify particular accounting requirements for NFPOs, tax-exempt organizations may be wise to segregate their expenses (including depreciation) and revenues between related activities and UOA.

The above setting and related accounting standards drew some criticism in the literature.

In 1988, a GASB survey showed that colleges and universities have least interest in depreciation data. Yet the FASB requires that it be reported by colleges and universities. The GASB also expressed its belief "that there are real differences between entities, environments and user needs in the public and private sectors that may justify . . . different financial accounting practices." Therefore, the GASB feels that the FASB approach of uniformity in reporting practices by NFPOs in both sectors is not justified.

Similarly, Falk (1992) argues that, unlike investors in business corporations, donors have no residual claim in the NFPO, and have different utilities for the various activities of the organization. Because these utilities cannot be aggregated, or do not have a common denominator, NFPOs should report on their activities and net assets in a fund accounting form. Each "fund account" should relate to a certain well-defined activity. Based on the so-called "club theory" (Buchanan, 1965; Hansmann, 1980), there is a distinction between clubs and charities. The former have five distinct characteristics: (1) the utilities of resource providers and beneficiaries are interdependent; (2) benefits are normally restricted to members and exclusion of others from benefiting by collective goods is possible; (3) they are normally controlled by elected members; (4) average periodic membership dues varies inversely with the magnitude of membership; and (5) exit and entry of membership is possible. Because of these characteristics, the membership contract is reciprocal and multi-period in nature, a type of contract for which accrual accounting is applicable. Charities, on the other hand, normally have no reciprocal or multi-period contracts with donors, and the utilities of resources provided by the beneficiaries are not necessarily interdependent. Therefore, the cash basis of accounting or a modified cash basis would be appropriate for such entities.

The FASB at the time of writing is in the process of drafting some modifications to the existing accounting standards.

Bibliography

Buchanan, J. M. (1965). An economic theory of clubs. *Econometrica*, Feb., 1–14.

Falk, H. (1992). Towards a framework for not-for-profit accounting. *Contemporary Accounting Research*, Spring, 468–99.

Hansmann, H. B. (1980). The role of nonprofit enterprise. *The Yale Law Journal*, Apr., 835–98.

HAIM FALK

oil and gas accounting Accounting for oil and gas producing companies has become a serious matter in the United States as many companies have claimed that certain accounting methods reduce their incentives to search for, and produce, oil and gas. The primary written standards defining the appropriate accounting procedures or GAAP (generally accepted accounting principles) for gas exploration and production (E&P) activities include the following pronouncements by the Financial Accounting Standards Board (FASB) and the Securities and Exchange Commission (SEC): Statement of Financial Accounting Standard (SFAS) No. 19, "Financial Accounting and Reporting by Oil and Gas Producing Companies;" SFAS No. 25, "Suspension of Certain Accounting Requirements for Oil and Gas Producing Companies;" SFAS No. 69, "Disclosure about Oil and Gas Producing Activities;" and SEC Regulation SX 210:4-10.

The major difference between the two main accounting methods (full cost (FC) and successful efforts (SE)) is their treatment of dry hole (i.e., unsuccessful well) exploration costs. Under SE, only those exploration costs that can be directly related to specific reserves discovered are capitalized. Exploration costs of dry holes are expensed. The capitalized costs for producing properties are amortized as the proved reserves relating to those properties are produced.

By contrast, under FC, all costs incurred in exploration within a relatively large cost center, such as a country, are capitalized when incurred. Thus, exploration costs relating to both dry holes and successful wells are recorded as assets. These capitalized costs are amortized as the reserves in the cost center are produced.

The use of two divergent methods spurred considerable debate within the accounting profession, although under both methods, all exploration costs are eventually expensed, either as dry hole costs or through amortization. Therefore, the choice of SE versus FC represents a timing issue. FC tends to push (dry hole) expenses into a later period and, correspondingly, to show higher asset levels than SE firms to the extent that there are unamortized dry hole costs on the balance sheet. In addition, the costs of development wells, whether successful or dry, are capitalized under both SE and FC and amortized over reserves when produced. Development wells are drilled within a proved area to provide facilities for producing proved reserves. Thus, they are not drilled to explore for oil and gas but to produce already proved reserves. Nevertheless, development wells can be determined to be dry.

The SEC in 1978 stated that traditional historical cost methods, such as SE and FC, are inherently limited in their ability to provide relevant information about E&P activities because of unique economic characteristics of the oil and gas industry. Under both methods, oil and gas properties are valued on the balance sheet at historical cost, which excludes information about the value of oil reserves.

Instead of requiring either FC or SE, the SEC introduced a new oil and gas accounting method in ASR No. 253 called "reserve recognition accounting" (RRA), which was based on a valuation of proved oil and gas reserves. In light of this conflict both FC and SE have been acceptable, with many variations on the basic FC and SE methods found in practice. Although FC firms are allowed to capitalize dry hole costs, the SEC requires them to test for impairment of their oil and gas assets on a quarterly basis. If the unamortized costs in a cost center exceed the present value of estimated future net revenues from production of proved reserves, the costs must be written down to the ceiling amount. Finally, accounting research has shown that, by comparison to SE firms, FC firms are younger, more highly leveraged, spend a larger proportion of their revenues on capital investments, and purchase more proved gas reserves. In addition, FC firms replace a higher proportion of the reserves they produce.

Supplemental Oil and Gas Disclosures

According to the US Securities and Exchange Commission's (SEC) reserve recognition accounting (RRA) method, proved reserves would be reflected on the balance sheet, and changes in the value of proved reserves (including discoveries) would be reflected on the income statement. Also supplemental RRA disclosure includes proved reserve quantities. The RRA reserve value measure was defined as the present value of estimated net revenues from future production of proved oil and gas reserves using a 10 percent discount rate. Thus, RRA reserve value disclosures were based on some estimates of *future* revenues and costs.

Critics argued that such reserve value estimates are unreliable and subjective. Three years later, the SEC issued ASR No. 289 in which it rescinded the RRA method, but continued to require *supplemental disclosures* of reserve values. Finally, in 1982, the US Financial Accounting Standards Board (FASB) presented a comprehensive package of disclosures in Statement of Financial Accounting Standard (SFAS) No. 69, "Disclosures about Oil and Gas Producing Activities," which was later also adopted by the SEC.

SFAS No. 69 requires publicly traded firms with significant oil and gas producing activities to report five sets of supplemental disclosures: (1) quantities of proved oil and gas reserves and changes therein; (2) capitalized costs relating to oil and gas producing activities; (3) costs incurred in oil and gas property acquisition, exploration, and development activities; (4) results of operations for oil and gas producing activities; and (5) a "standardized measure" (SM) of discounted future net cash flows, which is an estimate of the value of the firm's proved reserves, based on fiscal year-end oil and gas prices and costs, and a 10 percent discount rate.

After years of debate, both the traditional methods of successful efforts (SE) and full cost (FC) continue to be accepted alternatives, but the controversy has resulted in additional required disclosures about proved reserves and exploration activities.

Bibliography

Alciatore, M. (1990). The reliability and relevance of reserve value accounting data: A review of the empirical research. *Journal of Accounting Literature*, 9, 1–38.

Alciatore, M. (1994). New trends in reserve-based accounting research. *Petroleum Accounting and Financial Management Journal*, Spring, 50–68.

Securities and Exchange Commission (1978). *Accounting series release No. 253: Adoption of requirements for financial accounting and reporting practices for oil and gas producing activities.* Washington, DC: Securities and Exchange Commission.

Securities and Exchange Commission (1981). *Accounting series release No. 289: Financial reporting by oil and gas producers.* Washington, DC: Securities and Exchange Commission.

MIMI L. ALCIATORE

P

pensions

Types of Pension Plans

Pensions are a form of deferred compensation in which an employer provides monetary benefits to an employee after retirement. There are two principal types of pension plans in the USA – defined benefit plans and defined contribution plans. A defined benefit plan is one in which the amount of pension benefit to be provided depends on factors such as age, years of service, and compensation. A defined contribution plan is one in which the employer does not promise any specific level of benefits, but instead makes specified contributions into a pension plan, which determine benefits an employee receives.

Accounting for defined benefit plans is complicated by conceptual and practical issues in determining the cost today of a promise to pay future benefits.

Overview of Pension Accounting

Determining the pension obligation involves estimates of mortality, turnover, retirement dates, and rates of future salary increases. The future benefits to be paid are discounted to obtain the present value of the obligation. This is the *projected benefit obligation* which is the actuarial present value of all benefits attributed to employee service by the pension benefit formula, including any effects of estimated pay increases. The obligation can be viewed as deferred compensation, a portion of which is attributed to each period as an expense.

The assets which ultimately fund the benefit payments are held by the pension plan, which is a legal entity separate from the corporate sponsor. Pension plan assets are increased by contributions from the company and earnings on investment and are decreased by distribu-

tions to retirees and investment losses. Despite the legal separation, the plan assets and obligations are generally viewed as corporate assets and liabilities. The difference at any point in time between plan assets and the projected benefit obligation is the *funded status of the plan*.

The recorded net periodic pension cost consists of a number of components recognizing the consequences of events affecting the pension plan. *Service cost* is the actuarial present value of pension benefits allocated under the formula for employee services provided during the year. The effects of plan amendments changing benefits are amortized, with a portion recognized each year as a *prior service cost*. Since actual payments of benefits are delayed until retirement, the cost of financing incorporates the time value of money by including in pension expense an *interest cost* component, which measures the increase in the projected benefit obligation due to the passage of time. The *return on plan assets* offsets pension expense.

Included in the determination of pension expense are the gains and losses resulting from differences between the estimates used to project benefit costs and fund performance and the actual experience. Changes in the pension benefit obligation also result from changes in assumed discount rates, future compensation levels, turnover, mortality, etc. To smooth the volatility in pension expense, the accounting standard permits deferred recognition of such gains and losses.

Most of the pertinent information for assessing the status of the defined benefit pension plan can be obtained from notes provided as part of a firm's financial statements. Separate information is provided for underfunded and overfunded plans as well as for domestic and international plans.

A fundamental relationship in accounting for defined benefit plans is that the difference between pension benefit obligations and plan assets (funded status of the plan) equals the sum of amounts of:

- unrecognized transition gains and losses
- unrecognized prior service costs
- unrecognized gains and losses
- accrued or prepaid pension costs recognized on the balance sheet.

The unrecognized amounts are off the balance sheet, reported in the notes. Only the accrued or prepaid amounts are recognized and recorded on the balance sheet itself. Thus, the pension liability or asset recorded on the sponsor company's books is not simply the funded status of the plan, but is adjusted for amounts which have not yet received accounting recognition.

Measurement of Pension Obligation

Three measures of the pension obligation are disclosed. The *vested benefit obligation* is the most limited and is not contingent on future service or salary increases. The *accumulated benefit obligation (ABO)* includes the effects of future service, but not salary increases; the *projected benefit obligation (PBO)* includes the effects of both.

Pension Expense

Pension expense is recognized in the income statement. The notes to the financial statements show the periodic pension cost, broken down into components: service cost, interest cost on projected obligations, expected return on plan assets, amortization of net transition amounts, and other net amortizations and deferrals.

Service Cost

The determination of service cost requires a method of attributing pension cost across the accounting periods in which services are rendered. The service cost component reflects future salary levels including salary increases attributable to general price levels, productivity, seniority, promotion, and other factors.

Projected Benefit Obligation and Interest Cost

The projected benefit obligation is the actuarial present value, as of a specified date, of all benefits attributed by the pension benefit formula to employee service rendered prior to that date. The interest cost, which reflects the increase in the PBO due to the passage of time, is measured using a discount rate, which is commonly based on rates implicit in annuity contracts, the Pension Benefit Guarantee Corporation rates, or rates on high quality fixed instruments. Changes in the discount rate lead to significant changes in the liability estimates.

Actual Return on Plan Assets

The actual return is the difference between plan assets at the beginning and end of the year, adjusted for contributions and benefits paid. Plan assets are measured at their fair value as of the measurement date, e. g., the date of the financial statements, or, if used consistently, a date not more than three months prior to that date. The fair value of an asset is the amount that a plan could reasonably expect to receive in a voluntary sale.

The accounting profession permits a smoothing device to mitigate the volatility of actual returns experienced in the pension plans and ease the period-to-period impact on pension expense. The justification is that investments are made for the long term and plans do experience period-to-period volatility in returns.

Expected Return

The expected return on plan assets is based on the assumed long-term rate of return on plan assets and the *market-related value of plan assets*, which is either fair value or a calculated value that recognizes changes in fair value in a systematic and rational manner over not more than five years. It is expected return, rather than actual, which offsets pension expense.

Unrecognized Gains and Losses

Unrecognized gains and losses are a major source of off-balance sheet amounts (*see* Lilien & Mellman, 1994). One component is the difference between actual returns on investments and expected returns (deferred gains and losses). Additionally, the projected gains and losses can change due to other actuarial assumptions, as well as variances between actual experience and assumptions. These deferred gains and losses are amortized using an approach referred to as the *corridor method*, which is a powerful smoothing device that removes from the current period pension expense significant fluctuations in the fair value of plan assets and the benefit obligation. Recognition of these amounts is delayed and only gradually incorporated into the balance sheet.

Transition Amount

When Statement of Financial Accounting SFAS No. 87 was first adopted in the USA (effective 1986), a transition amount was calculated as the difference (at the beginning of the adoption year) between the PBO and the fair value of plan assets, adjusted for previously accrued pension amounts which were already on the balance sheet. The amortization of the transition amount is on a straight line basis over the average expected service life of employees to receive the benefits. When the service period is less than 15 years, the firm can still use a 15-year amortization period.

Prior Service Cost

A *prior period service cost* is the increase or decrease in the PBO attributable to plan amendments which increase employee benefits for services rendered in prior period. Prior period service costs are recognized as an additional component of pension expense over the average remaining service life of employees.

Minimum Liability

When the funded status of the pension plan (calculated using the ABO, i.e., without expected salary increases) is negative and exceeds the recorded obligation on the company's balance sheet, a company must make an adjustment to immediately recognize this minimum liability. The minimum liability adjustment does not affect the income statement, and the company simultaneously reports on the balance sheet an intangible asset attributed to future service of employees. There are limits on the amounts reported as intangible assets; if exceeded, additional offsets against shareholders, equity may be· required.

Research Issues

The market implications of pension disclosures, economic and financial statement effects of the accounting standard itself, and causes and effects of plan terminations have been the main areas of pension-related accounting research. Other research questions have included the determinants of funding policies, motivations for lobbying on the proposed standard, and the decision of some firms in the USA to adopt SFAS 87 early.

The relevance of pension assets and liabilities for the securities' markets in pricing the sponsoring firm's debt and equity has been examined by Daley (1984), Dhaliwal (1986), Landsman (1986), Reiter (1991), and Barth (1991). Essentially, these researchers found that prices reflect these liabilities and that pension obligations contribute to financial leverage in the stock market's assessment of the firm's financial risk.

Factors involved in the decisions to terminate pension plans were the focus of research by Haw. et al. (1991), Mittelstaedt (1989), and several other studies. Financial distress (as evidenced by decline in earnings, decline in marginal tax rates, and reduced cash flow), higher levels of owner control, and income-based management compensation plans were found to be associated with terminations, while higher levels of unionization mitigated against such actions. This research indicates that firms are able to draw on the surplus assets stored in pension funds, but at some cost: it appears that firms will first seek funds by reducing investment or cutting dividends. Even in the absence of asset reversions, termination may be undertaken to offset declines in reported earnings and to loosen restrictive debt covenant constraints.

Firms' pension funding strategies were examined by Francis & Reiter (1987) and Thomas (1988). Results show that financial considerations, including tax benefits and cash availability, provide incentives toward higher levels of funding, but labor and contracting incentives work in the opposite direction. Thus, funding strategy involves complex tradeoffs between different incentives, with tax considerations playing a major role.

Bibliography

Barth, M. E. (1991). Relative measurement errors among alternative pension asset and liability measures. *Accounting Review*, **66**, 3, 433–63.

Daley, L. A. (1984). The valuation of reported pension measures for firms sponsoring defined benefit plans. *Accounting Review*, **LIX**, 2, 177–98.

Dhaliwal, D. S. (1986). Measurement of financial leverage in the presence of unfunded pension obligations. *Accounting Review*, **LXI**, 4, 651–61.

Francis, J. R. & Reiter, S. A. (1987). Determinants of corporate pension funding strategy. *Journal of Accounting and Economics*, **9**, 1, 35–60.

Haw, I. M., Jung, K. & Lilien, S. B. (1991). Overfunded defined benefit pension plan settlements without asset reversions. *Journal of Accounting and Economics*, **14**, 3, 295.

Landsman, W., (1986). An empirical investigation of pension and property rights. *Accounting Review*, **LXI**, 4, 662–91.

Lilien, S. & Mellman, M. (1994). Time for realism in accounting for employers' pension plans. *CPA Journal*, **LXIV**, 6, 54–8.

Mittelstaedt, H. (1989). An empirical analysis of the factors underlying the decision to remove excess assets from overfunded pension plans. *Journal of Accounting and Economics*, **11**, 4, 399–418.

Reiter, S. A. (1991). Pension obligation, and the determination of bond risk premiums: Evidence from the electric industry. *Journal of Business, Finance and Accounting*, **18**, 6, 833–60.

Thomas, J. K. (1988). Corporate taxes and defined benefit pension plans. *Journal of Accounting and Economics*, **10**, 3, 199–238.

JANE BOZEWICZ and STEVEN B. LILIEN

postretirement benefits   In addition to pensions, many companies provide retirees and their dependents with benefits such as medical care, life insurance, housing, etc. In the USA, the costs of these other postretirement benefits (OPEB) tend to represent the largest portion of a company's total costs of benefits. For example, OPEB for General Motors Corp. exceeded $37 billion in 1993. Traditionally, the majority of OPEB plans in the USA have not been funded. Companies now have to accrue the projected cost of postretirement benefits during an employee's working life, as required by Statement of Financial Accounting Standard (SFAS) No. 106, "Employers' Accounting for Postretirement Benefits Other Than Pensions." In a single employer defined benefits plan, the benefits are specified in monetary terms or by type. The provisions of SFAS No. 106 are effective for fiscal years starting after December 15, 1992 for all public companies and for nonpublic companies with more than 500 plan participants (the relevant year is 1994 for companies with non-US plans and others).

Assumptions

The employer's best estimate of relevant future events are based on some explicit assumptions about:

Discount rate: The discount rate used to determine the present value of future expected benefit payments required to meet the plan's obligations should be based on currently available rates of return on high-quality fixed-income investments with similar timing of cash flows and benefits.

Expected long-term rate of return: This rate (for funded plans) reflects the average rate of return expected on current and future (contributed) plan assets, which considers the current returns being earned on the plan assets currently invested and returns expected to be available from reinvestment.

Demographic assumptions: These are assumptions regarding employee turnover, retirement age, mortality, dependency status, gender, and work force reductions.

Per capita claims cost: This represents the current cost of providing postretirement health care benefits for one year at each age of benefit eligibility.

Health care cost trend rate: This rate reflects the expected rate of change in average per capita claims cost, due to factors other than changes in the demographic characteristics of plan participants, which considers inflation, technological advances, health care delivery patterns, and changes in health status of plan participants.

OPEB Obligations

The expected postretirement benefit obligation (EPBO) is the actuarial present value of the postretirement benefits expected to be paid under the terms of the substantive plan (i.e., the plan as it is understood by the employer and the plan participants). The portion of the EPBO representing the present value of benefits attributed to the employee's service rendered to date, assuming the plan continues in effect and that all assumptions about future events are met, is referred to as the accumulated postretirement benefit obligation (APBO).

The APBO obligation and the plan assets are measured as of the company's reporting year-end date (or a date not more than three months prior to that date) based on the assumptions used for the previous reporting period or adopted during the current year.

Attribution

OPEB costs are spread over or attributed to the employee's service period using the projected unit credit actuarial method (also called the benefit/years-of-service method). Under this method, the same amount of expected post-retirement benefit costs is allocated to each year of the employee's attribution period.

Recognition of Net Periodic Postretirement Benefit Cost

The employer must recognize and report the net periodic costs of postretirement benefits (NPPBC) associated with the plan, which includes: (1) service cost for the change in expected postretirement benefit obligation (EPBO) attributable to employee service for the period; (2) interest cost for the increase in the accumulated postretirement benefit obligation (APBO) resulting from the passage of time; (3) actual return on plan assets calculated as the difference between the fair market value of plan assets at the beginning and at the end of the reporting period, adjusted for contributions and benefit payments made during the period; (4) prior service cost representing an amortized share of the increase in APBO due to retroactive plan amendments; and (5) gains and losses representing, in general, changes in the APBO and the plan assets resulting from changes in either assumptions or experience different from that assumed. In the case of funded plans, the gain or loss component includes the difference between the actual and the expected return on plan assets.

Balance Sheet Recognition and Disclosure

An asset, labeled prepaid cost of other post-retirement benefits, is reported in the balance sheet if the amounts contributed to the plan or paid to or for the plan participants during the reporting period exceed the net periodic costs of postretirement benefits (NPPBC). This asset represents the fair market value of plan assets in

excess of the accumulated postretirement benefit obligation (APBO).

A liability, labeled accrued cost of other postretirement benefits, is reported in the balance sheet if the NPPBC exceeds the amounts contributed to the plan or paid to or for the plan participants during the reporting period. This liability represents the amount of the APBO in excess of the fair market value of any plan asset.

Additional disclosures are required to inform the readers about plan assumptions, funding, and policy actions.

Defined Contribution Plans

These plans specify how contributions to the individual's account are to be determined. In such a plan, other postretirement benefits (OPEB) are limited to the amounts contributed.

Miscellaneous Issues

A multi-employer plan is one to which contributions are made by two or more unrelated employers (usually according to collective bargaining agreements) and is administered by a joint board of trustees comprised of management and labor representatives of the contributing employers. Each employer reports in its own financial statements: (1) NPPBC for the amount of the required contribution to the plan for the particular reporting period, and (2) a liability for any unpaid contributions required for the period.

Specific adjustments are also required for firms involved in business combinations, for settlements relieving the employer from APBO obligations, and for plan curtailments.

MARY STONE and JAN E. BARTON

present value and annuity

Present Value of Money

The concepts of present value and annuity are closely related to the time value of money. The time value of money, or interest, refers to the fact that a dollar received now is worth more than a dollar to be received on any other future date, even after adjusting for the effects of inflation or deflation. There are two different types of problems related to the time value of money:

future value and present value; each can be further classified into single amount and annuity (equal payments or receipts for a series of equal time periods). To understand the concept of time value of money, it is helpful to recall how interest is calculated upon a single-period deposit amounting P, given interest rate i:

$$\text{interest earned} = P * i$$

For example, if $100 is invested on an one-year fixed-term deposit with an interest rate of 10%, $110 ($100 principal plus $10 interest) is expected to be received at the end of this one-year period. The increased amount of $10 represents the time value of the principal over this period.

Present value is the amount that one or more future cash flows are worth currently, given a specified rate of interest. In present value problems, we are usually given the amount that will be available at some future date (principal plus interest; in the above example, $110), and we are asked to calculate the current cash equivalent of that amount ($100 in our example). Stated in a different way, $110 cash inflow received 12 months later is equivalent to $100 received now. Note that the present value is always a smaller amount than the known future amount because interest will be earned and accumulated on the present value to the future date.

Future value is the amount to which one or more sums of money invested at a specified interest rate will grow over a specified number of time periods. Since the future value is a reversed case of current value, and since the

present value is more relevant to many accounting issues, only the present value is covered here.

In computing future and present values, simple or compound interest may be used. Simple interest means that interest is earned or owed only on the original invested or borrowed (principal) amount. Compound interest means that interest earned in prior periods is added to the original amount so that, in each successive period, interest is earned or owed on both principal and interest. The time between each interest computation is called the compounding period. The more often interest is compounded, the higher the actual rate of interest rate being received or paid relative to the stated rate. Table 1 shows how compound interest is calculated and what is the impact of compounding period on the resulting interest amount.

From table 1, two variables determine how fast the principal grows into a future value in a compound interest problem: (1) the interest rate, and (2) the compounding period.

Present value of a single amount

To compute the present value of a sum (P) to be received or paid in the future, the sum is subjected to compound discounting at i interest rate for n periods:.

$$PV = \frac{P}{(1+i)^n}$$

Using the simple example given in the entry headed Present value of money, $PV = 110/(1+10\%)^1 = 100. The process of deriving the

Table 1: Compound interest calculation

Year	Compound annually			Compound quarterly		
	Beginning balance	Interest 10%	End-of-year balance	Beginning balance	Interest 10%	End-of-year balance
1	$100	$10	$110	$100	$10.38	$110.38
2	110	11	121	110.38	11.46	121.84
3	121	12	133	121.84	12.65	134.49
4	133	13.3	146.4	134.49	13.96	148.45
.	.	.	.	.	.	.
.	.	.	.	.	.	.
.	.	.	.	.	.	.
10	236	23.6	259.4	243.25	25.26	268.51

present value as shown here can be viewed as a reverse calculation of future interest compounding. The reverse of interest compounding is called discounting.

Although the *PV* can be calculated manually as illustrated here, it is more convenient to use present value tables that show the present value of $1 to avoid tedious computations. The present value table lists present value factors for (1) different interest rates which is often arranged in columns, and (2) the length of the time horizon in terms of the number of periods from the present time to the future event, often arranged in rows. With a known interest rate and the number of periods, a corresponding discount factor can easily be found from the table. To find the present value of an amount other than $1, we multiply the amount by the appropriate present value factor from the table. For example, you will receive $1,000 four years from today. With an interest rate of 10% per year, how much is that amount worth today (i.e., what is its present value)? From a present value table, we read down from 10% and across from period 4, the *PV* factor is 0.683. We then multiply 0.683 by $1,000, which gives $683.' This amount can be verified by using the formula $1,000/(1+0.1)^4 = 683$.

Present Value of An Annuity

An annuity means that instead of a single amount, there is a series of consecutive payments (called rents) characterized by:
1. An equal amount each interest period.
2. Interest periods of equal length (year, semi annual, or month).
3. An equal interest rate each interest period.

The concept of annuity exists not only in textbooks, but is also applied in daily life. Examples of annuities that can be found from daily life include: equal monthly payments on an automobile or a home, and equal yearly contributions to a savings account.

There are two types of annuity. In an ordinary annuity (such as bond interest), the first cash flow is at the end of a period. In contrast, the cash flows from an annuity due occur at the beginning of a period. The ordinary annuity has a wider application in accounting than does the annuity due.

The *PV* of an annuity can be found year by year by using the *PV* of $1 table, or calculated directly by using the formula:

$$PV = \frac{1 - \frac{1}{(1+i)^n}}{i}$$

The calculation of present value annuity is usually facilitated by using a present value of annuity table. The table is similar to the present value table in many ways. One notable difference is that the value of discount factors found in the present value table is always less than 1, while in the annuity table the value of discount factors is usually greater than 1 when the number of periods is larger than 1. This is because the annuity discount factors would be applied to multiple equal payments/receipts when there is more than one period.

Applications of Present Value in Accounting

Financial accounting. There are many situations in financial accounting in which transactions can only be reliably measured in present value of future cash flows. A typical example is the valuation of bonds payable which are measured to reflect the present value of (1) periodic interest payments during the life of the bond, and (2) the repayment of the principal when the bonds reach maturity. In this case, the periodic interest payments represent an annuity problem, while the principal represents a single sum problem. The current value of the bond combines the present values of the annuity and single sum payment.

Other issues in financial accounting which need to be measured in present values include:

1. Long-term receivable payable: Valuing receivables and payables that carry no stated interest or the interest rate is different from the current fair rate of interest.
2. Leases: Measuring assets to be capitalized under long-term leases, and determining the amount of periodic lease payments at a given rate of return and annual leasehold amortization.
3. Amortization of premiums and discounts: Computing interest expense and amortization of premiums or discount by the effective interest method.

4. Pensions: Measuring pension costs (past and current) and determining funding programs for pension plans.
5. Plant assets: Evaluating plant assets acquired by issuance of debt securities when interest is not specified or the interest rate is different from the current fair rate of interest. Also used in determining the value of assets acquired under deferred payment contracts.
6. Sinking funds: Determining the periodic payments necessary to accumulate a fund for the retirements long-term debt or preferred stock.
7. Depreciation: Measuring depreciation expenses under the sinking fund and the annuity methods.

FERHAD SIMYAR

prior period adjustments
Prior period adjustments are used to correct errors in previously issued financial statements. They are (1) not included in the determination of current year income but rather, charged, net of applicable taxes, directly to retained earnings, and (2) reported as adjustments to the beginning balance of retained earnings in the current year. Prior period adjustments are infrequent because most errors in financial statements are detected and corrected prior to issuance. Examples include errors due to mathematical mistakes, oversights, or improper analyses of facts existing at the time the financial statements are prepared that are not detected until after the statements are issued.

United States Standards

In June, 1977, the Financial Accounting Standards Board (FASB) issued Statement of Financial Accounting Standards (SFAS) No. 16, "Prior Period Adjustments," after concluding that, "with limited exceptions, items of profit and loss recognized during a period shall be included in the determination of net income in that period" (para. 8). The standard, as amended, allows for two exceptions that may be excluded from the determination of net income for the current period and thus accounted for as prior period adjustments: (a) an item of profit and loss related to the correction of an error in the financial statements of a prior period, and

(b) adjustments that arise from the realization of income tax benefits of preacquisition loss carryforwards of purchased subsidiaries.

SFAS No. 16 also defines adjustments for interim periods. Adjustments related to prior interim periods of the current fiscal year include adjustments or settlement of litigation or similar claims, income taxes (except for the effects of retroactive tax legislation), renegotiation proceedings, or utility revenue under rate-making processes. Any adjustment must be directly related to activities of a previous interim period of the current year (1994 current text of standard, para. 109).

In a related standard, the Accounting Principles Board (APB) Opinion No. 20 "Accounting Changes" of 1971 distinguishes between an error and an accounting change and covers the reporting requirements for the correction of an error in previously issued financial statements. "Errors in financial statements result from mathematical mistakes, mistakes in the application of accounting principles, or oversight or misuse of facts that existed at the time the financial statements were prepared. In contrast, a change in accounting estimate results from new information or subsequent developments and accordingly from better insight or improved judgment. Thus, an error is distinguishable from a change in estimate" (para. 13).

The reporting treatment of prior period adjustments is specified in SFAS No. 16 and in APB Opinion No. 9 of 1966, "Reporting the Results of Operations." As amended in SFAS No. 16 (para. 16a), in single period statements, prior period adjustments should be reflected as adjustments of the opening balance of retained earnings. According to APB No. 9, if prior period adjustments are recorded, the annual report for the year the adjustment is recorded should disclose the resulting income effects on prior periods both gross and net of applicable tax. If financial statements are reported for more than one period, then the disclosure should include the effects with applicable income tax, for each reported period.

International Standards

The international rules governing prior period adjustments are established by the International Accounting Standards Committee in International Accounting Standard (IAS) No. 8, "Net

Profit or Loss for the Period, Fundamental Errors and Changes in Accounting Policies," of 1994. IASs are not mandatory unless they are adopted by a particular country. However, they are used by some countries that do not have their own standard setting body and sometimes by multinational corporations to help users in different countries understand the financial statements (Coopers & Lybrand (International), 1991, (p. IAS-1). IAS No. 8 states that the correction of a fundamental error may be excluded from net profit or loss for the current period. Fundamental errors are defined as errors discovered in the current period that are of such significance that the financial statements of one or more periods can no longer be considered to be reliable at the date of their issue. The IAS proposes that corrections of such errors should be either (a) reported by adjusting opening retained earnings for the current period and amending comparative information for prior periods, or (b) disclosed separately in the current period income statement as part of net income. Thus, IASC regulations are less restrictive than US generally accepted accounting principles.

History

Adjustments that qualified for treatment as prior period adjustments were originally defined by APB Opinion No. 9. The intent of APB No. 9 was to limit the types of charges that would qualify as prior period adjustments. However, the US Securities Exchange Commission staff observed that the criteria set forth in APB No. 9 were not being strictly applied. Of particular concern was that out-of-court settlements of litigation were commonly treated as prior period adjustments. The question raised by the SEC staff was whether they met the criteria for prior period adjustments. During 1975, requests by the SEC staff prompted the FASB to reconsider the criteria to limit prior period adjustments for such settlements. The staff had taken the view that such settlements did not meet the criteria of APB No. 9 and therefore should not be treated with direct charges to retained earnings. The reconsideration undertaken by the FASB resulted in SFAS No. 16.

The effect of SFAS No. 16 was to significantly reduce the number of items reported as prior period adjustments. The FASB research staff surveyed the National Automated Accounting Research System (NAARS) database and identified firms reporting or referring to prior period adjustments in their 1973 and/or 1974 annual reports. The staff's research identified 112 and 79 firms that reported adjustments. A recent NAARS survey identified 13 firms reporting adjustments qualifying as prior period adjustments in 1993 and 2 firms in 1994.

Related Research

Kinney & McDaniel (1989) analyze the effect of prior period adjustments on stock returns of firms that correct previously issued quarterly reports. The authors identified 73 firms between 1976 and 1985 that had year-end restatements of previously issued quarterly reports, and categorized these restatements as either increasing or decreasing reported earnings. The results of the authors' statistical analyses are consistent with the claim that the market views corrections as bad news (a drop in stock price coincident with the public release of the annual report) regardless of the impact on earnings. The authors speculate that these results may be due to negative implications for management integrity or internal control/reporting systems of any type of corrections.

Bibliography

Coopers & Lybrand (International) (1991). *1991 international accounting summaries: A guide for interpretation and comparison.* New York: John Wiley and Sons, Inc.

Kinney, Jr, W. R. & McDaniel, L. (1989). Characteristics of firms correcting previously reported quarterly earnings. *Journal of Accounting & Economics*, 11, Feb., 71–93.

MARY ELLEN CARTER and
GREG TROMPETER

privatization, valuation of state-owned enterprises When enterprises change from being state-owned to being privately owned, some values need to be assigned to the enterprise's assets and obligations in order to determine the enterprise's equity. Because of the absence of market prices in the past, it is difficult to assign values to the enterprise's composition of assets and liabilities. Book values at the time of privatization may not be indicative of the underlying economic values of the assets because of the use of administered prices and arbitrary booking in the past. The problem is compounded by the existence of inflationary and unstable economic conditions, which render a higher degree of volatility in the prices observed in a newly created market system.

The process of coping with these problems differs among countries and became crucial with the breakup of the Soviet Union and the movement of numerous countries into privatization. In Poland, for example, the legal system requires the use of two different methods of valuation to assist in gauging the value of an asset or a liability. For example, the discounted future cash flow and the replacement cost can be used to check the validity of the calculation of one another. Furthermore, in Poland, the object of valuation might be the entire enterprise, a segment of an enterprise, or individual assets of a state-owned enterprise. This range of alternatives complicates the choice of valuation methods, especially since the anticipated cash flows are judgmental and subject to unknown inflationary effects.

In Poland the concept of "property" is defined by the Civil Code as being related to a specific entity and is synonymous with "possession." For accounting purposes, "property" means assets and, for a business entity, consists of both the material (tangible) substance and the intangible elements which are related to the organization and use of the material substance (e.g., goodwill). As with Western systems, tangibles include land, buildings and constructions with fixtures and fittings, technical equipment, and current assets. Fixed assets consist of intangibles, defined as fixed property elements, other than tangibles, including acquired computer software, patents, licenses, and goodwill. The object of valuation in the process of privatization is generally the enterprise "property," which is defined as the totality of various tangible and intangible elements. Indeed, an enterprise is defined in the legal codes as a set of tangible and intangible elements intended to perform economic tasks, which embraces everything that forms the enterprise's constituent parts that are to be directed at such functioning that allows a maximum utilization of their use value, i.e., their profit-yielding ability.

Methods of Valuation in Privatization

In the case of Polish privatization, appraisal of an enterprise follows one of three methods: property-based methods, income-based methods, and mixed methods (based on both property and income).

Property-based methods. Property-based methods consist chiefly in determining the value of the property components of a privatized enterprise on the basis of either book values (entries) or market values, where the latter includes (1) liquidation value, or (2) replacement value. The book value of net assets is the easiest method to apply because it is assumed that the value of an enterprise equals its book value minus liabilities in accordance with the basic balance-sheet formula.

The liquidation method allows one to establish the value of assets of an enterprise at a level closest to their terminal market value. Liquidation value is regarded as total cash realizable upon the liquidation of an enterprise or sale of its individual assets (usually by means of tender or liquidation). This method is particularly useful for an enterprise that is not considered a going concern. In contrast, the income-based method is preferred for profitable businesses.

The replacement value equals the amount of capital outlay needed to reproduce the same productive capacities at a given point of time. The replacement value relates mainly to fixed assets, but is also used in valuing patents, licenses and concessions, organization of distribution channels, and recruitment and training of employees.

Income-based methods. These methods assume that an enterprise is worth the asset based yielding the profits it can earn. Two such methods are in use: (1) the market multiplier method, which is a simple capitalization of the profit realized by the enterprise being privatized, and (2) discounting of future cash flows generated by such an enterprise.

For income-based valuation purposes, it is assumed that a given enterprise will continue to function as a state-owned enterprise in order to determine its value to the State Treasury, so the following generally accepted principles are adopted: (1) the enterprise is a going concern; (2) prudence, which is an expectation of average results that takes into account various external and internal prospects and threats in order to determine the enterprise's earning power; (3) most efficient use of assets; and (4) accurate, fair, reliable, and efficient valuation.

In order to measure the economic value of Polish enterprises, the privatization practice includes the assessment of: (1) volume of future income (revenue); (2) volume of expected costs; (3) volume of future profits; (4) discount rate of future income realized without the element of risk; (5) uncertainty in the realization of anticipated income; (6) terminal value; and (7) duration of an enterprise's life, constituting the basis for calculating future revenue and expenditure.

A crucial element in appraising the value of an enterprise is the choice of the discount rate. Due to the prevalent inflationary conditions in Poland, the chosen rate is often fixed at a higher level than is usually accepted for comparable undertakings in developed market economies. In general, however, the application of the discounted profit or cash flow method is difficult because there is an insufficiently developed capital market or transactions market to provide a relevant pricing frame of reference.

Mixed methods. Mixed methods of valuation (based on both property and income) assume that the worth of a business is a combined result of the value of assets and the discounting of income. Some of the mixed methods used include: (1) the average value method, also known in the literature as the German or Berlin method; and (2) the Anglo-Saxon methods in their original version, which have been employed by European Economic Community experts.

In general, each of the methods used in the valuation of privatized enterprises has its own limitations and reliance on appraisals by experts who use a combination of these methods is mandated by the long absence of established market prices and the reliance on administered prices. As these conditions change, market prices will form a more useful frame of reference and valuation will tend to be more structured.

ALICJA A. JARUGA and
ALDONA KAMELA-SOWINSKA

product cost determination   Accuracy in product costing is an important issue in managerial accounting and control. For purposes of product profitability analysis and continuous cost improvement, it is no longer considered sufficient to obtain aggregate cost figures only that are used for external financial reporting. With increasing global competition in the market place, the trend is towards setting a *target selling price* with a *target product quality* as a first step in new product planning. This is very different from the traditional approach where the selling price is set by estimating the product cost and adding to it a desired profit margin and where an acceptable level of quality is the aim. The new trend is to attain the highest product quality or at least to meet the target quality level at the target price. Thus, if the estimated product cost is below the target cost obtained by deducting a profit margin from the target price, the task is to increase quality further rather than to accept a higher profit margin. If the estimated product cost is higher than the target cost, then alternative product designs are sought or the profit margin reduced, rather than increasing the target selling price or reducing target quality. This is the currently proven way to obtain a desirable market share for the product. As a consequence, it is more important than ever to accurately determine product costs.

One of the major components of product cost, which affects the accuracy of its estimation, involves the application of overheads. This issue has lead to the development of activity-based costing approaches. However, a theoretically sound application of overhead should be based on the opportunity cost of producing the product including its consumption of common resources.

Opportunity Cost as Transfer Price

A transfer price is set for the service rendered by one organizational unit to another within the firm. The purposes of charging a transfer price are to accurately measure the full cost of the product and to induce the various organizational units to act in the best interest of the firm. There are two reasons for a transfer price to have an incentive role in a firm: these are (1) goal incongruence among the organizational unit managers and the firm manager, and (2) information asymmetries among the units. The measurement of product cost and the incentive issues are generally not tackled together in the literature on agency modeling. Multi-period considerations can mitigate the incentive issue but not the measurement problem. The approach proposed here addresses both the measurement and incentive issues: i.e., the extent of utilization of the common service center by decentralized units.

A theoretically sound definition for the transfer price when one unit provides a service to another unit within a firm is to set it equal to the incremental costs plus opportunity costs. The incremental costs are usually taken to be the incremental variable costs of providing the service but may include incremental fixed costs as well. In theory, opportunity costs are zero if there is excess capacity in the service center unit. If the servicing unit is operating at full capacity, the opportunity cost is calculated so that the total transfer price is equal to the market price of the product being transferred. In the case of a service, such as machinery repair, the market price is the price the outsiders will charge for this service. Thus, the opportunity cost apparently takes on only two extreme values. With the introduction of demand and scheduling uncertainty, however, this analysis is no longer appropriate.

Job Opportunity Cost in a Common Service Center

Consider a common service center that provides service to several jobs. The jobs may originate from many organizational units. Service rendered may be the repair of machinery, computer consultancy, or even a production process whose facility is shared by several jobs. The capacity of the service center is limited. If a specific job requires service when the center is occupied serving other jobs, it will have to wait in a queue for its turn. Viewing it in reverse fashion, if a job seeks to utilize a common service center, it creates a delay for jobs that may arrive later. The uncertainty involved in the actual arrival times precludes one from stating the exact delay caused by any specific job on the other jobs. Nevertheless, one can work with expected delays instead, provided one can determine the rate of demand by jobs for the service and the capacity of the service center. Formulas from queuing theory may be used to determine the expected delay experienced by

jobs at the service center. The cost due to delay experienced by the jobs is the opportunity cost of serving any other job. If this job is not processed, the delay and hence potential cost will not be experienced by the other jobs. Equivalently, this is the cost of consuming part of the common service center resource by the job.

The cost incurred to set up a service center is a sunk cost and should not directly enter into the determination of product cost needed for managerial decision-making. What should be part of the product cost is the opportunity cost of using the service. This idea is problematic if one assumes no uncertainty with respect to demand and service times. The problem arises because (1) either there is excess capacity in the service center, in which case the opportunity cost is zero, or (2) the service center is operating at full capacity, in which case the opportunity cost is at its maximum equal to the market price less incremental variable costs.

Taking into account the uncertainties with respect to demand and service times implies that capacity cannot be fully utilized (i.e., there must be times during which the center is idle) otherwise the queue length will become infinitely long. (For a proof of this statement, see a standard book on queuing theory.) It does not follow, however, that the opportunity cost is zero. Even though there is excess capacity, many jobs may be delayed prior to obtaining service due to the uncertain nature of demands and service times. Any job that seeks to use the center will, on average, cause a delay for other jobs that may arrive.

In order to provide concrete expressions for this idea, let us suppose that the cost of delaying a job by one unit of time is H and the expected delay experienced at the center by any job demanding service is D, so that the expected cost due to delay for one job is HD. If the demand rate is A per period, then the expected total cost due to delay per period for all the jobs using the service center is AHD.

If we consider a single job, the delay experienced by all the jobs in the service center by the entrance of this specific job is the marginal value of the total expected delay cost per period, which is equal to $[HD+\{AH\}.dD/dA]$ (where the symbol dD/dA denotes the derivative of D with respect to A). The first component is the delay cost for the entering job itself and the second component is the opportunity cost of serving the job, namely, the delay imposed on the other jobs.

For given probability characterizations of the demand and service processes, formulas for D are available from queuing theory. For example, if the demand process has a Poisson distribution and the service process has an exponential distribution with expected service time, S, the expected delay is given by the formula, $D = S/(1-SA)$. The opportunity cost is equal to $SAH/(1-SA)$. This is the amount to be applied to the job for utilizing the service in addition to all the variable costs of providing the service. This applied cost ranges from zero to a maximum equal to the market price for the service less variable service costs.

Service Center Capacity Determination

Suppose one treats the service center as a cost center. The capacity of the service center is chosen so that the benefit obtained from using the service center is equal to the fixed and variable costs of operating the service center. If the benefit is greater than the costs, jobs will find it advantageous to use the service center and consequently congest the center. This will reduce the benefit for all. This reduction is applied as the opportunity cost of delay. At equilibrium, equality will prevail.

The benefit obtained is the avoidance of paying the market price for the service, less the cost of delay in the service center. Symbolically, the expected benefit from the service center = the expected market price - the expected delay cost for the job. At equilibrium capacity, the market price = the transfer price for service+variable cost of service. The transfer price then is equal to the applied opportunity cost of delay caused to the other users.

Putting it all together, the expected benefit from the service center = applied opportunity cost+variable cost of service - expected delay cost to the job. At equilibrium capacity, equate this to the fixed and variable costs of providing service at the service center. Then, the fixed cost of operating the center = applied opportunity cost - expected delay cost to the job. If the equality does not hold and the fixed operating cost is greater than the right side, the firm should use an outside facility. If it is less, then there is underutilization of the center.

Service Center Volume Variance

Any positive difference between the fixed cost per period and the applied opportunity cost less the delay cost per period for all the jobs using a service center denotes the extent of underutilization. This is theoretically defined to be the service center volume variance.

By introducing an opportunity cost concept for application of service center costs an equilibrium usage of the center by its users will be induced such that the benefits obtained are equal to the costs of operating the center. This is a desirable property of a cost center.

Bibliography

Balachandran, K. R. & Srinidhi, B. N. (1987). A rationale for fixed charge application. *Journal of Accounting, Auditing and Finance*, **2**, Spring, 151–83.

Balachandran, K. R. & Srinidhi, B. N. (1988). A stable cost application scheme for service center usage. *Journal of Business Finance & Accounting*, **15**, Spring, 87–100.

Balachandran, K. R. & Srinidhi, B. N. (1990). A note on cost allocation, opportunity costs and optimal utilization. *Journal of Business Finance & Accounting*, **17**, Autumn, 579–584.

Balachandran, K. R. & Radhakrishnan, S. (1995). Delay costs and incentive schemes for multiple users. *Management Science: forthcoming*.

Cooper, R. D, & Kaplan, R. S. (1992). Activity-based systems: Measuring the cost of resource usage. *Accounting Horizons*, **6**, Sept., 1–13.

Cooper, R. B. (1981). *Introduction to queuing theory*, Elsevier North Holland, Inc.

Radhakrishnan, S. & Balachandran, K. R. (1995). Stochastic choice hazard and incentives in a common service facility. *European Journal of Operational Research: forthcoming*.

KASHI R. BALACHANDRAN and
JEFFREY L. CALLEN

profit center performance   Companies create business units to delegate decision-making authority to operating managers. When the financial performance of a business unit is measured in terms of profit (revenues less expenses), the business unit is a profit center, which allows senior management to use a comprehensive measure to evaluate the performance of the profit center. However, focusing on profits without consideration of the assets employed to generate those profits is inadequate. Nearly all performance evaluations of profit center types of business units include a measure of the assets employed as part of that evaluation.

In considering the performance of profit centers, two types of performance can be evaluated: first, the performance of the center as an economic entity and, second, a measure of management performance. The evaluation of these two performances can be different. For example, management performance can be very good while economic performance of the profit center is unacceptable. However, survey evidence (Skinner, 1990) suggests that most companies do not usually find it practical to disentangle managerial and economic performance. Survey respondents indicate that business unit net profitability is used for both managerial control and strategic decision-making. In this short discussion, no distinction will be made between economic and managerial performance.

Companies employ several alternative measures of business unit performance. Both financial and nonfinancial measures are used and surveys indicate companies use between 2 and 20 performance indicators in their internal reporting systems (Walsh, 1987; Drury et al., 1992). Various analyses of financial statement elements, cash flows, return on investment indicators, and a variety of volume of business and quality of outputs measures are employed by companies (Walsh, 1987).

Financial Performance Measurement

Three categories of financial measures are used: income-based measurements, rate of return indicators, and asset management indicators. Rate of return and income measurements are most widely used and are considered most important (Walsh, 1987). Several types of income measures are used. The two most commonly observed in practice are net income or operating income. Net income is computed as revenue less all expenses used in generating this revenue including allocated costs associated with corporate-wide charges. Income from operations typically varies as defined by senior management. Thus, operating profit can exclude interest charges, taxes, and/or other income. Occasionally, other noncontrollable expenses such as corporate allocations and depreciation on assets are also excluded. The use of simple income after taxes is useful when the business unit operates in several locations with a variety of effective tax rates. Operating income is used when senior management wants to evaluate the business unit based on controllable costs. The performance of the profit unit is assessed by comparing actual income results with budgeted amounts.

In addition to income, a rate of return indicator is useful for profit center performance evaluation because, as a ratio, it can be used for inter-business unit and inter-firm comparisons. These indicators take many forms including, rate of return on investments, assets, capital employed, and/or equity. Rate of return on assets, while widely used, varies considerably in how it is computed. This ratio of income to assets includes the variation in income measures discussed above and variation in measurement of the asset base. Asset measurement can be total assets minus liabilities, working capital plus net property, plant and equipment, or replacement cost. Rate of return on capital employed usually measures capital as the sum of whatever debt can be identified with the unit plus its net worth. Measuring equity for rate of return on equity can be troublesome. For most business units, it is difficult to allocate corporate assets and liabilities with fairness and accuracy so that a credible measure of equity can be generated. Companies are generally careful to use consistent definitions of assets, liabilities, equity and income measurement across their business units and must be equally careful when comparing computed rate of return indicators with external competitors.

Depending on the type of business unit, asset management is sometimes considered the most important financial measurement. Inventories and receivables may be the most important assets under the control of the business unit management. Thus, such indicators as inventory turnover (number of times the average investment in inventories is "sold" in each accounting period) and days' sales invested in such assets provide information on how profit center decision-makers are managing the inventory. Turnover measurements are also used for working capital, asset and capital management in general. Finally, other less commonly used financial indicators include cash flow, volume of sales, cost and expense control, and coverage measures.

Companies use a number of financial indicators because various types of measurements emphasize certain phases of business unit performance at the expense of other important considerations. Rate of return indicators have more significance over the longer term than income measurements but are criticized for being wedded to historical costs and having little relationship to current values. Income measurements are easiest to calculate and have direct pertinence to overall corporate profits, but are criticized for a short-term focus. Income measures also lack comparability across business units. Other financial indicators are useful in more restricted settings such as when a cash flow problem exists. However, the same set of financial indicators is typically used for all business units in a company.

Nonfinancial Performance Measurement

A large majority of companies use nonfinancial measures in addition to financial measures to evaluate profit centers. These measures capture marketing, production, human resource, and other types of performance. Market share and sales volume growth are used as indicators of the long-term health of a business unit. Levels of plant capacity utilization, production levels and operating productivity are tracked to evaluate production performance. Measures of employee headcounts, employee development, employee turnover, and absenteeism are tracked to evaluate human resource management. Quality and reliability of products and services and introduction of new products are also benchmarked in several companies. Finally, a variety of other categories, such as social responsibility, cooperation with other units, environmental factors, or management integrity are also assessed subjectively. The majority of senior management prefer financial measures to nonfinancial measures (Walsh, 1987). However, some executives believe nonfinancial indicators have more long-term significance. Financial indicators are believed to be more useful because of their objectivity and link to the enhancement of shareholder wealth.

Bases of Comparison. Surveyed firms indicate that the performance of other companies, especially competitors and the averages for industry groups, are the principal considerations in setting performance goals for profit centers. External sources such as trade association statistics, annual and quarterly reports and 10K's, Key Business Ratios from Dun & Bradstreet, Inc., Forbes statistics, and security and analysts' reports are used to gather and analyze information about competitors and peers. The firm's internal accounting system generates monthly, quarterly, and annual reports used to monitor actual results in comparison with established criteria.

Performance goals are generally constructed by participation between senior management and the profit center manager. The goals are used in bonus incentive schemes as additional compensation to the base salary of the profit center manager. Senior executives believe performance goals have a significant effect on business unit results. However, they express concern that the short-term, historical nature of financial measurements can encourage short-term thinking (Bhimani, 1993). To avoid short-term myopia, firms are tying incentives to attainment of long-term and nonfinancial goals in addition to the usual profit targets (Walsh, 1987; Bhimani, 1993).

Bibliography

Bhimani, A. (1993). Performance measures in UK manufacturing companies: The state of pay. *Management Accounting*, Dec., 20–22.

Drury, C., Braund, S. & Tayles, M. (1992). A survey of management accounting practices in UK companies. *ACCA Research Occasional Paper*, Chartered Association of Certified Accountants.

Merchant, K. (1989). *Rewarding Results: Designing and Managing Contracts to Motivate Profit Center Managers.* Boston, MA: Harvard Business School.

Skinner, R. (1990). The role of profitability in divisional decision making and performance. *Accounting and Business Research*, Spring, 135–41.

Walsh, F. (1987). *Measuring business-unit performance.* Research Bulletin No. 206. New York: The Conference Board.

SUSAN HAKA

R

red flags in accounting Red flags in accounting refer to a set of diagnostic checks to determine the riskiness of a client or a registrant filing financial statements. The importance of red flags in auditing has been highlighted by the US National Commission on Fraudulent Financial Reporting in a report of 1987 published by the American Institute of Certified Public Accountants (AICPA) that noted: "In 36 percent of the cases against independent public accountants by the Securities and Exchange Commission (SEC), the auditor failed to recognize or pursue with sufficient skepticism certain warning signs or 'red flags' that existed at the time the audit was conducted" (p. 113). Although individual auditing firms have developed their own set of proprietary red flags, there are at least two authoritative sources of red flags. The AICPA Statement of Auditing Standards (SAS) No. 53, (1988) is the most recent pronouncement on the issue. The US SEC through its Accounting and Auditing Enforcement Releases (AAERs) also has suggested red flags it considers in determining the targets of its enforcement actions.

Box 1 summarizes the red flags mentioned explicitly in SAS 53.

Box 1: SAS 53 Red flags
1. Management operating and financing decisions are dominated by a single person.
2. Management's attitude toward financial reporting is unduly aggressive.
3. Management (particularly senior accounting personnel) turnover is high.
4. Management places undue emphasis on meeting earnings projections.

---

5. Management's reputation in the business community is poor.
6. Profitability of the entity relative to its industry is inadequate or inconsistent.
7. Sensitivity of operating results to economic factors (inflation, interest rates, unemployment, etc.) is high.
8. Rate of change in entity's industry is rapid.
9. Direction of change in entity's industry is declining with many business failures.
10. Organization is decentralized without adequate monitoring.
11. Internal or external matters raise substantial doubt about the entity's ability to continue as a going concern.
12. Many contentious or difficult accounting issues are present.
13. Significant difficult-to-audit transactions or balances are present.
14. Significant and unusual related party transactions not in the ordinary course of business are present.
15. Nature, cause or the amount of known and likely misstatements detected in the audit of prior period's financial statements is significant.
16. New client with no prior audit history, or sufficient information is not available from the predecessor auditor.
17. Known circumstances that may indicate a management predisposition to distort financial statements, such as frequent dispute about aggressive application of accounting principles that increase earnings.
18. Evasive responses to audit enquiries.
19. Excessive emphasis on meeting quantified targets that must be achieved to

receive substantial portion of management compensation.

20. Indications that management has failed to establish policies and procedures that provide reasonable assurance of reliable accounting estimates, such as personnel who develop estimates appearing to lack necessary knowledge and experience, supervisors of these personnel appearing careless or inexperienced.

21. There is a history of unreliable or unreasonable estimates.

22. Lack of control activities. Constant crisis conditions in operating or accounting areas, disorganized work areas, frequent or excessive back orders, shortages, delays or lack of documentation for major transactions.

23. Indications of a lack of control over computer processing, such as a lack of control over access to applications that initiate or control the movement of assets, high levels of processing errors, or unusual delays in providing processing results and reports.

24. Indications that management has not developed or communicated adequate policies and procedures for security of data or assets, such as not investigating employees in key positions before hiring or allowing unauthorized personnel to have ready access to data or assets.

25. Effect of risk factors identified at the financial statement or engagement level on particular account balance or transaction class.

26. Complexity and contentiousness of accounting issues affecting balance or class.

27. Frequency or significance of difficult-to-audit transactions affecting balance or class.

28. Nature, cause, and amount of known and likely misstatements detected in the balance or class in the prior audit.

29. Susceptibility of related assets to misappropriation.

30. Competence and experience of personnel assigned to processing data that affect the balance or class.

31. Extent of judgment involved in determining the total balance or class.

32. Size and volume of individual items constituting the balance or class.

33. Complexity of calculations affecting the balance or class.

Box 1 provides only an illustrative list of red flags. Even the subset of 33 red flags listed here imposes severe constraints on information processing limits of a decision-maker. SAS 53 is also reticent as to the weight to be assigned to the individual risk factor in an audit judgment. The most relevant operational statement in SAS 53 follows: "The factors considered in assessing the risk should be considered in combination to make an overall judgment; the presence of some factors in isolation would not necessarily indicate increased risk" (para. 10).

Research addressing unresolved issues related to red flags falls into two categories: archival survey analysis and behavioral modeling. Archival survey analysis checks the correspondence between the red flags mentioned in authoritative sources against the case data available either from the auditors' archives or those of the SEC. Research results show correspondence between the SAS 53 red flags and those mentioned in AAERs and indicate that dominated decisions, weak internal control, dishonest management, and personality anomalies are primary predictors of management fraud and defalcations. However, research results also show that the use of red flags may not be efficacious as a decision aid.

In sum, red flags literature is an aggregation of potentially important but largely untested predictors of client (registrant) risks. Although, individual auditing firms and the SEC have been using subsets of these red flags for their own decision-making purposes, published scientific evidence regarding their efficacy is scarce. Much of the current evidence is based on case-based reasoning. While the internal validity of a case-based red flag is not an issue, the generalizability of case-based red flags remain an empirical question. Users of red flags are appropriately justified in being cautious until empirical evidence regarding their efficacy is widely documented. Finally, the increase in computerized fraud in financial reporting brings an added dimension of complexity to raise doubts about the efficacy of traditional red flags.

While the issue of deception in an evolutionary information processing context is still in its infancy, it is plausible that revolutionary changes in information processing technology will heighten the obsolescence of traditional accounting red flags.

Bibliography

AICPA (1987). Report of the National Commission on Fraudulent Financial Reporting, New York American Institute of Certified Public Accountants.

EHSAN H. FEROZ

reporting assumptions The domain of accounting consists of several areas that differ primarily in function and purpose. Financial accounting is concerned with the measurement and reporting of all the firm's transactions. An aggregate report of those transactions is made available to investors and other external users on a periodic basis. This report must follow accounting policies and standards considered generally acceptable. These are the policies adopted by the rule-making bodies of the profession, which are in constant flux to adapt to changes in the economic environment and business activities. Accountants who are not employees of the reporting firms, and thus are independent, must examine the financial report prepared by the firm's management and offer an opinion as to whether the report has followed the accounting policies in effect on the date the report is signed.

Managerial and cost accounting deals with measurement and reporting of information on the internal activities of the firm in such a way that would benefit management in decision-making, planning, and control. The nature of these tasks requires more disaggregated information and frequent measurement and reporting.

Another facet of accounting includes accounting for taxation, which in many countries is governed by the prevailing tax laws and regulations and is much less impacted by professional accounting rules. Over the years, the development of the accounting body of knowledge has resulted in adhering to certain broad assumptions, conventions, and concepts.

Going Concern and Valuation

As with any venture, the success or failure of a business enterprise could not be known with certainty until it is concluded. Consequently, entrepreneurs start business enterprises with life spans not known in advance. In fact, many firms outlast their founders. This uncertainty about the duration of a business enterprise has led accountants to assume indefinite survival unless compelling evidence to the contrary comes to light. Accountants refer to this assumption as the "going concern."

Adhering to the going concern assumption implies that (1) managers will continue making operating, investment, and financing decisions that add value to the firm, and (2) resources (assets) owned by the firm are then viewed as stores of benefits to be realized at future dates. To realize those benefits, the firm's assets are to be used in the normal course of business, not under distress conditions, which has implications for the measurement of values to be assigned to various assets. In particular, the value of an asset must emanate from the future benefits the asset is capable of generating. Those benefits are generally identified in terms of cash flows.

If the cash flow streams associated with those expected future benefits are known, they can be represented in a common denominator using present-time monetary units (say, the dollar). This is accomplished by discounting future cash flows to present values using appropriate discount rates and taking account of the timing of each flow. The present value of future flows to be generated by using an asset is the economic value of that asset.

It is a rare occasion, however, to know the amounts and timing of future cash flows. Thus, the economic values of various goods and services cannot be determined merely by a simple calculation. Yet, people exchange goods and services all the time even with this lack of knowledge. In a world of rational expectations, people use known information to predict future outcomes, including the cash flow stream expected to be generated from using an asset. Different people make different predictions, resulting in their making different bids or asking for different prices. An exchange takes place when bid and ask prices match. Thus, it is reasonable to assume that exchange prices represent the traders' best expectations of economic values at the time of the exchange. Accountants acknowledge this relationship and use the amount of cash given up to value the asset acquired in exchange.

As time passes and more information is generated about the performance of various assets, traders in the market place use the new information to revise their earlier predictions of the amounts, timing, and uncertainty of various cash flow streams. In the absence of perfect foresight, this revision is assumed to mirror changes in the economic value of the asset. Thus, assets similar to those held by the firm might be acquired at different times for amounts higher or lower than the firm is reporting them on the books; i.e., the current (replacement) cost differs from book values.

Similarly, assets held by the firm might be sold for prices higher or lower than their book values. In this case, exit values, or realizable values are different from book values.

Once an asset is acquired, accounting policy-makers have generally decided to use the value at the time of exchange for booking the asset, but typically ignore changes in values represented by deviations of either current replacement cost or exit values from book values. To make sure that users know that changes in asset values following acquisition are ignored, the market value at the time of acquiring the asset is denoted "historical cost." Because of the ability to verify the calculation of historical cost, it was considered more objective than other competing measures. Its relevance for decision-making, however, is questioned.

Another source of variation in asset values is the change in the purchasing power of the monetary unit used in valuation. Changes in the prices of assets, goods, and services do occur because of inflationary conditions and techno-logical advances. To reflect the effect of inflation on the financial conditions of the firm, financial statements that are based on historical costs are adjusted using a general price level index. The outcome of this process is known as financial statements in constant dollars.

The different reasons for changes in value has generated corresponding conceptual differences between historical cost, current (replacement) cost, exit values and historical cost adjusted for general price level changes. Although contem-porary accounting practice is essentially based on a historic cost model, the ad hoc nature of making accounting policies resulted in produ-cing financial statements that are in effect a depository of mixed measurements and judg-ments using different valuation rules. The end result of these measurement errors flows to the owners' equity section on the balance sheet.

Conservatism and Revaluation

While the heritage of accountants is to favor the use of historical cost due to its alleged objectivity, they deviate from this tradition when it becomes convenient to selectively update historical cost by adjusting for changes in market values. In some countries like the United Kingdom, Australia, and New Zealand, firms are allowed to substitute market values (or estimates thereof) for historical cost when the market values of assets held by the firm are judged to be materially different from historical cost (i.e., book values). Since many used assets have no ready second-hand markets, estimates and appraisals are often relied upon, which requires an extra effort in assuring users of information about the reliability of the newly reported information.

This practice of allowing upward revaluation of assets is not shared by the accounting profession in many countries. Universally, however, accounting policy-makers fully agree on the necessity of asset revaluation only when evidence shows material *decline* of market (or equivalent) values below book values. Only if there is a significant impairment of assets do accounting policies require substituting market values for historical cost.

This general asymmetric adherence to market value changes (i.e., ignore them if market value is higher than book values, but take them into account if the reverse is true) has been the hallmark of accounting policies for reporting information about the firm to its stockholders, creditors, and other external users of informa-tion. Adopting conservative policies is a deep-rooted tradition that has failed to adapt to changes in the socioeconomic environment. Up until the start of the 20th century, the typical business firm was small in comparison with modern corporations and was managed by their owners. Both features, the size and coupling of ownership and management, allowed owners to exercise control over the business firm's activities by means of direct observation and personal involvement. The need to inform others outside the firm was very limited. However, when owners sought financing from lending institutions, lenders, who were at an informational disadvantage as compared to the owner-manager, requested that: (1) the firm must follow conservative policies for investing and operating as well as in its accounting for financial reporting, and (2) the firm must disclose privately to bankers and lenders sufficiently disaggregated information about the performance of the firm so that they can undo the conservative reporting and understand the true economic picture of the firm. To date, these conditions have a lasting and, to a large extent, a progress-hindering effect on the development of accounting policies.

Conservative accounting policies essentially call for ignoring expected gains or anticipated increases in values, but must recognize the effects of expected losses or decline in values. Information users other than management must not be informed about good news until an exchange takes place, but bad news is to be told and taken into account as soon as it is anticipated with a reasonable degree of confidence. For example, if a firm holds goods in inventory, the decline in the market value of this inventory implies that a loss is likely to occur at a future date. To the extent that the market value falls below book value, a loss must be recognized when this expectation is formed. In contrast, an increase in the market value of inventories above book value must not be reported for external users until the earning cycle is complete. This conservative approach has led to concocting the lower-of-cost-or-market (LOCOM) measurement rule.

Since market values could refer to either current (replacement) cost or exit value, various combinations of LOCOM have evolved. In addition, the physical flow of inventory is irrelevant because accountants could assume an entirely different flow for costing purposes.

Because of its appeal to lenders and to those who fear the consequences of optimism, LOCOM was extended to other assets such as short-term investments. Even in recent times when policy-makers have shown more inclination to use market (or equivalent, fair) values for some accounting measurements, LOCOM was retained for some types of investments, while "management intent" has replaced LOCOM for other types. In fact, the book measurement of accounts and notes receivable also follow LOCOM, where market is defined as net realizable value; estimating uncollectible amounts effectively produces net realizable value.

Conservatism has also led to ignoring assets when measurements require judgment. While business firms undertake research and development activities with the anticipation of generating future benefits, most accounting policy-making around the world has followed the US lead by expensing R&D as incurred and thereby ignoring the valuation of those benefits.

Accounting Period and Temporal Allocation

Adhering to the going concern assumption was one way of recognizing that the business firm will live indefinitely, but it also raised the problem of evaluating the success of a business venture. The issue is complicated by the fact that the duration of expected future benefits that are associated with any asset varies by its interaction with other assets. Different assets are likely to have different expected productive lives, but often enough the practice of accounting allows using different productive lives for the same assets, especially under varying conditions. An accounting convention has evolved to partition the unknown life of the firm into known periods, which has the advantage of standardizing the period to which various activities can be attributed. The typical reporting period is one year, with corporations in the more developed countries reporting on a quarterly basis. External users, however, are demanding more timely and more frequent reporting. For assets having expected benefits longer than one year (i.e., long-lived assets) attribution of benefits to a given period can be conceptually undertaken by assessing the change in its economic value during that period. However, the accountants' preoccupation with objective and verifiable calculations, that has initially led to a preference for using a historic-cost basis, has also led to developing what are called "systematic and rational" methods of attributing costs to reporting periods. Typically, such methods involve estimating the useful life of an asset and choosing one of several alternative methods of allocating its historic cost to the different periods encompassed by that life. These intertemporal allocation methods are known as depreciation (for tangible assets) and as amortization (for intangible assets). Some allocation methods do not differentiate between the extent of asset use in different periods (e.g., straight line), while others attempt to allocate larger proportions to earlier periods (accelerated) based on various assumptions, including maintenance cost, technological obsolescence, and conservatism.

It is important, however, to note that none of these methods attempts to relate periodic allocation of cost to the actual degree of consuming the benefits stored in a long-lived asset. In effect, the so-called "systematic and rational" aspects of these methods lie in their calculation feature. It is, therefore, often argued that book values of long-lived assets are the products of two independent decisions: (1) the valuation, or more appropriately the cost measurement, decision that basically maintains the historic cost basis, and (2) the intertemporal allocation decision, which is rarely related to the degree of asset utilization or its economic depreciation.

A. RASHAD ABDEL-KHALIK

reporting extraordinary items Reporting for extraordinary items was born of the conflict between the all-inclusive concept of net income and the need to use income numbers to predict future profitability of a firm. Broadly defined, in the USA, net income is the dollar value of change in owners' equity from transactions other than those that affect ownership, such as the purchase of treasury stock. On the other hand, the income statement is one of investors' key sources of information for evaluating past performance and predicting future profitability. In particular, the results of normal operations can readily be expected to continue into the future. Items that do not occur regularly distort net income and create additional problems for predicting profits and measuring performance. Specifically, nonrecurring items are difficult to

assign to various reporting periods. These problems lead to segregating recurring events from nonrecurring events, including extraordinary items.

Measuring net income within set time periods is difficult. Defining revenue and matching expenses is sufficiently challenging at year-end. These difficulties are compounded by events that are nonrecurring. These items are not completely associated with the period in which they appear, and the recurrence may be difficult to predict (Bernstein, 1967). To meet these challenges, the exact nature of each item that makes up the income statement must be reported.

Two professional pronouncements were issued to give guidance by the US Accounting Principles Board (APB), of the American Institute of Certified Public Accountants. These were APB No. 9, "Reporting the Results of Operations," in 1966 and APB No. 30, "Reporting the Results of Operations-Reporting the Effects of Disposal of a Segment of a Business, and Extraordinary, Unusual and Infrequently Occurring Events and Transactions," in 1973.

Except for prior period adjustments, APB No. 9 firmly established the all-inclusive income concept as the standard for reporting income and the requirement of segregating nonrecurring items for decision-makers to assess their effects separately. Paragraph 17 stated: "*Extraordinary items* should . . . be segregated from the results of ordinary operations and shown separately in the income statement, with disclosure of the nature and amounts thereof." The segregation of extraordinary items and other nonrecurring items enabled net income to represent the all-inclusive concept, and at the same time allowed the user to assess the effects of nonrecurring items and to predict future profitability.

APB No. 30 further refined the delineation and reporting requirements of nonrecurring items. It provided two criteria that extraordinary transactions or underlying events must meet: "Extraordinary items are events and transactions that are distinguished by the unusual nature *and* by the infrequency of the occurrence." These criteria were defined as follows:

Unusual nature – the underlying event or transaction should possess a high degree of abnormality and be of a type clearly unrelated to, or only incidentally related to, the ordinary and typical activities of the entity, taking into account the environment in which the entity operates.

Infrequency of occurrence – the underlying event or transaction should be of a type that would not reasonably be expected to recur in the foreseeable future, taking into account the environment in which the entity operates. (para. 20)

The criteria were to be applied based on professional judgment. Extraordinary items must be evaluated in terms of the environment in which the entity operates, but cannot be affected by the size of the financial effects. Generally, the decision concerning the nature of an item has been left to the accountant's professional judgment. However, the early retirement of long-term debt has been specifically designated as an extraordinary item (FASB, 1975). In addition, the effect of the extraordinary item must be considered material "in relation to income before extraordinary items or to the trend in annual earnings before extraordinary items" (para. 24).

These criteria were significantly restrictive to drastically reduce the number of events or transactions which would qualify as extraordinary. Although APB No. 30 specifically excluded items that met only one criterion, these events and transactions would require adequate disclosure in the presentation of income from continuing operations (para. 26). Specifically, items that are not extraordinary include the write-down or write-off of assets, gains and losses from the exchange or translation of foreign currencies, gains and losses from the disposal of a business segment or the disposal of property, plant or equipment, and the effects of strikes or adjustments of accruals on long-term contracts (para. 23).

APB No. 30 reaffirmed the need to segregate only four items from income from operations. Gains and losses from the disposal of a segment of a business, extraordinary items, and the cumulative effects of a change in accounting principles should be segregated but included in the determination of net income, while adjust-ments to income from prior periods should be reported as adjustments to retained earnings. To maintain their extraordinary nature, these events or transactions must meet two rigid criteria, *unusual* and *infrequent*.

The disclosure of extraordinary items requires a separate line item which would appear after any gain or loss from the disposal of a segment of a business and before any cumulative effect from changes in accounting principles. The amount should be net of any applicable income taxes (para. 11). Finally, "Earnings per share data for income before extraordinary items and net income should be presented on the face of the income statement, as prescribed by *APB Opinion No. 15*" (para. 12).

In conclusion, the professional pronouncements concerning extraordinary items supported professional judgment and provided disclosure guidelines to meet the conflicting demands of the all-inclusive concept of income, the need to measure past performance, and the need to predict future profitability. In any given environment, the accountant must decide if the guidelines of both *unusual* and *infrequent* have been met. These criteria provide strong justification for the segregated information.

Bibliography

American Institute of Certified Public Accountants (1973). *Opinions of the Accounting Principles Board No. 30*, "Reporting the Results of Operations – Reporting the Effects of Disposal of a Segment of a Business, and Extraordinary, Unusual and Infrequent Occurring Events and Transactions," New York: AICPA.

American Institute of Certified Public Accountants (1966). *Opinions of the Accounting Principles Board No. 9*. "Reporting the Results of Operations," New York: AICPA.

Bernstein, L. A. (1967). *Accounting for extraordinary gains and losses*. New York: The Ronald Press Company.

Kieso, D. E. & Weygandt, J. J. (1995). *Intermediate Accounting*. 8th edn, New York: John Wiley & Sons.

FASB (1975). *Statement No. 4*. Reporting gains and losses from extinguishment of debt. Stamford: Financial Accounting Standards Board.

H. Francis Bush

research and development

Financial Accounting Standards for R&D

In 1974, the USA Financial Accounting Standards Board (FASB) issued Financial Accounting Standard No. 2, "Accounting for Research and Development Costs" (SFAS 2). Research and development (R&D) includes all direct costs – in particular, materials, equipment facilities, personnel, purchased intangibles, and contract services obtained from others – and also includes reasonable allocations of indirect costs. All costs that satisfy these criteria and that have no alternative future use are to be deducted when computing net income in the period when they are incurred. Moreover, the amount deducted is to be disclosed in the financial statements. The USA Securities and Exchange Commission (SEC) Accounting Series Release No. 178, effective 1981, endorses the application of SFAS 2 for publicly-traded firms.

Statement of Financial Accounting Standards No. 68 "Research and Development Arrangements" stipulates that accounting and financial disclosure practices be carried out for R&D conducted under contract. Costs to enterprises that purchase or fund such contracts are treated in accordance with SFAS 2. Costs to enterprises that conduct contract research for others are expensed if the contractor bears the financial risk of the endeavor, and deferred if the risk is transferred to other parties. In particular, the contractor, informed by the terms of the contract, recognizes both the revenue and the costs according to the appropriate revenue recognition principle. Accountants are encouraged to look beyond contractual details to consider the economic substance of R&D arrangements. For example, an obligation to repay can take the form of a special option to purchase research output, rather than an unconditional obligation in cash. Terms of contractual arrangements and the amounts involved are to be disclosed in the notes to financial statements. The SEC Staff Accounting Bulletin clarifies the application of SFAS 68 for publicly-traded firms, stressing the relevance of percentage ownership and degree of influence by entities that fund R&D contracting arrangements.

USA practice with respect to the accounting treatment of R&D is, to an extent, discordant with the practices of other developed countries. For example, International Accounting Standards Committee Statement No. 9 (IASCS 9) (effective January 1, 1980) permits the inclusion as development costs of certain market research costs incurred prior to commercial production, whereas SFAS 2 proscribes the designation of market research costs as either research or development. The primary difference between the standards, however, is in the accounting treatment of development costs. As with SFAS 2, research costs incurred under IASCS 9 are normally treated as an expense when they are incurred, but if technological and commercial feasibility can be demonstrated, and if management has both the wherewithal and the intention to market the product or process, then "it may be appropriate" to defer development costs. Such deferred costs are to be amortized on a "systematic basis." If a deferral policy is used, then it must be applied generally to all products or processes. The total R&D expense for the period, including the amortization of deferred development costs, must be disclosed. The balance of unamortized deferred development costs and the basis for amortization also must be disclosed.

Research on Accounting for R&D

Studies in the academic accounting literature that consider financial accounting practices for R&D expenditures typically address one of two general issues of practical significance. First, the debate about whether R&D costs should be treated as an expense when they are incurred or as a deferrable cost to be amortized over subsequent accounting periods raises the issue of whether such costs yield future economic benefit. In the context of standard financial accounting theory, the establishment of future benefits is necessary, albeit not sufficient, to justify cost deferral. Thus, the implications for practice of this class of studies are straightforward. An ancillary question, one that is germane to the establishment of amortization periods for R&D costs that are deferred, is the duration of economic benefits. Recent studies that are designed to consider these questions appeal primarily to the notion that future benefits, to the extent that such benefits exist, are impounded in security prices.

Hirschey & Weygandt (1985) employ Tobin's Q-ratios (the ratio of firm market values to replacement values) to investigate possible future benefits to both R&D and advertising expenditures. Their analysis suggests that benefits last for five to ten years.

Bublitz & Ettredge (1989) find that these correlations differ, and, moreover, the direction of the differences suggests future benefits accrue from R&D.

The methodology employed in a more recent study by Sougiannis (1994) is both more comprehensive and more sophisticated than these antecedent studies. One distinguishing feature of the study is its consideration of the income tax consequences of R&D spending, a factor largely ignored by the earlier studies. Results indicate that economic benefits from R&D expenditures continue for periods up to seven years.

A second issue is whether or how the mandated adoption of SFAS 2 influenced R&D spending decisions. Vigeland (1981) hypothesizes that if investors anticipate that the statement will cause managers to reject positive net present value investments in R&D activities, then security prices of firms that defer R&D costs are adversely affected by events that increase the probability of the SFAS 2 adoption. The evidence indicates that security returns to a sample of firms that deferred R&D are comparable to returns to a matched sample of firms that expensed R&D currently.

Four studies, Dukes et al. (1981), Horwitz & Kolodny (1981), Elliott, et al. (1984), and Shehata (1991), employ a more direct approach to investigate the consequences of SFAS 2. In particular, using relatively small samples composed of R&D-intensive industrial firms, these studies compare R&D expenditures prior to the adoption of SFAS 2 with expenditures after its adoption. These investigations typically indicate modest declines in R&D to sales ratios after SFAS 2, especially for small firms.

Finally, Baber et al. (1991) report that investment in R&D, but not investment in tangible assets where costs are deferred, tends to be less when R&D spending jeopardizes the ability to report either positive or increasing income in the current period. Further analysis reveals that the results cannot be attributed to arrangements where management compensation is explicitly tied to accounting income.

Thus, considered as a whole, expensing R&D seems to influence decisions to invest in R&D activities.

Bibliography

Baber, W., Fairfield, P. & Haggard, J. (1991). The effect of concern about reported income on discretionary spending decisions: The case of research and development. *The Accounting Review*, **66**, 4, 818–26.

Bublitz, B. & Ettredge, M. (1989). The information in discretionary outlays: Advertising, research and development. *The Accounting Review*, **64**, 1, 108–24.

Dukes, R., Dyckman T. & Elliott, J. (1980). Accounting for research and development costs: The impact on research and development expenditures. *Journal of Accounting Research*, **18**, supplement, 1–37.

Elliott, J., Richardson, G., Dyckman, T. & Dukes, R. (1984). The impact of SFAS No. 2 on firm expenditures on research and development: Replications and extensions. *Journal of Accounting Research*, **22**, 1, 85–102.

Hirschey, M. & Weygandt, J. (1985). Amortization policy for advertising and research and development expenditures. *Journal of Accounting Research*, **23**, 2, 326–35.

Horwitz, B. & Kolodny, R. (1980). The economic effects of involuntary uniformity in the financial reporting and R&D expenditures. *Journal of Accounting Research*, **18** (supplement), 38–74.

Shehata, M. (1991). Self-selection bias and the economic consequences of accounting regulation: An application of two-stage switching regression to SFAS No. 2. *The Accounting Review*, **66**, 4, 768–87.

Sougiannis, T. (1994). The accounting based valuation of corporate R&D. *The Accounting Review*, **69**, 1, 44–68.

Vigeland, R. (1981). The market reaction to Statement of Financial Accounting Standards No. 2. *The Accounting Review*, **56**, 2, 309–25.

WILLIAM R. BABER and SOK-HYON KANG

revaluation   The revaluation of non-current assets is an accepted accounting practice in a number of countries, including the UK, Australia, and New Zealand. Revaluations, by their nature, lack a degree of objectivity because they are based on estimates of current value. Furthermore, empirical evidence supports the view that, under certain conditions, there are managerial incentives to revalue. It is therefore possible that the revalued amounts may be distorted by management's desire to produce a certain outcome, although the scope of choice is constrained by the requirement for an audit.

In deciding whether to accept a valuation as reasonable, the auditor should first assess the risk of material misstatement. This will involve an evaluation of the client's business, its financial structure and the integrity of its management. In particular, the auditor should identify any underlying motives for revaluing non current assets that may lead to a desire to overstate asset values.

Next, the auditor should determine the extent and nature of evidence needed to form and support an opinion. This evidence will involve two broad categories of audit procedures: first, those related to an assessment of the person or firm undertaking the valuation, and second, those pertaining to the valuation itself.

Issues Relating to the Valuer

In New Zealand, accounting standards require that revaluations of fixed assets be carried out by a person holding a recognized professional qualification. That person should also have experience in both the location and the category of the fixed asset being valued. Valuations are either conducted or reviewed by an independent valuer. In contrast, Australian standards permit "directors' valuations" as well as independent valuations. While the latter should be carried out by a person "who is an expert in relation to valuations of that class of non-current assets," there is no requirement concerning the expertise of those undertaking directors' valuations. From the auditor's perspective, a valuation carried out internally by the client has a greater risk of misstatement than one carried out by an independent qualified valuer. In those circumstances, auditors can request the client to obtain an independent valuation or else they may need to qualify the audit report.

The audit issues relating to valuations undertaken by independent valuers are covered by auditing standards and guidelines concerning using the work of an expert. (Auditing Standard AS-5, "Work Performed by Other Auditors and Experts" in New Zealand; Statement of Auditing Practice AUP-22, "Using the Work of an

Expert" in Australia, and International Standard on Auditing ISA-620, "Using the Work of an Expert," (formerly IAG-18), issued by the International Federation of Accountants). The valuer here is an independent expert appointed by the client. The auditor should be satisfied with the valuer's technical qualifications such as (1) evidence of competence indicated by a professional qualification and (2) the valuer's reputation and experience in the field. The auditor should also evaluate the valuer's independence by considering his/her relationship to the client. Lynn (1993) suggests that, in evaluating independence, the auditor should consider whether clear instructions were given by the client to the valuer; whether the valuer was permitted to exercise his/her own professional judgment on key issues; and whether the client exerted any pressure on the valuer concerning the selection of methodology or assumptions.

Auditing Methods and Reporting

Normally, the valuer prepares a formal report giving details of the assets being valued, together with background information about the methods used, data sources, and any assumptions on which the valuations have been based. The auditor must then assess the appropriateness of the valuations contained in this report. The assessment may need to be supported by information obtained from the client, from other experts within the audit firm, or from sources outside the firm.

The auditor should assess the need to communicate with the valuer to ensure that the scope of the valuer's work is adequate for the purpose of the audit. (ISA) International Standard on Auditing 620 "Using the Work of an Expert," suggests that a review of the written instructions given by the client to the valuer may provide the necessary audit evidence. Statement of Auditing Practice AUP-22 "Using the Work of an Expert," in Australia and Auditing Standard AS-5 "Work Performed by Other Auditors and Experts," in New Zealand suggest that, where the auditor knows in advance that the valuer's work will be relied on, then the auditor should communicate with the valuer to confirm the terms of the appointment and other matters relating to the valuations.

Two related issues that can pose problems for auditors are the appropriate methodology for valuing specialized assets and the need to ensure that a revalued asset is not recorded at an amount which exceeds its recoverable amount.

In Australia, accounting standards do not specify the basis of valuation when assets are revalued. In New Zealand, standards require revaluations to be undertaken on the basis of net current value, which is essentially market value based on the existing use of the asset. However, problems can arise when assets are specialized and there is no market price for reference. In this case, it is generally accepted that replacement cost (less depreciation) is an appropriate surrogate for market value. The auditor should check the source data used to establish replacement cost and assess whether depreciation adjustments are adequate.

Regarding recoverable amount, directors must ensure that assets held for use are not recorded at amounts that exceed the amount of net cash flows expected to arise from use and ultimate disposal. This depends on the on going profitability of the client and should be embraced in the auditor's going concern assessment.

To conclude, while non current assets have traditionally been regarded as a low-risk audit area requiring the application of routine verification procedures, when those assets are revalued, the auditor's task becomes more complex. While various procedures can be undertaken to obtain evidence to support an opinion, the decision to accept a valuation as reasonable inevitably involves the exercise of professional judgment.

Bibliography

Australian Accounting Research Foundation, Auditing Standards Board (1985). *Statement of Auditing Practice AUP 22 Using the Work of an Expert.* Melbourne.

International Federation of Accountants (1994). *International Standard on Auditing ISA 620 Using the Work of an Expert.* New York.

Lynn, R. S. (1993). Asset valuation: The auditor's perspective. *The Valuer and Land Economist*, Feb., 342–5.

New Zealand Society of Accountants (1986). *Auditing Standards and Explanatory Notes (Auditing Standard 5–Work Performed by Other Auditors and Experts).* Wellington.

JENNY GOODWIN

revenue recognition, expenses, gains and losses

Revenue Recognition

Early accounting practices focused on the listing of assets and liabilities at periodic intervals. Changes in the values of assets and liabilities were noted directly in these accounts. As the transactions of entities became more numerous and more complex, another method of measuring and explaining the changes in assets and liabilities emerged, resulting in the income statement or statement of operations. Income statements became common only during the current century.

Assets and liabilities are considered real or permanent accounts because they reflect the actual resources of an entity and the claims against those resources. Income statements include the nominal or temporary accounts of revenues, expenses, gains, and losses. These are termed nominal or temporary accounts because they represent explanations of the changes in the real or permanent accounts. Nominal or temporary accounts are closed out at the end of each period after their explanatory purposes have been captured in the income statement. With the development of the income statement, direct measurement of changes in assets and liabilities gave way to indirect measurements guided primarily by concepts of revenue recognition and expense matching. Although not always articulated clearly, the concepts of revenue recognition and expense matching have dominated the measurement of income in practice for several decades.

Revenues are often described as the accomplishments and expenses as the efforts for an operating period. Revenues are defined in US Financial Accounting Standards Board (FASB) Statement of Financial Accounting Concepts No. 6, "Elements of Financial Statements" (1985) (SFAC 6) as, "inflows or other enhancements of assets of an entity or settlements of its liabilities (or a combination of both) from delivering or producing goods, rendering services, or other activities that constitute the entity's ongoing major or central operations" (para. 78). Revenue would result from the sale of merchandise in the typical merchandising or manufacturing entity and the performance of services for organizations such as accounting, engineering, or legal firms.

Judgment is often required to determine the appropriate time period to record revenue. "Revenue recognition" occurs when the revenue is formally recorded in the accounting records. A current explanation of the revenue recognition concept is found in FASB Statement of Financial Accounting Concepts No. 5, "Recognition and Measurement in Financial Statements of Business Enterprises" (1984) (SFAS 5). Paragraph 83 of this document states " . . . recognition involves consideration of two factors: (a) *being realized or realizable* and (b) *being earned*, with sometimes one and sometimes the other being the most important consideration." Realization is the process of an asset being converted to cash or claims to cash. The FASB made an important distinction between revenue realization and revenue recognition. Prior accounting literature often referred to the realization concept using explanations similar to what is now more clearly defined and labelled as the revenue recognition concept.

Revenue Realization

Revenue recognition requires sufficient evidence of revenue realization. This often involves the exercise of judgment although standards have been issued in several areas to guide the judgment process. The point of sale or delivery of product is the most common time where evidence of realization is judged to be sufficient. This has been described by at least one author as the critical event (Myers, 1959). There are numerous exceptions made to the point of sale for revenue recognition especially in specialized industries outside the traditional manufacturing and merchandising entities. Exceptions having a relatively long accounting history include production under construction contracts and the production and acquisition of inventories of precious metals or agricultural products. There are several other exceptions made to the common point of sale with a shorter accounting history in newer industries such as franchising and computer software development. Installment sales, where collection of all of the cash installments is highly uncertain, is another exception where revenue may not be recognized at the point of sale.

The nature of an asset received in a potential revenue transaction can make a difference in determining the state of realization. The receipt of cash or cash equivalents generally is regarded as proof of realization. The receipt of noncash assets inherently represents an earlier state in the realization process, may or may not offer sufficient evidence of realization, and may also create measurement problems concerning the value of the assets received. Notes and accounts receivables are generally viewed as acceptable evidence of the amount of cash to be realized after estimates of uncollectible amounts have been made and, therefore, constitute sufficient realization. In case of extreme uncertainty of collection and insufficient information to estimate the uncollectible amount, realization is not sufficiently assured and the installment method exception of revenue recognition that defers profit to the time of collection may be followed. The receipt of an asset similar to the one given up is generally regarded as proof that realization has not occurred and revenue is typically not recognized. An example would be the exchange of one tract of land for another. US Accounting Principles Board Opinion No. 29, "Accounting for Nonmonetary Transactions" (1973), describes the accounting treatment for this type of exchange transaction.

The second major factor in the recognition of revenue is the earning process. It is commonly understood that all major functions of an entity support the earning process and that the "earning" of income or profit is a continuous process from the acquisition of revenue-producing inputs to the completion of collection and product warranty service activities. Allocation of a portion of the earnings or income to each of these activities would be difficult and arbitrary. For example, there is no natural basis for determining how much of the profit from the sale of an item was "earned" by the efforts of the salesperson versus the efforts of the production foreman. Therefore, the major earnings test for revenue recognition is whether the earning process has been sufficiently completed. As with realization, this requires judgment, although accounting guidelines exist in several areas to guide the judgment process. The point of sale again serves as the most common point where the earning process is judged as sufficiently complete, with follow-up activities such as collection and product warranty service viewed as incidental.

Further consideration of the two major revenue recognition factors of realization and the earning process assist in an understanding of the normal emphasis placed on point of sale as well as the common exceptions noted above. For most manufacturing and merchandising entities the point of sale is the first time that a known exit market value (sales price) exists. The market price is established at that point in a bargained transaction between two parties with an assumed conflict of interest. Typically either cash is transferred or a receivable is established in a fixed amount at that time. As for the earning process, most of the significant activities have been completed by that point. Exceptions are made for production under construction contracts, precious metals, and agricultural products largely because the sales price is either established or highly determinable in advance of sale or delivery and the acquisition and production activities significantly outweigh sale and any other potential subsequent activities.

Revenue and Expense Matching

The recognition of revenue is only the first step in the measurement of net income. The matching of expenses with revenues is the second step. There are three levels of matching. The best matching is achieved where expenses can be directly associated with the resulting revenue. Sales commissions paid to salespersons is an example of such an expense. A second category of expenses is where an association between revenues and expenses is assumed but cannot be determined directly. Depreciation of assets used in the production of revenues and the determination of cost of goods sold using an assumed flow of goods (e.g. FIFO) are examples of this category. This matching is generally referred to as systematic and rational allocation. While depreciation and inventory cost flow methods are systematic, the degree of rationality is often difficult to access in the absence of stated criteria for the selection of a particular method. The third level of matching is typically referred to as period expensing. These expenses are costs that have been determined to have

expired during the period of measurement but cannot be associated with the revenue for that period or any other specific period. Administrative salaries and depreciation on office equipment are two examples of expenses in this category.

Many expenses allocated to specific time periods are estimated. Expenses resulting from future costs such as bad debts, product warranty service, and employee retirement are estimated. Expenses determined through systematic and rational allocation of prior costs such as depreciation are also estimated. Determining product costs in a manufacturing process requires many estimates and assumptions.

Gains and losses are also components of net income but are differentiated from revenues and expenses. The primary basis for differentiation lies in the nature of the transaction, event, or circumstance that caused or created the item. Gains and losses are associated with nonoperating peripheral and/or incidental transactions and events. A loss created by damage from a fire or flood, inventory that became unsalable, and assets seized in a foreign country after a revolution are potential examples. A gain or loss from the sale of an operating asset is another example. The use of an operating asset is a central or major continuing activity that creates an expense such as depreciation or maintenance. The sale of an asset normally used in operations is considered to be a peripheral or incidental transaction since an entity does not operate for the purpose of selling its productive assets. Another characteristic of a loss, unlike an expense, is that it represents a cost that expired without producing a benefit.

Gains and losses are determined on a net rather than a gross basis. Due to the influence of conservatism, gains require a higher degree of certainty than losses for recognition to occur. Gains generally need to have been validated by a specific transaction involving the item while the incurrence of losses need only be probable to be recognized. US Financial Accounting Standards Board (FASB) *Statement of Financial Accounting Standard No. 5*, "Accounting for Contingencies" (1975) (SFAS 5), offers guidance on the recognition of contingent gains and losses. Although this standard is not widely criticized, one could argue that the recognition of both gains and losses should be based on the same level of probability without differentiation in treatment.

The FASB has issued several standards providing specific accounting and reporting guidance, including revenue recognition, for certain industries. For example, SFAS 45, "Accounting for Franchise Fee Revenue" (1981), established accounting and reporting standards for the unique circumstances created in franchise agreements. Revenue recognition guidelines are given for both initial and continuing franchise fees. SFAS 48, "Revenue Recognition When Right of Return Exists" (1981), lists six criteria that must be fulfilled before revenue can be recognized when return rights exist. SFAS 50, "Financial Reporting in the Record and Music Industry" (1981), discusses how to account for revenue from license agreements. SFAS 51 "Financial Reporting by Cable Television Companies" (1981), establishes accounting and reporting standards for costs, expenses, and revenues relating to the construction and operation of cable television systems. SFAS 53, "Financial Reporting by Producers and Distributors of Motion Picture Films" (1981), discusses how to account for revenue generated by films licensed to movie theaters and to television. SFAS 60, "Accounting and Reporting by Insurance Enterprises" (1982), offers guidance on accounting for insurance premium revenue. SFAS 63, "Financial Reporting by Broad-casters" (1982), primarily focuses on cost issues but also discusses how to account for barter revenue. SFAS 65 "Accounting for Certain Mortgage Banking Activities," addresses how to account for fees related to mortgage banking. SFAS 66, "Accounting for Sales of Real Estate" (1982), establishes how to recognize revenue and profit from real estate sales.

Although the nine standards identified above address different situations, all are similar in offering specific guidance to assist in determin-ing when the realizability and earnings criteria set forth in SFAC 5 have been met in these specialized situations. For example, SFAS 53 indicates that a film distributor should recognize revenue from films licensed to television when the license period begins and all of the following five conditions have been met: the license fee for each film is known, the cost of each film is known or reasonably determinable, collectibility of the full fee is reasonably assured, each film has been accepted by the licensee in accordance with the agreement, and the film is available for its first showing. Fulfillment of these conditions provides strong evidence of the amount of cash inflows to be received from the license agree-ment (realization) and the earnings process efforts of the film producer/distributor are deemed to be substantially completed when the film is made available for the first showing.

The exercise of judgment is supported but not eliminated in situations where specific revenue recognition guidelines exist. Revenue recognition is a very broad and pervasive issue in accounting. Specific guidelines do not exist for the majority of circumstances. The measure-ment and determination of the appropriate point to record revenues often require the exercise of good professional judgment. The revenue recognition criteria set forth in SFAC 5 and specific financial reporting standards are impor-tant and valuable guidelines to assist in making these critical judgments. In conjunction with revenue recognition, the proper matching of expenses against revenues is necessary in order to determine net income. Matching criteria assist in arriving at a proper matching of revenues and expenses, but considerable judg-ment is often required and sometimes arbitrary allocations are necessary. Gains and losses are reasonably clear concepts and are appropriately distinguished from revenues and expenses. The exercise of good professional judgment in accounting for gains and losses is also required, especially in determining the amount and status of a loss.

Bibliography

Myers, J. (1959). The critical event and recognition of net profit. *Accounting Review*, Oct. (1959).

JOHN K. SIMMONS

S

securities The US Financial Accounting Standards Board (FASB) issued Statement of Financial Accounting Standard No. 115 (SFAS 115), entitled "Accounting for Certain Investments in Debt and Equity Securities," in May 1993, setting forth new accounting procedures for marketable securities.

SFAS 115 greatly expands the use of "fair value" accounting beyond previous standards in this area. The prescribed financial reporting varies among three categories: held to maturity, trading securities, and available for sale.

The "held to maturity" classification only pertains to debt securities. To be classified as such, the management must have the positive *intent* and ability to hold the debt instrument to maturity. These securities are reported at amortized cost.

The "trading securities" category, comprised of both debt and equity securities, are those that are "bought and held principally for the purpose of selling them in the near term" (FASB, 1993, p. 5) They are bought and sold frequently with the objective of generating trading profits. Trading securities are reported on the statement of financial position at fair value, which might be higher than historical cost. An "unrealized holding gain or loss" is recorded to reflect changes in fair values of investments in trading securities, and are included in current year's earnings.

The third classification, "available for sale," includes all other securities. This category is also reported at fair value. However, any unrealized holding gains and losses (changes in fair values) are reported as a separate component of stockholder's equity. This treatment is intended to reduce volatility in reported earnings.

Also, at the time of transfer between categories, the unrealized holding gain or loss shall be recognized in current earnings for a security transferred into the trading category. For securities transferred from the trading category, any unrealized holding gain or loss is already included in earnings and should not be reversed upon transfer. Any unrealized holding gain or loss pertaining to a security transferred into the held to maturity category from the available for sale category should continue to be reported as a separate component of stockholder's equity. However, such unrealized gains and losses should be amortized over the remaining life of the debt investment as an adjustment of yield in a manner similar to the amortization of a premium or discount. Finally, for a debt security transferred from the held to maturity category to the available for sale category, any unrealized holding gain or loss at the date of transfer should be reported as a separate component of stockholder's equity. However, transfers from the held to maturity category should be rare since such transfers would call into question an entity's positive intent and ability to hold to maturity the remaining securities in this category.

It is interesting to note that prior to the issuance of SFAS 115, a common theme among the few published papers in this area was a call for market value reporting of marketable securities. Recently, the majority of articles outline the provisions of SFAS 115 and provide a listing of potential weaknesses of the current generally accepted accounting procedures.

See also **marketable securities**

JOHN D. NEILL

statistical sampling in auditing

Professional Standards

The American Institute of Certified Public Accountants (AICPA) has promulgated two Statements on Auditing Standards (SASs) that apply to the use of statistical sampling in auditing. These are SAS No. 39, "Audit Sampling," issued in June 1981 and SAS No. 47, "Audit Risk and Materiality in Conducting an Audit," issued in December 1983.

SAS 39 describes the use of sampling in auditing and the role of uncertainty and its relationship to risk. Sampling risk associated with incorrect decisions is described, as is the disaggregation of risk into four categories that pertain to auditors: inherent risk, control risk, analytical procedures risk, and tests of details risk. Two types of sampling applications, account balances tests and internal controls tests, are also described.

In SAS 47, audit risk and materiality and their impact on planning and implementing audit procedures are described. SAS 47 complements SAS 39 by more fully defining and describing inputs required to conduct audit sampling applications.

Research Summary

The earliest discussions of applications of audit sampling occurred in the 1940s (Editorial, "Testing 'very small' percentages," *Journal of Accountancy*, 72, 2–3, (1942)) when it was suggested that consideration of a small portion of a population might be an acceptable way of learning about the entire population. In the 1950s and 1960s most applications were in the compliance area with accounts receivable and inventories soon added to the list of audit sampling objects. Emphasis then was on *estimating* dollar balances rather than *testing* hypotheses about the balances. Elliott & Rogers (1972) criticized the continuing emphasis on estimation in audit sampling applications and went on to present a hypothesis-testing model that controlled the two primary risks an auditor must face when deciding whether or not to accept a client's book value balance. These risks are the risk of incorrect acceptance when a balance is materially misstated and the risk of incorrect rejection when a balance is not materially misstated. They used large sample normal distribution theory to calculate the necessary sample sizes to achieve the desired risk levels.

Throughout this period classical statistical procedures were introduced for use in auditing and they included simple random and stratified sampling, and the mean-per-unit estimator and a set of auxiliary information estimators. The estimators' expected uses were all based on large sample normal distribution theory. However, extensive research revealed that none of the estimators consistently achieved the nominal reliability levels (Kaplan, 1973; Neter & Loebbecke, 1975; Beck, 1980). The unreliability of the classical estimators and large sample theory in auditing applications prompted a need to know more about accounting populations so that the problems could be explained and possibly overcome. In the late 1970s and mid-1980s two major auditing firms made actual audit sampling databases available for study. These databases included both book and audit values so that error rates and error amounts could be studied. Analyses of these databases were conducted by Ramage, Krieger & Spero (1979); Johnson, Leitch & Neter (1981); Neter, Johnson & Leitch (1985); and Ham, Losell & Smieliauskas (1985).

The results of these analyses were consistent. Accounts receivable tended to have very low error rates with the preponderance of errors being overstatements. Inventory accounts tended to have larger error rates than accounts receivable with errors split approximately evenly between overstatements and understatements. While these databases were not selected randomly and could not be claimed to be representative of all accounting populations, the analyses provided support for the problems that had been reported in simulation studies.

In view of the problems with classical sampling theory and accounting populations, there has been a large volume of research into methods not requiring classical theory. One such development in sample selection methods is dollar unit sampling (DUS). When using DUS the probability of selecting an account is proportional to the number of dollars in the account, while in random sampling of individual accounts, the probability of selection is the same for all accounts. Auditors are naturally inclined to prefer DUS since larger individual accounts have a larger exposure to potential error amounts and also have a larger probability of selection.

Along with the attraction to DUS sampling, an attraction to a new estimator for audit sampling applications took place in the early 1970s. The Stringer bound, named for the person who developed it, was based on DUS. It became the subject of many simulation studies designed to test its reliability (Anderson & Teitlebaum, 1973; Goodfellow, Loebbecke & Neter, 1974a and b) since there was no underlying theory by which to demonstrate its reliability. The Stringer bound was constructed for use in a hypothesis testing context and is a "one-tail test" designed to provide protection against the most serious of the two possible decision errors, i.e., the probability of incorrect acceptance of a materially misstated balance. Without exception the reliability level achieved in all simulation studies exceeded the planned nominal level.

However, while these studies revealed conservatism in providing protection against the worst decision error, they prompted questions concerning how well the other decision error was controlled, i.e., the probability of incorrect rejection. Subsequently, simulation studies revealed that in most cases, the probability of making this error was surprisingly large. Despite this, the Stringer bound has become the most widely used of all the methods discussed here.

During the 1970s and 1980s many other bounds based on DUS were proposed. The general objective of bound construction was reliability, at least at the nominal level, and less conservative than the Stringer bound.

All of the DUS-based research reviewed above involved bounds designed for overstatement errors only. While auditors do not have the same aversion to understatements as they do for overstatements, not explicitly including understatements in the sampling design can help lead to the conservatism found in the Stringer and other bounds.

In the mid-1980s Dworin & Grimlund (1984) introduced the moment bound which accommodated both overstatements and understatements. It was based on a three-moment representation of the sampling distribution of the mean error in an accounting population. It used DUS and, similar to the Stringer bound,

simulation was required to evaluate its potential usefulness. Many simulation studies have been conducted since the moment bound's introduction. These studies have shown it to be generally reliable and much less conservative than the Stringer bound with significant reductions in the probability of incorrect rejection. In the early 1990s one of the largest US Big Six auditing firms adopted it for use in its ongoing audit engagements.

In 1993 the augmented variance bound (AVE) was introduced by Rohrbach (1993) and was based on probability proportional to size (PPS) sampling without replacement. This is similar to DUS sampling except that once selected, an account is removed from the population and further sampling is conducted from the remaining population items. AVE accommodated both overstatements and understatements and it also had to be studied by simulation. In the single published study of AVE so far (Rohrbach, 1993), it was shown that AVE achieves nominal reliability and also tends to be less conservative than the moment bound. In a working paper, Wurst, Neter & Godfrey (1994) also found that AVE generally had a smaller probability of incorrect rejection than the moment bound which supports the "less conservative" claim made in the Rohrbach study.

Current Status of Research

The use of statistical sampling by auditors has varied greatly over the past thirty years. Some audit firms have used it extensively, e.g., at one point one of the US largest firms required justification for not using statistical sampling on practically every audit engagement. Other firms have not insisted on its use, leaving it up to the auditors at the local operating level. It appears that in recent years overall use has diminished, although in the early 1990s, one of the largest US audit firms formally adopted the moment bound for use throughout the firm.

Statistical sampling in auditing has reached a stage where further improvements through research will be difficult. All recent advancements, beginning with the Stringer bound, have been based on DUS and their performance determined by simulation studies. The ideal research discovery would be a closed form model that guarantees control over the two primary decision risks and requires sample sizes small enough to be cost-effective for auditors. However, based on the progression of past research, attaining this ideal does not appear likely in the near term.

Finally, auditors have been extensively investigating other approaches to assessing and controlling audit risk and from a cost/benefit standpoint this may reduce the need to search for new developments in sampling.

Bibliography

Anderson, R. & Teitlebaum, A. D. (1973). Dollar-unit sampling. *Canadian Chartered Accountant*, **102**, 4, 30–9.

Beck, P. J. (1980). A critical analysis of the regression estimator in audit sampling. *Journal of Accounting Research*, **18**, 16–37.

Dworin, L. & Grimlund, R. A. (1984). Dollar-unit sampling for accounts receivable and inventory. *The Accounting Review*, **59**, 218–41.

Elliott, R. K. & Rogers, J. R. (1972). Relating statistical sampling to audit objectives. *Journal of Accountancy*, **134**, 46–55.

Goodfellow, J., Loebbecke, J. & Neter, J. (1974a). Some perspectives on CAV sampling plans, Part I.' *CA Magazine*, **105**, 4, 23–30.

Goodfellow, J., Loebbecke, J. & Neter, J. (1974b). Some perspectives on CAV sampling plans, Part II. *CA Magazine*, **105**, 5, 47–53.

Ham, J., Losell, D. & Smieliauskas, W. (1985). An empirical study of error characteristics in accounting populations. *The Accounting Review*, **60**, 387–406.

Johnson, J. R., Leitch, R. A. & Neter, J. (1981). Characteristics of errors in accounts receivable and inventory audits. *The Accounting Review*, **56**, 270–93.

Kaplan, R. S. (1973). Statistical sampling in auditing with auxiliary information estimators. *Journal of Accounting Research*, **11**, 238–58.

Neter, J. & Godfrey, J. T. (1988). Statistical sampling in auditing: A review. *Essays in honor of Franklin A. Graybill*, J. N. Srivastava, (Ed.), Netherlands: Elsevier Science Publishers BV.

Neter, J., Johnson, J. & Leitch, R. A. (1985). Characteristics of dollar-unit taints and error rates in accounts receivable and inventory. *The Accounting Review*, **60**, 488–99.

Neter, J. & Loebbecke, J. K. (1975). *Behavior of major statistical estimators in sampling accounting applications – An empirical study*. New York: AICPA.

Ramage, J. K., Krieger, A. M. & Spero, L. L. (1979). An empirical study of error characteristics in audit populations. *Journal of Accounting Research*, **17**, supplement, 72–102.

Rohrbach, K. J. (1993). Variance augmentation to achieve nominal coverage probability in sampling from audit populations. *Auditing, A Journal of Practice and Theory*, **12**, 79–97.

Wurst, J. C., Neter, J. & Godfrey, J. T. (1994). Additional findings on effectiveness of rectification in audit sampling.Unpublished working paper.

JAMES GODFREY

stock compensation

Accounting Standards for Stock Compensation

Corporations employ various stock-based plans to provide employees incentives, compensation, and a means for increasing stock ownership among employees. These arrangements may include the granting of stock options, stock purchase plans, stock thrift or savings plans, stock bonus or award plans, the granting of stock appreciation rights (SARs), and performance plans. The latter two as well as the granting of stock options usually comprise a portion of compensation packages for key employees or executives. Accounting for stock-based compensation in the USA is currently governed by Accounting Research Bulletin No. 43, Chapter. 13B, "Compensation Involved in Stock Option and Stock Purchase Plans" (1953); Accounting Principles Board (APB) Opinion No. 25, "Accounting for Stock Issued to Employees" (1972); and Financial Accounting Standards Boards (FASB) Interpretation No. 28, "Accounting for Stock Appreciation Rights and Other Variable Stock Option or Award Plans" (1978) as amended by FASB Interpretation No. 31, "Treatment of Stock Compensation Plans in EPS Computations" (1980).

Compensatory versus Noncompensatory Stock Compensation

The accounting treatment differs for various stock-based plans, depending on whether the plan is deemed compensatory or noncompensatory. A "noncompensatory" plan is one for which the corporation need not recognize compensation expense. To qualify as a noncompensatory plan the following criteria must be met: (1) participation allowed by substantially all full-time employees meeting limited employment qualifications; (2) equal or uniform percentage of salary offers of stock purchase to eligible employees; (3) allowance of a limited, reasonable time period for exercise of option or purchase right; and (4) any discount from the market price would be no greater than that granted in a reasonable offer to stockholders or others (in practice this discount ranges from 10 to 15 percent). All other plans are designated as "compensatory" and usually include stock option plans, thrift or savings plans to the extent of employer contribution, stock bonus and award plans, SARs, and performance plans.

Tax and Accounting Considerations

Stock option plans have been classified as to their tax treatment in the USA as either incentive or nonqualified plans. Tax laws require that the market price of the stock for which options are granted be equal to the option price on the grant date for a stock option plan to be deemed an incentive plan. For incentive stock option plans, the corporation does not recognize compensation expense and correspondingly receives no tax deduction. Upon the exercise of the options, the difference between the stock's market price on the purchase date and the option exercise price becomes taxable income to the employee but payment of tax on this income is deferred until the employee subsequently sells the securities. Alternatively, under a nonqualified plan, the issuing corporation would recognize this difference as an expense and would be entitled to a tax deduction while the employee is concurrently taxed based on the difference between the market price of the stock and the option price at the exercise (purchase) date. From the corporation's perspective, incentive stock option plans may be useful in attracting key high-quality employees, especially for high-tech start-up companies with meager cash and little need for a tax deduction.

Two other accounting issues pervade the literature relative to stock option plans and stock appreciation rights: (1) the determination of amounts to be charged as compensation expense, and (2) the timing of the recognition of such expense. US Accounting Principles Board (APB) Opinion No. 25 specifies that compensation cost be measured as the excess of the market price of the stock over the option

price at the *measurement date*. The measurement date is defined as the first date at which both the number of shares to which the options apply and the option or purchase price are known. For fixed plans (wherein both the number of shares and the exercise price are known on the grant date), the measurement date is deemed to be the date that the options are granted.

Since compensation cost is incurred for service, the expense should be allocated in a systematic and rational manner over the periods in which the employee performs the related services, the *service period*. When an employee fails to fulfill his or her obligations and thereby forfeits his or her options, an adjustment in the charges for compensation expense is allowable and is accounted for as a change in accounting estimate. However, in the case where options merely expire or are not exercised, the cost of services stands and no adjustment to compensation expense is allowed.

Stock Appreciation Rights and Similar Plans

Complications merit modification of the aforementioned measurement and allocation of the compensation cost associated with stock appreciation rights and awards under other compensatory plans with variable terms. These are plans for which the number of shares of stock an employee may receive or the share price is unknown at the date of the grant or award. By definition, stock appreciation rights involve the right to receive amounts known as share appreciation measured by the excess of market price over a pre-established price at the date of exercise.

In its Interpretation of Accounting Principles Board (APB) Opinion No. 25, the Financial Accounting Standards Board (FASB) deemed that the measurement date for these types of arrangements is the exercise date, as this is the first date on which the number of shares (or in the case of stock appreciation rights awarded in cash, the liability incurred) becomes actually known. The service period over which the charge to expense is accrued is designated as the *vesting period*, unless otherwise defined in the plan or other related agreement.

The above accounting treatment presents an allocation problem for the accounting periods falling between the grant and exercise dates. Current accounting standards call for an adjustment to compensation expense in these periods for changes, in the quoted market value of the shares covered by the grant. This adjustment is made directly to compensation expense for the current period, but should never result in a cumulative compensation expense less than zero.

The technical process involves an allocation of compensation expense based on percentages. In the initial accounting period, wherein the grant occurred, compensation expense is determined to be the product of (1) the excess of current quoted market price over the pre-established price, (2) the number of shares covered by the grant, and (3) the portion of the service period expired or the percent vested. In the second period or year, a similar computation using the then current market information would be made, resulting in the cumulative compensation accrued. The difference between cumulative compensation and the compensation expense accrued in the initial period would be the expense accrued for the second period. A similar process is adopted for subsequent periods. Unlike stock option plans with fixed terms, the determination of periodic compensation expense for stock appreciation rights and variable option plans involves the use of contemporaneously quoted market prices in each accounting period and, depending on stock price movements, may result in a reduction of compensation expense in some periods.

Current accounting treatment for compensatory stock option plans therefore involves measuring compensation expense that may result in charges against income over a specified allocation period. The determination of the actual compensation expense depends on whether the terms of the plan are fixed or variable. In the case of fixed stock option plans, a charge to earnings will result if the market price of the stock is in excess of the exercise price at the grant date. This discount from fair market value is then apportioned equally over the service period. Currently most fixed executive grants in the USA do not result in such a discount. Variable plans, on the other hand, receive "stock appreciation right accounting." Earnings are charged for an "emerging" value by marking to market every period until such time as the options are exercised. A similar

process is utilized for stock-based awards in performance plans.

Current disclosure requirements include information about the status of the option or plan at the end of the period, the number of shares under each option, the option price, the number of shares exercisable under each option, the number of shares exercised during the period involved, and the option exercise price.

Accounting for stock-based compensation has become controversial. This has been caused by some counter-intuitive results spawned by the accounting treatment, by the publicity surrounding excessive executive compensation packages, and by the lack of full disclosure. For example, "a stock option and a SAR with similar terms may provide an employee with an identical economic benefit but do not result in the same expense amount" (Rouse & Barton, 1993). Furthermore, no compensation expense is recorded for stock options if the exercise price at grant date is equal to the market price. In contrast, variable stock option plans, which are usually contingent on performance, require the estimation and accrual of compensation expense between the grant date and a final (exercise) measurement date.

Bibliography

Rouse, R. W. & Barton, D. N. (1993). Stock compensation accounting. *Journal of Accountancy*, June, 67–70.

ELLEN L. LANDGRAF

stockholders' equity   The stockholders' equity section of the balance sheet (also referred to as shareholders' equity) represents the book value of the ownership interest in the assets of a business entity. Ownership interest is normally increased by issuing shares of stock and by earned income; ownership interest is decreased by net losses of the entity and by distributions of assets to owners. The ownership claim on the assets is secondary to claims by creditors, but the residual interest that accrues to owners encompasses all remaining assets after creditor claims are satisfied. Ownership bears the maximum risk of loss associated with the enterprise, but is also entitled to all of the residual rewards. Organization of the stockholders' equity section is by sources of capital formation. The primary sources of capital are contributed capital and earned capital.

Contributed Capital

Contributed capital refers to investment by owners in the capital stock of the corporation. Amounts paid in for capital stock are usually accounted for in two parts: par or stated value, and additional paid-in capital. The par or stated value of stock is a designated dollar amount (in the USA) per share and is set by the corporation. In the USA, the par value or stated value per share times the number of shares issued usually comprises legal capital. If there is no par or stated value, the entire investment may be defined as legal capital. Restrictions may exist on the ability of the corporation to make distributions to owners that would reduce stockholders' equity below what is considered legal capital.

Additional paid-in capital, or share premium, occurs if the investment per share exceeds the par or stated value per share of stock. Other sources of additional paid-in capital include the sale of treasury stock (i.e., shares temporarily reacquired by the issuing firm) or transfers from retained earnings through certain stock dividends. Accounting Principles Board (APB) Opinion No. 14 (March, 1969) states that the portion of the proceeds of debt securities issued with detachable stock purchase warrants that is allocable to the warrants shall be accounted for as additional paid-in capital.

The segregation of additional paid-in capital by source is recommended by Accounting Research Bulletin (ARB) No. 43 (June, 1953) and APB Opinion No. 5 (September, 1964). However, APB Opinion No. 5 also acknowledges that state corporation laws may specify treatments other than those preferred by generally accepted accounting principles and that these should be deemed acceptable. Since state corporation laws generally do not require segregation, many corporations do not maintain sufficiently detailed records to identify additional paid-in capital by source.

Earned Capital

The second primary source of corporate capital is earned capital, which is accounted for in the retained earnings account. Retained earnings represents the accumulation of undistributed earnings over the life of the corporation. A negative balance in retained earnings, or deficit, indicates the corporation currently has a cumulative net loss.

The most common event to affect the balance in retained earnings is the declaration of a dividend. According to the "Framework for the Preparation of Financial Statements" [International Accounting Standards Committee (IASC), 1989] and consistent with Statement of Financial Accounting Concepts (SFAC) No. 6 (December, 1985), distributions to owners decrease ownership interests in an enterprise; the declaration and payment of dividends do not lead to the recognition of an expense. Dividends become an obligation of the corporation only when they are declared by the board of directors; at declaration, the aggregate amount of the dividend is subtracted from retained earnings. Most dividends are paid in cash. Dividends can also be paid in kind; i.e., noncash assets such as inventory are distributed to the stockholders. APB No. 29 (May, 1973) mandates that dividends in kind be recorded at the fair value of the assets transferred.

Protection of creditors has high importance. Under the European Community (EC), Fourth Directive, recognition is given to the need for a company to establish a minimum share capital and to ensure that it is maintained. In the UK, there is no requirement to recover past losses of capital before a dividend is paid out of current profits. In general, however, the EC view is that a company should not be permitted to pay a dividend unless all prior losses, revenue and capital, have been recovered.

A second form of dividend is the stock dividend, which is a corporate distribution on a pro rata basis of additional shares of its own common stock to its common stockholders without payment of additional consideration. Accounting techniques for stock dividends are stated in ARB No. 43 (June, 1953). Stock distributions of additional shares totaling less than 20 to 25 percent of the previously outstanding shares are considered "small" stock dividends; for these distributors distributions, the fair market value of the shares distributed should be transferred from retained earnings to the common stock (for par or stated value of the shares issued) and additional paid-in capital (for amounts above par value) accounts.

Stock distributions involving issuance of additional shares totalling more than 25 percent of the number previously outstanding may be accounted for as a "large" stock dividend or as a stock split. If it is considered a stock dividend, the par value of the issued shares is transferred from retained earnings to the common stock account. If the distribution is considered a stock split, the par or stated value per share is adjusted so that legal capital remains unchanged. When a stock split is clearly for the purpose of effecting a reduction in the unit market price of the shares, no transfer from retained earnings is called for unless required by local law.

Certain conditions require a restatement of the beginning balance of the retained earnings account. In July 1990, the IASC issued "Statement of Intent: Comparability of Financial Statements," which proposes that the preferred accounting treatment for correction of fundamental errors and omissions, and variation resulting from accounting policy changes should be a restatement of the beginning balance in retained earnings. Alternatively, income effects of changes in accounting policy could be included in the determination of net income. The alternative treatment is consistent with accounting practice in the USA. According to APB No. 20 (July 1971), errors in financial statements are defined as errors resulting from mathematical mistakes, mistakes in the application of accounting principles, or oversight or misuses of facts that existed at the time the financial statements were prepared. SFAS No. 16 (June, 1977), as amended by SFAS No. 109 (February, 1992), states that only corrections of errors are properly recorded as prior period adjustments. SFAS No. 109 states that any item of profit and loss related to the correction of an error in the financial statements of a prior period shall be accounted for and reported as a prior period adjustment and excluded from the determination of net income for the current period. According to SFAS No. 15 (June, 1977), those items that are reported as a prior period adjustment shall, in single period statements, be reflected as adjustments of the opening balance of retained earnings. APB Opinion No. 9 (December, 1966) mandates

that for comparative statements, corresponding adjustments shall be made of the amounts of net income, its components, retained earnings balances, and other affected balances from all of the years presented to reflect the retroactive application of the prior period adjustment.

Normally, a change in accounting principle is accounted for prospectively. However, certain items specifically identified in the standards are given retroactive treatment. A retroactive adjustment is made by recasting the statements of prior years on a basis consistent with the newly adopted principle. Any part of the cumulative effect attributable to years prior to those presented is treated as an adjustment of beginning retained earnings of the earliest year presented.

Treasury Stock

When a corporation acquires its own shares, these shares must either be retired or be placed in treasury. When shares are retired, they reassume the status of authorized, but unissued, shares. When shares are placed in treasury, they are considered issued, but not outstanding, shares. Some state corporation laws do distinguish between treasury shares and unissued stock on some dimensions. Treasury shares may be exempt from certain legal limitations on the issuance of authorized, but previously unissued, common shares. In the USA, in jurisdictions that have adopted the Model Business Corporation Act (MBCA), there are virtually no legal differences between treasury shares and retired shares. However, even in these states, many corporations retain the designation of treasury shares for financial reporting purposes.

Shares held in treasury are not assets of the corporation because these shares do not provide a future benefit that will result in revenues or income. Consistent with SFAC No. 6 (December, 1985) definitions, these distributions to owners decrease ownership interests and do not lead to recognition of revenue or expense.

Treasury stock is most commonly shown at cost, and it is a contra–equity account. The most common method of presentation is to deduct the aggregate cost of treasury shares from the total of all other equity accounts. GAAP also permits valuation of treasury shares at par value.

Donated Capital

Some corporations show a donated capital account in their stockholders' equity section. Donated capital arises from the contribution of assets to corporations without a commensurate issuance of equity claims. The donated assets are recorded at their fair market values as increases to the related asset accounts, and the credit is to an additional paid-in capital account. SFAS No. 116 (June, 1993), effective for reporting years beginning after December 15, 1994, mandates new accounting techniques to account for donations. Under this Statement, contributions received will be recorded as an increase in the related asset accounts, but the credit will be made to a revenue or gain account instead of being made directly to a capital account. Rather than a direct effect on stockholders' equity, the donation will indirectly increase stockholders' equity when the revenue and gain accounts are closed to retained earnings.

Other Adjustments to Stockholders' Equity

Quasi-reorganizations. Some US state laws permit a quasi-reorganization. This procedure eliminates an accumulated deficit in retained earnings and may be appropriate if new products or new management have substantially improved the economic conditions and operating results of a company. Some state laws prohibit declaring or paying dividends until a deficit has been replaced by earnings which could hinder a company's ability to obtain new capital. A quasi-reorganization eliminates the deficit in retained earnings through a reclassification of the stockholders' equity accounts but does not require intervention of the courts in a formal reorganization. To accomplish a quasi-reorganization, an amount equal to the cumulative deficit is removed from the additional paid-in capital accounts, resulting in a zero balance in the retained earnings account. In subsequent financial reports, the retained earnings must be dated for a period of five to ten years to show the fact and the date of the quasi-reorganization.

Foreign currency translation. In 1981, the US Financial Accounting Standards Board (FASB) issued SFAS No. 52 (December 1981), which calls for postponing the recognition of unrealized exchange rate gains and losses on foreign currency until the foreign operation is substantially liquidated. This postponement is accomplished by creating a stockholders' equity account to carry the unrealized amounts.

Marketable securities adjustments. Certain readily marketable debt and equity securities, not actively traded but available for sale, are valued at fair value at the end of the accounting period. According to SFAS No. 115 (May, 1993), the unrealized gain or loss associated with the change in asset value is captured in a stockholders' equity account.

Presentation of Contributed Capital According to the Fourth Directive

The Fourth Directive, which prescribes formats for financial statements, was issued by the European Community (EC) in 1978. With respect to contributed capital, subscribed capital is the first item disclosed in the equity section. If national law provides for called-up capital to be shown under this heading, the amounts of subscribed capital and paid-up capital must be separately disclosed. The share premium account immediately follows subscribed capital.

Classifications of Stock. All corporations have at least one class of capital stock identified as common stock; in addition, some corporations issue one or more classes of preferred stock. Common stock is the basic ownership equity of a company. Four rights normally accrue to each share of common stock: voting rights, dividend rights, liquidation rights, and preemptive rights. Each share of common stock is entitled to one vote; common stockholders elect the board of directors. When dividends are declared and paid, each share of common stock is entitled to receive a pro rata distribution. In liquidation, the residual assets of the company (assets remaining after the claims of all creditors and stockholders with preferred claims are satisfied) are distributed on a pro rata basis to each share of common stock. The preemptive right entitles stockholders to purchase a percentage share of any new stock offering equal to their current ownership percentage. Occasionally, there is more than one class of common stock with differences in the rights associated with each stock issue or class.

Preferred stock usually is entitled to senior claims on the net assets of the corporation relative to the common shares. Preferences usually relate to dividend and liquidation rights. Preferred stock has the right to receive a predetermined dividend each year before any dividends can be paid to common stock. The dividend may be expressed as a percentage of par or stated value, or as a cash amount per share. The preferred dividend may also be cumulative, which means that any dividend preferences not paid in previous years must be paid in full before common stockholders may receive a dividend. Unpaid cumulative dividends relating to prior years are referred to as "dividends in arrears." If the dividends are not cumulative, a dividend missed in prior years need not be paid. While the right to dividends is normally fixed on a per share basis, preferred stock may also be participating, which means that preferred stockholders may be entitled to additional dividends under contractual conditions. Claims of preferred stockholders in liquidation are senior to the claims of common stockholders, and are predetermined on a per share basis. Preferred stock normally does not have a right to vote.

Convertible preferred stock may be converted into another security, normally common shares, at a predetermined ratio. Callable preferred stock can be redeemed at a fixed per-share price at the option of the company. Normally, missed cumulative dividends must also be paid when the preferred stock is called. The preferred features, particularly the fixed dividend rate and the fixed liquidation value, give preferred stock some of the characteristics of debt. Important differences are that the preferred stockholders are not entitled to demand either the redemption of their shares or the declaration and subsequent payment of dividends. There may be multiple classes of preferred stock, each with different priorities and preferences relative to dividend and/or liquidation rights.

Fourth Directive Requirements

The Fourth Directive allows considerable flexibility in financial statement presentation. The overriding reporting standard is a "true and fair view," and this consideration overrides specific reporting requirements. If required disclosure is not sufficient to provide a true and fair view any necessary additional information must be provided in the financial statements or in the notes. Relative to stockholders' equity, notes to the financial statements should disclose: (1) the number and nominal value (or accounting par value) of shares subscribed during the year; (2) the number and nominal value (or accounting par value) of each class of share in issue; and (3) a description of any participation certificates, convertible debentures, or similar securities or rights, with an indication of their number and the rights they convey.

Disclosure Requirements in the USA

According to Accounting Principles Board (APB) Opinion No. 12 (December), 1967, proper disclosure requires an analysis and explanation of changes in the number of shares of stock issued and/or outstanding during the period. Disclosure may be included on the face of the financial statement or in the footnotes. Increases in capital stock may result from sale of additional shares of stock, conversion of preferred stock or debentures, issuance of stock through stock dividends or stock splits, issuance of stock in acquisitions or mergers, or issuance of stock pursuant to the exercise of stock options or stock warrants. Decreases may result from the purchase and ·retirement of stock, purchase of treasury stock, or reverse stock splits.

The need for disclosure in connection with complex capital structures is stated in APB No. 15 (May, 1969). Financial statements should include a summary description sufficient to explain the pertinent rights and privileges of the various securities outstanding. Disclosure requirements for capital stock include contractual obligations to potentially increase the number of shares outstanding of a given class of stock. Such obligations include: (1) conversion rights of debentures or preferred stock into common shares; (2) warrants outstanding entitling the holder to exchange them for shares; (3) stock options under compensation and bonus plans that call for the issuance of capital stock over a period of time at prices fixed in advance; and (4) commitments to issue capital stock under certain merger agreements. These disclosures are necessary to alert investors to potential increases in the number of shares outstanding and the related potential for dilution of earnings per share and book value per share.

Disclosures specific to preferred stock include the terms to which preferred stock may be subject. In particular, dividend rights, including participating and cumulative features, and liquidation rights must be disclosed. APB No. 10 (Dec. 1966) encourages disclosure of the aggregate liquidation value of preferred stock parenthetically rather than on a per-share basis or by disclosure in the footnotes.

The Use of Reserves in the Financial Statements

Restrictions on the availability of retained earnings to support distributions to owners may be accomplished by an appropriation of retained earnings, which is accomplished in some countries by legal provisions. Generally a reserve is created by a specific act of the board of directors, and it is recorded by crediting a special equity account called appropriated retained earnings or a specific purpose reserve account, and by debiting retained earnings. Appropriations of retained earnings can be reversed by a vote of the board. This appropriation has sometimes been called a reserve, and this is the only acceptable use of the term "reserve" under US generally accepted accounting principles.

In some countries outside of the USA however, the term reserve is used more broadly. Under the Fourth Directive, revaluation reserves and other legal reserves are to be disclosed on the balance sheet immediately after the share premium accounts. These reserves may be used for certain income items that do not flow through the income statement but instead increase or decrease stockholders' equity directly. In addition, common practice in certain countries permits shifting of income between accounting periods to either minimize income taxes or smooth earnings. The accounting mechanism used to accomplish this reporting result is also called a "reserve." Reserve accounts may appear on the balance sheet as a component of stockholders' equity. This use of reserves does not misstate total stockholders' equity, however. Instead of recognizing an item on the income statement and closing the item through retained earnings, thereby indirectly adjusting stockholders' equity, the use of the reserve allows a direct adjustment to the value of stockholders' equity. A company's ability to pay dividends may be limited by the existence of these reserves.

In countries other than the USA, firms may use reserves to revalue assets without showing an income effect for the current period. Accounting principles in the UK permit periodic revaluations of fixed assets and intangible assets to their current market value. The increased valuation of assets that usually occurs leads to an increase in a revaluation reserve account included in stockholders' equity.

Accounting principles in some countries (e.g., Japan, Germany, and France) require the establishment of reserves through appropriations of retained earnings. Annual appropriations of earnings are accumulated until the balance in the reserve account equals a percentage of outstanding share capital. The purpose of this reserve is for the protection of creditors since assets of equal amounts would not be available for distribution to owners.

CYNTHIA JEFFREY

substantive auditing tests   Substantive tests performed by the auditor consist of tests of details of transactions and account balances, and analytical procedures. The objective of substantive tests is to detect material misstatements in the financial statements. The auditor selects particular substantive tests to achieve audit objectives and considers, among other things, the risk of material misstatement of the financial statements, including the assessed levels of control risk, and the expected effectiveness and efficiency of such tests (US Statement on Auditing Standard No. 31, "Evidential Matter" 1980). The evidential matter provided by the combination of the auditor's assessment of inherent risk and control risk and by substantive tests provides a reasonable basis for the resulting opinion on the fairness of the financial statements.

Audit Evidence

The auditor's responsibility is to design audit procedures that will provide reasonable assurance that any material misstatements due to errors or irregularities will be detected and removed from the financial statements. Errors are unintentional mistakes including clerical mistakes, mistakes in the application of accounting principals, and misinterpretation of facts. Irregularities result from intentional distortions such as fraud or defalcations. It is important to note that an audit does not include procedures specifically designed to detect illegal acts (Statement on Auditing Standard No. 54, "Illegal Acts by Clients" 1988).

The auditor must collect evidence and document the collection process. Evidence requirements are found in the Third Standard of Fieldwork, which states: "sufficient competent evidential matter is to be obtained through inspection, observation, inquiries, and confirmations to afford a reasonable basis for an opinion regarding the financial statements under audit." More specifically, the evidence is obtained to support or refute the assertions that pertain to the accounts in the financial statements. Financial statement assertions can be classified as follows: existence or occurrence, completeness, rights and obligations, valuation and allocation, and presentation and disclosure.

For evidence to be useful to the auditor it must possess to some degree each of four characteristics: relevance, freedom from bias, objectivity, and persuasiveness. Six types of audit evidence are available to the auditor to support a given audit objective: physical evidence, representations by third parties, mathematical evidence, documentation, representations by client personnel, and data interrelationships.

Test Objectives. The overall test objective relates either to tests of controls or substantive tests. Tests of controls determine the effectiveness of the design and operation of control structure policies and procedures. The results of these tests assist in determining the nature, timing, and extent of substantive tests. Substantive tests determine if material dollar or disclosure misstatements exist in the financial statements. If the client has established a good internal control structure, the auditor may decide to restrict substantive testing because the client's internal control structure is likely to prevent or detect material misstatements. This relationship means that if the financial statements are less likely to contain material misstatements, the auditor may properly do less substantive audit work than if the financial statements are likely to contain material misstatements.

Types of Substantive Tests. Substantive tests can be classified as follows: analytical tests, observation and inquiry, tests of transactions, and tests of balances. Analytical tests are evaluations of financial information and nonfinancial data, and may be used as substantive tests. In fact, some audit objectives may be difficult or impossible to achieve without relying to some extent on analytical tests because they may be more effective or efficient than tests of details. For example, analytical tests may be more effective than tests of details in testing the completeness assertion for income statement accounts.

Although not used extensively, inquiry can be used as a substantive test. For example, inquiries regarding subsequent events would be a substantive test because they provide evidence regarding the adequacy of disclosures in the financial statements. Tests of transactions are the auditor's examination of the documents and accounting records involved in the processing of a specific type of transaction. A substantive objective is accomplished when the purpose of the auditor's examination is to determine if dollar errors have occurred during the processing of the transaction. Tests of balances are audit tests performed directly on a balance to identify misstatements in an account. Two specific examples of tests of balances are confirmation and observation.

Specific Audit Techniques. The major types of tests can be classified into specific methods to gather evidence as follows: physical examination, confirmation, vouching, tracing, reperformance, reconciliation, inquiry, inspection, and analytical procedures.

Physical examination is the activity of gathering physical evidence. As a substantive test, it involves the examination of assets that have a tangible existence, such as cash or equipment. Physical examination is an activity used in the observation of inventories. This activity is a generally accepted auditing procedure used as a substantive test. The independent auditor who issues an opinion when he or she has not employed this procedure has the burden of justifying the opinion expressed

(Statement on Auditing Standard 1, 1982, "Inventories"). The primary audit assertion tested by physical examination is existence. However, it also provides evidence about valuation. The completeness assertion may also be tested through physical examination in that items omitted from the financial statements may be discovered.

The confirmation technique requires the auditor to request a written response from a specific third party about a particular item affecting the financial statements. The primary assertions tested by confirmation are existence and rights and obligations. This technique can also provide evidence about the valuation or allocation, completeness, and presentation and disclosure assertions. The auditor's decision to use confirmation procedures rather than, or in conjunction with, tests directed toward documents or parties within the entity is based upon a desire to use substantive tests to obtain more or different evidence about a financial statement assertion. For example, confirmation of accounts receivable is a generally accepted auditing procedure that will be performed unless certain conditions are met (Statement on Auditing Standards No. 67, 1991, "The Confirmation Process").

Vouching is the examination of documents that support a recorded transaction or amount. Because the purpose of the vouching technique is to obtain evidence about a recorded item in the accounting records, the direction of the search for the supporting documents is crucial. The direction of testing is from the recorded item to supporting documentation. Vouching can best provide evidence addressing existence or occurrence, valuation or allocation, rights and obligations, and presentation and disclosure.

Tracing is the following of source documents to their recording in the accounting records. This procedure is performed by selecting source documents and tracing them through the accounting system to their ultimate recording in the accounting records. Tracing is often used as a test of the completeness assertion. The reperformance of client activities involved in the accounting process is a common substantive technique. Evidence is obtained about client activities by repeating the activities and comparing the result with the client's result.

Reconciliation is the process of matching two independent sets of records. In an audit, one set of records is usually the client's and the other set is the third party's. Reconciliation primarily serves the assertions of completeness and existence or occurrence. The preparation of a bank reconciliation is a common example of this technique.

Inquiry is a broad audit technique that entails asking questions. Inquiry is used extensively in an audit and as a substantive test it may address any of the assertions. Inspection is the examination of documents in other than the vouching or tracing techniques. It is the critical reading of a document comparing the information therein with other information known to the auditor or recorded in the accounts. Because of the variety of documents that auditors may inspect, the inspection technique addresses all the financial statement assertions.

Analytical procedures encompass a number of specific procedures the auditor may perform. Auditors employ specific procedures to assess the reasonableness of data and to identify unusual relationships. Because unusual relationships among data can occur for a number of reasons, analytical procedures may address all five financial statement assertions.

Audit Risk

The auditor's responsibility is to reduce the possibility of audit risk to an acceptably low level. The auditor uses the assessed levels of control risk and inherent risk to determine the acceptable level of detection risk for financial statement assertions. The auditor then uses the acceptable level of detection risk to determine the nature, timing, and extent of substantive procedures to be used to detect material misstatements in the financial statement assertions. It is not appropriate, however, for an auditor to rely completely on the assessments of inherent risk and control risk to the exclusion of performing substantive tests of account balances and classes of transactions where misstatements could exist that might be material when aggregated with misstatements in other balances or classes (US Statement on Auditing Standards No. 47, 1983, "Audit Risk and Materiality in Conducting an Audit").

As the acceptable level of detection risk decreases, the assurance provided from substantive tests should increase. Consequently, the auditor may do one or more of the following (Statement on Auditing Standard No. 55, 1988, "Consideration of the Internal Control Structure in a Financial Statement Audit"):

– change the nature of substantive tests from a less effective to a more effective procedure, such as using tests directly toward independent parties outside the entity rather than tests directed toward parties or documentation within the entity;

– change the timing of substantive tests, such as performing them at year-end rather than at an interim date;

– change the extent of substantive tests, such as using a larger sample size.

In considering efficiency, the auditor recognizes that additional evidential matter that supports a further reduction in the assessed level of control risk for an assertion would result in less audit effort for the substantive tests of that assertion. The auditor weighs the increase in audit effort associated with the additional test of controls that is necessary to obtain such evidential matter against the resulting decrease in audit effort associated with the reduced substantive tests. When the auditor concludes it is inefficient to obtain additional evidential matter for specific assertions, the auditor uses the assessed level of control risk based on the understanding of the internal control structure in planning the substantive tests for those assertions.

Although the inverse relationship between control risk and detection risk may permit the auditor to change the nature or the timing of substantive tests or limit their extent, ordinarily the assessed level of control risk cannot be sufficiently low to eliminate the need to perform any substantive tests to restrict detection risk for all of the assertions relevant to significant account balances or transaction classes. Consequently, regardless of the assessed level of control risk, the auditor should perform substantive tests for significant account balances and transaction classes.

An auditor must determine when to perform each audit procedure. (Statement on Auditing Standards No. 47, 1983, "Audit Risk and Materiality in conducting an Audit"). Audit procedures performed before year-end are known as interim procedures. In deciding whether to perform interim procedures, the auditor should consider the entity's internal control structure, changing business conditions, the risk associated with the various account balances, and the predictability of account balances at year-end. If interim substantive tests are performed, additional tests must be performed at year-end. Then year-end tests may involve further tests of details or analytical procedures.

RICHARD TABOR and BARRY BRYAN

sunk costs   Decision-makers invest resources with the hope of realizing some goal or goals. However, after having made the investment, there are instances in which decision-makers may receive negative feedback, suggesting that they have not realized their goals and that additional investments may not result in goal realization. The manager now must decide whether to pursue or retract from the previous investment decision. This scenario often is similar to many managerial decisions that consist of a series of choices rather than separate decisions. Research findings imply that individuals are prone to a particular bias in sequential decisions, namely, a tendency to escalate commitments. Decision-makers improperly consider sunk costs, which is part of a general behavioral trait carrying various titles such as "escalation commitment," "sunk cost phenomenon," and "sunk cost problem."

Determinants of Sunk Cost Escalation Behavior

Staw & Ross (1987) proposed a model consisting of project, psychological, social, and organizational determinants. *Project* determinants suggest that: if performance feedback is negative, commitment of resources are more (less) when the determinants of failure are exogenous (endogenous). *Psychological* determinants include reinforcement traps, such as difficulties in withdrawing from a previously rewarded activity; individual motivations, such as the need for self-justification; decision errors, such as trying to recoup sunk costs; and biases in information processing, such as paying more attention to confirming than disconfirming information. *Social* determinants include interpersonal processes that may lead to excess commitment, such as the need for external justification for a sub-par performance project. Under *organizational* determinants are variables such as a project's institutionalization within the organization, job security, infrastructural resources expended on the project, and political support for the project in the organization.

Escalation errors may also be driven by the manager's desire to manipulate others' perception of his or her performances.

Reducing Sunk Cost Escalation Behavior

There are two approaches to reducing escalation: (1) lessen the impact of those variables that invoke escalation tendencies (Simonson & Staw, 1992), and (2) develop control mechanisms that improve decision quality, since escalation research considers overcommitment as a departure from decisional accuracy (cf. Ghosh, 1994).

Research findings suggest that escalation behavior may be reduced by decreasing the need for self- or external justification.

An approach for reducing escalation is to adopt certain control mechanisms for capital projects where the sunk cost effect is most prevalent. These projects have streams of revenues and costs; further, funds are expended incrementally and precede revenues. Assuming a well-formulated capital budget, there are three essential steps to control capital projects: (1) provide unambiguous feedback on outcomes of previous expenditures; (2) evaluate the impact of any changes in the initial plan on the project's outcome, which includes evaluating future benefits of additional expenses prior to their commitment; and (3) monitor whether the project is following the plan, which typically entails submission of a performance report on the initial expenditure prior to making any decision on additional expenditures. Mechanisms (1) and (2) are *implicit* controls because they do not actively regulate the investment decision; instead they are intended to make the decision-maker focus only on the incremental investment decision. In contrast, mechanism (3) is an *explicit* control mechanism because it takes a more active role in regulating decision by requiring a submission of the performance report. These mechanisms are discussed below.

Implicit control: The role of feedback.
Feedback that the course of action is not achieving the desired goal is believed to enhance escalation.

The concept and manipulation of negative feedback, which would indicate a failed course of action, is not well defined in previous research on escalation. The research also showed that a greater amount was committed by those who were personally responsible for the negative consequences.

Negative feedback is perceived to be less accurate and accepted less readily than positive feedback. In addition, providing unambiguous negative feedback of prior investment decisions should reduce the perpetuation of additional commitment of resources to the same course of action.

Implicit control: Information on future benefits
Prior research indicates that decision-makers improperly attend to historical costs instead of basing decisions exclusively on future costs and benefits. For example, Arkes & Blumer (1985) show that people who pay full price for season theater tickets go to more performances during the season than people who paid a discounted price for the tickets. This suggests that people are not marginal decision-makers because the amount expended for a theater ticket – a sunk cost – affects the decision to attend performances. Nevertheless, getting *only* an increased commitment reaction to historical cost indicates some underlying problem with prior studies in this area, e.g., absence of information on potential future benefits from the additional investment to the initial course of action.

Explicit control: The role of monitoring.
Information asymmetry is considered a prerequisite for committing escalation errors (Narayanan, 1985). The adverse selection problem arises with information asymmetry because managers may have incentives to hide or misrepresent their private information so that they can be judged only by their observable actions and results. This allows managers to continue with a course of action that may not provide acceptable results and not admit to previous incorrect choices without an incentive to do so. Thus, managers will escalate and will subsequently be compensated for the results they achieve.

Penno (1983) analytically investigates several issues of information asymmetry in managerial accounting. He specifically addresses reporting/incentive and monitoring systems. In a reporting/incentive system, subordinates report some of their private information to superiors, who then revise the standards by which subordinates are evaluated. Participative budgeting is an example of reporting/incentive system. A major problem with this system, however, is that subordinates may have incentives to distort the information they report.

In controlling capital projects, the availability of a monitor may act to reduce the level of information asymmetry between the subordinate divisional manager and the senior manager. A monitor requires setting up minimum performance standards for capital projects, forcing managers to compare actual performance with these standards, and providing possible reasons for the variance. If the subordinate manager knows there is a possibility that discriminating private information about the project will be disclosed via the monitoring mechanism, he/she will be less likely to commit an escalation error. From an organizational standpoint, this suggests that there is a need to reward good decisions over impression management.

There are steps an organization may take to reinforce the control mechanisms discussed above:

(1) Although unambiguous negative feedback has a de-escalation effect, people are reluctant to communicate negative feedback or selectively focus on the positive aspects. Using multiple channels for feedback, increasing its frequency, and displaying a willingness to help a subordinate help to mitigate this problem.

(2) Information on expected benefits for additional investment reduces the sunk cost phenomenon; however, marginal decisions are not easy to make in capital projects. Therefore, toward the end of the project, commitment may escalate since marginal investments produce an increasingly high expected return. Project segmentation could reduce this problem.

(3) Although monitoring has a de-escalation effect, its purpose will be better served in an organization where there is a delineation between those who are actively engaged in the capital project and those who make the decisions on funding and possible discontinuation of a line of business. The monitor can serve as an effective communication link between the two groups. This approach is common in the banking industry where those making the decision to embark on a course of action (e.g., loan officers) are often assisted by others in the bank (e.g., a workout group) in recouping bank assets.

Bibliography

Arkes, H. R. & Blumer, C. (1985). The psychology of sunk cost. *Organizational Behavior and Human Decision Processes*, **35**, 124–40.

Ghosh, D. (1994). De-escalation strategies of sunk cost effect: Some experimental evidence. Accounting, Behavior, and Organization Research Conference. San Antonio.

Narayanan, M. (1985). Managerial incentives for short-term results. *Journal of Finance*, **40**, 1469–84.

Penno, M. (1983). Issues of information asymmetry in managerial accounting.Unpublished dissertation Northwestern University.

Simonson, I. & Staw, B. M. (1992). Deescalation strategies: A comparison of techniques for reducing commitment to losing courses of action. *Journal of Applied Psychology*, **77**, 419–26.

Staw, B. M. (1981). The escalation of commitment to a course of action. *Academy of Management Review*, **6**, 577–87.

Staw, B. M. & Ross, J. (1987). Behavior in escalation situations: Antecedents, prototypes, and solutions. *Research in Organizational Behavior*, B. M. Staw & L. L. Cummings, eds, **9**, 39–78. Greenwich, CT: Jai Press.

DIPANKAR GHOSH

T

technological auditing In the current technological environment, traditional, manual procedures have been replaced by computer programs that undergo constant revision. The computer requires monitoring by trained "technology auditors."

This relatively new profession is referred to as (electronic data processing) EDP auditing, IS (information systems) auditing, or technological auditing. Technological auditors now audit a wide variety of technology as diverse as radio, cellular, infrared, satellite, fiber optic, public switched, LAN, and WAN communications technologies. Technological auditors are not only concerned with financial auditing; they evaluate alternative hardware, software, and procedures; they act as internal consultants for technology issues; and they occasionally assume an operational role when no one else within the organization can.

Standards For the Practice of Technological Auditing

Types of audit
Attestation. Auditors establish what should be done and verify compliance. When the auditor's work product is the expression of an opinion on the quality of, and compliance with the rules, that audit is an attestation audit. The most common type of audit performed by public accountants is financial auditing in which the auditor attests that the client has followed the rules (generally accepted accounting principles); that the transactions and assets the client reports are "real"; and that nothing important has been omitted. Usually, financial audits are about how fairly (in agreement with the rules) the client's accountants have processed the financial transactions.

Compliance audits. Auditors apply the methods used for attesting to monitoring how well non-accounting transactions are processed. Non-accounting transactions may or may not be financial in nature. Compliance audits are primarily restricted to ensuring that non-accounting rules are followed. Examples include audits that verify compliance with internal controls, bank examiner's audits, and audits of compliance with environmental laws. Compliance auditing is particularly important in the governmental and regulated environment.

The quality assurance audit combines the features of both the attestation and compliance audit. Regulations within the European Community have created the need for quality assurance audits known as ISO 9000 audits. ISO 9000 audits are named after the ISO 9000 standard which establishes how to document a production process. Once a process is documented, compliance with the procedures can be audited, which increases quality assurance. ISO is not an acronym. It comes from the Greek word for equal, as in isosceles triangle or isobar. In this case it refers to standards to ensure an equal or consistent production process. In this type of audit, audit skills are employed to certify that an entity's production is processed according to established guidelines.

Operational audits. The objective of operational auditing is to improve the way things are done by reducing the resources necessary to accomplish a goal (efficiency) and/or by ending up with better results (effectiveness). For example, before an organization submits to an ISO 9000 quality assurance audit, the organization usually engages a quality control expert to review and modify their procedures to ensure an acceptable production process. This review and modification process is an operational audit.

Operational auditing is also known as value-added auditing because auditing success is usually measured by return on investment; for every dollar spent on operational auditing, a multiple of those dollars are saved by the organization.

Technological auditor's role

The technological auditor develops procedures that are routine enough for more traditional auditors to apply, thus freeing the technological auditor to conquer new frontiers. Sometimes, it is necessary for the technological auditor to continue auditing an area for years.

Standards for technological auditing by profession

Standards for technological auditing are found in each of the auditing disciplines such as independent public auditing, internal auditing, governmental auditing, and information systems auditing. These standards are attempts to establish a minimum level of competence necessary for organizing and performing auditing tasks. In the USA, Government Auditing Standards (GAS) are promulgated by the General Audit Office (GAO) as well as the standards of three professional organizations: the American Institute of Certified Public Accountants (AICPA), the Information Systems Audit and Control Association (ISACA), and the Institute of Internal Auditors (IIA). Other auditing standards exist, but they are too narrow to be of interest.

Authority for standards. In the USA the AICPA promulgates standards for the practice of auditing and consulting by Certified Public Accountants (CPAs). Throughout the USA, CPAs are regulated by state boards. The courts and state boards have recognized generally accepted auditing standards as yardsticks for the measurement of professional performance. Therefore, the AICPA auditing standards have become, in effect, the law governing the minimum performance of auditing work by external professional auditors. In some cases, IIA standards have a similar impact when they are adopted by governments for the performance of internal auditing. Professionally, IIA standards apply to those who hold the certified internal auditor designation or those who are members of the IIA. Government auditing has a separate set of Government Auditing Standards known as the *GAO Yellow Book*, which also

have the effect of law for federal government audits and many local and state audits under a variety of provisions. The ISACA's auditing standards are of interest primarily because they are designed to cover any information systems auditor.

All the four sets of standards contain provisions to ensure that auditors are trained, collect adequate evidence, maintain an appropriate degree of professional independence, carry out their duties in a sufficient and professional manner, and adhere to the appropriate ethical conduct. However, the AICPA and the *GAO Yellow Book* give special recognition to the problems of technological auditing.

AICPA. The AICPA standards generally refer to the process of auditing for compliance or fairness as attestation work. There are separate but related standards for attestation of financial statements and other attestation such as quality assurance audits or internal control audits. The hallmark of these audits is compliance with some published or generally accepted methodology and an audit report that expresses the auditor's opinion about the degree of compliance with those benchmarks. CPAs also perform operational audits, which are more judgmental and are advisory to the client. The AICPA calls this type of work "Management Advisory Services" and it is covered by much less detailed standards then those covering financial auditing. The AICPA traditionally has included developments in its standards after technological auditing approaches have evolved.

GAS. Government Auditing Standards (GAS or *GAO Yellow Book*) refer to all attestation-type audits as financial audits. Performance auditing, which is like operational auditing, requires auditing for compliance with applicable laws and regulations. Government auditors may be called on to participate in nonaudit work such as advisory services.

GAS are intended for both internal and external auditors. The financial audit standards strongly rely on AICPA audit standards; they are basically modifications and enhancements to AICPA standards. Performance auditing standards address audits that may be conducted for unique audit objectives.

IIA. The IIA has become a leader in technological auditing research. The IIA's

Advance Technology Committee's projects such as *Systems Auditability and Control Study*, *Advanced Technology Conference*, and forthcoming publication of technology auditability projects ensures the IIA will continue to be an authority in this area.

ISACA. ISACA is devoted to developing technological auditing procedures and certifying information systems auditors. These are auditors who have to perform accounting-type audits in computer environments. The ISACA auditing standards are constructed to accommodate members of all three of the professional organizations, the American Institute of Certified Public Accountants, the Information Systems Audit and Control Association, and the Institute of Internal Auditors, without creating a conflict of interest.

ALAN H. FRIEDBERG

transfer pricing Transfer prices are the prices of goods sold by one division (or other responsibility center) to another within the firm. The prices of such internal sales do not directly affect the profits of the firm as a whole, since the selling division's revenue is offset by the buying division's expense. Transfer prices affect the firm indirectly, however, through their effect on manager's decisions. A well-designed transfer pricing system provides top management with meaningful information on individual responsibility centers' performance and provides responsibility center managers with both the incentive and the information needed to make the decisions that are best for the firm as a whole.

Surveys of practice (Tang, 1992; Price Waterhouse, 1984; earlier studies summarized in Grabski, 1985) have shown that market prices and full cost (actual or standard, with or without a markup to provide profit to the selling division) are the most common bases for transfer pricing. In the case of either market-based or cost-based prices, two alternative procedures for price-setting are available. A general rule may be established which defines "cost" or "market price" (e.g., standard full cost plus 10 percent or the average price offered by the three principal suppliers, updated at the end of each month), and the rule is thereafter followed mechanically. Alternatively, buyer and

seller may negotiate transfer prices periodically, using market or cost data as a basis for the negotiation.

The appropriate basis and procedure for transfer pricing depend on characteristics of the firm and its environment. Market-based pricing is impossible in some settings because the goods to be transferred are not available in the market. In other cases, goods traded on the market may be similar to those produced in the firm but not identical in terms of quality, timeliness of delivery, etc. Adjustments to market prices may be necessary to allow for these factors, or for the reduction in the selling division's marketing and collection expenses that occurs when it sells internally instead of in the open market. When comparable market prices are available, however, and adjustments are trivial or easily agreed on, market-based transfer prices provide an objective measure of performance for both buying and selling divisions and provide an incentive to the selling division to control production costs.

Transfer prices based on actual cost may remove the incentive for cost control and provide an incentive for the selling division to distort reported costs for products transferred internally (e.g., by allocating more indirect costs to products sold internally). The use of standard rather than actual costs may reduce the magnitude of these problems, if the method of setting standards is sufficiently objective; other measures to encourage cost reduction and accurate costing can also help to make cost-based transfer prices effective.

If the selling division is a profit center rather than a cost center, transfer prices are often set at full cost plus a profit margin comparable to that which the division would earn on outside sales. Without such a profit margin, the selling division will prefer to sell to outsiders rather than sister divisions whenever possible, in order to maximize its own profits; and this may be disadvantageous to the firm as a whole. The potential difficulty with adding a profit allowance to cost, however, is that it can lead the buying division to price the final product too high, if the buyer adds its usual profit margin on top of costs that already include the seller's usual profit margin.

A general rule (either market-based or cost-based) which automatically adjusts transfer prices with every change of market prices or production costs saves the time and effort managers spend when price changes must be negotiated. The portion of this time and effort which managers spend in trying to get the larger share of the firm's profits for their own division does not benefit the firm; however, the negotiation process also includes exchanges of information that may lead to decisions increasing the size of the firm's overall profits. Experimental studies (De Jong et al., 1989; Chalos & Haka, 1990) have shown that transfer price negotiations grow more efficient (less likely to end in impasse, and more likely to increase total profits) when the negotiating parties gain more experience with the process and each other.

Theoretical economic studies (e.g., Hirshliefer, 1956; Banker & Datar, 1992) have suggested marginal cost as the optimal basis for transfer pricing. Although variable cost may appear as an appropriate surrogate, it is rarely used (Grabski, 1985; Tang, 1992). Recent studies suggests that in a multi-product firm, full cost is a reasonable proxy for long-run marginal cost. For a firm that maximizes profit in a competitive market, market price should be equivalent to marginal cost.

Mathematical programing approaches to transfer pricing have also been developed (*see*, e.g., Abdel-Khalik & Lusk, 1974; Kanodia, 1979; Harris et al., 1982), but are mainly useful as a way for top management to learn more about the characteristics of production in the divisions. While mathematical programing techniques allow top management to set transfer prices and quantities at (theoretically) profit-maximizing amounts, this procedure reduces the autonomy of divisional managers, thus undercutting one of the principal goals of transfer pricing systems. Such techniques could also generate divisional profit figures that fluctuated widely in response to small changes in conditions and would not be informative about divisional managers' performance.

In multinational firms, transfer prices play an important role in allocating costs and profits to national sub-units of the firm. High transfer prices to subsidiaries in high-tax jurisdictions and low transfer prices to low-tax jurisdictions may arouse suspicions of tax evasion. Local tax codes must be consulted for acceptable transfer price methods for tax purposes.

Bibliography

Abdel-khalik, A. R. & Lusk, E. J. (1974). Transfer pricing – a synthesis. *The Accounting Review*, **49**, Jan., 8–23.

Banker, R. D. & Datar, S. M. (1992). Optimal transfer pricing under postcontract information. *Contemporary Accounting Research*, Spring, 329–52.

Chalos, P. & Haka, S. (1990). Transfer pricing under bilateral bargaining. *The Accounting Review*, **65**, July, 624–41.

DeJong, D., Forsythe, R., Kim, J.-O. & Uecker, W. (1989). A laboratory investigation of alternative transfer pricing mechanisms. *Accounting, Organizations and Society*, **14**, Jan., 41–64.

Grabski, S. V. (1985). Transfer pricing in complex organizations: A review and integration of recent empirical and analytical research. *Journal of Accounting Literature*, **4**, 33–75.

Harris, M., Kriebel, C. H. & Raviv, A. (1982). Asymmetric information, incentives and intrafirm resource allocation. *Management Science*, June, 604–20.

Hirshleifer, J. (1956). On the economics of transfer pricing. *Journal of Business*, **29**, July, 172–84.

Kanodia, C. (1979). Risk sharing and transfer price systems under uncertainty. *Journal of Accounting Research*, Spring, 74–98.

Price-Waterhouse (1984). *Transfer pricing practices of American industry*.

Tang, R. Y. W. (1992). Transfer pricing in the 1980s. *Management Accounting*, **70**, Feb., 22–6.

SEVERIN V. GRABSKI and JOAN LUFT

trial balance (unadjusted and adjusted) Preparing a "trial balance" is an intermediary process that precedes preparing financial statements. The "trial balance" (unadjusted or adjusted) is a listing, in account number order, of all account balances of an entity as of a particular date prepared before and after *adjusting entries* have been made. From a clerical accuracy standpoint, a trial balance is taken to verify the equality of the sum of *debit and credit balances* in the *general ledger* accounts.

Accounting Systems and Adjusting Entries

Accounting systems are essentially transaction oriented, and most day-to-day recordkeeping consists only of recording transactions entered into on open account or settled in cash. Hence, at the end of an accounting period (which may be a month, quarter, or year), the effects of many important economic events would have not yet been recorded in the accounts. In particular, end-of-period *accruals* (which reflect items of revenue or expense that have not yet been realized or paid in cash) are likely to be omitted from the unadjusted trial balance, as are adjustments to reflect the *amortization* (i.e., wasting away) of previously recorded limited life assets. In addition, *valuation allowance* accounts usually require adjustment at period-end to reflect effects of new developments, as will other types of accounts for sundry reasons.

Adjusting a Trial Balance

An unadjusted trial balance, drawn from the general ledger after routine transactions of the period have been recorded, is carefully scrutinized by an accountant to identify accounts that require adjustment so as to reflect end-of-period transactions that have not been recorded during the relevant accounting period. Individual companies document the account adjustment process differently.

Table 1 illustrates various types of adjusting entries. Adjustment A, an accrual for salaries payable at year-end, concisely illustrates the central theme of the accrual method of

Table 1: Example of a trial balance worksheet

Act No.	Account title	Unadjusted trial balance	Adjustments		Adjusted trial balance
			debit (credit)		
101	Cash	$ 5,000			$ 5,000
110	Accounts receivable	9,000	(500)	D	8,500
111	Allowance for uncollectables	(200)	(650)	C	(850)
250	Equipment	30,000			30,000
260	Accumulated depreciation, equipment	(10,000)	(5,000)	B	(15,000)
301	Salaries payable	0	(2,500)	A	(2,500)
501	Owner's equity, beginning of year	(23,800)			(23,800)
601	Revenues	(60,000)	500	D	(59,500)
701	Salaries expense	50,000	2,500	A	52,500
710	Bad debt expense	0	650	C	650
750	Depreciation expense	0	5,000	B	5,000
	Total	0	0		0

Entry explanations:
A   To accrue salaries payable at year-end; assume amount represents salaries earned but not yet paid during last two weeks of year.
B   To record depreciation for year; assume equipment is depreciated over a six-year life with no residential value.
C   To adjust allowance for uncollectable accounts to 10% of adjusted accounts receivable; assume percent is based upon company's experience.
D   To correct a pricing error on a sales invoice.

Note: A trial balance verifies the equality of the sum of debt and credit balances in the general ledger; the above worksheet "balances" since the sum of debt and credit balances add to zero. The unadjusted trial balance is carefully scrutinized by an accountant to identify accounts that require adjustment. The adjusted trial balance serves as a reference source for preparing numerous end-of-period reports.

accounting, i.e., recording the economic effects of transactions in the period in which the transaction occurs, which may differ from the period in which the transaction is settled in cash. Thus, in Adjustment A, the salaries accrue (or "accrete") to employees with the passage of time; accordingly, the related expense and liability are recorded in the period in which the services are rendered, even though the employees will not be paid until next period. Also, it should be noted that if this adjustment were not made, net income of the current period would be misstated, because revenue would not be matched with the cost of the effort to generate them.

Items B through D in Table 1 illustrate other common types of adjustments. Adjustment B illustrates the amortization (use) of a usable fixed asset, specifically, depreciation on equipment. Item C illustrates adjusting the allowance for uncollectibles, a valuation allowance account, to 10 percent of adjusted receivables. Adjustment D illustrates the correction of a random clerical error. Finally, in terms of worksheet's mechanics, it should be noted how the unadjusted balances, when combined with the amounts in the adjustments column, are added across the schedule to produce the adjusted balances.

Use of an Adjusted Trial Balance

An adjusted trial balance principally is a repository document that reflects the final end-of-period balance, reflecting all period-related transactions, in each of the entity's general ledger accounts. The document is commonly used as a reference source in the preparation of other financial statements and reports. Such reports may range from detailed internal reports for management to highly summarized financial statements for external investors.

THOMAS R. CRAIG

turnover ratios

Turnover Ratio Types

Turnover or activity ratios typically relate net sale or cost of sales to some assets. These ratios often are used to assess efficiency of operations,

effectiveness in carrying out operating policies and attaining objectives, quality of financial conditions, and liquidity of a firm. Empirical studies have documented the richness of information in turnover ratios and the importance of including turnover ratios in decision models. The survey conducted by Walsh (1984) also indicates that activity ratios are widely used by management for various types of decisions. Three types of turnover ratio are considered here.

Accounts Receivable (A/R) Turnover

A/R turnover = net sales/year-end net accounts receivable

A measure related to A/R turnover is the average collection period (days) for accounts receivable, or the number of days accounts are outstanding.

The A/R turnover ratio (or average collection period) provides a measure of the quality and liquidity of account receivables, and the effectiveness of a firm's credit collection activities. A low turnover ratio or long collection period suggests that the accounts receivable may be of low quality and it is likely that the firm will suffer losses in collecting accounts receivable. Generally, the longer receivables remain outstanding the lower is the probability of their collection in full. Liquidity of receivables refer to the speed with which receivables will be converted into cash.

The A/R turnover ratio also serves as a gauge of the effectiveness of the firm's credit policy and its implementation. An average collection period that remains within the terms of payment set by the firm vouches for the effectiveness of the firm's credit policy. A collection period that exceeds the terms of payment suggests that the firm either has an improper credit screening policy or has done a poor collection job. A collection period of excessive length also can be a result of tardiness in payment by one or two substantial customers. The firm can detect such an instance by aging the accounts receivable.

Limitations

(1) Many users prefer to use the average of beginning and ending balances of accounts receivable, rather than the year-end figure, to compute the ratio. Others argue for the

average of quarterly or even monthly balances. The more widely sales fluctuate, the more important it is to use an average so that the turnover ratio will not be distorted due to nonrepresentative accounts receivable affecting the denominator. Most of the industry ratios provided by financial data companies such as Dun & Bradstreet Inc., Robert Morris Associates, and Standard & Poor's Corporation, however, use the year-end number, which assumes no seasonal fluctuation in sales.

(2) The numerator should be net credit sales (merchandise sold on accounts) only. Net credit sales, however, rarely is available to external users and net sales is used as a proxy.

(3) The denominator should include all outstanding receivables arising from normal sales (see ACCOUNTS RECEIVABLES: RECOGNITION, VALUATION, AND REPORTING).

Inventory turnover ratio

Inventory turnover = cost of goods sold/year-end inventory

The related measure, average days' sales in inventory:

Average days' sales in inventory = 365/inventory turnover ratio

The higher the turnover ratio is, the lower the average days' sales in inventory, or vice versa. The inventory turnover ratio shows the number of times a firm sells its inventory on hand during the year. The corresponding average days' sales in inventory is the average number of days the firm takes to sell its inventory. ABC Pharmaceutical Company inventory has sold its inventory 2.23 times during 1991. Alternatively, it takes the company, on average, 163.68 days to sell the inventory. We conclude the firm maintains an inventory sufficient for sales of more than five months.

Inventory turnover ratio (or average days' inventory on hand) measures the efficiency of the firm in managing and selling inventory. It also is a gauge of the liquidity of the firm's inventory and quality of the current assets. Generally, a high inventory turnover ratio (or a low days' inventory on hand) is a sign of efficient inventory management. A high inventory turnover ratio, however, may also be an indication of not having sufficient inventory on hand to meet all demands and, as a result, sales might have been lost due to products being out of stock.

A low inventory turnover requires the firm to invest more heavily in inventory and storage space, and incur higher operating costs to store and retrieve inventory. It also subjects the firm to a higher risk of inventory obsolescence. This is a primary reason why many world-class companies adopt a just-in-time inventory policy. These firms have minimal inventory on hand and thereby have a very high inventory turnover ratio. The sum of days' inventory on hand and days to collect receivables is often referred to as the operating cycle.

Operating cycle = days to sell inventory+days to collect receivables

The operating cycle of a firm is the total number of days a firm requires to purchase merchandise, sell the merchandise, and collect accounts receivable. For firms with mostly credit sales, the difference between its operating cycle and its credit term for purchases is the number of days the firm needs to finance its purchases.

Limitations

(1) The year-end inventory is often used to compute the inventory turnover ratio if there are no significant fluctuations in inventory levels during the period. Otherwise, a quarterly average or monthly average is considered more appropriate.

(2) Inventory valuation methods can affect the inventory turnover ratio markedly. Generally, a last-in, first-out (LIFO) firm will show a markedly higher inventory turnover ratio than that of first-in, first-out (FIFO) firm.

(3) Regardless of the inventory valuation method a firm used, an inventory turnover ratio calculated based upon accounting numbers tends to be inflated. This result occurs because the generally accepted accounting principles (GAAP) prescribe use of historical cost, not the current price, as the basis for inventory valuations. Older prices are usually lower than the current prices, which understates ending inventory, resulting in a higher inventory turnover ratio. This problem exists regardless of the valuation method the firm uses.

(4) Using a LIFO method may render the inventory turnover ratio, as well as the current ratio, meaningless when the inventory in the LIFO layer was acquired several years ago at significantly different price levels.

(5) Management of a firm can obtain a better evaluation of inventory turnover by computing separate turnover rates for the major components of inventory such as (a) raw materials, (b) work in process, and (c) finished goods. Departmental, divisional, or product-line turnover rates can similarly lead to more useful conclusions regarding inventory quality.

Asset turnover ratio

Asset turnover ratio = net sales/year-end total assets

An asset turnover ratio measures the extent to which total assets are used to generate sales and provides a gauge on the effectiveness in utilizing a company's assets. In the example, ABC Pharmaceutical Company utilized its assets 0.69 times to generate sales in 1991. Or, one dollar of assets generated 0.69 dollar of sales.

Generally, the higher the asset turnover ratio is, the smaller is the investment required to generate the same amount of sales and thus the more profitable is the firm. A low asset turnover ratio indicates that a firm either has excess assets on hand or is not using its assets efficiently. For example, Peter Drucker (1980) attributes the higher returns GE enjoys compared with the returns of its competitor, Westinghouse, to GE having a higher asset turnover.

Limitations

(1) Financial statements report assets on historical cost bases. As a result, the asset turnover ratio usually is inflated because historical costs of assets generally are lower than their current value or market prices.

(2) The accounting method a firm chooses to use also affects its asset turnover ratio. Use of an accelerated depreciation method, for example, would certainly yield a lower total assets valuation than using a straight line depreciation method would.

(3) The total assets included in the calculation of an asset turnover ratio should include only operating assets; nonoperating assets such as land purchased for a future factory site are excluded. Some analysts choose to calculate the asset turnover ratio using only the net fixed assets (gross fixed assets minus accumulated depreciation) for the denominator.

Activity Ratios in Financial Analysis

Financial ratio analysis often involves comparisons to norms. The norm can be a firm's past records, the same ratio of the firm with the best performance, or the industry norm.

Financial ratio analysis is a useful and efficient tool in assessing firms. Users, however, need to keep in mind its limitations. Financial analysis examines only selected aspects of the firm. Many other important factors such as the economy, outlook of the industry, and the uniqueness of the firm, are not considered in the analysis.

All financial ratios relate closely to each other. They share either a common component in their derivations or are affected by the same operating activities. An overzealous attempt to improve a ratio would almost certainly be accomplished at the expense of one or more other financial ratios or operating characteristics. A financial ratio analysis needs to be conducted in its entirety by examining all aspects of the operation. An analysis of selected financial ratios can produce, at best, a partial picture of the firm. At its worst, such an analysis can lead to a misleading conclusion.

As a firm's short-term and long-term interests may conflict with each other, so may its short-term and long-term financial ratios. To improve a ratio in the short run may jeopardize the long-term welfare of the firm. Tradeoffs between long-term and short-term interests should also be considered in analyses.

Some General Comments

(1) A ratio is calculated using data from financial statements. Financial statements report only past operations. A ratio does not tell anything about the future. A comparison of past records will give only a crude indication about the trend of the ratio. To have a more precise prediction, an analyst has to rely on more sophisticated statistical

methods such as regression analysis or time series analysis.

(2) A frequent criticism of corporate financial reporting is the diversity allowed in accounting methods used by firms. Such diversity makes it difficult to compare financial ratios of different firms. Some analysts adjust the reported financial statements to make data more comparable among firms before conducting financial analyses. Adjustment techniques include incorporating information provided by the firm in footnotes to financial statements, management's discussions and analyses, reports filed with the Securities Exchange Commission (in the USA) or other regulatory agencies, and news items reported in the *Wall Street Journal* (in the USA) or other news media.

(3) Horrigan (1968) and Lev & Sunder (1979) criticize the lack of concrete theoretical foundations that specify appropriate conditions for using ratios analysis and the consequences of using ratios when these conditions are not met. Unfortunately, this problem still remains unresolved. Among unresolved issues are: (a) whether a proportional relationship does exist between financial ratios and the economic reality that the ratios purport to measure; (b) whether the industry norms of a specific ratio are normally distributed; and (c) what are the theoretical bases for selecting financial ratios as the predictors in positive financial analysis. Barnes (1987) reviews some of these issues.

Bibliography

Barnes, P. (1987). The analysis and use of financial ratios: A review article. *Journal of Business Finance and Accounting*, Winter, 449–61.

Drucker, P. F. (1980). *Management in turbulent times.* New York: Harper & Row.

Horrigan, J. (1968). A short history of financial ratio analysis. *The Accounting Review*, Apr., 284–94.

Lev, B. & Sunder, S. (1979). Methodological issues in the use of financial ratios. *Journal of Accounting and Economics*, Dec., 187–210.

Walsh, F. (1984). *Measuring business performance.* New York: The Conference Board.

KUNG H. CHEN and PAY YU CHENG

W

warrants A warrant is an option to buy additional shares in a company. The option is tendered by a certificate that conveys to the bearer the right to acquire a stated number of shares at a specific price within a stated period of time. Companies are motivated to issue warrants for three common reasons: (1) as a preemptive privilege to existing shareholders; (2) as a sweetener or "equity kicker" when issuing debt; and (3) as compensation to employees and executives. If the option is not exercised at the expiration date, then all rights are voided.

Subscription Rights for Additional Shares

Each share of common stock owned normally gives the owner one voting right. Issuing new shares of stock to raise capital can dilute the proportion of ownership among existing shareholders, unless they can protect themselves and maintain their proportion of voting rights. The preemptive privilege of existing shareholders in this respect is referred to as a "stock right." Both the number of shares and the price at which the new shares can be purchased are stated on the warrant certificate as well as the date on which the "right to purchase" expires. The time period between the date of issuance and expiration is variable; however, it is usually of short duration in the case of stock rights relative to warrants issued with other securities.

To recognize the "loyalty" of existing shareholders, company directors tend to specify in the warrants the new issue price of shares at an amount less than their current market value. This creates a value for the rights and the warrants can be traded on organized markets like any other security.

For the accounting profession, warrants of this type are nonproblematic. No substantive exchange transaction has occurred when a warrant is issued and, thus, there is no change in the accounting record. Upon exercise of the warrants, cash is received by the company and shares are issued accordingly. This transaction increases both sides of the balance sheet by an equal amount. There is no effect on the profit and loss statement.

Stock Warrants Issued With Other Securities

Warrants may be issued with stock or debt. These types of financial packages are long-term options to buy common stock at a fixed price, usually over a period of five years.

Warrants issued with stock. Warrants issued with stock are detachable, which creates two independent securities that trade separately on financial markets. From the point of view of the issuer, this type of financial package is not problematic because both elements are treated as capital.

Warrants issued with debt. Stock purchase warrants issued with debt, such as bonds, constitute one class of compound financial instruments available to investors in world financial markets. Normally referred to as bond–cum–warrants, or loan stock with warrants, the detachable stock warrant feature means that the initial hybrid security is decomposable into two separate and independent securities. The bond is viewed as a debt instrument while the detachable stock warrant is an equity instrument.

In the USA, Accounting Principles Board Opinion (APB) No. 14 issued in 1969 requires that bond–cum–warrants be treated as part debt and part equity. Technical Release (TR) No. 667, issued in 1987 by the Institute of Chartered Accountants in England and Wales, recommended similar treatment. These two authoritative pronouncements are in contrast to the traditional generally accepted accounting principles (GAPP) utilized in the larger international accounting community. Under the traditional method, a firm capitalizes the bonds at their principle value and charges interest against profit and loss accordingly. No value and, hence, no recognition is given to the outstanding warrants.

Exposure Draft 48 (E48) was issued for comment by the International Accounting Standards Committee (IASC) in January 1994. E48 subsequently became International Accounting Standard 32 (IAS 32) in June 1995. Since detachable stock warrants and bonds have separate values, the IAS 32 guideline is in accord with APB No. 14.

The authoritative pronouncements pertaining to detachable stock warrants issued with debt are intended to correct two deficiencies associated with the traditional method of accounting for such compound financial instruments: (1) the overstated liability and understated equity on the balance sheet; and (2) the artificially low interest cost on the profit and loss statement.

The first deficiency is resolved by initially recording the separate components at their fair market value by either the proportional method or the incremental method. The proportional method measures each component separately and adjusts the amounts so determined on a pro rata basis such that the sum of the components equals the price paid for the compound financial instrument. The incremental method focuses on the security for which the market value is determinable and allocates the remainder of the purchase price to the security for which the market value is not known.

There is no differential cash effect between the two methods and this has been the favourite counter-argument of the business community against regulation. However, the higher interest expense under accounting regulation produces a lower net income each year for the duration of the life of the debt (Yeo & Williams, 1994). This effect may cause firms to change their contracting arrangements if net income is tied to employee bonus or compensation plans. Finally, the debt/equity ratio is lower under accounting regulation and the overall weighted average cost of capital relevant to the firm's investment decisions becomes higher because of the larger proportionate increase in equity.

Warrants in Stock Compensation Plans

Warrants may be issued to employees of a firm in conjunction with a stock option plan or a stock purchase plan. The latter is considered noncompensatory in nature and reflects the interests of the company to raise additional equity capital. Generally, four conditions are required to classify warrants as noncompensatory:

(1) All eligible employees may participate.
(2) Each employee has rights to an equal number of shares.
(3) The time period for exercise of the rights is limited.
(4) The reduced price from the market value of the stock contained in the warrant offer must be compatible to a similar offer to other shareholders.

Satisfying these conditions essentially reduces a stock purchase plan to the status of rights to subscribe for additional shares and it poses no difficulties for accountants. The warrant offer may expire or be exercised in which case cash is received and stockholders' equity is increased by the amount of the option price.

Stock option plans are compensatory in nature if they represent a payment for current or future factor services from employees. Bonus plans or employee award plans fall into this classification and become problematic because they represent an element of expense to the company. The difficulties here are very complex in nature and fall outside the scope of accounting for ordinary stock warrants per se.

Conceptual Issues

There are few instances in the world accounting community that feature de facto issues of debt with detachable warrants and which are under the purview of international accounting standards.

However, one current financial market which has experienced the issuance of bond-cum-warrants is Singapore. Williams & Rangan (1994) report that the stock exchange of Singapore has taken unprecedented action by requiring those firms with bond-cum-warrants to disclose the effects according to the guidelines set forth by E48 or IAS 32 as at present. A common argument is that a securities market which is efficient can see through cosmetic differences (i.e., no cash flow effect) in reported results arising from the use of either method. However, regardless of market efficiency, there may be risk effects from this mandated disclosure or wealth redistribution effects.

A more serious conceptual issue arises with the issuance of debt with nondetachable warrants which many view as equivalent to the features of convertible debt. In 1990, the US Financial Accounting Standards Board (FASB) issued a Discussion Memorandum which attempts to deal with the separate recognition of the debt and equity components of these types of financial instruments. The arguments here are normative and there has been no empirical research on market effects. Essentially, the accounting profession refuses to acknowledge the separation of the equity feature in these circumstances. It is argued that such hybrid securities are incapable of being separated into the debt and equity components. One either exercises the option feature or holds the debt to maturity and redeems the debt for cash. Critics of this current accounting treatment for nondetachable warrants and convertible debt claim that the accounting profession is only considering the form and not the substance of these transactions.

There is universal agreement on how to account for stock warrants issued separately.

With the release of IAS 32, there is solid indication that the world accounting community has moved toward unanimity in accounting for the separate debt and equity features of detachable warrants issued with debt. The empirical findings in the Singapore context should motivate other countries which follow the International Accounting Standards Committee's pronouncements to recognize the potential economic effects in security markets having similar characteristics to those of Singapore. However, agreement on how to account for the debt and equity components of nondetachable stock warrants will be contingent on the general reaction of financial and business communities to the FASB Discussion Memorandum and IAS 32.

Bibliography

Williams, J. J. & Rangan, N. (1994). Regulatory accounting changes: Issues, conflicts and implications of E40. *Accounting and Business Review*, 1, Jan., 107–26.

Yeo, G. H. H. & Williams, J. J. (1995). Market reaction to bond cum warrants modified disclosure: The case of the Singapore stock market. A working paper presented at the MIT/NTU conference on Current Developments and Globalization in Financial Markets and Services, Singapore, Jan.

JOHN JOSEPH WILLIAMS and
GILLIAN HIAN HENG YEO

— INDEX —

Compiled by Liz Granger (Registered Indexer)